Children and Their Art

CHARLES D. GAITSKELL

Director of Art, Ontario Department of Education

UNDER THE GENERAL EDITORSHIP OF

WILLARD B. SPALDING

Chairman, Division of Education
Portland State College, Oregon

HARCOURT, BRACE
& WORLD, INC.

Children and Their Art

Methods for the Elementary School

CREDITS: Title page photograph—Gilda Rosenblum.
Diagrams interpreting Cézanne's *Card-Players*—Howard Fussiner.
Drawings—Charles Gottlieb, Herbert Marcelin, Fred McCarroll.

To Margaret

Contents

part two

TEACHING ART

Editor's Foreword

The teaching of art in the elementary schools today is light-years removed from the formal training in drawing skills that plagued my generation during its early years. Art has become the province of all children, not just those with the dexterity of hand and eye required to draw cubes in perspective or to paint flowers in accurate detail. Today's children are encouraged to explore freely in many art media, using a variety of subjects for expression. In their work they thus approximate the process and discipline of the mature artist, and they learn, as my generation rarely did, a great deal about the meaning of art.

For the student preparing to become an elementary teacher, today's art program is both a liberation and a responsibility. He will be given an opportunity, denied many of his predecessors, to challenge the pupils' natural creativity to the utmost, and at the same time he will be required to present as rich and varied a program as the resources of his school will allow. Sometimes the prospective teacher who has little or no aptitude for art finds this responsibility more intimidating than challenging. To him I can make no better recommendation than that he acquire a copy of Dr. Gaitskell's *Children and Their Art*, for this book will give him the understanding, experience, and skill necessary to build a well-rounded and modern art program. This is a book which will serve the student well as a basic text in the college course in art education and later will be an invaluable reference when he begins his classroom teaching.

Dr. Gaitskell does two things better in my opinion than anyone has done them before. He describes fully the philosophical and theoretical basis of modern art education—that is, our belief that education should reflect democratic ideals, our insistence that the teaching of art be consistent with the disciplines of genuine art, and our understanding of how children's artistic capabilities develop. Then he gives many practical suggestions about the ways in which the various art media—painting, sculpture, paperwork, printing, and so forth—can be used to implement this philosophy. In Dr. Gaitskell's book, practice illuminates theory and theory guides practice in perfect integration. The result is an eminently sound and usable text.

Portland, Oregon   W. B. S.
February 1958

Preface

During the twenty-five years in which I have taught art in the elementary school and supervised the teaching of others, art education has taken many new directions.

Recent advances in general educational thought, a deepening insight into the nature of art itself, and an ever-growing understanding of the true character of democracy all give rise to the problems which concern the teachers who either are preparing to teach art or are actually engaged in teaching it. These teachers want to know how art teaching today is influenced by educational practice as a whole; they want to discover the relationships existing between art in general and art in the classroom; and they want to understand how democracy in life influences the practice of art in school. In my own teaching I have attempted to work out answers to these problems, and in my supervisory work I have repeatedly discussed them with teachers who are looking for their own solutions. My purpose in writing this book has been to put down the ideas that I have gained in teaching and supervision in the hope that they may be of use to teachers, whether in-training or in-service, who are concerned with the important task of teaching art to young people.

During the four years required to prepare the manuscript for this book, I have received much help and many kindnesses from a large number of people. Lacking the support of these people, it is safe to say that I could never have written this volume. Unselfish in sharing their knowledge and abilities, my friends and colleagues have supported me to an extent which never fails to arouse my deepest gratitude.

Many people have contributed to the illustrations to be found in this book. Among those who have selected excellent pieces of children's work to emphasize certain statements in the text are the following: Mr. F. K. Shaw, Supervisor of Art and Crafts for the Township of North York; Miss G. Campbell, formerly Art Supervisor for the Board of Education in the City of Fort William; Mr. Garnet Humphrey, Supervisor of Art and Auditorium in the City of Windsor; Mr. George Buckland, Supervisor of Art for the Ottawa Public Schools; and Mr. Geoffrey Tomkinson, Supervisor of Art for the Board of Education, Etobicoke. Members of the staff of the Summer Courses in Art sponsored by the Ontario Department of Education for teachers-in-service have also selected work for my use, as have the staff members of the special classes for gifted children also sponsored by the Department. My daughter Adrienne, a teacher of third-grade youngsters in the county of North York, has kindly taken up special topics in her classroom so that certain illustrations could be obtained. To all these people, whether administrators, artists, or teachers, I offer my deepest thanks. Not least, I also wish to thank the many children whose work appears herein.

A number of fine photographs are also to be found in this book. These testify to the skill and taste of several photographers. My especial thanks must be directed toward Mr. Jack Engeman of Baltimore and Mr. Bob Ellis of the Royal Studio in Toronto, who supplied most of the photographs selected for publication.

No statement of my gratitude would be complete without mention of Professor Harold A. Schultz of the University of Illinois, who criticized the entire manuscript and made many valuable suggestions, and Professor Willard B. Spalding, who has provided good counsel at every stage in the writing of this book.

Of all those others who have assisted me in one respect or another in the preparation of the manuscript, one person stands out above the rest—my wife, Margaret. For some years she was my assistant, and it was she who did so much of the painstaking research with thousands of children of various types and ages. From her mountains of data I have been able to select valuable facts of which otherwise I should probably never have become aware. Now in the role of mother of two little girls she has relinquished her professional duties, but she still finds time (especially when Vicki and Susan are asleep) to give me sympathetic attention and advice. There is really no adequate way of expressing my debt of gratitude to Margaret.

Toronto   C. D. G.
March 1958

Some Examples

of Children's Art

Some Examples

of Children's Art

The first seven pictures in this sequence are examples of children's pictures arranged according to their ages. They can most profitably be studied in connection with Chapter 6. The last five pictures illustrate a few of the various media in which elementary school children can work and which are described in Part Two of the text.

"The circus clown in Santa's parade," an example of an early symbol for a man, painted in tempera with round hog-bristle brushes by a girl, age five years.

a   *"Playing with my train," a five-year-old boy's painting in tempera which contains several symbols. Note the "fold-over" delineation of the track.*

b   *"I want to be a teacher," painting in tempera by a six-and-a-half-year-old girl. Note the use of several "base lines" and the overlapping of objects.*

"*Playing ball,*" *drawing in chalk by a seven-and-a-half-year-old boy, which* *demonstrates his interest in group activity. The picture has a complete* *background and a well-established center of interest.*

a   *"Trees at Christmas," poetic painting in tempera by a gifted girl (I.Q. 130), age nine years and two months.*

b   *"Trick or treat," painting in tempera by a ten-year-old boy. The boy has developed a strong design to depict a personal aspect of an often stereotyped subject.*

"The slalom," painting in tempera by an eleven-year-old girl. Note the subtle rhythms which give movement to the painting.

A print made by a fourth-grade boy with a turnip and red, blue, and green tempera paint. (See Chapter 10.)

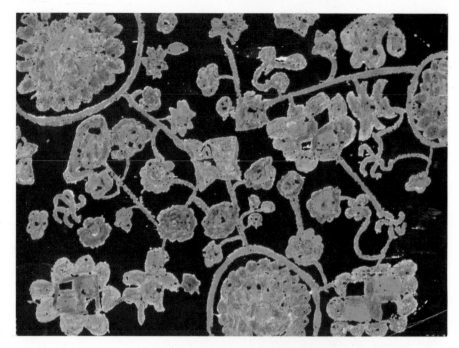

a *"In our garden," a picture made with repellents by a third-grade girl.*
   (See Chapter 7.)

b *A picture made with torn paper by a sixth-grade boy in a rural school.*
   (See Chapter 8.)

a   *Embroidery made by a slow-learner, an eleven-year-old girl with an I.Q. of 70. (See Chapter 12.)*

b   *A chance technique by a ten-year-old boy: tempera paint is dribbled on the paper and then blown around to make "spidery" areas of color. (See Chapter 12.)*

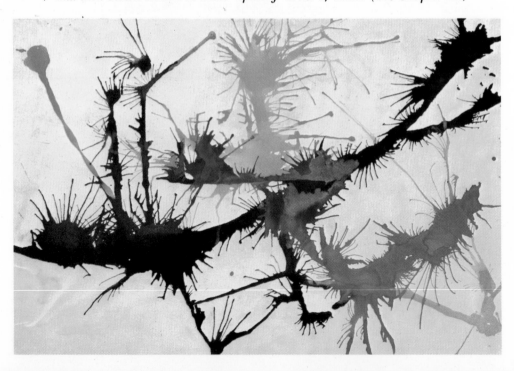

Children and Their Art

PREPARING TO TEACH ART

This book is divided into two parts. Part One presents theoretical information for the teacher so that he may develop his professional background before he enters the art classroom. Part Two suggests actual classroom activities in art.

Over the years great changes have occurred in the teaching of art. The type of art program our parents followed in school possessed purposes and followed procedures quite distinct from those of the present-day program. What caused these changes? What is preferable about today's program compared with the programs of other days? Have we any reasons to regret the disappearance of the old programs? Have we retained anything from them? What exactly are our contemporary purposes in teaching art in our schools? What theoretical knowledge does a teacher need to be professionally equipped to teach art? These are among the basic questions to which a teacher of art today should have answers.

Unquestionably, teaching methods are gradually being improved in all areas of learning in our schools. We know, for example, that children learn to read and to think with numbers more quickly and with greater accuracy than they did some years ago. Indeed, they learn facts and develop skills of all kinds with ever increasing efficiency in all subjects. This is as true for art as it is for language, mathematics, or science. What is the nature of the new methods of teaching which have proved to be so effective in the classrooms of the nation? What must a teacher do so that efficiency in teaching may be maintained? Here again are professional questions for which the art teacher will want to have answers.

There is one aspect of art education which holds peculiar importance for the teacher of art. This is what we call *design*. Design is a fundamental component of all art. It enters into every art activity. Without a knowledge of this aspect of art and art education, a teacher would be handicapped indeed. Fortunately, an understanding of design can be readily gained by those who study the subject. What is design? How is it produced? How may it be taught? How may good design be recognized in the work of children? These are some of the important problems about which the contemporary art teacher should hold opinions.

The teaching of any subject invariably raises problems about a program of studies. While the development of every educational program is largely governed by a number of basic principles, each subject exhibits certain peculiarities demanding special consideration. What are the peculiarities of art that tend to influence program planning? What strategies must teachers and others employ so that the pupils may follow an art program which will result only in learning of great worth? Since the teacher should be a major influence in the development of an art program, he must be familiar with its problems and procedures.

No one can expect, upon entering a classroom, to find physical conditions ideal for art education. Almost invariably, alterations and improvements must be made before supplies and equipment can be distributed efficiently and work can proceed smoothly. What are some of the most efficient physical arrangements to be made in any type of classroom and for pupils in any grade level? Here are more questions to be answered by the art teacher.

Finally arise the problems associated with the actual art production of the pupils. To the uninitiated, the art of children often appears either merely amusing or puzzling, or even downright untidy and annoying. Children's art, however, has been the subject of much earnest study, and its artistic qualities have been greatly admired by reputable artists and critics. What is good about the art of children? What differences are to be found in the production of children of varying stages of development? How can one understand what the child is doing and saying in his art work? These and other similar questions are of paramount importance to the teacher of art. So important are they, in fact, that it is doubtful if anyone could teach art successfully in school without having first attempted to find answers for them.

To each of the above six sets of questions, a chapter has been devoted in the first part of this book. Chapter 1 outlines the changes which have occurred in art education throughout the years and relates these changes to developments in general education. Chapter 2 reviews a number of teaching methods which are effective in art. Chapter 3 discusses design. Chapter 4 presents a theoretical basis for the development of a program of studies in art, and Chapter 5 describes the physical arrangements of the classroom. The final chapter in this first section, Chapter 6, discusses some current methods of classifying and analyzing children's production in art. With a grasp of these six topics, a teacher should feel ready to approach tools, materials, and, of course, all children who may profit from the delights and disciplines of contemporary art education.

Developments

in Art Education

Three main influences have affected art education in our schools. The first of these is the nature or tradition of art; the second, the philosophy of democracy; and the third, the development of theories of teaching based largely upon the discoveries of psychology. Art education today, therefore, is the result of an evolutionary process, and whatever degree of efficiency we now enjoy in our school program has not been achieved suddenly. By means of philosophical deliberation, systematic experimentation, and, sometimes, it must be admitted, trial and error, we have arrived at methods of art teaching which appear to be acceptable from the standpoint both of contemporary aesthetics and of education in a democracy. This chapter is intended to show how the characteristics and objectives of a good contemporary art program have arisen out of the three influences mentioned above. The chapter opens with a statement of the chief characteristics of a good contemporary program of art education, followed by a discussion of the influences of theories of art, the democratic credo, and the psychology of learning.

Some Characteristics
of Contemporary Art Education

The contemporary program of art education can be distinguished from its predecessors by several characteristics. Since education does not stand still, these characteristics will, no doubt, change as time goes on. At present, however, they appear to be six in number.

Belief in the Creative Ability of All Children

One of the most obvious characteristics of present-day art education is the belief of teachers in the creative ability of all children. Not so many decades ago the ability to create was usually thought to be an attribute of only a few learners, particularly those having artistic talent. Today, creativeness apparently is no longer considered a special ability reserved for a gifted minority nor is it assigned to a limited number of human activities. Kilpatrick [1] gave recognition to this fact when he said that creativeness is a characteristic of all learning, although it differs in degree from one situation to another. It is present in any of the novel situations which people continually face in life. Everyone can and, indeed, must create to live a normal life. Spearman,[2] a distinguished British psychologist, endorsed this view. Dewey [3] and Hartmann [4] went so far as to assert that the rediscovery of a solution to any problem, when achieved without a knowledge that the solution had already been found, might be considered a creative act and might be placed, from the standpoint of learning, in the same category as an original discovery. Such interpretations of the creative aspect of learning have encouraged the widely held belief that learners of almost any age in an art class have the ability to produce something which for them is new, superior, or unique when compared with previous performances.

Belief in the Integrated Acquisition of Skills

Probably no other phase of the present-day art program has caused more controversy than the beliefs of teachers concerning the acquisition of skills and the importance of these skills in expressive acts.

---

[1] W. H. Kilpatrick, *A Reconstructed Theory of the Educative Process* (N.Y.: Teachers College, 1935).

[2] C. E. Spearman, *Creative Mind* (N.Y.: Appleton-Century, 1931).

[3] "All thinking is original in a projection of considerations which have not been previously apprehended." A child, says John Dewey, who realizes for the first time that 5¢ and 5¢ make 10¢ is a discoverer. See his *Experience and Education* (N.Y.: Macmillan, 1938), p. 187.

[4] George W. Hartmann, *Educational Psychology* (N.Y.: American Book, 1941). It is interesting to note that Harold Rugg considers Hartmann (together with Raymond Wheeler) an author who interprets Gestalt psychology in a manner which is "by far the best for American conditions." See Harold Rugg, *Foundations for American Education* (N.Y.: World Book, 1947), p. 149.

It will be shown later in the chapter that earlier art programs set forth a number of exercises which were graded according to the difficulty of the skills required for their successful completion. It cannot be denied that those who were subjected to this program developed skills. The skills they developed, however, were of the "watertight compartment" variety. That is to say, although a person might learn to draw a chalk box, shade in pencil, or lay down a water-color wash acceptably, he was given little or no opportunity to use these skills in acts involving creative thinking.

Dewey pointed out in this connection that narrow modes of skill in any field cannot be of much service to the learner. To be of practical use, skills must be gained in such a manner as to allow the learner to achieve a deepening knowledge and an increased insight into the subject under consideration. As skills are being acquired, he said, they must be readily put to use in new situations which are under the personal control of the learner.[5]

Contemporary practice in art education, then, is influenced by the concept that the acquisition of skills should be related to the needs of the learner. It is believed that skill in art must develop as an integral part of an expressive artistic act, rather than by means of a mechanical exercise. Artistic acts involve intellectual and emotional activity on the part of the artist, and hence growth in artistic skill automatically includes his broader personal growth.

Belief in the Necessity for Freedom of Thought

A third characteristic of the contemporary art program derives from both political and aesthetic sources. This is the strong belief of teachers that learners must enjoy freedom of thought when they are engaged in artistic pursuits. Without such freedom, it is claimed, no one can produce art.

In those earlier art programs which were built upon the acquisition of formal skills little attention was paid to the individual thought of the learner. Rules and regulations were laid down for both production and appreciation of art forms, and pictures were produced according to standard rules of composition. A masterpiece was considered good because it was conceived according to a formula. The struggle to think was taken away from the pupil by a step-by-step method of teaching.

The task of developing teaching methods which allow for freedom of thought in aesthetic matters and which will contribute to the development of citizens worthy of the democratic state has challenged the ingenuity of art teachers. Today, the ideals of art education have become almost identical with those of democracy itself, to the extent that each is founded upon a belief in freedom of thought.

[5] John Dewey, *Democracy and Education* (N.Y.: Macmillan, 1916).

Belief in Experience
as the Basis for Expression

Artistic expression never emerges from a void. As mentioned previously, any artistic expression worthy of the name reflects the thoughts and feelings of its author. His thoughts and feelings are the result of his reaction to his experiences. Such is the traditional nature of art, and any attempt by painters and other artists to express what they have not experienced results in shoddy and insincere performances unworthy of the name of art.

As we shall see further on in the chapter, one of the chief reasons for the failure of much of the school art of the past was that the children's experiences were not utilized for expressive purposes. Subject matter employed in drawing and painting was derived more from the experiences of adults than from those of children.

In contrast, art teachers today try to build their programs around the traditional basis of artistic expression. An activity which does not engage the children's experiences in life as a motivating force for expression is rarely seen in the contemporary art program. This practice in no way limits the range of expression because children have an unlimited variety of experiences which lend themselves to expressive acts. In any situation which moves the child emotionally and stimulates him intellectually, it is believed, a basis of expression will be found.

In the art program of today, experience refers not only to the subject matter of expression, but also to the tools and materials employed in an expressive act. In former years, children were often presented with materials and tools and told in minute detail how to produce an object designed by someone else. Little if any previous experience had been gained by the pupils before they began work on the project selected by the teacher. As a result, the children's insight into the properties of the materials being employed and into the potentialities of the tools being used remained insufficiently developed. Whatever learning they gained was too narrow to apply to any activity but the one in progress. Today, it is believed that the child should experiment freely with tools and materials.

Emphasis upon the Development
of Taste

It must be admitted that former art programs did little to develop taste. Almost the only conscious effort made in this direction was a spasmodic, formal, and often literary study of "famous pictures" or of "historic ornaments."

Beginning in the 1920's critics began to express serious concern about the general level of aesthetic taste. Roger Fry stated that in aesthetic matters we were "satisfied . . . with a grossness, a sheer barbarity and squalor which would have shocked the thirteenth century profoundly." [6]

In 1934, Dewey asked the question, "Why is the architecture of our cities so unworthy of a fine civilization? It is not from lack of materials nor lack of technical capacity . . . yet it is not merely slums but the apartments of the well-to-do that are aesthetically repellent." [7]

Statements such as these offered a challenge to education, for such condemnations referred not to artists but to the mass of the people who were the product of public schools. The inference could be made, and indeed was made, that the program of art education was not effective in developing people with the ability to discriminate good design from bad. As a result, art educators have comparatively recently begun to give serious consideration to methods of developing taste.

How effective art teachers may be in their attempt to improve taste is still a matter of speculation. The world is full of bad taste—in books, in pictures, in music—which unquestionably overwhelms in volume the objects of good taste. We find at every turn the pulp booklet with its themes of lust and violence; we hear from countless outlets the recorded ware of the popular singer with his false sentiment. Garish and unnecessary decoration is to be seen in almost every aspect of daily living—in automobiles, in houses, in furniture. "Our unmastered crafts," asserts Teague, "have produced a squalid disorder as a too common setting of modern life." [8] In Gill's opinion, "Step by step things have been sacrificed to entries into account books." [9]

Perhaps it is still too soon to judge the effects of the new art program; perhaps the desire of men for display and ostentation, together with the pressure of advertising which often appeals to snobbishness and a desire to be up to date rather than to a respect for craftsmanship and honest quality,

---

[6] Roger Fry, *Vision and Design* (N.Y.: Meridian, 1956), p. 23. This is the currently available edition of Fry's book, published originally in 1920. Throughout the text we give wherever possible the most recent editions of all books cited.

[7] John Dewey, *Art as Experience* (N.Y.: Minton Balch, 1934), p. 341. See also G. Holme, *Industrial Design and the Future* (London: Studio, 1934).

[8] Walter Dorwin Teague, *Design This Day* (N.Y.: Harcourt, Brace, 1940), p. 115.

[9] Eric Gill, *Art and a Changing Civilization* (London: John Lane, The Bodley Head, 1934), p. 98.

The recent trends in the design of the Studebaker automobile are worthy of note in this connection. In 1953, Raymond Loewy, a U.S. designer of repute, redesigned this vehicle. In a display that year of outstanding automobile designs, the Museum of Modern Art in New York included Studebaker but no other U.S. automobile (see *Eight Automobiles*, Museum of Modern Art). But after this year the Studebaker—"one of the few really beautiful cars to come out of the United States . . . was loaded with irrelevant decoration, and finally replaced by something square, aggressive, and pretentious; something 'within the design trends of the industry,' as the handout said."— "Cars," *Design*, No. 92 (August 1956), p. 14. Studebaker, of course, was forced to make the change to sell its wares.

will hold back the efforts of the art educator. However, the need to develop taste has been recognized and an attempt to do so is an important characteristic of the present-day art program.

Belief That Art Can Help
Develop Worthy Citizens

The final characteristic of art education today is the tendency of art teachers to look upon art activities as a means of developing good citizens. This characteristic is, of course, closely related to the five characteristics previously mentioned, particularly the belief in the necessity for freedom of thought.

Art teachers today see in the artistic process a traditionally worthy occupation. The person engaged in artistic matters harnesses and directs his intellect and emotions, relates himself to his environment, and attempts to bring order out of disorder. The greatest personal disciplines must be exerted if an expressive act is to be successful and worthwhile goals achieved. The aesthetic act, in other words, engages the whole personality of the creating person and channels his actions into constructive modes of behavior.

Art, as such, then, is good for people and demands of its creators the highest standards of endeavor. There are indications, also, that under certain conditions, art tends to have permanently beneficial effects upon the personalities of those who create it. Any activity which engages the individual so deeply may exert a broad and lasting influence on the whole personality.

Since in art education today emphasis is placed upon the development of the individual as a person and not merely as a producer and consumer of art forms, the individual's behavior in relation to his associates takes on considerable significance. Contemporary art education has been affected by the idea that the school "must be a place where pupils go, not merely to learn, but to carry on a way of life." [10] Hence, the art program of today is not considered adequate unless it tends to bring about growth in the child's social intelligence, and one may find in the art class certain group activities designed to bring about this end.

The form and order inherent in art are thus utilized in the contemporary art program to help bring about a similar form and order in the lives of individuals and a more harmonious pattern of group life.

The Traditional Nature of Art

As we have suggested above, perhaps the most important influence upon contemporary art education is the nature or universal tradition of art. The

---

[10] Boyd H. Bode, *Democracy as a Way of Life* (N.Y.: Macmillan, 1937), p. 77.

1 *Even in the relatively impersonal religious art of the Middle Ages, a great work bears the stamp of the personality of its creator, as this statue of a prophet (School of Chartres) reveals.*

2 *This etching by Goya in the "Horrors of War" series portrays the intensely personal reaction of the artist to his environment, another characteristic of great art.*

Con razon ó sin ella.

failure of past art programs was a consequence of their divergence from this tradition. What is the tradition? What, in other words, is art? The question is a difficult one to answer and for centuries has been the subject of philosophical discussion. However, we may arrive at a definition of art to suit our present purpose and to indicate some of the chief and most enduring characteristics of art through the ages.[11]

Perhaps the most obvious characteristic of art is that it is the result of forming, or making. Anyone who attempts to form or make anything is an artist in embryo. If art is to be produced, however, the maker must have mastery of tools, materials, and processes. He usually achieves such mastery only through a rigorous self-discipline which keeps him striving for excellence of production. Every artist worthy of the name engages in this search for excellence, never ceasing in a struggle to surpass in quality his former output.

As a result of his struggle for mastery, an artist may produce an organization, or assembly, of materials to which we respond favorably. This assembly is usually given such names as "composition," or "design." "The musical composition is arresting," we say, or, "The design of the bridge is excellent." Bell called an arresting artistic assembly a "significant form." "In each [work of art]," he said, "lines and colors combined in a peculiar way, certain forms and relations of forms stir our aesthetic emotions . . . these aesthetically moving forms I call 'significant form' and 'significant form' is the one quality common to all works of art." [12] While Bell's statement is an important one, he failed to make entirely clear the meaning of "significant." To do so one must recognize the fact that art possesses qualities in addition to that of fine form, or design.

Common to all art, although perhaps more apparent in the art of our Western civilization than elsewhere, is the individual quality of expression. All great art bears the imprint of the personality of its creator. "Even the art that allows the least play to individual variations," says Dewey, "like, say, the religious painting and sculpture of the twelfth century, is not mechanical and hence bears the stamp of personality." [13]

The personal nature of art arises largely from two conditions of production, the first being the source of its subject matter and the second the manner in which its design is developed. The subject matter used by all artists

---

[11] For the student, one of the most complete and scholarly histories of art is Élie Faure, *History of Art,* tr. by Walter Pach, 5 vols. (N.Y.: Harper, 1921–30).

[12] Clive Bell, *Art* (N.Y.: Stokes, 1914), p. 8.

[13] John Dewey, *Art as Experience*, p. 251. See also Paul Zucker, *Styles in Painting* (N.Y.: Viking, 1950); Sheldon Cheney, *A Primer of Modern Art,* 11th Ed. (N.Y.: Tudor, 1945); and Herbert Read in his *History of Modern Art* (N.Y.: Horizon, 1953); all illustrate the intensely personal nature of contemporary art.

of reputation has been derived from a similar source. All great art presents a personal reaction of its creator to his experiences. The genius of El Greco, Breughel, Goya, Cézanne, Matisse, and a host of other great men is reflected through the thought and emotion generated by their contact with their environment. Again, the greatest artists are those who have discovered a personal mode of expression that suits the reaction to experience they wish to convey. Thus, we can glance at a work of art and say immediately, "That is a piece of sculpture by Henry Moore," "That is a painting by Chardin," or "That is an etching by Rembrandt." In the individuality of the work rests its timeless and universal quality.

We see, therefore, that art results from an act of self-expression involving emotions and intellect. Thus we may say that *art is a significant expression giving form and order to a human being's reaction to his environment.*[14] It is this concept of art—a traditional one—which governs to a great extent the art program in our schools today.

Some Periodic Changes in Artistic Theories

The history of art contains many periods in which thinking about the nature of art has changed, leading to changes in modes of expression. In some periods artists have emphasized subject matter of local interest at the expense of design. In others, design, because of new discoveries such as those of the Cubists or the Vorticists, was given greater attention than subject matter. From time to time, scientific discoveries, such as the laws of linear perspective, have dominated both design and subject matter.

As we saw in the previous discussion of the traditional nature of art, artistic expression must rely both upon personal expression of the artist's reactions to experience and upon a design which is suitable to the subject matter selected. Both aspects of expression—subject matter and design— must be developed in an art form. When one is sacrificed for the other, as for example design was neglected in the work of Landseer and some other nineteenth-century painters, or as subject matter has been slighted in the output of some nonobjective painters, the quality of art inevitably suffers.

These tangential developments in art, of course, are often good because they reveal new potentialities of expression. While they may upset the standard of production for a little while, they tend to enrich the main stream of art. Eventually each mode sinks into this stream, leaving some influence

---

[14] See Dewey, *Art as Experience*, pp. 64–65 for further elaboration of this idea.

3 *A dominant theme of primitive art is the expression of fear in an unknowable world. In this work the Maori sculptor obviously has not been concerned with expressing his reaction to ideal beauty!*

or disappearing entirely, according to its merits, while the great artistic tradition lives on.

At least four developments, which overlap to some extent, are worthy of our consideration since each has influenced, or continues to influence, art education in varying degrees. The first of these is the dominance of "beauty" as an ideal of artistic expression; the second is the influence of a movement called "Neo-Impressionism"; the third, the influence of "Expressionism"; and the fourth, the movement known as "nonobjective."

The Concept of "Beauty"

The idea that art should exhibit a reaction to beauty is of limited significance in the history of art. As Read points out, it probably arose in Greece as the offspring of a humanistic philosophy of life, was inherited by Rome, and was revived by the Renaissance.[15]

---

[15] Herbert Read, *The Meaning of Art* (N.Y.: Pitman, 1951).

The chief theme of Greek art was the portrayal of a perfect type of humanity, an ideal which naturally gave great emphasis to physical beauty. But this, continues Read, is only one of several possible artistic ideals. The Byzantine ideal is divine rather than human. The primitive ideal is often the expression of fear in an unknowable world; much of the oriental is abstract, nonhuman. It would be difficult to bring beauty into service of all aesthetic expressions of these several ideals.

While many artists have relied upon beauty as a basis for expression, it is merely one of many possible themes. Goya, for example, found inspiration in the horrors of war as well as in the beauty of a woman's body; Daumier found themes for expression in political revolution; Toulouse-Lautrec, in the degradation of the body and soul. Art, in fact, embraces all of life and not only that small segment of it which may be considered ideally beautiful. So powerful, however, is the Greek-Roman-Renaissance influence upon Western civilization that even to this day the limiting concept of ideal beauty as a single theme of art still exerts a major influence upon professional art and hence upon art education in our schools. Nevertheless, to impose such a limitation upon children, as some teachers have done, is to deny children the opportunity of exploring all the themes that artistic expression traditionally includes.

Neo-Impressionism

In the closing years of the nineteenth century one finds the origins of a second major influence upon art education. Starting with a consideration of color, certain writers and painters attempted to interpret design in terms of physical laws and by means of intellectual analyses of surface composition.[16] Georges Seurat and Paul Signac—both painters of ability—attempted to find a logic in the use of pigment which their predecessors, the Impressionists, had employed with great charm but wholly intuitively.[17] Scientists such as Chevreul, Helmholtz, and Ostwald provided an intellectual and theoretical

---

[16] The reader is referred to Jay Hambidge, *Dynamic Symmetry* (New Haven, Conn.: Yale Univ. Press, 1936), in which the ultimate in intellectual analysis of pictorial composition is to be found. Here the author resolves a number of masterpieces into mathematical formulas. How wrong one may go by following a formula may be seen in Faber Birrin's *Monument to Color* (N.Y.: McFarlane, 1938). One can only describe the illustrations in color as shockingly bad. The book, however, contains considerable technical and historical information about color theory.

[17] Seurat's painting *Les Poseuses* is especially interesting as an example of Neo-Impressionism since he includes as a background a part of his masterpiece *La Grande Jatte*. A good book on Seurat and his painting is the volume in French, Jacques de Laprade, *Georges Seurat* (Monaco: Les documents d'art, 1945). Even if the reader cannot understand French, the volume is still worth looking at because of its well-selected and well-reproduced illustrations.

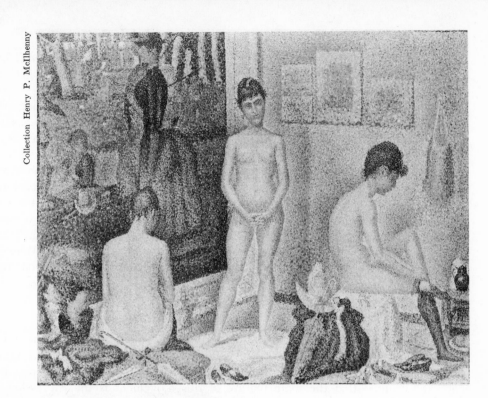

4 In the background of this Neo-Impressionist masterpiece,
Les Poseuses *by Seurat, we see a portion of his even
more famous* **La Grande Jatte.** *Notice the carefully arranged dots of pigment, characteristic of the method of
painting known as "pointillism" developed by Seurat and
his followers.*

summation of much that had been discovered intuitively by many artists
in the past.

Although the Neo-Impressionists first emphasized color, it was not long
before they either invented or resurrected formulas for other elements of
pictorial composition. Some of the classic formulas of the Greeks were re-
studied to find "the perfect proportion" so that a formula could be offered
for the most pleasing oblong. The idea of a "line of beauty," first formulated
by the English critic John Ruskin, was also revived. Ruskin had stated that
the most acceptable line which could be employed in art was an S-curve,
later occasionally called the "Hogarth line of beauty" because it was discovered that this sprightly artist had used it to good effect.

In the United States appeared such influential books as A. W. Dow's

Composition [18] and Denman Ross's *The Theory of Pure Design*.[19] Each of these publications presented theoretical analysis of design, together with some formulas for the production of aesthetic compositions.

Many of the findings of the Neo-Impressionists have been important to us. Through the work of the colorists, a series of hues in pigment has become standardized. Today, when we order a certain hue of paint, for example, we know exactly what color to expect from the manufacturer. One cannot deny, furthermore, that the efforts of many of the early Neo-Impressionist painters were within the artistic tradition in the sense that they were reaching into the unknown and engaged in the never-ending task of all good artists—the search for excellence of expression. It was not the fault of these men that others of less stature, both teachers and artists, unthinkingly adopted the formulas which the Neo-Impressionists had evolved creatively. When artists resorted to formulas, their work became sterile; when classroom teachers did so, the children's work suffered similarly.

Expressionism

Van Gogh

In revolt against the intellectualism of Neo-Impressionism came Expressionism. Expressionism, while difficult to define because it took numerous forms, was clearly the opposite of Neo-Impressionism. Some people have claimed that the main feature of this movement is the expression of the artist's feelings, rather than his ideas, in the face of his environment. Others have stated that the movement relies chiefly upon design used nonobjectively, or at least very abstractly, to achieve an order and a rhythm which have greater significance than can be found in art which relies upon nature as a basis for expression.[20] Still others assert that Expressionism is mainly decorative.[21]

Matisse, Rouault, and Derain may be taken as representative painters

[18] N.Y.: Doubleday, Page, 1899. One should note here that Dow's contribution is considered by some to be an important forward step in art education. Italo de Francesco, in "Changing Ideas about Art Education," *School Arts,* Vol. 56, No. 8 (April 1956), 8, says: "Dow's contribution lifted art education from a traditionally academic position to a recognition of basic principles and elements of composition. It was argued that with the new approach a measure of personal interpretation could be evoked."

[19] Boston: Houghton Mifflin, 1907.

[20] See the following section for a discussion of abstract and nonobjective means of expression.

[21] See some of the following concerning the nature of Expressionism:
Clive Bell, *Since Cézanne,* (N.Y.: Harcourt, Brace, 1922). Sheldon W. Cheney, *The Story of Modern Art* (N.Y.: Viking, 1941), and *Expressionism in Art* (N.Y.: Liveright, 1941), Herbert Read, *Art Now* (N.Y.: Pitman, 1949). A sprightly and entertaining account of Expressionism in America may be found in parts of Rudi Blesh, *Modern Art U.S.A.* (N.Y.: Knopf, 1956).

5 *In this painting, which is called* **The Black Circle,** *Kandinsky,* *"the father of nonobjective painting," has depended solely upon a manipulation of the elements of design for expressive purposes.*

The Museum of Modern Art, New York.
Acquired through the Lillie P. Bliss Bequest.

of the movement. An analysis of their work leads to a number of conclusions concerning Expressionism. Generally speaking, it may be said that the Expressionist painter places emphasis upon emotions, sensations, or ideas, rather than upon the appearance of objects. He presents his reactions in a form which is almost invariably a pronounced distortion of the camera view of the environment. Frequently his expression takes the form of extreme abstraction. The liberating effects upon painting which attended Expressionism can be well imagined.[22] Later we shall see that it had similar effects upon art education, which are still being felt.

Nonobjective Art

From Expressionism arose nonobjective painting. Wassily Kandinsky, a Russian who lived in Germany and France, is considered to be the father of nonobjective painting.[23] Until the advent of the nonobjective, the subject matter of painting derived almost universally from the natural world, although the degree of correspondence ranged widely from photographic to

---

[22] The reader is referred to Appendix II, "Series of Books for Art Appreciation," for titles dealing with Expressionistic artists.

[23] Kandinsky wrote an exposition of his art for the Guggenheim Foundation (N.Y.: 1946) under the title *On the Spiritual in Art.* Piet Mondrian is another well-known nonobjectivist; see his *Plastic Art and Pure Plastic Art* (N.Y.: Wittenborn, 1945).

highly abstract statement. The nonobjective painter, however, asserts that he bases his expression upon the manipulation of the elements of design— line, mass and space, light and shade, texture, and color [24]—without reference to the visible world so that subject matter is in a sense eliminated. Although nonobjective painting has perhaps declined in popularity recently, it has taught us much about media, techniques, and pictorial composition, and art education has profited greatly from this knowledge.

The Influence of the Democratic Credo

Since art is of a highly personal nature, the creating person must be the controlling agent of the activities which engage him. To be in control of his work the artist must enjoy a high degree of freedom in the choice of both subject matter and manner of expression.

At certain periods in the political and aesthetic life of the world, restrictions have been placed upon artists. Sometimes these restrictions have re-

[24] See Chapter 3 for a discussion of these elements.

6 *Classic façade of the Pennsylvania Station, New York, built in the first decade of the twentieth century. Until the second decade, submission to the classic mode of architectural design tended to impede the development of a creative building art.*

Pennsylvania Railroad

sulted not from the normal discipline of artistic production, but rather from the repressive actions of dictators. One of the most recent examples of such a period was the Nazi regime in Germany. The Nazi repression was, of course, promulgated for political reasons, as are the similar restrictions on Soviet artists today. In other periods, various groups of artists, salons, and academies have attempted to restrict artistic activities, often for the purpose of maintaining a *status quo* in which their members strongly believed. In England, in France, and elsewhere, individuals or groups of influential artists have from time to time attempted to set forth canons for art from which deviations were greatly discouraged. Sometimes one man of remarkable ability and persuasive power was able to influence artistic thought around him until it became derivative rather than creative. Under all such conditions, the art production of the times has suffered.

Cheney has offered a number of examples which demonstrate the disastrous effects which unnecessary restriction has upon artists' output.[25] He mentions the Chinese, who, with their passion for regulating design, did not escape the cramping effects which attend the codification of rules related to composition. Cheney also cites the codification of the rules of architecture by Vitruvius. Originally written in the first century A.D., these rules were rediscovered and enthusiastically adopted by the architects of the Renaissance. The supremacy of Vitruvius' "orders" has touched the environment of all of us. Cheney maintains that until the second decade of this century submission to the classic mode of architectural design seriously impeded the development of a creative building art based upon human need.

One of the most clear-cut examples, of course, of dictatorial practices which almost completely stifled aesthetic expression may be found in educational systems of the past. The lessons which we have learned, therefore, from a study of artistic practice, and which today we apply to art education in our schools, are concerned with two freedoms. We believe that art cannot flourish, either in professional circles or in school, unless the creating person is free, first, to employ those aspects of experience which truly arouse his emotions and stimulate his intellect and, second, to develop a form of expression which he finds sympathetic to the theme he wishes to express. Today we believe that the success of a program of art education depends largely upon adherence to these traditional freedoms. Furthermore, we believe that the quality of any art program may be judged by the degree to which the teacher advocates these freedoms and the means by which he encourages them.

It will be realized that the freedoms necessary for the success of an aesthetic act are closely related to those freedoms of thought and action in

---

[25] Sheldon Cheney, *A New World History of Art* (N.Y.: Viking, 1956), pp. 203, 333–34.

general which are the privilege of the individual living in a democracy. These democratic freedoms have been won slowly. The governments of most democracies and the public institutions for which these governments have been largely responsible have not always provided liberties in keeping with the democratic ideal. Schools were often notorious for the dictatorial character of their teaching procedures. While believing in democracy and indeed preaching it, most schools were governed by a methodology which today we might expect to find only in totalitarian states.

At the time when these procedures were current, democracy had received no real challenge. Karl Marx had written *Das Kapital,* but leading democratic countries were in no way threatened by dictatorial states. Britain had her magnificent navy which kept her possessions safe, and the North American continent was safeguarded from the turmoil of the European scene by the expanse of the Atlantic. The Orient was a quaint but negligible factor in the political life of the world. Russia had suffered from internal political upheavals and had neither the ability nor the strength to act as an aggressor.

Up to World War I, there was thus little need to defend democracy against nondemocratic ideas, external or internal. Dictatorship in the schools was shrugged off with the adage "spare the rod and spoil the child." The experience of freedom could be postponed until adulthood. New methods of warfare and the rise of the dictator states, however, forced the democracies to fight for an existence which in the past had largely been taken for granted. The democratic way of life was thus shaken. Many of its institutions had to be reappraised in the light of the new situation in the world, and the schools were included in the scrutiny. The question was asked, how could dictatorial methods within the classroom be reconciled with the democratic ideal? Obviously, if children were to be prepared for democratic life within the classroom, teaching methods had to be devised to produce democratic citizens. It was obviously wrong that children living in a democratic state should emerge from its schools with uniform opinions derived from dictatorial teaching procedures. The inculcation of uniform beliefs was the tool of the dictators; democracy could exist only in an atmosphere which allowed freedom of thought. One writer on education, Robert Ulich, went so far as to assert that democratic education must stake everything on a program for the liberation of intelligence.[26]

A fact which perhaps has not been as freely recognized as it might have been is that art educators have been among the pioneers in developing a pedagogy which is compatible with democratic practices. What assisted them as much as anything was the recognition of the fact that such a form

---

[26] Robert Ulich, *Fundamentals of Democratic Education* (N.Y.: American Book, 1940).

of pedagogy was in keeping with the requirements of artistic expression. Indeed, art could not be taught successfully unless it was presented in an atmosphere of democratic freedom.

Art and General Educational Thought

Modern education, of which art education is a part, is not entirely a product of the last three or four decades. Many of the basic ideas to be found both in aesthetics and in teaching today may be traced to ideas held by philosophers and teachers who lived long ago.

What a modern ring some of the ancient writings have! In the *Republic* of Plato (427–347 B.C.), for example, we find the germ of the concept called the "search for excellence" discussed earlier in this chapter. Again, both Montaigne (1533–1592) and Bacon (1561–1626), who published his first treatise on education in 1605, emphasized the need to base teaching upon first-hand experience rather than upon "logic chopping." Comenius (1592–1671) developed this idea in his *Didactica Magna* and later made it practical in his *Orbis Pictus*. In the latter, it is also interesting to note, he affirmed that children should not memorize what they do not understand. Rousseau (1712–1788) believed that teaching should be related to childhood interests and that education should be concerned with the everyday life of the child. He emphasized these ideas in his *Émile:*

> What must we think of the barbarous education, which sacrifices the present to the uncertain future, which loads a child with chains of every sort, and begins by making him miserable, in order to prepare him, long in advance, for some pretended happiness which it is probable he will never enjoy?

Let children be children, Rousseau advocated, and let them learn through self-initiated activities. He also touched on the matter of competition—a question we are still debating in education—and declared that self-competition is to be preferred to a rivalry between a child and his fellows. It must be admitted that Rousseau was a theorist and a dreamer, and that some of his ideas about teaching appear to be quite impractical. It remained for future teachers to bring pedagogical order out of Rousseau's theories. Three men, Pestalozzi (1746–1826), Herbart (1776–1841), and Froebel (1782–1852) contributed to this process.

Unlike most of his predecessors, the gentle Swiss Pestalozzi gave particular emphasis to the idea that education is more than a process of recording sense impressions upon a passive mind, or "tabula rasa" as he put it. The

7 *Froebel established the first kindergarten in 1837. His influence upon art education, while considerable, is not always acceptable to modern art teachers.*

learner must, himself, be an active participant and must reorganize the experiences which come to him. It was Pestalozzi, also, who saw as the chief aim of teaching the development of good citizens.[27]

As a pioneer and experimenter, Pestalozzi made many mistakes, and he lacked the ability to systematize his thoughts into a teaching methodology. The task of developing a systematic pedagogy was left to the learned German Herbart. Herbart gained inspiration to perform this task, however, from Pestalozzi's school in Yverdon.[28] Although Herbart's methodology seems cold and formal to teachers today, his teachings nevertheless recognize in the learning process the natural capacities, interests, and activities of children.

Froebel, also a German, who was something of a mystic, established his first kindergarten in 1837 after visiting Yverdon. His methods of teaching were founded upon the naturalism preached by Rousseau and practiced by Pestalozzi. His mystical ideas prompted him to make use in the kindergarten of objects having a basic geometrical shape—cube, circle, prism, and so on, on the theory that a child would gain an awareness of unity, and indeed Deity, by being in contact with some of these "perfect" forms. Froebel has exerted a profound influence upon art education in kindergartens, but his influence is not always acceptable to modern art teachers, for reasons which

---

[27] See Pestalozzi's novel, *Leonard and Gertrude* (1781) and his book on education, *How Gertude Teaches her Children* (1801).
[28] Herbart wrote *ABC of Sense Perception* to explain Pestalozzi's views.

will be explained later. His strong belief, however, derived from Pestalozzi, that children should be taught from the concrete to the abstract and that a school should form a miniature society, we admit today as sound.[29]

Although the educational theories and practices just described have had their effects upon art teaching, an even stronger influence is to be found in the developments of psychological thought. A complete and detailed study of the effects of psychology upon methodology is manifestly impossible here. One may indicate, however, one or two of the most important influences in psychology which have affected teaching methods in art. These influences include, first, what are known as "faculty" and "Herbartian" psychology, both of which are associated with the so-called "introspective" school of psychological thought; second, the "functional" school of psychology from which developed E. L. Thorndike's "S–R" theory of learning and much of John Dewey's philosophy; and third, the "Gestalt" school of psychology. Although psychology has in recent years developed still other theories of learning, these new developments have so far exerted little influence on art education.

The "faculty" psychologists believed that the mind was composed of a series of separate compartments each of which housed a "faculty" such as "memory," "will," or "reason." In order to train his mind, a person must, according to them, perform a series of intellectual exercises. "Those whose 'faculties' had not been trained by suitable exercises or who were deemed lacking in 'faculties' as the masses were sometimes thought to be had to be content with lowly social positions."[30] Because the faculty psychologists taught that the mental powers developed through exercise could be applied to all areas of human endeavor, including artistic effort, their influence upon early art education was great.

Herbart thought that the mind acted as a unity, maintaining that it has the power of what he called "apperception." This, he said, is the capacity to assimilate new ideas through ideas already acquired. Herbart developed teaching methods which he believed assisted the mind to make use of the power of apperception.

Herbart's methods "elevated the importance of the teacher and made the pupil a listener, whose mind was to be molded according to a preconceived plan of studies and by formal steps of method. . . ."[31] By the middle of the nineteenth century, the Herbartian steps of teaching had become current practice—indeed, slogans—in almost every North American

---

[29] His most important book is *Education and Man*, published in 1826.

[30]. James Mulhern, *A History of Education* (N.Y.: Ronald Press, 1946), p. 389.

[31] *Ibid.*

normal school and soon determined the methods used in "drawing" lessons as well as in those of other subjects.[32]

In America, interest later developed in a concept of mind related to Darwinian biology in which mind was considered to be the chief factor in adaptation to environment. Hence it was said to consist of functions rather than of the static structures suggested by earlier psychologies; this concept led to the so-called "functional" school of psychology.

John Dewey (1859–1952) was in his early years closely associated with the functional school of psychology, of which he is considered to be one of the founders. As a philosopher, of course, Dewey ranged far in his ideas, but they were unmistakably colored by functionalism. Dewey was greatly concerned with the relationship of the learner to the environment and society in which he lives.[33] He saw education as the "continuing re-creation of experience." He pointed out that experience and education are not synonymous; education involves the direction and control of experience, and a good experience implies some measure of control for future experiences. Knowledge is not static, Dewey said, nor is it gained in a static environment to be used in a static society. Learning must lead to more learning, and the end of knowledge can never be reached. Dewey's ideas readily lend themselves to the teaching of art. Indeed, he was a philosopher of aesthetics as well as of education and produced an admirable book on the subject to which we shall again refer.[34]

A psychologist also associated with the functional school of thought was E. L. Thorndike (1874–1949). Thorndike joined the staff of Teachers College, Columbia University, in 1901 and remained there until his retirement in 1940. Among his achievements were the development of a systematic animal psychology, the production of the first standardized tests in education, and the investigation of many problems of learning.[35]

Thorndike based his educational theories upon what is called a stimulus-response, or "S–R," theory. According to this theory, learning consists in the establishment of a series of connections, or pathways, in the brain, re-

---

[32] The Herbartian steps of teaching are as follows: preparation, presentation, association, generalization, and application. The student is referred to Herbart's *Text Book of Psychology,* published in 1816, and his *Outlines of Educational Doctrine,* published in 1835.

[33] Of the vast amount of writing Dewey produced on this theme, perhaps his *Democracy and Education* might be selected for reading by the student.

[34] *Art as Experience.*

[35] In 1913 and 1914 he published his three-volume *Educational Psychology,* comprising the following: Vol. I, The Original Nature of Man; Vol. II, The Psychology of Learning; Vol. III, Work, Fatigue and Individual Differences.

8 *John Dewey, a philosopher of aesthetics as well as of education, profoundly influenced contemporary art education.*

Brown Brothers

sulting from a specific stimulus which causes an equally specific response.[36] Between each nerve ending is a gap, or synapse, which tends to resist the impulse of the stimulus but which can be bridged by repeated stimuli. This physiological condition led Thorndike to believe that learning should be a matter of repetitive drill. The most efficient form of teaching would result from breaking a school subject into minute parts. Drill based upon these minute details would then allow the learner to develop "a wonderfully elaborate and intricate system of connections." [37] When Thorndike's system was applied to art, it exhibited certain deficiencies. While learning may undoubtedly occur as a result of a methodology based upon such a system, the S–R theory failed, as we shall see, to promote the kind of creative thinking which art demands.

Having strong influence upon contemporary art education is a system of psychology called "Gestalt." Some of the limitations of earlier approaches to learning were demonstrated by the Gestaltists. Kurt Koffka (1886–1941) in his book *The Growth of the Mind* [38] produced evidence to show that in learning an organism acts as an entity and not by exercising certain parts.

---

36 See Thorndike's description of this phenomenon in *The Psychology of Wants, Interests, and Attitudes* (N.Y.: Appleton-Century-Crofts, 1935), pp. 17–18.

37 E. L. Thorndike, *Educational Psychology: Briefer Course* (N.Y.: Teachers Coll., 1914), p. 173.

38 N.Y.: Harcourt, Brace, 1928.

Wolfgang Köhler, a German psychologist, while caught in neutral Tenerife during World War I, performed experiments with primates which supported the Gestaltist theories. In his experiments primates show "insight" in solving problems.[39] From such experiments, the Gestaltists maintained that wholes are primary; parts derive their properties and their behavior from them. The learner, in other words, acquires knowledge not by building bit by bit a system of nervous connections, but by achieving "insight," that is, *understanding of the relationships among the various aspects of the learning situation.* How deeply this idea has affected contemporary art education we shall see in the subsequent chapters of this book.

Changes in Art Education

Having studied the three major influences upon art education as we find it today, we may now examine in some detail the changes which have occurred in this area since it was first offered as a part of general education. Although art activities have apparently engaged the attention of man almost since his beginning on earth, art as a part of general education is relatively new. Many other fields of study had become traditional before the 1850's when art, in a restricted form, was placed on most programs of studies. Even when art began to be offered in some schools, leaders in public education were usually reluctant to recognize its importance or give it support as a serious part of the school program. Even fifty years ago, educational thinkers such as Herbert Spencer held that art should be considered only as a leisure-time activity.[40] Spencer's position may be explained by the fact that he was greatly influenced, like the "functionalists," by Darwin's *Origin of Species,* so that, to him, the fundamentals of a good education depended upon activities contributing largely to human survival in a world of fierce biological competition. Art, therefore, was a luxury which might be indulged in only after all other "necessary" human activities had received their fullest share of attention. The Spencerian attitude toward art was long current in schools; even today a few educators may still be found who agree with Spencer.

Around the 1850's, a type of work which in some respects might be considered the beginnings of school art began to make its appearance in some European and American institutions of learning. This work was usually called "linear drawing," and while it did not include expressive work, it involved some of the media associated with art. In its beginning, linear drawing consisted for the most part of the making of maps, but as time went on, the content of the program was broadened. By the 1880's it included map-

---

[39] *The Mentality of Apes* (N.Y.: Harcourt, Brace, 1927).
[40] *Education—Intellectual, Moral and Physical* (N.Y.: Appleton, 1906).

drawing and "the delineation of common objects on paper, slates, and blackboard," by which advanced pupils might master the intricacies of linear perspective. The thirty-year advance may seem pitiful to us today, particularly in view of the tremendous strides being made at the time by such artists as Manet, Degas, Toulouse-Lautrec, Pissarro, and, above all, Cézanne.[41] Nevertheless even this limited advance had the effect of breaching a hitherto impregnable and almost universal wall of academic resistance to anything resembling art in general education.

The nature of the program of linear drawing may be studied in several series of exercise books which were published beginning in the 1870's. These series consisted usually of eight books—one for each grade. They remained in vogue until the early 1900's when "drawing" became "art," and a new point of view became apparent.

Influenced by the "faculty" type of psychology, the drawing books outlined a curious mixture of mechanical drawing and freehand copying and were planned according to an adult standard of draftsmanship. They were built upon the idea that it is necessary to master the elements of one small skill before progressing to an exercise involving another skill.

In North America, the *Smith Drawing Books* were one of the first of the series to be adopted for general use in schools. Walter Smith, their author, was at one time Headmaster of the Leeds School of Art and Science, a training school in England for art teachers. He later became State Director of Art Education in Massachusetts. In 1872 he published a volume called *Art Education, Scholastic and Industrial*.[42] Smith seems to have been a man of considerable learning, for in this volume he made many fitting remarks concerning the design of industrial objects. Unfortunately, his pedagogy was characterized by the limitations of his day.

The many series of drawing books which appeared during the period of "linear drawing" were very much alike in format. Most of them provided on the cover a statement concerning their educational objectives. It was usually stated that the purpose of the series was "the laying of a good foundation for more advanced art training." The following statements as to the particular aims of the books are typical:

1. To train the eye in the accurate perception of form, size, and proportion, and to exactness in the measurement of distances and angles.
2. To train the hand to freedom and rapidity of execution.

---

[41] Professional developments in "drawing" as illustrated in etchings of this period are strikingly displayed in Edward T. Chase, *The Etchings of the French Impressionists and their Contemporaries* (N.Y.: Crown, 1946).

[42] Boston: James R. Osgood & Company.

9 *A page from a drawing book published in the 1880's.*

10 *This page from Smith's* Art Education, Scholastic and Industrial, *which appeared in 1872, illustrates the prevailing rigid authoritarianism in so-called art education.*

hand heavy line, draw a vertical line parallel with the diagonal of the square and to the centre of the nearest semi-diameter. Observe me.
Pupils. — We have drawn it.

This will give the result which is seen at C.

Teacher. — How many corresponding lines does symmetry now require to be drawn?
Pupils. — Seven.
Teacher. — Draw them, and erase the construction lines.
Pupils. — We have, and it gives us a cross.

The result may be seen at A, less the construction lines. It is a simple combination of straight lines; but, because the lines are symmetrically arranged about a centre, the effect is pleasing.

A Rosette, illustrating Symmetrical Arrangement about the Centre of a Square.

Here, at D, we have another simple illustration of the principle of symmetrical arrangement about the centre of a square. The form may be used for a blackboard lesson in this wise: —

Teacher. — Draw a square on its diameters; add the diagonals. Thus. From the upper end of the upper left-hand semi-diagonal, mark off one-eighth of its length. Thus. What does symmetry now require?
Pupils. — That the same length be marked off

D.

3. To train the memory to accurate recollection of the forms and arrangements of objects.
4. To cultivate and refine the taste by the study, delineation, and recollection of beautiful forms.

In the teachers' colleges of this period, the drawing books were often used as guides to methodology. The teachers-in-training were subjected to the same type of formal discipline in drawing as was advocated in the drawing books. A study of the drawing examinations which teachers-in-training had to pass gives further insight into the emphasis placed upon technical skill in drawing rather than upon expression. The following are sample questions placed on an examination paper set at a teachers' college in 1878:

1. Give instructions in full as you would give them to a class for drawing a water pitcher. Be especially particular about the *lip* and *handle*. Show your construction lines.
2. Sketch a doorway with a door half open.
3. Draw a Roman cross showing its thickness; first, with the eye *below* it and to the left; second, with the eye *above* it and to the right.[43]

As time went on, a number of art schools became interested in the drawing program in the public schools and some of them established courses for prospective teachers. In this way, the influence of the drawing books tended to diminish. Unfortunately, the early program in the art schools apparently was as rigid as that set forth in the books. When state departments of education brought their influences upon such courses, they apparently made it clear that no nonsense was to be condoned in art classes. As one official in an education department put it:

> The subjects [in the art course] will be of a practical character. Take drawing, for example; it is not the purpose of the government to encourage amateurs whose sole object is to draw something agreeable, merely for the sake of representation, but rather to provide instruction which will assist in explaining the technicalities of that which is represented.

A representative "elementary" course for teachers-in-training might consist, therefore, of the following studies: "freehand outlines; model drawing; perspective; practical geometry." An advanced course might contain a continuation of the subjects found in the elementary course, with the addition of "historical ornament and painting of objects in oils." By the turn of

---

[43] While teachers today might be expected to answer such questions, they would, of course, not be judged solely upon their ability to find correct answers to mechanical problems of this kind.

the century, "nature study" was sometimes added to the list, while a study of famous paintings might appear in some programs.

That the program of "linear drawing" was anything but creative and expressive is obvious. Nevertheless, it left deep-set influences upon art education. Even to this day, one may find in some classrooms certain so-called "art" activities which are based upon the program of linear drawing. Where they are not used merely to keep children quiet, coloring exercises, for example, are still offered in some schools in the belief that the hand and eye should be trained dissociated from thought. Step-by-step exercises in which the teacher does the planning and organizing of an art form, and by which the children are taught to follow directions passively, are another manifestation of the fact that neither linear drawing nor the Herbartian methodology is yet dead in our educational systems. That exercises of this type are educationally inefficient has been proved over and over again, and yet these practices persist.

The influence of the S–R theory of learning was equally unfortunate. It led to an overemphasis of the intellectual content of art programs, rigidity, and the acceptance of the worst aspects of Neo-Impressionism. Children were encouraged to make color wheels and value scales. They made prearranged designs to illustrate some of the standardized color arrangements known as "monochromatic," "complementary," "split-complementary," and the like. Exercises in the use of "classic proportion and line" were to be found in many schools.

11 *Examples of the use of Froebel's "basic shapes." "Art" lessons which teach children to copy these forms are harmful to educational development.*

12　*A picture produced in Cizek's school in Vienna. Cizek proved that children are capable of expressing themselves in a personal, creative, and acceptable manner.*

Certain activities found in the program of linear drawing were retained. Linear perspective was given even greater prominence because it provided a collection of neat intellectual tricks for teachers and pupils. The chalk box, drawn in "two- and three-point perspective," was laboriously delineated by many a weary pupil, as were lines of telephone poles and railway tracks. In connection with most activities, a number of "principles" were established which the pupils were expected to commit to memory.

Even the youngest children did not escape. Froebel's "basic shapes" were employed to teach "drawing" to them. Teachers designed "men" and "birds" out of circles, "houses" out of triangles, and a host of objects out of oblongs. These the children copied. In so doing they were denied the opportunity for expressive work resulting from first-hand observation of their environment.

Until the advent of Expressionism, art education remained remarkably aloof from the artistic tradition, and even then artistic thinking affected education only slowly. Expressionism first had its effect upon art education largely through the work of one outstanding teacher, Franz Cizek.[44] Cizek,

---

[44] See W. Viola, *Child Art and Franz Cizek* (N.Y.: Reynal & Hitchcock, 1936). See also Thomas Munro, *Art Education, Its Philosophy and Psychology* (N.Y.: Liberal Arts Press, 1956), pp. 237–47.

an Austrian, went to Vienna in 1865 to study art. At the close of his formal period of study, he turned to art education. In 1904, after achieving success in several teaching posts, he accepted the position of chief of the Department of Experimentation and Research at the Vienna School of Applied Arts. His now famous art classes for children were developed in this department.

Cizek eliminated from these classes such activities as the making of color charts and the photographic drawing of natural objects. Rather, he encouraged children to present in visual form their emotional reactions to happenings in their lives. In the output produced under his guidance, much of which has been preserved to this day, one finds that the young artists depicted themselves at play, attending happy gatherings, and in general doing the things which naturally engage the attention and interest of the young. Cizek always maintained that it was never his aim to develop artists. Instead, he held as his one aim the development of the creative power which he found in all children and which, he felt, could blossom "in accordance with natural laws." [45]

Much of the work produced in Cizek's classrooms reveals the charm of expression of which children, under sympathetic teachers, are capable. There are indications, however, that Cizek and his staff discouraged the young from venturing much beyond the concept of beauty as a theme for artistic expression. Some of the output seems oversweet and discloses pretty mannerisms, such as a profusion of stars in the sky areas of compositions or, again, a stylized expression of childish innocence in the drawing of faces. These mannerisms lead one to deduce that there may have been overvigorous teaching in some of the classes, and that the artistic development of the children was brought about as much by some of Cizek's teachers as by "natural laws." Nevertheless, Cizek is a most important figure in the story of art education, and his work deserves the widespread admiration it has received. The contemporary belief that children, under certain conditions, are capable of expressing themselves in a personal, creative, and acceptable manner derives largely from his demonstrations in Vienna.

During the years in which Cizek held his classes, many visitors from abroad came to him. Word spread, in particular to England and America, of the "new system of art teaching." [46] Those who understood its basic prin-

---

[45] R. R. Tomlinson, *Picture Making by Children* (London: Studio, 1934), p. 27.

[46] Tomlinson made Cizek's methods well known in England; see his *Picture Making by Children*. His *Crafts for Children* (N.Y.: Studio, 1955) is also an excellent book in which children's three-dimensional art activities are discussed in relation to Expressionism. Munro was among the many influential writers who brought word of Cizek to the U.S.A. Developments along Cizek's lines in Canada were largely the result of the work of Arthur Lismer; see John McLeish, *September Gale, A Study of Arthur Lismer* (Toronto: Dent, 1955), especially Chapter 8.

ciples used the new system to bring about desirable modifications of their art programs. In education as elsewhere, however, there are always those who embrace new movements without understanding them. Expressionism as related to art education was no exception. Several observers of Cizek's methods who found merit in the idea of "creative expression" were unable to develop an adequate pedagogy to make his ideas practicable. Such teachers were convinced that the child could grow naturally, untrammeled by adult interference. Freedom to grow "according to natural laws" meant for them that the child should have license to do pretty much as he liked without adult supervision.

When certain educational administrators witnessed some of the artistic results of the program of "freedom without restriction" they were evidently disturbed. Instead of the orderly, neat, and disciplined delineation of railway tracks and chalk boxes and the bright circles of color charts, here were meaningless daubs of paint produced in noise and confusion. If this was art, they wanted no part of it. Said one official in an educational report: "There is no pretense at teaching the subject. . . . It is a method to keep children busy. The results obtained are deplorable."

Much of this criticism was justified. When children are left to their own devices and lack stimulus and guidance from a teacher, the results are indeed often "deplorable." [47] While art, as we observed earlier, cannot be produced without certain democratic freedoms, progress in expression cannot take place unless an acceptable pedagogy underlies classroom procedures.

These false moves toward freedom of expression in art education were often responsible for delays in bringing art education closer to the artistic tradition. But today the future of art education in America appears bright. Guided by a broad human philosophy, a practical psychology, and a traditional aesthetic, it should continue to flourish, no matter what problems the future may bring.

The Objectives of Contemporary Art Education

A study of the trends in art education over the last century and a consideration of its contemporary characteristics lead us to the assertion that the main objective of art education today is to assist in the intellectual, emotional, and

---

[47] We still have the *laissez-faire* teachers with us and, paradoxically, there are none more dictatorial than they. Even if the child requires instruction, they insist on withholding it from him, and maintain that he will learn without urging or guidance. See also Monica Haley, "Contradictions in Art Educational Theory and Practice," *Art Education,* vol. 9, No. 5 (June 1956), pp. 6 ff.

social growth of the learner according to his needs and capacities. In addition to this general objective, art education today has certain specific objectives.

Art is included in the school program so that children

a) may gain insight into the nature of creative, artistic acts;

b) may acquire artistic skills in relation to activities involving their emotions and their intellect;

c) may learn some of the possibilities and responsibilities which accompany freedom of thought and action in relation to artistic pursuits;

d) may gain insight into their environment by expressive acts based upon their experiences;

e) may develop their taste by broad artistic experience with many materials and techniques;

f) may by artistic endeavors develop greater insight into the nature of the democratic ideal.

Art today is a field of study which can help to develop worthy citizens—people who enjoy intellectual and emotional control, people with skill and initiative, and people who are aware of the world in which they live. Art lends itself readily to the accomplishment of these aims. Perhaps no other field of study can quite equal art in the flexibility with which it can accomodate itself to the most divergent types of personalities. Obviously, art has always challenged the most gifted. Contemporary teaching methods, however, have demonstrated that all normal children can find success in this work. Recently proof has been forthcoming that children of retarded mental development can engage profitably in art activities.[48] Further discoveries have shown that with children suffering from various psychoses, art has been used successfully for therapeutic purposes, and it is claimed that some unfortunate mental conditions have been corrected by means of creative artistic activities.[49] In short, as we shall attempt to show in the following chapters of this book, art is a worthwhile activity for nearly all children.

---

[48] See for example C. D. and M. R. Gaitskell, *Art Education for Slow Learners*, (Peoria, Ill.: Bennett, 1953).

[49] See Emery I. Gondor, *Art and Play Therapy* (N.Y.: Doubleday, 1954), an excellent book for the layman. See also Viktor Lowenfeld (Ed.), "Art Education for the Exceptional Child," *Research Bulletin*, Kutztown, Pa., Eastern Art Association, April, 1956. This pamphlet does not pretend to offer much information, but it reviews the scope of the subject.

ACTIVITIES FOR THE READER

1. Study a group of children enrolled in (a) a kindergarten or first grade and (b) a fifth or sixth grade. Observe the children at work and at play. Make a note of what you consider to be their creative acts.

2. Study an art session under the supervision of an expert teacher. Make observations of the following: (a) the ways in which the children develop artistic skills; (b) the ways in which freedom of thought is encouraged; (c) some of the experiences the children use as bases for expression.

3. Ask a group of students in a teachers' college or pupils in school (whichever suits your situation) to bring to class objects costing no more than 25 cents each which they consider to be well designed. Discuss each object and arrange a show of the objects with explanations of the choices lettered or typed on small cards.

4. Select a reproduction of a well-known painting or some other professional art form and discuss the nature of the artist's reaction to experience which the work exhibits.

5. Select reproductions of two art objects that are limited to an expression of beauty and compare them with two that are not.

6. Observe an art lesson and describe it, making particular note of any Neo-Impressionistic or Expressionistic influences upon the teaching methods.

7. Describe any attempts at dictatorial control in any area of the arts which you may have experienced personally and explain their ill effects.

8. Outline an art lesson according to the "five Herbartian steps." Appraise it for its strong and weak points.

9. Devise an art lesson based on the S–R theory of learning. Explain how it might fail.

10. See if you can find some old art education books hidden away in school cupboards, attics, and the like. You may find an interesting and instructive hobby in collecting them. Analyze the educational theories on which they are based. Make a display of them for students of education and others to see.

11. See if you and your associates can find some old drawings and paintings to illustrate some of the historical developments in art education. Make a show of them with suitable captions.

Some Teaching Methods

in Art Education

As was noted in the preceding chapter, art as a field of study in the elementary school can be either beneficial or harmful to the learners. What determines in no small measure the value of art instruction to children is the teaching method employed. Faulty teaching can create in children a thorough dislike for art which may remain with them for the rest of their lives. Inadequate methods of teaching, moreover, apparently tend to produce other unfortunate attitudes. A feeling that any artistic activity is wasted effort, a resentment against original thought in all forms of artistic endeavor from architecture to literature, a sense of insecurity when called upon to make choices involving aesthetic judgment or taste—these are but a few of the possible effects of faulty teaching. Added to these may be a thorough disrespect for the school which forces upon the learner a subject in which he can see no value and find no personal challenge, and from which he derives no knowledge of lasting worth. Likewise, as a result of inappropriate teaching methods, more than one teacher in the past has experienced "discipline problems" during the art sessions. Many young boys react unpleasantly when forced to paint a tulip in delicate hues of water color and with photographic realism. Little girls become inattentive when told to draw a chalk box in two-point linear perspective.

On the other hand, children may be enthusiastic over art as a school activity. When such is the case, art can influence the whole tone of a school, and other fields of study seem to benefit by its good effects. Thinking in general becomes livelier, and children take a greater interest and pride both in their school and in themselves. School halls and classrooms can be changed from drab areas into places of sparkling interest. Children proudly bring their parents to school to see exhibitions of work. Principals report a greater degree of cooperation, not only among the children themselves, but also among members of the teaching staff, and between the public and the school.

Since the degree of success achieved in an art program depends largely upon teaching methods, it will be well at this time to discuss some of the contemporary methods by which teachers achieve outstanding success in art. As was stated in the previous chapter, a number of teaching techniques used in the present-day art program achieve the aim of developing good citizens through art activities. No formulas, of course, can be offered for the details of teaching, since teaching is an art depending upon individual situations and allowing for wide variations in method. As well as discussing some recommended teaching practices, this chapter will describe some methods which appear to be either ineffective or actively harmful to the artistic development of children.

Some Sound Teaching
Practices in Art

Who can teach art? The answer must be: any successful teacher in an elementary school system. The teacher who has sufficient ability, tact, and liking for children to teach, say, language, arithmetic, or social studies may be considered equally capable of teaching art. Art, like any other subject, of course, contains a certain content and requires of the teacher some specific knowledge and skills. A knowledge of pictorial composition and of other forms of design, an acquaintance with some professional art production, and some ability to use such media as paint, wood, or clay are required. However, the insights demanded of an art teacher in an elementary school are no more exacting than for any other subject. With relatively little effort, a competent teacher may gain the knowledge and master the skills associated with art education. The problems in teaching art, including classroom management and control, discipline, presentation of lessons, assistance of pupils, and appraisal of the success of the program are, broadly speaking, not distinct from the general school program. One may assert, therefore, that any proficient teacher in an elementary school may be a capable teacher of art.[1]

---

[1] Luella Cole's summary of the characteristics of a good teacher in *Teaching in the Elementary School* (N.Y.: Rinehart, 1939), pp. 33 ff., might be read at this time. The trouble, of course, with many such summaries is that most frail humans cannot measure

Phil Fein from Monkmeyer

13 *As a guide and counselor, the teacher has a vital role to play in the art program.*

The reader will doubtless take note of the fact that the following discussion about teaching methods contains nothing new.[2] Almost anyone who has ever taken a course in methods of teaching will have become familiar with the ideas presented below. They are outlined merely as a reminder of certain facts about pedagogy which any teacher, whether in service or in training, would do well to keep in mind.

One important lesson we have learned in the past is that a *teacher* is needed while art is engaging the attention of pupils in an elementary school.

up to the list of excellent traits suggested by the authors. In real life, however, these same frail humans often make good teachers.

Probably Marion Richardson was one of the greatest art teachers of children the world has ever seen. Unconsciously, she reveals in her book *Art and the Child* (Peoria, Ill.: Bennett, 1952) the qualities of a great teacher, among them tact, sympathy, knowledge of subject, sensitivity to art and children, and a number of intangibles. She never lists the "traits" of a good teacher—perhaps she never thought of them!

Pearson gives special emphasis to the successful teacher's mental attitude: "She must have the creative as against the copying attitude of mind." Ralph M. Pearson, *The New Art Education*, Rev. Ed. (N.Y.: Harper, 1953).

[2] Earl C. Kelley and Marie I. Rasey, *Education and the Nature of Man* (N.Y.: Harper, 1952), contains excellent generalizations about teaching and learning and is highly recommended for reading in conjunction with this chapter.

As mentioned previously, some teachers who were influenced by an Expressionistic type of program failed to play a sufficiently strong role as teachers of children. As a result, their art programs, although largely founded upon commendable ideas, failed through lack of suitable teaching methods. The contemporary program, on the other hand, rests upon the foundation of a strong belief in the need for both teaching and a reasonably consistent pedagogy. This pedagogy is most concerned with motivation and actual teaching, and with the media and tools of expression.

✓Motivation

As children live from day to day, they have many experiences. These experiences arise from life at home, at play, at school, and in the community in general. As a result of his contact with the world which surrounds him, and with his associates, the child's intellectual curiosity may be stimulated and his feelings aroused. To each new experience, he brings the insight he has acquired from previous experiences. If the new experience arouses his interest, and if it has a sufficient number of elements which are reminiscent of some of his former experiences, learning should occur. If he lacks interest in the new experience, on the other hand, he will probably fail to profit from it.[3]

The majority of experiences which a child enjoys are suitable for artistic expression. Any situation in life which has aroused his intellect and stimulated his feelings may be considered suitable subject matter for art. Indeed, there is no other subject matter worthy of a place in art education. Art is a peculiar field of study in that its subject matter, in one sense, remains constant throughout the child's entire school life. In some other subjects, such as mathematics, a series of topics is often developed, and teachers find that it is expedient to follow such a series if learning is to be efficient.[4] No such series can be prescribed for a program of art. From the time a child enters kindergarten until he leaves the school system, he will be occupied with only one theme—his own personal experiences.

[3] Paul R. Mort and William S. Vincent, *Modern Eductional Practice* (N.Y.: McGraw-Hill, 1950), have good sections on motivation and "motivational devices" in general. See, for example, the section called "Stimulating Situations and Problems," pp. 35 ff.

Also, included in the book are excellent summaries under the title "Reasons Why . . ." in which the authors give succinct statements derived from psychology and sociology to justify their suggestions about method. Every statement of this type might profitably be read by art teachers.

[4] This does not mean to say that a logical sequence of topics need always be followed. Indeed, recent studies seem to challenge the idea of logical sequences of subject matter in any field. However, in certain subjects a number, but not necessarily an order, of topics require study. See John Dewey, *Experience and Education* (N.Y.: Macmillan, 1938), Chapter 7, "Progressive Organization of Subject Matter," in which the philosopher relates subject matter to experience in life.

A sequence of a kind, however, appears in a child's art. Although his subject matter remains constant in the sense mentioned above, the child's developing skills with tools and materials, and his growing insights into the nature of his existence, cause a recognizable progression in his output. As the years pass, and as his insight into artistic expression goes deeper, his output reflects his development.[5] The development which occurs, however, unlike that to be found in many other subjects in school, is dependent primarily upon the child's selection of subject matter and not upon that of the teacher. The logical sequence of a child's artistic expression, in other words, is a reflection of the developing mind of the child and entirely dependent upon his personal growth.

The subject matter of a child's art, then, is derived wholly from his experiences, and as was mentioned previously, he has many experiences every day. It is important to remember, nevertheless, that children do not normally connect these experiences with artistic acts. If a teacher tells children to paint a picture of any item of experience that appeals to them, or, in other words, "to do whatever they like" in art, the results are usually disappointing. Under such circumstances, the children are often at a loss to paint or make anything. A well-known cartoon of children looking up at a teacher and asking with rueful expressions, "Do we have to do anything we want to?" illustrates the point.[6] It was not that the children in the cartoon lacked experiences suitable for expression, but rather that they had not connected them with expressive artistic acts.

In order that children may be successful in relating their experiences to their art activities, the teacher must see that they are motivated. In the art program, motivation means first that the teacher will assist children to recall those stimulating experiences which are most suitable for expression, and second, that the children will establish as goals for themselves successfully completed artistic acts.[7]

What the teacher does for children with regard to motivation, the adult artist does for himself. The artist selects those items of experience which he considers suitable for his particular kind of artistic expression. In his mind's eye, he visualizes the finished work, not completely perhaps, but clearly enough for him to set a goal which he strives to reach. This goal carries him forward in his undertaking and is the real motivating force for all his en-

---

[5] See Chapter 6.

[6] "No competent and responsible educational leader has ever said anywhere at any time that the pupil is to do what he wants to do." William H. Burton, *The Guidance of Learning Activities,* 2nd Ed. (N.Y.: Appleton-Century-Crofts, 1952), p. 65.

[7] "Children ordinarily are not motivated to learn anything; they are rather motivated to relieve tension," *ibid.,* p. 69.

deavors.[8] In resorting to the educational technique of motivation, therefore, the teacher is in no respect departing from a traditional artistic process. Rather, he accepts the nature of childhood and by means of an acceptable pedagogical device draws it closer to the nature of the artist.

The teacher, then, must help children to recall an experience for expression. To do so successfully, he must be well aware of the areas of interest of the group of children with whom he is working. What these interests are will be discussed in some detail in subsequent chapters. Only a brief summary of the varying interests of children at different levels of development need be offered at the present time.[9]

The most immature child is interested largely in the materials of expression. As he grows older, the child begins to depict subjects which are egocentric in character. Later, a number of physical features in the environment catch his attention. Still later, the relationship of the child to his associates becomes more significant for him, so that themes related to the social group in which he finds himself are given expression.

✓ Isolating and Defining a Theme

Motivation in art must be built upon the child's existing interests. With the most immature children, the teacher may rely entirely upon materials themselves as a motivating force for creative activity. It is not long, however, before the children require assistance in defining themes for expression. Then the teacher must begin to observe carefully children at school, at play, and, when possible, at home and in the community in general. Once the teacher has discovered a theme which he considers to be of general interest, and, of necessity, one in which all children have had some experience, the problem of motivation confronts him.

Let us say the school has reassembled after Thanksgiving. In Thanksgiving may be found themes which are broad enough to suit any pupil, and in which all children have probably participated in one way or another. Usually, a series of well-chosen questions followed by discussion serves to focus the pupils' attention upon the experience. The questions should be sufficiently broad in scope to include many activities associated with the Thanksgiving season such as shopping with Mother for Thanksgiving dinner, decorating the table, the guests who came for dinner, or the religious significance of the day. The discussions which take place between the teacher

---

[8] "When an organism is ready to act, it is painful for it not to act." Mort and Vincent, *Modern Educational Practice*, p. 38.

[9] Chapter 6 treats this subject in detail. See also Viktor Lowenfeld, *Creative and Mental Growth* (N.Y.: Macmillan, 1952), for children's art interests; and Arthur T. Jersild, *Child Psychology*, 4th Ed. (Englewood Cliffs, N.J.: Prentice-Hall, 1954), Chapter 16, for general interests.

and the pupils are a powerful means of recalling not only the facts of the experience, but also the feelings connected with it.[10]

Sometimes the teacher should make arrangements for new experiences which would be suitable for expressive purposes. Visits to a farm, a dairy, a park, and a zoo might all be appropriate. It is to be assumed that the teacher will plan any trip well in advance. He should discuss the expedition with the principal, so that all arrangements may be made through the proper channels. Then he should make a preliminary survey of the ground subsequently to be covered by the children. Also, before the trip occurs, a discussion should be held with the class concerning some of the salient features to be observed. Upon return to class after the expedition, another discussion should take place, after which expressive work should immediately begin.

The highly educative nature of these procedures will be readily recognized. Mere experience is of little value to the learner. It is only when one resolves experience into coherent form that it has significance. The definition which children give to events in their lives, by performing expressive acts, allows them to come to grips with their environment and to profit from their contact with it. For this reason alone, art may be considered an extremely valuable part of general education.

---

[10] See Daniel A. Prescott, *Emotion and the Educative Process* (Washington, D.C.: American Council on Education, 1938), for a detailed study of emotion and learning. See also Jersild, *Child Psychology,* Chapters 7, 9, 10, and 11, in which some of the positive as well as the negative values of the emotions in learning are described.

14 *The teacher of these pupils, in arranging the trip to a nursery, has provided them with a new experience suitable for artistic expression.*

✓ Establishing Goals

It was mentioned earlier that a teacher has the task of helping children not only to recall experience, but also to establish goals or purposes.[11] Although assisting a child to establish a goal is a vital part of art education, it does not present a teacher with a particularly difficult task. By the time children have arrived at the stage of development at which they are ready to use personal experiences as subject matter for expression, they have manipulated many art media. The mere mention by the teacher that painting, sculpture, and the like are to be produced in connection with the theme is usually all that is necessary for the children to establish goals for expression.

Should any child be unable to begin work, the teacher must give him particular attention. One of the most usual difficulties is that the child has not found sufficient interest in an experience to prompt him to express himself. In this case, a teacher may find it necessary to help him select another theme. The teacher might eventually resort to vicarious experiences, such as stories from literature or themes from films, radio, or television. New bases for expression, from either actual or vicarious sources, must be brought to the child's attention, however, until he is prompted to action.

A further difficulty may be that a child has failed to clarify his thinking about the theme to the extent of isolating one main thought about or center of interest in his subject. The difficulty which this child is experiencing may perhaps be more clearly exemplified in the writing process. Unless the writer constructs a topic sentence, his subsequent paragraph may be chaotic. Similarly in the visual arts the child cannot begin work if he has not selected one main topic. A few simple questions may help the learner in this predicament to sort out his ideas. He might be asked what is the main object or event he thinks about in connection with the topic; what is his outstanding feeling about the topic? Questioning of this sort, while requiring delicacy, can continue as long as the child displays a strong interest in the subject.

✓ Teaching [12]

Teaching in art is the technique of helping children to say what they want to say, in the terms in which they want to say it. Teaching is concerned,

---

[11] A valuable discussion about goals, or purposes, will be found in Dewey, *Experience and Education,* Chapter 6, "The Meaning of Purpose." See also Lee J. Cronbach, *Educational Psychology* (N.Y.: Harcourt, Brace, 1954), Chapter 14, "Purposes and Aspirations."

[12] At one time the term "guidance" was used to describe this part of the art program. Now "guidance" is gaining another meaning and hence such words as "assisting," "teaching," "helping," "instructing," and so on must replace it. Perhaps the old word

therefore, with the enlargement of a theme once the main topic has been selected, with the use of tools and materials, and with composition or design. Since the child must remain in control of the ideas being expressed and of the tools, media, and composition used to express them, the teacher should in no way resort to dictatorial methods. It will be shown later how disastrous are the results if a child suffers from dictatorial pressures.

The two most important problems facing a teacher who offers assistance of the type being discussed are, first, the timing of teaching, and, second, the amount of teaching to be done.

The teacher must time teaching so that it is given neither too soon nor too late. Once each child has an idea for expression in mind and has selected the tools and medium he intends to use, there comes a period of "hesitation or doubt" which any creating person, whether child or artist, experiences.[13] Although the teacher has assisted the child to select a topic, and has prompted him to set up as a goal an act of expression, the child's thoughts about both the theme and the goal tend to be nebulous. It would be a most extraordinary case in which the child knew exactly what his subject matter, his composition, and his handling of media were to be. Should a child have stereotyped answers to all these aspects of his work, his efforts would no longer be creative, and he would be better employed in some other activity. Once a child has settled upon a theme, therefore, he should obviously be allowed to think about it and to explore it, both mentally and with the medium he has selected.

During this period of exploration, some of the child's ideas may lead to blind alleys. False moves resulting from controlled experimentation are, of course, not a waste of educational time and materials, since they narrow the number of choices the learner has at his disposal to arrive at a satisfactory solution to his problems and the achievement of his goals. The experimentation which occurs at this time does not consist of random activity, but rather it is highly controlled by the problems and goals previously established. The testing and retesting of ideas, the sifting, discarding, and coordinating which go on, are all traditional functions of a creative act and, at the same time, are highly educative. Lacking this period of personal struggle, an activity

---

"teaching" is the most suitable now. Burton, *The Guidance of Learning Activities,* p. 213, says: "Teaching is the guidance of the natural activities of the learner. . . ." He elaborates on the statement in Chapter 7 especially.

[13] Described in detail by John Dewey in *How We Think* (N.Y.: Heath, 1935). See Chapter 6, "The Analysis of a Complete Act of Thought." In his *Democracy and Education* (N.Y.: Macmillan, 1916), p. 182, he says: "The most significant question . . . which can be asked . . . about any situation or experience proposed to induce learning is what quality of problem it involves."

Jack Engeman Studio

15 *In producing art, children are confronted with many problems, most of which they may be expected to solve themselves.*

does not fall within the definition of art. It is safe to say, in fact, that no real art has ever been produced without it.

The artist knows he must face this period of exploration before he can produce an art form. He must rely upon his own initiative to arrive at a satisfactory solution to his problems. Because children, on the other hand, are immature, they cannot be expected always to solve their problems and to reach their goals to their own satisfaction. Sometimes they must rely upon the teacher for help. The important question, therefore, arises: when should a child receive help? The answer must be dictated largely by common sense.[14] When the child, because of his limited experience, has exhausted the possibilities of experimenting and without help can no longer proceed in his work, he must receive assistance from the teacher. Because each child is different from his fellows, each requires individual treatment. One child may show need of assistance soon after work has begun, while another may not indicate that he is in difficulty until he has been working for some time.

In deciding when to offer assistance, therefore, the teacher must constantly study every child engaged in art work: John is not wiping his brush

[14] Principles are involved, of course. See Burton, *The Guidance of Learning Activities,* Chapter 7, for a good summary.

free of excess paint and hence is spoiling his page with unwanted drops of paint; Mary is making her main figures too small; Elizabeth is unable to draw a house; the background in Peter's picture interferes with the center of interest he has established. When each child has reached the end of his resources, when each has struggled to the full extent of his capacity with the problem in hand, he must receive help. There is no formula upon which the teacher can rely in giving help; no rule-of-thumb for him to follow. Only a personal knowledge of every member of the class, together with his own good judgment, can tell him when help must be forthcoming. To step in too soon will take away the child's initiative; to be too late will leave the child frustrated in his creative efforts. The solution to the problem of the timing of teaching demands all the resources which a teacher can muster.

The preceding remarks on the timing of teaching have application to the amount of teaching which should be given. The teacher has noted John's difficulty with the brush, Mary's trouble with small figures, Elizabeth's dilemma with the house, and Peter's problem with background. He knows that the children need help, but how much assistance should they have? If too much help is given, the teacher will be thinking for the children; if too little is offered, the children will still be unable to proceed. An exact amount of assistance must be offered so that the child is helped to overcome his difficulty, while at the same time he is left free to face further problems as they may occur. Moreover, wherever practical and possible, the help provided must be of such a nature as to lead the child to the position where he can solve the problem for himself.

It is obvious, of course, that the help provided must be governed by the stage of development of the child receiving it. Because John is only six years old he must be shown how to dip a brush in paint and how to wipe it free of excess drops. He may require several demonstrations of this process before he will use the brush successfully. Mary is seven and the teacher can ask her to observe her work from a distance and tell why it is difficult to see. Then, he may ask Mary how she would change the picture so that everyone in the class may enjoy looking at it. Some of her classmates may help her arrive at a satisfactory solution. Elizabeth is ten, and she may be helped to observe houses closely, and perhaps make some sketches of them. Peter, who is twelve, may have his attention drawn to the work of others so that he may study how they overcome difficulties of painting backgrounds. Later, he may be taught how to mix tints and shades of color for use in the background.

Much of the help in art offered by a teacher must be provided on this individual basis. On occasion, however, the teacher may observe that many members of the class seem to have a similar difficulty. This, of course, means that he may give a short general lesson to the group. Unless the majority in a lass will profit from a group lesson, however, the act of teaching should remain an individual matter.

In summary, then, before help can be successfully offered, the teacher must ask himself these two questions: first, is the child ready for help, and second, does he really feel the need of help? The learner who has not exhausted his resources obviously should be encouraged to continue his experiments, in the hope that he will discover his own solutions to his problems. Only when he finds his problems insoluble, but, at the same time, more clearly defined as a result of his personal efforts to master them, is the child both ready for teaching and in need of it. Only at such a time, and under such conditions, can teaching occur with maximum efficiency.

Selecting the Media and Tools of Expression

Media are the substances, such as paint, clay, and paper, which a pupil employs in art activities. Their proper use in class depends upon the teacher's observation of certain facts concerning them. These facts have a distinct influence upon teaching methods.

The physical development of pupils has bearing upon the types of media which suit them best. At certain stages of development, for example, children find some difficulty in using soft chalk and instead require a harder substance such as wax crayon. Too hard a medium, however, makes it difficult for children to cover paper readily and hence will interfere with their expression.[15] Little children, who have not learned to use the smaller muscles with dexterity, require large surfaces upon which to paint or to assemble large objects. As they grow older and gain greater muscular control, the size of surfaces and objects with which they work may be smaller. Some children, on the other hand, may wish to work on a large scale, no matter what stage of muscular development they have reached.

Some children tend to exhibit marked preferences for a particular medium. One child may find greater satisfaction in using clay than he will in using cardboard; another may prefer colored inks to tempera paint. Unless these children are given reasonable, although of course not exclusive, opportunities to employ the media of their choice, they may fail to reach a point of adequacy in their art output.

The fact that children vary in the media they prefer to use leads to the recommendation that as many different materials as possible should be placed at their disposal. Indeed, unduly to restrict the variety and kinds of materials tends to inhibit expression in art. It is unlikely that every member

---

See Chapter 7, "Drawing and Painting," for a further discussion of suitable media.

of a class will find a challenge or an inspiration in one kind and color of paper, one type of paint, or one variety of cloth. Unless children are given some choice of materials they cannot explore sufficiently to discover those media which best suit their needs of expression. Being confronted with variety, they will have an opportunity to think for themselves and to make practical judgments in their art work.

What has been said about media applies also to tools. A certain size and type of brush may suit one child, but not another. A fine pen point may appeal to some, while coarser nibs may be right for others. Just as a variety of materials must be offered, so also must a selection of tools be provided.

The teacher who makes some effort to provide a variety of materials and tools is following an accepted practice in art. The artist is always an explorer in the media and tools he uses. Nearly every artist, of course, develops a few preferences among the many media and tools at his disposal. This does not prevent him from exploring further possibilities of his favorite materials, or from testing new materials.

Some Faulty Teaching Practices in Art

We have just reviewed a number of sound teaching practices in art, and throughout this book we shall find repeated examples of their use. Before passing on to other subjects concerning art education, it might be well to consider a few examples of faulty teaching practices, some of which occur not as infrequently as one might wish. A study of these examples may serve not only to clarify the principles of good teaching practice, but also to assist the student in avoiding some of the pitfalls of faulty teaching methods in art.

The Teacher Who Advocates Copying

Every year when spring approaches, Miss L, a conscientious teacher of the second grade, provides the class with yellow and green construction paper. She has designed a pretty pattern of a daffodil in which the leaves are green and the flower yellow. She demonstrates first how to cut the petals and later shows how to make the leaves. "The children," says Miss L, "love to make a daffodil. It provides a most effective art lesson."

Miss L is correct in saying that the children love to make a daffodil. Spring is in the air and the bright new paper is fascinating. Motivation is no difficult for Miss L, a friendly, likeable, sympathetic person, who has timed her activity well.

Miss L is incorrect, however, in saying that the work constitutes an effective art lesson, because the activity is not art, but "busy work." In producng the flower, no one but Miss L has done any planning. She has not only done all the planning and solved all the problems, but if she has any feelings about the flower (which she probably has if one may judge from her own compositions), hers are the feelings expressed. The children have developed some skill, but have done so in isolation from thought and feeling. The pupils, in other words, have been subjected to a form of teaching based upon a mechanistic psychology.

While it is true that the children like to make the flower, the liking is no criterion of the worth of the activity. With very little motivation, children may be led to break windows or to chop down trees in public parks. Given sufficient approval, they will like these activities even more than they do making daffodils according to Miss L's directions. Children like art, but their liking for an activity does not necessarily mean that the work they like is either art or even an educationally sound pursuit. Actually, Miss L has wasted good educational time and materials in this work. Among the basic teaching principles discussed earlier, she has failed to observe those which demand that children must establish their own goals and that they must face problems which arise during their work. Miss L has taught, not according to the childrens' needs but, rather, dictatorially.

The Teacher Who Advocates
Extreme Neatness

Miss G is a tidy person; she is of neat appearance and her classroom is a model of order. "I like things to look right," says Miss G, as she goes about her duties in a fourth-grade classroom. "I have no use for sloppy work," she asserts, "either in drawing, painting, or in any other subject, for that matter."

So vigorously does Miss G encourage neatness that her pupils have grown afraid to experiment. Those who first tried experiments with ideas and media naturally ran into difficulties with both the media and Miss G. Now they hold fast to thoroughly familiar materials and well-tried clichés in artistic thought, and this pleases their teacher.

Sometimes even under these conditions Miss G is not altogether satisfied with the neatness of some of the children's work. Then, with bold application of chalk or paint, she "touches up" the youngsters' work. She is so clever at this that the output of her class sometimes wins prizes. Only an expert in child art could tell where the children's work had been doctored, and very few such experts are to be found on juries established to judge children's art work upon a competitive basis, because well-informed art educators are skeptical about competition of this kind.

When the children in Miss G's room make murals, their work must also be neat. Sometimes in this activity, too, the children do not meet Miss G's

standards of neatness and this embarrasses her, particularly when the principal visits her. However, she has developed what she calls a "good" system
of mural-making. Now the children draw and paint only the backgrounds
in which work they cannot be too untidy if properly supervised. After that
they cut out figures from magazines and glue them into place. The new system is much easier because no real effort is required, but the children
scarcely want to draw or paint at all now.

Miss G would be insulted if she were told that she is being dishonest.
She would be furious if someone described her as a dictator, an enemy of
art, a destroyer of creative thinking in general.

No one in his right mind would advocate untidyness for its own sake
in a classroom. Children, however, must be allowed to experiment freely
with ideas and media. Before ideas and the materials employed to express
them are mastered, lack of skill in the organization of both subject matter
and materials makes it inevitable that their art production is often untidy.
Tidiness in the execution of artistic acts will occur only after the skills associated with them are acquired. To demand extreme neatness at all times is
to handicap children in producing creative work in art. Among the basic
principles of teaching neglected by Miss G are the following: expression
must arise from personal experience; the goals of expression must be the
child's own; teaching must be built upon the children's interests; mental exploration, even if it leads to blind alleys of thought, is valuable.

The Effective Teacher
Who Lacks an Understanding of Art

Mr. W is a social studies specialist and holds a degree in history from a
reputable university. He says he believes that art is quite a suitable subject
for his sixth-grade class of boys. Privately, he does not hold a particularly
high regard for "this modern art" and feels that art ought to be "sane and
practical." Accordingly, Mr. W encourages his boys to correlate art with
history. "This teaches them both history and art," he explains.

Mr. W is a vigorous teacher of history. Following one of his excellent
lessons, he discusses with the boys the possibilities of picture-making in connection with the historical theme in question. When the boys have suggested
the aspect of the theme which most appeals to them, Mr. W, amid great enthusiasm, sends them about their research. The boys have collected many
clippings from magazines, and the classroom houses a well-stocked library
of books and periodicals. It is not long before each boy has found a picture
suitable for his topic which he copies with great care. Mr. W never fails to
commend the boys for their close attention to detail and their painstaking
efforts to make their work look "real."

Obviously, Mr. W understands the technique of motivation and can rouse enthusiasm over a theme for expression. If Mr. W enjoyed as much understanding of art as he does of history, his work would be most effective. But he lacks even a rudimentary knowledge of the nature and place of art in general education. The moment that copying begins, education, not only in art, but also in history ceases. If he were to guide the boys into creative work related to the historical theme, art would probably be produced. Moreover, because recall of a historical experience would be effected creatively, the pupils would probably gain greater insight into Mr. W's favorite field of study. In short, Mr. W has failed to observe the following important principle of teaching: the learner must think for himself, testing and retesting his own ideas through controlled experimentation.

The Artistic Teacher
Who Lacks an Understanding of Pedagogy

Down the hall from Mr. W's classroom is Miss deP. She is tall and dark and looks artistic because she wears extraordinarily large pieces of jewelry. Miss deP spends each summer painting first-rate landscapes and is a vigorous supporter of *avant-garde* art. It is rumored that she and Mr. W do not get along.

Miss deP says she is a lover of freedom, to the extent that she feels reluctant to interfere with any form of childlike expression in art. "Art is an informing spirit," she says. The output of her pupils seems to be lacking in sparkle. The principal claims that the pupils are noisy and inattentive and inclined to be rude to Miss deP. Quite often, when not obstreperous, the pupils are listless. They say that they often do not know what to do. The situation is unfortunate because Miss deP has much to offer. Her feeling for art apparently is deep, but she has failed to master the art of teaching. She would have more success as a teacher if she recognized the following basic teaching principles: first, the pupils must be assisted to establish personal goals for expression; second, teaching must occur when the situation indicates a need for it.

The Teacher
Who Has Developed a Formula

Miss Z is a teacher of a third-grade class who is clever at mathematics. One of her favorite art lessons consists of having the children resolve objects into triangles, squares, oblongs, and circles. She admires the precision resulting from this activity. "The children are learning to handle basic forms," she explains. Thus the children are taught to draw houses by means of a triangle supported by a rectangular oblong; a chicken by using two circles; a man, strangely enough, by resorting to triangles.

Miss Z is another example of a teacher who prevents children from performing art activities. The designs she insists upon are false in relation to the objects depicted. Houses, chickens, and men may have basic forms, which will be discovered in time by children, but certainly these forms cannot be successfully arrived at through mathematical shapes supplied by the teacher. Rather, they may be depicted adequately only by means of personal experience and experiment on the part of the children. Miss Z's system is, in reality, a false and rather ugly one of pictogram shorthand and is certainly anything but art. Miss Z should recall at least two basic principles of teaching: personal experience is the basis of learning, and skill (precision in the use of tools and materials) is best gained in close connection with expressive acts engaging the thoughts and feelings of the learner.

A Study of the Effects of Some Inappropriate Teaching Methods Upon Children

The methods of the teachers described above are based upon practices inappropriate to artistic development. By studying both art and children one may readily deduce that these methods are either ineffective or harmful. The question arises: how ineffective or harmful are they? Among numerous experiments, two will be described which indicate an answer to this question.[1] The first of these is concerned with dictatorial teaching practices, and the second with *laissez-faire* practices.

Some Effects of Dictatorial Teaching Practices

An experiment was performed with 250 children between six and eight years of age to attempt to discover some of the effects of dictatorial teaching practices upon their artistic development. Until the experiment was performed, all the children had enjoyed a creative program of art. They were in what is known as the "symbol" stage of expression and were able to relate these symbols to their environment.[17] In brief, they were capable of producing pictures creatively about their experiences. The children were paired

---

[16] These are part of a program of research sponsored by the Ontario Department of Education and under the direction of the author.

[17] The "symbol" and other stages of development will be discussed in detail in Chapter 6.

according to their mental ages into two groups called Group A and Group B.

Group A, consisting of 125 children, had their creative program in picture-making brought to an abrupt halt. In the place of creative work, their teachers substituted ten activities of a restrictive or dictatorial nature. These activities were as follows: cutting a triangle and a square in colored paper, later to be pasted on paper to form a house; drawing an apple in the form of a circle which the teacher had previously drawn on the blackboard; copying the outline of a tree which had been drawn on the blackboard; coloring a flower which had been drawn by a teacher and mimeographed; copying a drawing of a bird from a mimeographed outline; drawing a snowman according to the teacher's verbal directions; tracing the outline of a car prepared by a teacher; copying from the blackboard a drawing of a girl; drawing a tulip according to visual demonstrations on the blackboard; and following verbal directions in the use of circles to draw a cat.

While Group A was engaged in this work for ten days, Group B, consisting of the remaining 125 children, continued to make pictures creatively.

On the eleventh school day, both groups were taken to a fire house where the firemen had consented to act as hosts. The children explored parts of the building and the equipment, after which the firemen completed the visit by supplying light refreshments. The day was an obvious success and a stimulating experience.

On return to school the next day, all the pupils were subjected to the usual forms of motivation. Then, they were asked to develop a picture from their experiences. All the children in Group B were, in varying degrees, successful in this work. Their drawings and paintings illustrated personal reactions to their observations and were produced in a variety of media and with different techniques. In Group A, however, 44 percent (55 of the children), instead of presenting their reactions to the outing, resorted to the drawing of houses, birds, and the like, in the manner in which they had been taught during the previous ten school days. Others reverted to a manipulation of the media, a stage of development which precedes that of the production of symbols.

The children in Group A were studied intermittently for a period of two years. At the end of this time, no fewer than eight percent (ten children) were still inclined to make use of the stereotyped work which they had been taught during the ten days. If only ten days of dictatorial work in art [18] interfere to this extent with children's artistic expression, one may well ask himself how inhibiting, say, a whole year of this kind of work may be on the minds of children, and how durable may be its results.

---

[8] We must not forget to take into account also the effects of variable interval reinforcement which usually accompanies such a program.

The Effects of Laissez-faire
Teaching Practices

In order to discover the extent to which children can get along withou an art teacher, 200 children were selected for observation. One hundred c them, whose age range was from five years to six years and three month: with an average chronological age of five years and eight months, were i the first group studied. Sixty-two of these children were still in the manipu lative stage. The remainder were making symbols to represent some object in their environment.

For five days, their teachers provided a variety of materials alread familiar to the children, including tempera paint, clay, plasticine, and cor struction paper and glue. No aid in motivation and no teaching were offerec

During the first day and largely during the second, the children g along well without help from their teachers. They kept themselves bus either manipulating materials or forming symbols. On the second day, 1 children showed a lagging interest in the work, while on the third, 59 ind cated this tendency. On both the fourth and fifth days, nearly every chil indicated lack of interest in his activities, and all the work produced ex hibited a lack of vitality. It was interesting to note, furthermore, that th older children in the group seemed to miss the attention of the teacher to greater extent than did the younger. This may be accounted for by the fact: first, that they had grown more used to motivation and guidance than th younger pupils and, second, that the symbolic stage of expression require more help from the teacher than does the manipulative stage. Of furthe interest was the fact that about 22 percent of the children who originally ha reached the symbol stage reverted to the manipulation of materials an failed to produce any symbols.

The above procedures were repeated with another group of 100 chi dren. This time the age range was from seven years and two months to nir years and one month, with an average chronological age of eight years an three months. Results were similar to those obtained with the first group wit the exception that from the first day a noticeable lack of interest in the wor was apparent. This attitude was almost universal on the second and subse quent days.

It was concluded that the youngest children, particularly those in th manipulative stage, may apparently benefit from an occasional art perio in which the teacher does not resort to motivation or assistance. Too mar such sessions in sequence quickly have adverse effects upon the art activiti of all children, but particularly on the production of those children wh have advanced beyond the manipulative stage of development.

ACTIVITIES FOR THE READER

1. Tell of any situation you have experienced in which children disliked art. Explain how the dislike arose and indicate the means you might use to alter the children's attitude.

2. Describe the traits of a personal acquaintance whom you consider to be an efficient teacher of art.

3. Observe some art lessons by expert teachers and note especially (a) the motivational devices employed; (b) the manner in which themes are defined; (c) the way in which goals are established; (d) the problems which arise and the means by which a solution to them is found.

4. Describe the steps you might take to improve the following situations:

(a) A third-grade art class whose members are outrageously untidy and wasteful of materials.

(b) A class of fifth-grade children who have always been taught to copy during their art sessions and feel they are unable to create.

(c) A group of sixth-grade boys who think art is "sissy."

(d) A group of kindergarten children whose parents or older brothers and sisters have given them formulas for the drawing of objects.

Studying Design

In considering art education, the teacher is soon confronted with problems about design. What is a design? How is a design produced? How can a good design be recognized?

It should be kept in mind that design (or form, or composition) is not a separate and distinct part of art. Design is the structure of any art form. It is the organization by which a creating person presents his reactions to experience. The message he wishes to convey is made apparent by means of the design he produces. Whenever any art form is being produced, whether by a child or an adult, a design is automatically included in the production. A piece of clay modeling by a child in the first grade, a Sung stoneware vase, a painting by Cézanne, a symphony by Beethoven, or a play by Christopher Fry—all involve design.

The remainder of this chapter will present in some detail a discussion of design largely as it applies to visual forms of expression. The discussion will include an analysis of the parts, or elements, which go to make up a design, together with an outline of the methods employed by artists and others to bring about a satisfactory coherence in the use of these elements. Lacking a knowledge of design the art teacher would suffer some handicap. The information to be found in this chapter, however, like that in the first and second chapters, is presented as professional background knowledge, little of which can be used directly in the classroom, as Chapter 7 will explain.

The Elements of Design or Form

A good design is a highly integrated organization. In studying the designs of artists of repute, we have a feeling that nothing could be changed without violating their structure. Lines, colors, textures, masses and spaces, patterns of light and shade form a complete and, as far as we can judge, a perfect whole. This perfection of organization has been called "form," and Abercrombie says of it:

> Whatever art gives us is given as an instance of a world of unquestioned order, measure, government, a world in which experience occurs with perfect security, knowing that the firm inter-relationship of its process can never be dislocated by chance—a world which is the desire of the mind. . . .[1]

Abercrombie continues by stating that "form," as he calls it, is the chief excellence of art:

> It is because art presents its matter as Form that it effects this profoundly desirable impression of coherence, of inter-relation, and so of significance both of parts and of whole.[2]

As Abercrombie suggests, the act of designing is common to all human beings. The savage brings about some order and coherence in the jungle when he constructs a village; the office worker does the same when, on Saturday afternoon, he works in his garden. The housewife follows the "desire of the mind" as she rearranges the furniture in her living room, as does the law-maker in a parliamentary session. Because the desire for order is found in us all, artistic acts, which demand that we achieve an organized form, composition, or design, have a potential significance for every person who studies them.

Philosophers have been fascinated by the faultless organization of good design, and have attempted to analyze it. Repeatedly the question has been asked: What are the parts or elements which go to make up these splendid organizations? Philosophers ask this question in order to gain a greater understanding of design as a whole, knowing full well that any intellectual dissection of the work being observed can never adequately explain the significance of the design when considered in its entirety. From observations of life in general, man has sensed for a long time what the Gestalt psychologists stated a relatively short time ago, that the whole is greater than the sum

---

[1] Lascelles Abercrombie, *An Essay Toward a Theory of Art* (London: Secker, 1926), pp. 105–07.

[2] *Ibid.*

16 *Cézanne's* **Card-Players**—*a significant organization of
the elements of design.*

of its parts, and that to separate the whole into parts is to destroy the object
we attempt to analyze. Any form of intellectual analysis when applied to
design is attended by danger of destroying the organization we study.

With the realization that by intellectual analysis we can arrive at neither
a complete understanding of design nor an adequate formula for its production, we are nevertheless justified in searching for its elements. The physi-
ologist who probes into a corpse and dissects nerves and organs knows that
the body before him is less than the living being.[3] The chemist who analyzes

[3] A figure used by Benedetto Croce, in his *Aesthetic* (N.Y.: Noonday, 1956). See especially pp. 20–21 for Croce's anticipation in aesthetics of the Gestalt principle, "The
whole is greater than the sum of its parts."

a drug realizes that the individual elements cannot produce the healing effects of the compound. In both instances, however, those engaged in the research of the parts feel that from their study an insight may eventually be gained into the nature of the complete object. While the original object, in other words, can be fully understood only in terms of itself and not its parts, the partial knowledge acquired may be helpful later when considering the object in its entirety.

Those who have attempted to isolate the elements of design have reached only a partial agreement.[4] At the present time, nevertheless, a number of elements have been defined which appear to be acceptable to the majority of thinkers in this field. These elements of form or design are line, mass and space, light and shade, texture, color. It is these elements which will be discussed in the following paragraphs. The discussion is offered so that teachers may not only acquire some intellectual insight into design as it appears in the work of children, but also develop a vocabulary for this segment of art education.[5]

Line

Line, the path traced by a moving point, is perhaps the most flexible and revealing element of design. If we are angry and "doodle" a line, our anger is clearly revealed in the marks we have made. If we are placid, calm, or pleased, our doodle takes on a different character.

An artist may readily express his feelings by means of line. In commu-

---

[4] For example, compare the following: Ray Faulkner, Edwin Ziegfeld, and Gerald Hill, *Art Today*, 3rd Ed. (N.Y.: Holt, 1956), Chapters 9 and 10; Roger Fry, *Vision and Design* (N.Y.: Meridian, 1956), pp. 33–34; and Viktor Lowenfeld, *Creative and Mental Growth* (N.Y.: Macmillan, 1952), pp. 265 ff., "The Meaning of Aesthetic Criteria."

A good system of analysis of pictorial composition may be found in Erle Loran, *Cézanne's Composition*, 2nd Ed. (Berkeley & Los Angeles: Univ. of California Press, 1946).

[5] A curious analysis of design which was once popular in schools, and even today has some adherents, is that of Adolfo Best-Maugard, *A Method for Creative Design* (N.Y.: Knopf, 1926). Best-Maugard believes that all design may be resolved into seven "motifs," and by combining these motifs any number of original designs may be created. As one might expect, all designs made according to this system look much alike. N. I. Cannon, *Pattern and Design* (N.Y.: Pitman, 1949), says of Best-Maugard, "while agreeing with his choice of seven motives, I would add two more to this list." Cannon's designs in the book likewise suffer from a uniformity reminiscent of that seen in Best-Maugard's designs. In a sense, the scribble patterns of William Johnstone, *Child Art to Man Art* (London: Macmillan, 1941), Chapter 2, "How to Develop the Natural Drawing Instincts of Children," are equally remote from the nature of art and contain pedagogical dangers similar to those described in Best-Maugard and Cannon. The children look for the depiction of objects in their scribbles or "doodles." By referring to the illustrations accompanying the text we may observe that the system, not expression, is dominant.

17 *A diagrammatic indication of the movement of the lines in* The Card-Players.

nicating his hatred of war and brutality in general, an artist, like Picasso in his *Guernica,* may use slashing, angular, abrupt lines. In presenting his feelings about the soft beauty of a summer landscape, his lines might be gently undulating, flowing, rippling.

Notice the line used by Cézanne in his painting *The Card-Players,* of which a reproduction may be seen in Fig. 16. In the line diagram in Fig. 17, one can see how the movement begins over the back of the card-player on the right, then swings down over his arm, only to be caught up by the line across the back of the center player. Swirling around this center card-player's hat, it moves up over the arm and around the back of the standing man and, falling across the shoulders of the player on the left, ends in the sweep of the chair. Folds in the draperies and shadows in the background augment the sweep of Cézanne's expressive line.

Just as most people, by means of practice, develop a personal style of handwriting, so the artist develops a line peculiar to himself. By developing a skillful command of line the artist can make the element speak of his experiences. Line, therefore, is a revealing path of action, letting us know something of what its creator thinks and feels, and helping us to respond to whatever he has in mind. Small wonder that line has sometimes been called "the nervous system" of a work of art!

There are generally two kinds of line: that which is free flowing and that which is measured. The upsurging line of a Gothic cathedral or of a modern skyscraper, the lines found in a formal Italian garden are the result of mathe-

18 *A diagrammatic indication of the distribution of masses and spaces in* **The Card-Players.**

matical measurement. Because these lines follow mathematical rules, they may be less personal than lines created freely. They are, nevertheless, selected by human judgment and taste and, because of this constitute an aesthetic element.

Mass and Space

Mass refers to the shape or bulk of objects in an art form, and space to the areas which surround mass. The nature of mass as an element of design is perhaps most readily grasped in architecture and sculpture. The great mass of an office building or the soaring spire of a church has power to move us. In sculpture, we are affected by the delicacy, weight, or arresting shape of the mass created by the sculptor. The same effect is found, of course, in the masses delineated in a good drawing or painting. Here, the artist draws or paints the masses so that they are as significant as those found in three-dimensional art forms.

Every mass has as an environment the element of space. Space is a void of no significance until one can detect landmarks or points of reference within it. Then it becomes an environment for other elements. One may appreciate the importance of space as an element of design by referring once more to architecture. Think of the courtyards separating the buildings in a modern housing development. Here the architect has carefully considered the amount of space which should be provided between one building and another. If he had planned the spaces to be smaller, the buildings might have appeared huddled together; wider, the buildings would not appear to belong to a coherent plan.

The artist working in two dimensions must also regulate the spaces between masses. His is the problem of providing an environment for the objects he draws and paints in such a way as to give the semblance of architectural coherence to his design. Often he gives an illusion of depth or of a third dimension. Not all painters wish to make use of a third dimension, of course, and instead produce designs having only a two-dimensional effect. If a three-dimensional effect is required, however, the artist may overlap masses, make use of linear perspective, tone his color, and so on.[6]

In Fig. 18 we find a diagram of the masses and spaces in Cézanne's *Card-Players*. The masses formed by the players, the table, and the draperies are presented in a sculptural unity relieved by variations in the light and shade, texture, and color. The simplicity of the spaces offers a significant contrast to the detail of the masses.

Light and Shade

In producing an art form, the creating person may make use of the elements of light and shade. In drawing with chalk, the pressure applied to the

---

[6] Some writers, in mentioning the three-dimensional effects which may be achieved in painting, have said that another element is involved which they have named "volume." In her analysis of El Greco's *Assumption of the Virgin,* for example, Helen Gardner speaks of his "organization in space of cylindrical and cubical volumes." *Art Through the Ages,* 3rd Ed. (N.Y.: Harcourt, Brace, 1948), p. 564 (A).

19 *A diagram of the distribution of the chief areas of light and shade in* **The Card-Players.**

medium regulates the degree of lightness or darkness of the marks produced. By adding black or white to a standard hue of paint, light and shade are controlled. Architects and sculptors control these elements by a variety of devices. A building may be designed with deep recesses to produce shadows in contrast to a façade which catches the light. Sculptors, likewise, take great pains in controlling the hollows and bumps they make in a medium so that light and shade may be used to their best advantage.

In Fig. 19 we find a diagram of the arrangements of light and shade in *The Card-Players*. Every dark area seems to have its corresponding light area which gives significance to the dark place. Notice, for example, the white face of the left-hand player against the dark clothes of the standing figure, or the dark hat and profile of the right-hand player against the light space of the background.

Light and shade may create most dramatic effects. These have been well demonstrated, for example, in black-and-white films, where, if the elements of light and shade are used effectively, we may be quite content that color is absent. The etchings and paintings of Rembrandt and the work of Mantegna move us largely because of the clever handling of these elements. Light and shade, then, when well controlled, are powerful elements to which we may react strongly.

Texture

Texture may be thought of as the degree of roughness or smoothness of any surface. Every surface has a texture; a pebble on the seashore, a veined leaf, the wrinkled face of an old man, a brick wall, a sheet of glass, all display varying kinds and degrees of texture.

Figure 20 illustrates some of the textural qualities to be found in *The Card-Players*. We find various degrees of roughness and smoothness in, say, the relative smoothness of the wall background compared with the rougher surface of the drapery. Again we see the smooth quality of the wooden surface of the table contrasted with the rougher quality of the right-hand player's cloak.

Very often we derive a sensual enjoyment from texture. We like to run our hands lightly over the surface of a tweed jacket or a fur coat. We may enjoy holding a small stone lightly in the hand or gently stroking a baby's hair. When we go to bed we may take delight in the smoothness of the sheets or, on the other hand, in what Rupert Brooke called "the rough male kiss of blankets." The rough kiss of a bearded male himself is said by our grandmothers to have been a textural pleasure of some significance.

Texture also appeals, of course, for aesthetic as well as sensual reasons, although it is doubtful if the two can be entirely separated. Artists often go

20 *A diagram of some of the varied textures to be found in* The Card-Players.

to great pains to control texture as an element of design. Paper for water-color paintings is chosen with extreme care for its textural qualities. Some painters will stipple a surface with gesso or white lead before painting upon it with tempera or oils. The application of paint, also, is made with careful regard for its textural qualities. In certain areas, paint may be applied thickly and with a degree of roughness, while in others the paint may be put on with silky smoothness.

Sometimes artists devise textural effects which are not actually rough or smooth, but which appear so. In some parts of a drawing, for example, lines may be criss-crossed or a pattern of dots devised so that the area thus treated may have a rough appearance. Other areas may be left untouched or washed in smooth color to create a textural contrast.

Textures, therefore, may be of two kinds, actual or devised. Whatever type of texture is used in design, it must be as carefully controlled as any of the other elements.

Color

The importance of color in comparison with the other elements of design has been a matter of debate. Roger Fry points out that nearly all the elements of design are connected with essential conditions of our physical existence. Texture has been discussed already in this connection. Mass and space appeal to the various adaptations to the force of gravity which we must make every day; light and shade represent a necessary condition of our existence; line appeals to our muscular activities. In connection with color, however, he says:

> Colour is the only one of our elements which is not of critical or universal importance to life, and its emotional effect is neither so deep nor so clearly determined as the others.[7]

However debatable the importance of color may be in relation to the other elements, it must be emphasized that color is a powerful element. Its misuse can be disastrous in any design. A room, no matter how good the furnishings may be, can be ruined by painting the walls the wrong color. The design of a painting, likewise, can disintegrate if the colors have not been chosen wisely.

Color serves to emphasize the extent to which the elements are interdependent. Although we have discussed the elements separately, in reality they cannot be disassociated from one another. The moment we make a mark upon paper, we involve both mass and space. If the mark is made with black crayon, light and shade are involved. If paint has been applied, color is present. Line, no matter how thin, establishes itself in space as a mass. Only for the sake of convenience, as was pointed out above, have we spoken of the elements as distinct.

Of all the elements, color thus seems to be the least essential. Many art forms are produced in which this element is lacking. The black-and-white film has been mentioned previously. To films may be added most forms of sculpture, many of the etching processes, drawings of all sorts in which black-and-white media are used, and so on. Any design, moreover, to which color is applied before due consideration is given to the arrangement of the other elements would undoubtedly be most unsuccessful. Color, then, is a mysterious element—at once dependent, powerful, and very moving.

Organization of the Elements in Works of Art

The design of a work of art consists of a satisfactory arrangement of the elements. The design is satisfactory when it is coherent, organized, and com-

---

[7] Fry, *Vision and Design*, p. 35. In Faber Birren's *Monument to Color* (N.Y.: MacFarlane, 1938), we find illustrations which probably follow accurately enough a scientific color theory so that they are technically acceptable. Since the other elements seem to be ill-conceived, however, the technically correct use of color cannot save the designs. What is to serve as a "monument to color" appears to end in a salute to bad taste. For a complete scientific analysis of color, see Maitland E. Graves, *Color Fundamentals* (N.Y.: McGraw-Hill, 1952).

plete in itself so that we, the observers, respond favorably to it and can continually return to it with interest and approval.

It would be convenient to offer a formula for the production of satisfactory designs. If the formulas of the Neo-Impressionists regarding design had been valid and acceptable, how simple a matter the organization of the elements would be! But, of course, if designs could be produced according to a formula and could in any other manner be subjected to rules and regulations, art would cease to exist.

The truth of the matter is that every good design is different from every other design. Every artist, moreover, has a unique way of producing designs, just as every design he creates is distinct from all others of his creation.

With the idea firmly in mind that there are no reliable formulas for producing designs, we are safe in attempting to ask whether or not there exist any common denominators to be found in all satisfactory designs. In conjunction with the knowledge that every design must be personal to its author and hence must be unique, can we discover some further general principles which are broad enough to allow for the variations to be found between one good design and another, but without which no design could be considered satisfactory? What, in other words, makes a design good?

Unity of Design

At the opening of this chapter, the highly integrated nature of design was mentioned. Design was described in terms of order and coherence and was made analogous to a world of perfect security. These are unquestionably the most obvious characteristics which result from a successful organization of the elements, and they may be found in any successful art form whether musical, dramatic, literary, or graphic. Each element is so arranged that it contributes to a desirable wholeness, or oneness. In a drawing, a line ripples across a certain area to be caught up elsewhere; masses set up beats and measure; while spaces contribute to the visual music established by the masses. Colors, textures, areas of light and shade all contribute to a kind of orchestration of the visual pattern. This oneness or wholeness we call *unity*, and unity of design seems to be the first characteristic of all successful output in art. To appreciate the nature of unity one must expose oneself to many art forms and must attempt actively to respond to them. A symphony, a play, a building, a piece of sculpture, a piece of ceramics, or any other example of art will offer clues to the nature of unity.[8]

At the risk of oversimplifying and of placing too great a reliance upon the intellectualization of a process which is largely one of feeling, we may

---

[8] See Walter Dorwin Teague, *Design This Day* (N.Y.: Harcourt, Brace, 1940), Chapter 7, for a good discussion of unity, much of which refers to machine production.

analyze to some extent how unity is achieved in a visual design. Three interdependent devices, or arrangements of the elements, may be observed in a unified work of art. These are rhythms, balances, and centers of interest.

RHYTHMS: As we study a recognized masterpiece, we became fascinated by the numerous pathways of its design. A line may ripple in one direction, then change to an undulation in another direction. This movement may be momentarily halted by an obstruction of a brightly colored mass before it darts away elsewhere along a pathway formed by areas of light and shade. The controlled movements which are to be found in all good design are called rhythms. Rhythm is a device used by designers to give orderly movement to the manner in which our eyes move over a work of art and to control the pace at which they travel.

Some of the rhythms in *The Card-Players* have been diagramed in Fig. 21. We see the sweeping rhythm of the line, rising, falling, twisting, and turning in all its subtle variations of movement. Again we see the little beats formed by the pipes in the rack hanging on the background wall and in the pattern made by the fingers of the central player.

21 *A diagram of some of the rhythms to be found in Cézanne's* Card-Players.

There appear to be at least two main types of rhythms to be found in works of art. The first has the character of a flow and is usually achieved either by lines or through the elongation of masses and spaces. The work of El Greco, particularly in his later period, comes to mind as an outstanding example of this type of rhythm.

The second type has the character of a beat. An element may be used in one area of an art form and repeated elsewhere. The repetition may be an exact duplicate of the original theme or motif, or it may be only reminiscent of it. In the radiator grille of an automobile we may often observe an exact duplication of a motif. In paintings we are more likely to find reminiscences of an original theme.

Perhaps a reference to music by way of illustration may clarify the two types of rhythm mentioned. In a waltz, for example, the line type of rhythm may be found in the melody, while the beat type may be found in the *one*-two-three of the time signature.

Rhythms may be established through the use of any of the elements. Lines, areas of light and shade, spots of color, repetitions of masses and spaces, and textured surfaces may all contribute to a rhythmic movement throughout a composition.

CENTERS OF INTEREST: In describing the nature of rhythm in a composition, we noted that the pace in which the eye travels about a composition may be carefully regulated by the design. Sometimes the observer's glance rushes along, sometimes it slows, and occasionally it halts. These places at which the eye pauses are called centers of interest. They are established by the designer so that the observer will dwell upon an artistic statement which, in the opinion of the designer, is important. Centers of interest, like rhythms, unify a design.

Figure 22 illustrates for us the main center of interest to be found in

22 *The main center of interest in* The Card-Players.

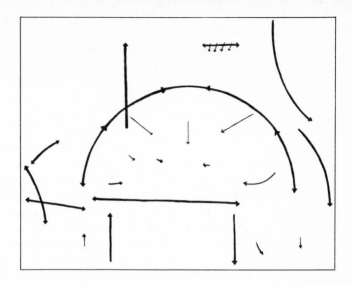

23 *A diagram of the balances in* **The Card-Players.**

The Card-Players. It is obvious that our eyes pause longest around the hands of the players on the table. Not only are these hands in a central position, but their presence is emphasized by strong contrasts of light and shade, by the flickering pattern they make, and by the lines which continually lead us back to this central area.

Many works of art—perhaps the majority—are arranged so that one center of interest has paramount importance. Georgia O'Keeffe's painting *Black Abstraction* or Balla's *Street Light* are illustrations of the use of this type of arrangement.[9]

Particularly in recent years, compositions have appeared in which a distribution of several centers of interest is established. Léger's *Propellers* or Mondrian's *Color Squares in Oval* serve as examples of this kind of arrangement.

As in the development of rhythms, so also in the establishment of centers of interest—any of the elements may be used. A large mass centrally placed or of peculiar shape, a bright color area, a sharp contrast between light and shade, an area more heavily textured than its surroundings, a series of lines leading to a certain place are some of the means at the disposal of the designer to attract and hold the observer's attention.

BALANCES: A third device for developing a unity of design is found in the use of balances. Balances occur when the eye is attracted equally around imaginary axes of a composition.

---

[9] The paintings mentioned in this and the next paragraph may be seen at the Museum of Modern Art, New York.

Many writers, particularly the Neo-Impressionists, attempted to explain balance in terms of physics, and this concept seems still to be the most widespread in public education even today. The figure of a seesaw is usually used by these writers to explain the nature of balance.[10] Unfortunately, the concept does not seem to be quite accurate, since physical balance and aesthetic balance, while probably related, are not synonymous. It seems highly necessary, therefore, that the question of balance in aesthetics be considered rather as attraction to the eye than as gravitational pull. Aesthetic balance refers to all parts of a picture—the top and bottom as well as the sides—and not merely to the sides as the seesaw analogy suggests. Size of the masses, moreover, while having some influence upon aesthetic balance may easily be compensated and, indeed, outweighted by a strong contrast of elements. A small, bright spot of color, for example, has great aesthetic weight in a field of gray; an area of deep shade next to a highlight has the same property.

In many books on art, there is still considerable discussion about "formal" *versus* "informal" balance. The arrangement of a composition with one well-defined center of interest placed centrally and with balancing elements placed similarly on either side of this center, such as, say, Duccio's *Maestà* or Fra Angelico's *Coronation of the Virgin*, is called "formal" balance. All other arrangements are called "informal," "active," or "occult." The "informal" type, found in Miro's *Composition, 1933* or Orozco's *Barricade,* is sometimes considered more creative and mysterious but less dignified than the "formal." [11] In recent writings these terms appear to be rapidly disappearing from the vocabulary of design, largely, it appears, on the grounds that balance, like other aspects of design, must under all circumstances be considered in terms of the expressive needs of the artist. The distinction between "formal" and "informal" appears to be, in short, largely an artificial one reminding us of the Neo-Impressionists' formulas. The more dynamic concept, with emphasis upon the idea that the artist's expressive requirements determine balance, will no doubt be of greater service to education.

Variety of Design

We have observed that the elements of design must be arranged into a unity if the resulting work is to be successful. One must point out, however, that it is possible to produce a design having all the attributes of unity, which is neither interesting nor distinguished. A checkerboard, for example,

---

[10] See, for example, Harriet and Vetta Goldstein, *Art in Everyday Life,* 4th Ed. (N.Y.: Macmillan, 1954), p. 87, fig. 87 a–c, "The principle of the seesaw applied to balance in art."

[11] *Ibid.,* Chapter 5; see also Faulkner, Ziegfeld, and Hill, *Art Today,* pp. 218–19.

is a design displaying a rhythmic beat, a series of centers of interest, and a balance, but no design could be duller. Likewise, a picket fence, a line of identical telephone poles, and a railway track, while maintaining a degree of unity from a design standpoint, are as uninteresting as the ticking of a clock.

Eminent painters like Thomas Hart Benton, Charles Burchfield, and John Piper [12] have used house gables, telephone poles, and railway tracks as subject matter for their work. But in doing so, while maintaining an over-all

---

[12] The Englishman John Piper seems not yet as well known in the U.S. as one might expect. He is an experimentalist in techniques and paints with a healthy vigor. See *John Piper*, Penguin Modern Painters Series, Sir Kenneth Clark, Ed. (Harmondsworth, Eng.: Penguin, 1948). This is an excellent series of inexpensive booklets. The plates, especially those in color, are superb. U.S. artists are also represented in the series.

24 *In this painting,* Six O'Clock, *Charles Burchfield develops an interesting variety in a design from objects which in reality are monotonous.*

Collection of the Syracuse Museum of Fine Arts

unity, they have introduced subtle variations into the delineation of these objects, as Fig. 24 illustrates. Mondrian has even used what might be likened to the basic form of the checkerboard as a basis for many of his compositions. He has treated each area, however, in such a manner as to bring a high degree of *variety* to his paintings.

Every design, then, requires, together with a unity, a subtle variety in the way in which the elements are treated. Lacking this variety, a design is uninteresting and consequently fails to hold our attention. Every element, therefore, must be employed to bring about a desirable variety within unity.

Variety Within Unity
as an Expression of Life

Philosophers have postulated that design, or form, is a manifestation of man's deepest and most moving experiences. In the design he produces, man is said to express his relationship to the universe. Dewey [13] has mentioned the mighty rhythms of nature—the course of the seasons and the cycle of lunar changes—together with those movements and phases of the human body, including the pulsing of the blood, appetite and satiety, and birth and death, as basic human experience from which design may arise.

The concept of variety within unity, furthermore, rather than being paradoxical, is said to be reminiscent of the pattern which a satisfactory life takes. Unity in life is a necessity to well-being. We must feel, as Thorndike has often stated, that we "belong"—that we have loved ones and friends and a place in life we can call our own. We must know some security in an environment which we have so far satisfactorily mastered, and which we may hope to master in the future. Only under these conditions do we experience a unity in life. Should any sudden disruption to the even tenor of our lives occur through war, sickness, death of a loved one, or loss of a job, the unity of life is broken, and until we create a new coherence to our broken existence, we feel lost and unhappy.

Too great a unity in life, as in design, however, can lead only to monotony. To follow a similar routine of living day after day, year after year, without change, is a life of boredom. Hence, we welcome variety in the form of planned events such as holidays, and in those little exciting surprises which occur to all of us. In the unity of our lives we find our security and indeed our sanity; in life's variety we find its zest. This is the "dance of life" reflected, as Ellis [14] points out, in every art form produced by man.

---

[13] John Dewey, *Art as Experience* (N.Y.: Minton Balch, 1934).
[14] Havelock Ellis, *The Dance of Life* (N.Y.: Modern Library, 1929).

Attitudes and Mental Processes
Involved in the Production
of Design

Much discussion has revolved around the nature of the attitudes and mental processes involved when an artist produces a design. What does he think and what does he feel? How does he know when his work is "right"? We have already studied some divergent views on this subject. Some Neo-Impressionists felt that the act of designing was a feat of intellect; some Expressionists, in opposition to the Neo-Impressionists, held that it was an emotional adventure. The Gestalt psychologists have reminded us, however, that the human organism acts in totality; when a person is occupied with an act of artistic expression, both his feelings and intellect are involved.

It would appear, then, that in the creation of a design, an artist must employ both the intellectual and emotional aspects of his personality. Some creative people, like architects and industrial designers, lean towards an intellectual approach to design, while some painters and poets favor an emotional emphasis. Nevertheless, both the intellectually and the emotionally inclined designer apparently alternates between feeling and thinking. "I feel that this should be done" is followed by "I think that this is right," or *vice versa*. Thus, emotion livens an artistic statement, while intellect tempers it. Exactly when intellect is the dominant force in artistic acts, or precisely when feeling replaces intellect, would be difficult to detect. Often the creative person himself would be unable to analyze his approach.

While engaged in developing design the artist manipulates the elements until he has arrived at a unity and a variety of composition which satisfy his mind and his heart. This manipulation is performed creatively and is never the result of adhering to a formula. Whatever is produced is unique.

To be successful, however, the artist must approach his task with certain traditional artistic attitudes. Not the least of these is a desire to be completely honest. An honesty of purpose embraces not only a faithful adherence to the true nature of the artist's reactions to experience, but also a respect for the materials and techniques related to his work. Having selected the materials which he considers as a worthy vehicle for the ideas he has in mind, he treats their qualities with respect. Wood retains its qualities as wood; stone as stone. He resorts to no subterfuge to disguise the nature of the substance in use. Even in producing designs of a utilitarian nature, later to be mass-produced on a machine, the true artist-designer will countenance no camouflage. In many articles of this kind, his design is governed by the function which the product must perform. Efficiency cannot, of course, be associated entirely with aesthetic quality since extreme functionalism as

25 *Although the two are not identical, efficiency often coincides with aesthetic quality, as in the graceful Oakland Bridge.*

26 *Gilt-bronze clock, French, late 18th Century. A principle of good design has been violated.*

required in, say, high-speed airplanes, must eliminate the personal choices which are necessary to artistic acts. As Dewey says, "A good deal of intellectual effort has been expended in trying to identify efficiency for a particular end with 'beauty,' or aesthetic quality. But these attempts are bound to fail, fortunate as it is that in some cases the two coincide and humanly desirable as it is that they should always meet." [15]

Nevertheless, in producing a design for functional purposes, such as a design for a building, a piece of pottery, or an item of furniture, which provides a certain scope for personal judgment, the designer must let his decisions be governed by an honest respect not only for the materials used, but also for the purpose to which they are put.[16]

Design in art, therefore, involves considerations related to unity, to variety, to materials, and to function, in which the feelings and the intellect of the designer are brought into play.

Some Principles of Design

Having studied design in some detail, the reader may ask himself to what extent principles of design may be enunciated. It will be realized that art does not lend itself readily to rules and regulations, and that any statement concerning principles must be outlined with caution.[17] Nevertheless, we should attempt from time to time to set down principles about design. To systematize thinking about previous experience in this way is often desirable, since this philosophical activity tends to clarify the nature of the experiences related to it. There are dangers, of course, attendant upon the enunciation of general principles. Should the learner come to rely upon the principles he has developed from his experiences to such an extent that he ceases to look for new, deeper truths in art, his thinking will become static. Whatever universal beliefs one may hold about art must, it seems, be subject to continued revision and further enquiry. General truths about art, in short, must always

---

[15] Dewey, *Art as Experience*, p. 115.

[16] See Herbert Read, *Art and Industry* (N.Y.: Horizon, 1954) for many fine illustrations of these ideas. See also Teague, *Design This Day*. A magazine with the highest ideals and standards in respect to "materials" and "purpose" is *Design* (see Appendix 4).

[17] "The emergence of many systems of theory dealing with formal elements in art is, I believe, an indication of a not altogether healthy state in art education. In periods of confusion as to standards . . . the purely formal theory seeks certainty and safety. . . ."—Robert Iglehart, "Theories of Design: An Evaluation," in *Art Education Today*, 1941 (N.Y.: Teachers College, 1941), p. 26. Iglehart goes on to point out that in clinging to the "safety" of theory, the artist can no longer explore. Ralph M. Pearson, in *The New Art Education*, Rev. Ed. (N.Y.: Harper, 1953), pp. 7–9, shows the unfortunate results which occur when the so-called classic or scientific principles are applied blindly by children.

be regarded in a pragmatic light. Like William James, we must say to ourselves, "This principle appears to be true about all art because at the present it works for us. Tomorrow the principle may not be adequate because by then we shall have enjoyed new experiences and gained new insights into design." If the learner scrupulously maintains this dynamic and open-minded attitude, the formation of principles will then tend to have value for him.

Each learner will arrive at a personal statement of principles dependent upon his experience and his resulting insights. If he has worked thoughtfully with all the elements of design and has mastered, with some degree of personal success, problems related to unity and variety of composition, he may, for example, have arrived at two principles of design somewhat as follows:

> Every successful design exhibits a unity of composition.
>
> Within its unity, every successful design exhibits a variety in the use of the elements.

If the learner has studied and worked with many materials, he will probably have a third principle to enunciate:

> In a successful design, the materials used are treated so that their inherent qualities are respected.

If the learner has studied and produced some functional objects which allow sufficient scope for personal choice, he might be inclined to state:

> The successful design of a functional object is largely governed by the function for which it is produced.

In summarizing his experiences with all types of design activities, the learner will probably advance a principle as follows:

> All successful design in art bears the stamp of the personality of its creator.

To these principles, some readers will wish to add others, emerging from their own thinking. No matter what principles one may formulate, however, they should be employed only as temporary working hypotheses.[18]

---

[18] A helpful list of questions which may be applied to machine-made goods is suggested in *Design Index* (Ottawa: National Industrial Design Council, 1957), p. 1, as follows:

FORM

1. Is the form suitable to the functions of the object? (This implies further that the object be both comfortable and easy to handle.)
2. Is there an harmonious relationship of all parts? (This implies further that no part or section be overemphasized or dramatized at the expense of the object as a whole.)

The preceding discussion about design consists of a verbal and intellectual analysis of a process which is visual and, in considerable measure, emotional. At best, such a discussion can afford the reader only a partial insight into the nature of the act of designing. It would be well, therefore, for the reader to attempt the production of some designs in order to experience directly what designing actually involves. Accordingly, several activities will be described in which the reader may try for himself to achieve this end.[19]

ACTIVITIES EMPHASIZING LINE

1. Select black chalk and a sheet of inexpensive paper such as newsprint measuring about 18" × 24" and having a natural color. Play some stimulating music and begin to draw a line, not to depict an object but rather to develop a nonobjective arrangement. Draw a line freely without attempting to produce a particular effect. Repeat the operation, but in this second case, consider the question of the variety of the line. See that it swoops and glides, ripples and pauses. Repeat again, this time thinking of the unity of the composition produced. Play music of a completely different mood and produce some further compositions in line.[20]

2. Place a piece of cardboard in your coat pocket. With a stub of a pencil draw "blind" an object under observation, such as a park bench, a person, or a flower.

---

3. Is the design as simple as it can be in relation to its function and the manufacturing components involved?
4. Is there no unnecessary or meaningless ornament? (This also implies the absence of any attempts to add unnecessary material in order to give a false appearance of solidity or a false appearance of "streamlining.")
5. Is the use of texture and color both honest and logical in relation to the material used and the function of the object? (This also implies that the object has not been made to look as if it were a handicraft product.)

PRODUCTION
1. Is it mechanically efficient?
2. Is the material used a suitable one in regard to the function of the object and the manufacturing processes used?
3. Is it firmly constructed, durable, and safe?
4. Has ease of maintenance and repair been considered?

[19] See Cannon, *Pattern and Design,* for further activities listed at the ends of the chapters. Activities suggested by the following are also worthy of note: Pearson, *The New Art Education,* especially Part II, pp. 71 ff. Ralph L. Wickiser, *An Introduction to Art Activities* (N.Y.: Holt, 1947); this book deals almost exclusively with discussions of elements of design, with each discussion followed by "problems" in design emphasizing the elements being discussed. Kimon Nicolaïdes, *The Natural Way to Draw* (Boston: Houghton Mifflin, 1941), demonstrates some excellent "organic" approaches to objective drawing.
[20] See the film *Design to Music* (see Appendix 6).

"Blind" drawing of this type tends to place emphasis upon line rather than upon any other element. Withdraw the cardboard from the pocket and analyze the lines and general composition produced. Use this drawing as a basis for another, but make the improvements in composition thought necessary.

3. From observation, draw an object in the environment, such as a person or a house, with reference only to the line quality of the object seen. Remember that a line is being produced, not a photographic statement.

4. Study some drawings of recognized masters of line such as Picasso, Rembrandt, or Henry Moore. Make a line analysis of one of them. Such an analysis should emphasize the main flows of line in the composition without copying any of the elements. Pen and ink or Conté crayon are suitable media.[21]

ACTIVITIES EMPHASIZING MASS AND SPACE

1. Cut some rectangular shapes from paper of various tones but generally neutral in color. Place these shapes on a piece of white cardboard. Move them about until a satisfactory arrangement of the masses and spaces has been found and glue into place.

2. Select a piece of well-seasoned softwood. With a jacknife, gouge, and chisel, carve bumps and hollows having interesting variety. Repeat with another piece of wood so that the second carving is reminiscent of the first but not exactly like it. Carve both until the unity is considered satisfactory when they are brought into close proximity with each other.

3. Take toothpicks or medical swabs and glue them together to form a nonobjective three-dimensional mass having interesting internal space relationships.

4. Study the drawings and sculpture of artists such as Blake, Toulouse-Lautrec, Degas, Maillol, Lachaise, Lehmbruck, and Brancusi for the manner in which they have arranged masses and spaces. An analysis might be made by a drawing in which these elements are emphasized.

ACTIVITIES EMPHASIZING LIGHT AND SHADE

1. With black chalk about one-half inch in length placed flat on the paper, make a nonobjective line drawing. Alter the pressure of the chalk while drawing, and occasionally use the point of the chalk. Analyze the results, particularly for variety in light and shade.

---

[21] See Ray Bethers, *Composition in Pictures*, 2nd Ed. (N.Y.: Pitman, 1956), for some interesting analyses of the elements in pictorial compositions.

2. Place the sculpture produced previously (to illustrate problems of mass and space) in the path of a strong source of light. Manipulate them until the shadows and highlights on the objects themselves, together with the shadows cast from one object to another, form an acceptable unity.

3. Analyze the work of well-known artists such as Cézanne, Miro, Marin, O'Keeffe, Davis, and Guido for their arrangements of light and shade. Make an analysis of a painting to emphasize the use of these elements.

ACTIVITIES EMPHASIZING TEXTURE

1. Cut pieces from printed pages so that the various kinds and arrangements of type appear to have different textural qualities. Paste the pieces to a piece of cardboard or paper so that an interesting textural arrangement is developed.

2. Draw with pen and ink a continuous line so that enclosed spaces occur. By using dots, crossed lines, small circles, and the like, create a design having an interesting textural quality.

3. Repeat (2) using a sheet of silver foil, but this time merely press the foil with a pen without using ink.

4. Study the textural effects produced by artists such as Matisse, Braque, Piper, Kuniyoshi, and Epstein.

ACTIVITIES EMPHASIZING COLOR

1. Repeat any of the activities previously mentioned in which color may be employed.

2. Paint freely with a large brush, placing one hue next to another. Note the apparent changes in hues as one is placed adjacent to another.

3. Dampen a sheet of paper and drip tempera paint or water colors so that different hues may "run" and blend. Note the new colors so formed.

4. Study the work of some great colorists, such as El Greco, Tintoretto, Rubens, Van Gogh, Seurat, and Orozco.

ACTIVITIES RELATED TO FUNCTION AND TO ADEQUATE USE OF MATERIALS AND TOOLS

1. Start a scrapbook and collect for study "families" of similar objects such as automobiles, chairs, yachts, and kitchen equipment. Compare one brand with an-

other from the point of view of function. How does a Jaguar car, for example, compare with a Buick or a Jeep in this respect? What concessions have the manufacturers made to "style" at the expense of function? Why have they done so? To what extent are they justified in so doing?

2. Try to find a number of objects in which a certain material, such as cardboard, has been processed to resemble leather, or plastic to look like woven cloth. Why has the manufacturer resorted to such practices? What are the opinions of designers and critics about them?

Developing a Program

of Studies in Art

Having considered the broad nature of both art and art education, together with some related teaching practices which have proved effective, the teacher will next be concerned with problems associated with the development of a program of studies for art. What should be included in the program? Who will ultimately choose the types of work to be done and what are the most important factors governing a choice of activities?

The development of a program of studies must, like other aspects of art education, be considered a creative endeavor. Indeed, one may say that to carry out the art program successfully engages the teacher in what amounts to an educational strategy. As the pupils progress in their studies, they arrive at carefully arranged "choice points," arising from (1) the selection of themes for expression, (2) the selection of media and tools and techniques, (3) the social setting in which the work is carried out, and (4) the standards of accomplishment in the work produced. As the art program unfolds in the classroom the teacher looks ahead, discovers the points at which he must choose and the points at which the pupils must choose, and plans alternative procedures at each point.

As well as the teacher and the pupils, others, of course, are concerned with the art program. The principal of the school and other supervisors and administrators, whose authority often ranges from the particular locality of the school to the entire state, will be interested in the type of art program being conducted. Just as the range of authority varies, however, so also do the interests of those in charge. The local art consultant, for example, may largely wish to help the teacher with details of classroom procedure, while the state director of art (if the state is fortunate enough to have such an official) will be more concerned with the broader, more philosophic aspects of the program.

No matter how many teachers and educational officials may have some responsibility for the development of an art program, they must rely upon a limited number of criteria for choosing which particular activities it shall include. Among these criteria of choice are the following: the discipline of art; the readiness of the learner; the readiness of the teacher; the school setting; and finally, the community setting.

This chapter, therefore, will open with a short description of the choice points of an art program. It will then turn to a discussion of those who choose an art program. This section will be followed by a description of the criteria of choice. The chapter will close with some case histories which illustrate wherein the development of an art program is an educational strategy.

The "Choice Points" in an Art Program

We observed in the opening chapter that the nature of art demands that the creating person must be in control of the theme of expression. This is as true for artists as it is for children. Nevertheless, we pointed out that while an artist is sufficiently mature to select from the whole range of experience particular themes suitable for his expressive acts, such is not usually the case with children. Children who are told to do "anything they like in art," it will be remembered, often are disinclined to express themselves artistically, simply because they lack a sufficiently specific stimulus to prompt this expression. Nevertheless, within the range of a limited number of specific stimuli sufficiently strong to motivate expression, the young person must have full freedom to select that aspect of the theme which interests him. Choice of theme, then, while it may be limited to a specific rousing experience, must otherwise always allow freedom for the selection of subject matter. While a class of third-graders, for example, might be temporarily encouraged to deal only with the actual trip in the theme "We went to the aquarium," expression might range from a picture of an octopus to that of a group of children listening to an official of the institution.

Just as a controlled freedom appears desirable in the selection of a theme for expression, so also it may often be recommended in choosing media and tools. Most themes may be given expression in a number of differ-

27 *Children work on their paintings in one of the four studios
of the Young People's Art Center of the Baltimore
Museum of Art.*

ent media and with a variety of tools. The trip to the aquarium could be
depicted in a painting in which water color, tempera paint, chalk, or wax
crayon was used; it could be shown in sculpture employing paper or clay;
it could be developed in a textile design, carved in linoleum, or even woven
in colored yarns. Obviously, however, for most teachers, to allow the simultaneous use of all these materials and their attendant tools would create an
impossible teaching and administrative burden in the classroom. Nevertheless, all of these materials would provide valuable educative experiences for
most children. Hence, arrangements must be made by which they may
eventually be selected for classroom use.

The third choice point is that of technique. In using each medium, the
child may select more than one method of manipulation. In painting he may
stipple with the brush as well as employing it in a stroking fashion.[1] He may
use thin paint over a "resist" area where wax has been placed. In clay work
he may "add to" a basic body of this substance, or he may "draw out" from
it.[2] He might work with an inner support for the clay mass or, more likely,
he might work directly without this prop. Many of these techniques require
the teacher's demonstration and subsequent supervision, and everyone will

---

[1] See Chapter 7 for drawing and painting techniques.
[2] See Chapter 9 for work in clay.

agree that the number of techniques being used at one time in a classroom must be limited. Yet each technique may be of value for a child to help him realize his expressive potentialities.

In the art class there are the choice points related to the social setting. Sometimes a type of work like mural-making or puppetry demands that children pool their efforts in order that the project may succeed. At the same time much artistic effort demands solitary individual effort, in which a group of people cannot profitably be employed. Whether the art work shall be performed by a group which would doubtless provide valuable social learning, or whether the work shall be performed by an individual so that he may gain valuable artistic insights are important choices to be made by both teacher and pupils.[3]

In some communities, furthermore, some types of art are acceptable and some are not, so that further choice points arise.

Finally, we have the choice points arising from expected artistic standards. How "excellent" must the children's work be?[4] Children are experimenters, and sometimes as a result of experiments the artistic quality of their work deteriorates. How much should one encourage experimentation at the expense of an artistic standard? This of course is an age-old question in art education. While unnecessary untidyness, undue lack of completeness, and similar shortcomings in artistic production are detrimental to the finished expression, too great an emphasis upon neatness may not only inhibit experimentation, but also damage artistic standards themselves. In working out suitable standards, both pupils and teacher are faced with perhaps one of the most crucial choice points of the art program.

Children, subject to the carefully developed strategy of a teacher, are evidently capable of making a wise choice in their art activities. Some years ago, an experiment was conducted in which children were allowed to participate in the development of an art program.[5] For four years, every child in a representative experimental group of pupils from the first to the sixth grade was encouraged to select with a certain freedom the art work he wished to perform. The choices which the pupils could make were necessarily restricted to ensure that the teachers could offer adequate stimulation and assistance. At the beginning of the experiment, only two choices of theme, tools, media, and technique were open to the children. Thus a child in the first grade

---

[3] See Chapter 11 for a discussion of group activities.

[4] See Chapter 15 for a discussion of the appraisal of children's work in art.

[5] In the Powell River and District Schools, British Columbia, Canada, 1940–1943, during which time the writer was the Supervisor of Art for this area. About 150 pupils in Grades I to VI participated. No kindergartens at that time were operated in the publicly supported educational system of British Columbia.

could, for example, work at picture-making in paint or could construct objects out of boxes. Soon, however, four choices were allowed, and this range of choice was maintained in all classes for the remainder of the four-year study.

At the close of the four-year testing period it was found that out of the range of choices presented by their teachers the children had selected for themselves a broad and comprehensive art program. Every child had included in his program both two- and three-dimensional work. The children had also chosen activities involving individual and group effort. What pleased and perhaps surprised some of the teachers, furthermore, was the fact that the children had from time to time selected work of a theoretical or historical nature.

In order to bring about these results, the teachers, of course, were careful in arranging the choices in the types of work which the children could make at any one time. Such was their strategy that the four available activities always included at least one involving two-dimensional work, while the remainder might include work in three dimensions. From time to time, moreover, activities requiring some historical or theoretical work, such as a study of local architecture or a survey of the output of local painters, were included, particularly in the higher grades. Also in the higher grades, work involving a group was frequently introduced.

In the early 1940's, when this experiment was conducted, many teachers were guided by a fairly rigid art program. At that time, programs in art were often designed in detail by a central committee, and every teacher was supposed to follow these programs closely. A comparison of the output in art by the children in the experimental group with that of pupils who were more restricted revealed that the freedom which the experimental program allowed appeared to have beneficial effects upon the children's output. Their work exhibited a greater variety of technique, a wider range of subject matter, and, strangely enough, superior qualities of design.[6]

It was concluded, therefore, that children should be given considerable freedom of choice in their selection of art activities. Under conditions of freedom, modified only by a necessary pedagogical strategy, they appeared to select a reasonably broad program of art and to improve the artistic standard of their output.[7]

---

[6] This experiment was conducted also in Grades VII to XII, where similar results were observed.

[7] A general trend, not only in art but in many subjects, towards cooperative planning of a program of studies involving teachers, supervisors, administrators, and children is noted and described as "a satisfactory . . . wholesome trend," by Harold G. Shane and E. T. McSwain, *Evaluation and the Elementary Curriculum* (N.Y.: Holt, 1951), pp. 278 ff.

The Choosers
of the Art Program

At the highest levels of administration we find some curriculum makers and general administrators concerned with art education. It is these officials who often supervise the writing of courses of study, and it is usually their concern to ensure that these courses, once designed, are effective. At the same time, they are faced with the fact that the teacher cannot place much reliance upon others to solve for him the problem of developing a detailed program of studies in art. Some authors have attempted to present in exact detail what they consider to be a suitable day-by-day, week-by-week, or month-by-month series of activities. In the past, some city and state educational authorities have done the same, setting down exact statements of what to do from fall to spring, or for January, or for Easter, or in preparation for the Fourth of July. While the statements made may be studied with interest, the teacher usually discovers, if he attempts to follow closely the directions set down, that much of the work prescribed may be unsuitable for his particular class. It is difficult, if not impossible, for anyone in any way remote from the classroom situation to prescribe adequately a detailed program of art. Only those who are directly engaged in art—the pupils and the local teaching and supervisory staff—can attempt to determine in any detail the nature of the program to be followed.

General administrators, especially in parts of the United States, Canada, and the United Kingdom, are giving tangible evidence that they accept these facts. During the past decade or so, a considerable change is manifest in the art publications emanating from some central offices of education in the United States. The former tendency for central offices to set down a detailed program of art has largely changed. Now the teacher is frequently encouraged to assist in the development of the program to suit local conditions and hence to meet local approval. Pamphlets and booklets about art are still published by larger administrative bodies in the United States, but these publications deal with the broad aspects of art education—philosophy, general pedagogy, and sometimes a few broad directions for the production of two- and three-dimensional art forms.[8]

In Canada there appears to be a tendency for provincial departments of

---

[8] One of the most succinct and attractive of these publications is *Creative Art* (Denver, Col.: Denver Public Schools, 1949). An excellent example of a state bulletin is *Art and Youth* (Richmond, Va.: Commonwealth of Virginia, 1955). The latter, however, is largely for secondary schools, although the teachers in elementary schools will find it valuable. Not as attractive in format, but full of excellent material, are *A Course of Study in Art Education* (Harrisburg, Pa.: Department of Public Instruction, 1951) and *Art in the Lives of Florida Children: A Tentative Guide* (Florida: State Department of Education, 1950). See Appendix 5 for a full list.

education to provide not one, but a series of publications for the schools of a province. In some respects these bulletins are more detailed than those of United States origin, but in spite of this, they do not prescribe a program to be followed rigorously.[9]

An informative and well-illustrated, but at the same time not prescriptive, bulletin published in England is a pioneer among the publications in art education issued by a central educational authority.[10]

Most of the art bulletins appearing today, when offering information about techniques, do so only broadly. Mere hints about how to perform a project rather than detailed, step-by-step instruction are offered. In this way the teacher not only is encouraged to gain information about materials and processes through first-hand experience, but also is reminded that art experiences demand such exploration, as opposed to the slavish copying of directions.

As well as state, county, or city supervisors of art, the teacher frequently finds that a local art supervisor or consultant, together with the principal of the school, shows interest in his art program. These officials, if they are up-to-date, will believe that the program must develop according to a number of educational circumstances peculiar to the classroom in which art is taught.[11] To ensure that this idea will prevail locally, some state departments of education are issuing attractive pamphlets, which urge that superintendents of education rely upon the local art specialists and teachers to devise suitable art programs and that principals cooperate with the teacher in developing a program to suit local conditions.[12]

Even with the philosophical and broadly administrative advice of departmental officials and school principals, and more particular assistance of art supervisors and consultants, the classroom teacher is still a major chooser of an art program. He must decide upon such items as the broad themes of

---

[9] See the three-volume series by Elizabeth Jaques, *Art Activities* (Grades I–VIII) (Quebec: Department of Education–Protestant, 1954). In Ontario, the Department of Education has published five books to supplement its outline of an art program: *Art and Crafts in the Schools of Ontario* (7th Ed. Rev., 1956), *Children and Their Pictures* (1951), *Art Education in the Kindergarten* (1952), *Art Education for Slow Learners* (1954), and *Art Education During Adolescence* (1955). Other books are planned for the future for which research is now in progress.

[10] *Art Education: Pamphlet No. 6* (London: H. M. Stationery Office, 1946).

[11] The question of professional relationships between the art teacher and others will receive detailed attention in Chapter 18.

[12] One of the most effective pamphlets of this description is *The 3 R's and Art* (Harrisburg, Pa.: Department of Public Instruction, 1955). See also *Junior Primary in Hillsborough County* (Tampa, Fla.: Hillsborough County Board of Public Instruction, 1948). The latter is a more general type of pamphlet aimed also at the general public; ideas about art programs, however, are emphasized. For a further listing see Appendix 5.

expression, number and types of media to be used, and the possible techniques within the capabilities of the pupils. Likewise, he must decide within what limits the pupils must act as choosers of the program. Again, he must make arrangements so that the pupils may choose creatively and not according to any fixed formula laid down from above. The teacher's strategy of developing a program of studies in art, then, involves both many people (especially the children) and many educational considerations which make great demands upon his professional and personal capabilities.

The Criteria of Choice
in an Art Program

To assist the teacher in developing a suitable art program, one may refer to a number of criteria of choice.[13] As the art work progresses, a variety of choices will be apparent to both pupils and teacher. The best choice in any given situation is more likely to be taken if the following criteria are given adequate attention.

Art as a Discipline

Every major area of learning has developed traditional attitudes, traditional subject matter, a series of activities, and a historical background peculiar to itself. The traditional attitudes of art, that is, honesty of expression, freedom of action in respect to subject matter and design, willingness to work to capacity, and the like have been discussed previously. We have suggested in another chapter also that the subject matter of art has remained constant throughout the centuries, in the sense that it has always reflected the reactions of the artist to his environment.

The activities which have engaged men in this capacity are likewise traditional. Art is a field of forming, or, as we might more commonly say, of making or producing. The raw products which come under the artist's hands are manipulated until they say for him what he wants them to say. In the educational background of most artists will be found experience in both two- and three-dimensional art forms, although most artists tend to reach eminence in just one form. It is well known that expression in drawing and painting, for example, has often tended to be more powerful if the artist has enjoyed some experience in three-dimensional output. Likewise, sculpture and ceramics—to name but two examples of three-dimensional work—

---

[13] Some interesting criteria to assist in determining the adequacy of the teacher's plans are listed in Harold G. Shane and Wilbur A. Yauch, *Creative School Administration in Elementary and Junior High Schools* (N.Y.: Holt, 1954), p. 273. Although these criteria refer to education in general, rather than to art in particular, the art teacher will find them interesting.

28a and b

The comparison of Henry Moore's drawing Two Seated Figures in a Shelter *with his sculpture* Family Group *illustrates the value to the artist of having experience in both two- and three-dimensional art forms.*

DEVELOPING A PROGRAM IN ART

have tended to be more successful if the artist has worked in some two-dimensional fields. Recognition of these facts means that every child should be given an opportunity to produce both pictures and various types of sculpture and modeling.

No one who lacks acquaintance with the development of art through the ages can be said to be adequately educated. Study of the historical background of art cannot begin too early in the elementary school. Even a kindergarten child has much to gain merely by being exposed to carefully chosen works. Naturally, the limited understanding of the child will restrict his insight into the nature of the work on view. If, however, examples are chosen, not for formal study, but rather to be related to the expressive work which is engaging the young learner's attention at the moment, a beginning may be made in acquainting him with his vast cultural heritage in art.[14]

Thus we see that the artistic tradition, as well as the needs and capacities of pupils of any particular stage of development, is a major factor tending to keep all art programs similar. Every art program demands of the learners a wholehearted, personal, and active participation in the various projects under consideration. The content of any art program will include work with many materials by means of which the learners may express their reaction to their environment. The historical background, moreover, must be given some attention. In these respects, the art programs in all elementary schools will be related.

Readiness of the Learners

So flexible is the subject matter of art that it may be accommodated to a learner of practically any age, personality type, or experience. Competent teachers realize that, just as no two children are alike, so also classes or groups of children differ. A program of art which was suitable for the class of a year ago, may not be suitable this year.

The previous educational background of children has an important bearing upon the art program. Sometimes a group of children will be found who have, up to the present, enjoyed little creative work in art, but instead have been taught according to dictatorial methods. Then the teacher's task must be to help the pupils think for themselves, instead of relying upon their teacher. Other children may have had an exceptionally rich background of experience, and the teacher must then offer a more challenging program. In former classes, children may not have been given sufficient group work in art, with the result that they are at a loss as to how to proceed in an activity involving a number of individuals. Some children, on the other hand, may not have mastered sufficiently the technique of working individually, and

---

[14] Chapter 14 discusses in detail the development of an appreciation of art.

hence will require help in this regard. In some classes, children may be discovered who have suffered from an overemphasis of certain types of art work at the expense of others. A former teacher, for example, may have laid undue stress upon "craft," or three-dimensional projects, and may have failed to provide opportunities in picture-making. In attempting to develop a balance of art experiences for children, the teacher must be prepared continually to modify the nature of the program.

The capacities of the children to learn will obviously influence the art program. In classrooms where grouping is not arranged according to a homogeneity of intelligence, the mental capacities of the individual learners will differ markedly. Variations in intelligence, contrary to popular opinion in some quarters, affect art output, as well as general learning about art. Slow learners in academic fields of study are usually slow to profit from art activities, and because of this, their program must be arranged so that undue pressure is eliminated. Intelligent children, on the other hand, will usually profit from art work which presents a continual challenge to their creative energies. Again, children who tend to be nervous in temperament, or, on the contrary, to be phlegmatic require various and carefully arranged degrees of stimulation.

The needs and capacities of the children, therefore, demand diversification of art programs. Indeed, the strong recommendation is made that children should be given every reasonable opportunity to select the activities in art they wish to follow. Even at the kindergarten level, as soon as the pupils have enjoyed experiences with various types of work, they should be encouraged from time to time to select the activities which most appeal to them. As the children grow older and gain further experience with art media, they require an increasing latitude. All art programs should be designed to allow the children to act as the controlling participants, and often the initiators, of the activities performed.

Readiness of the Teacher

The success of an art program depends primarily upon the teacher. When the teacher of art knows materials and tools and is acquainted with some of the techniques associated with them, he can provide his pupils with adequate assistance and sponsor an efficient and stimulating program.

Art is so important in the general education of children in the elementary school that each teacher should be eager to provide adequate opportunities for exploring all practical aspects of this field. Teachers who feel inadequate in handling some tools and materials can readily acquire skill through practice after school hours, often with the assistance of a supervisor or of another teacher. The feeling that "I can teach a little picture-making, but when it comes to craft work, I'm hopeless," soon disappears after relatively little experience with craft work. Likewise, sufficient skill in picture-making can be readily acquired should the teacher feel inadequate in this form of art.

Actually, a teacher should have had some experience with any medium, tool, or technique which he hopes to introduce into the classroom. Even if he plans to promote the use of the simplest medium such as wax crayon, he should experiment with it, however briefly. The various types of paint and the materials lending themselves to three-dimensional work, such as clay or folded paper, should similarly be tested and subjected to experiment. In this way the teacher not only anticipates difficulties in the classroom, but also gains insight into the potentialities of the media. Preparation of this nature is as necessary for the teacher as reading a poem, working out a mathematical problem, or performing an experiment in science before presenting it to the pupils.

Teachers with emergency certificates or those who are recent graduates of a teachers' college, of course, cannot be expected so early in their professional career to be familiar with all the art materials, tools, and processes. It is expected, however, that every graduate will have become acquainted with a reasonable number of two- and three-dimensional activities while studying to become a teacher. His necessarily limited experience, nevertheless, will tend to restrict the art program until he enlarges his knowledge of media and processes. As time goes on, the beginning teacher should make it his business to explore more and more activities which can be added to his art program. Attendance at art workshops and conventions, together with the continued assistance of an art consultant if one is available in his school system or if not, of fellow teachers, will help the young teacher to expand his capabilities in art.

Sometimes, during his in-service training a teacher will develop a particular enthusiasm for a specific type of work. He may, perhaps, be especially attracted to the silk-screen process, or to sculpture in wood. The enthusiasm he exhibits is often catching, so that many of his pupils may also take delight in the activity. When such is the case, teaching tends to be inspiring and consequently the art classes often exhibit a commendable eagerness for their work.

Enthusiasms in teaching are to be encouraged. Two cautions, nevertheless, are in order. In the first place, the enthusiasm should arise in relation to an activity which is of reasonable importance in art education and which is suited to the pupils' level of development. If painting in oils catches the attention of a sixth-grade teacher, the subsequent classroom activities could be extremely practical and beneficial. If making shell-work pictures of "old-fashioned" ladies and roses becomes a passion with the teacher, it is recommended that he follow his vice secretly in a secluded room and present other work in the classroom. Secondly, it is common sense for the teacher to guard against inflicting any enthusiasm for particular work beyond the point of interest and efficiency in his class. No matter how strongly he favors his chosen activity, moreover, he should always make adequate provision for optional activities in cases where the pupils cannot find inspiration in the current activity.

A strong, but at the same time, subtle influence upon an art program is that of the teacher's artistic taste. Just as we all enjoy different kinds of cooking, so also do we all possess different preferences about art. There is a minimum aesthetic standard, however, by which each of us determines whether or not the thing we are observing or producing is art. Those who have this insight will not countenance that which is shoddy, insincere, trite, debased, or contrived. Rather, they admire only those art forms which are conceived honestly and sincerely and produced with sensitivity and sure artistic judgment.

What good taste actually is and how is it acquired are difficult to determine.[15] Apparently, however, an individual acquires a reasonably good standard of taste partly through an acquaintance with good art forms. His taste can also be improved by attempts to produce some art forms. The development of artistic taste is said to begin in childhood and to continue throughout one's life. Some people seem to improve their taste more readily than others, but all can do so to a considerable degree. If the teacher's taste is reasonably sensitive and his aesthetic standards sufficiently high, every art activity in his classroom will tend to be acceptable, and he will be likely to praise, or in some other manner emphasize, the admirable aspects of artistic production. In his classroom, a subtlety of decoration, a proper use of material and technique—in short, a high standard of thought and feeling—will be found which cannot fail to have fortunate effects upon the young learners.

One may hope, then, that all teachers of art will, from time to time, make honest and searching analyses of their personal taste in aesthetic matters and, by taking trouble to gain greater insight into the true nature of art, will maintain in the classroom the highest possible artistic standards.

Personal analysis of any kind is, of course, not easy; in the matter of taste it is admittedly especially difficult. Good taste is as elusive as the *chic* in a woman's costume. It is there or it is not there, but it can neither be measured nor, like design, be completely analyzed. However, a periodic self-examination will remind us of the need to develop and maintain high

---

[15] This topic will be discussed in greater detail in Chapter 14.

standards. Then, having the will to keep our taste at a high level, we may more readily achieve this goal.

The necessity of maintaining high standards of taste in general education has never been stated more forcefully than by Clive Bell:

> If standards go, civilization goes. To hear people talk you might suppose there had never been such things as dark ages. . . . Besides taste in art there is such a thing as taste in life; a power of discerning and choosing in life's minor matters; and on this taste in life, this sense of the smaller values, is apt to flourish that subtler and more esthetic sense. Without this taste no civilization can exist.[16]

Hence, we may say, perhaps of all the items affecting art education, the teachers' good taste is the most important.

Influences from the School Setting

Manifestly the art program is greatly affected by the school setting. The climate of opinion in the school in respect to art education, the classroom accommodation, the supplies and equipment available will all have bearing upon what the teacher can hope to see accomplished. A wide variation exists in these respects from one locality to another. Sometimes, but fortunately rarely, the school authorities may be of the "old school" type and resent monetary expenditures upon anything but the more "basic subjects." In some schools, virtually no special provision is made in classrooms for art and little money is allocated for the purchase of supplies and equipment. Occasionally the teacher finds himself in a school where the schedule is inflexible, and art has to be taught at certain periods and must deal with specific themes.

No matter how discouraging the situation may be, the teacher must firmly resolve to include art in the school curriculum. With determination and ingenuity, he will always find a way to develop a reasonably acceptable art program. If specified themes must be considered, then he must see that the children become sufficiently conversant with them, and excited over them, to express themselves in a creative manner. If sufficient supplies cannot be purchased, then he must make use of scrap materials and whatever supplies may be gathered from the natural environment. Again, various conveniences may be built in the classroom at little or no cost. While an initial lack of supplies and accommodation may limit an art program, this condition need not prevent art from being taught.[17]

---

[16] Clive Bell, *Since Cézanne* (N.Y.: Harcourt, Brace, 1922), pp. 149–50.

[17] Subsequent chapters will indicate how a teacher may improve upon conditions for art education with regard both to supplies and equipment and to accommodation. See Chapters 5 and 7–11.

Influences from
the Community Setting

As has been pointed out previously, the substance of art is to be found in the immediate environment. Artists have invariably discovered subject matter in those experiences which arise from the part of the world which they know. In this sense, art is always local. If the work of the greatest artists displays a universality, it does so because its producers have discovered this comprehensive quality in the local scene. The art of children, of course, will be greatly affected by their community, and it is fitting that this should be so. Only thus will their art activities rest upon the sole reliable foundation for aesthetic forms of expression.

It is the teacher's duty to encourage artistic expression which is derived from immediate experience. In the past, some teachers have felt that art should arise from something romantically remote from the humdrum local scene. Hence, one might discover children living in an eastern seaboard city drawing pictures of the Rocky Mountains, and those in a rural community depicting the skyscrapers of some mythical metropolis. As with adults, the strength and vitality of children's expression do not, in the long run, arise from objects and events remote from their lives. Such attributes are more likely to come from their own backyards.

Some teachers have been concerned with the "development of the imagination" through art activities and have organized art programs almost exclusively around activities which they consider will "stimulate the imagination." Their concern over the imagination is, of course, commendable, but, unfortunately, the type of work which they have encouraged has often tended to lead the children away from their own environment. Among these activities may be the making of "fantastic" fish, birds, or flowers, the painting of "weird landscapes," the delineation of distorted faces, and the like. While such work occasionally might be acceptable, as steady artistic employment it is undoubtedly inhibiting. The imagination works best when it has something tangible to work upon. What is more local, yet more imaginative, for example, than Cézanne's pictures of his native Aix-en-Provence? Indeed, from this locality sprang, if not a new, then at least a revived Western aesthetic.

The community served by the school not only will provide much of the subject matter for an art program, but will perhaps supply some materials for expression. In the most populous cities, any original local materials have largely ceased to exist, and supplies must be purchased and gathered from scrap. Elsewhere, however, suitable woods for sculpture, clays for modeling and ceramics, grasses for weaving, and so on may be found locally. These materials, of course, should be exploited to their full, and their use will have bearing upon the development of the art program.

Sometimes the general character of the community will influence the program. In some areas, well-established local interests, such as the "Little Theater" movement, may suggest that some emphasis be placed upon stagecraft or puppetry. Communities in which there is a well-defined interest in local history might again influence some of the activities in the art program. In certain locations, ethnic groups still maintain a few traditional arts and crafts of which they are proud. The teacher might profitably give some recognition in the art program to work which has its basis in these time-honored and locally approved techniques. The teacher should be alert to capitalize upon the healthy interests or the obvious needs of the region in which the school is located. In doing so, he will not only tend to stimulate a stronger local support for the school in general, and art in particular, but also to develop a more unusual art program.

Some Case Histories Demonstrating the Development of an Art Program

From the foregoing, it will be observed that the development of an art program demands much strategic thinking on the part of the teacher. Many local factors affect the character of the program. At the same time, the teacher must keep in mind the traditional nature of artistic effort, so that whatever work is produced in the name of art will have the attributes of art.

Many teachers have been eminently successful in developing a program of art in keeping with these concepts. It is instructive to study the efforts of some of them, to observe how they have coped with the various factors affecting the program. Accordingly, four case histories are presented to illustrate the manner in which some teachers solved, to the general satisfaction of all concerned, the problems associated with the development of an art program.[18]

A School in an Isolated Community

Mr. Y accepted his first teaching position in an isolated community in the Tennessee mountains. Only seven families supplied the twenty-six children enrolled in his school. Mr. Y noticed that many of the parents had little good to say for their neighbors and that their conversation about them contained many unkind references. No social gatherings in the community had occurred for some years; instead, the people were in the habit of seeking

---

[18] Should the reader consider some of the settings somewhat unusual, it must be pointed out that often an unusual problem more clearly demonstrates an educational strategy.

their entertainment in the nearest small town some fifteen miles away. In summer, the people were able to drive to this town, but in winter traveling became almost impossible because of the snow or mud.

Mr. Y was young and liked people. He determined to organize a social gathering at the school during the winter. He hoped that he might thereby bring about fraternization and that a better feeling might develop in the community. Eventually, he organized a dance to take place in the schoolhouse. Two hired men—one who played a fiddle and the other a guitar —consented to make the music. Each family was asked to bring food.

As far as Mr. Y could discover, no art had ever been taught in the school. However, he found some colored blackboard chalk and some dusty paper in a cupboard. He managed to obtain a quantity of wrapping paper, some old newspapers, and some catalogues from his boarding house.

The children were excited about the forthcoming dance. The drab appearance of the classroom, however, had escaped their notice. Indeed, in that country no one seemed to be concerned with interior decoration, either at home or elsewhere. Mr. Y brought the matter before the class. "What could we do to make the classroom pretty for the dance?" he asked, producing a few art supplies. After much discussion, a theme for decoration was agreed upon: summer in the mountains. The children drew or fashioned in paper sculpture the flowers, birds, and trees of the surrounding country. They painted a mural depicting a trip to the neighboring town. They made paper doilies upon which food was to be placed, and finally, they modeled paper hats and funny faces from papier-mâché for the revelers.

When the parents and a few visitors arrived at the schoolhouse on the night of the dance, every item of decoration was in place. Not many words were passed concerning the gay appearance of the schoolroom, but the decorations were nevertheless noticed. "That teacher's a smart artist," the people said. When they learned that the work was entirely that of the children, they could scarcely credit the fact. Later, after they realized that the children had been responsible, some small bickering developed as to whose children were the smartest artists. Fortunately the paper hats, masks, and finally food created sufficient amusement and general diversion to prevent any serious disagreement on the subject.

Let us examine the most obvious choice points in this situation and at the same time observe the influence of the five criteria which influenced the choices. Media and tools caused few problems arising from choice; in fact anything which the children might use artistically was welcome. A possible choice of theme arose between the local scene and perhaps some more usual semisophisticated topic the young teacher might have observed in nightclubs or dance halls. The size of the job demanded that the children should work as a group so that little choice was open in this respect. Also because the children were inexperienced in art work and hence possessed neither good nor bad taste, as long as they worked honestly toward a functional goal, which the decoration of the classroom offered, the matter of standards could be expected to cause little concern.

Hence the criteria began to operate, with the discipline of art exerting itself largely from the standpoint of the "function" of the project. The problem being well within the understanding of the children, one finds them ready for the activity; the art activities being of a simple nature largely because of the lack of supplies, one sees the young teacher ready to assist the pupils. Since the community was primitive artistically and otherwise, nothing but a "practical" or functional form of art, such as this clearly proved to be, would probably have been acceptable to the parents. Finally, since the community had much stimulating material for a theme for decoration, a local theme was the logical choice to appeal to the parents and to evoke real artistic responses from the children.

Mr. Y, as well as doing the community a social service, had cleverly launched an art program in a region where if art had ever been considered at all, it had been related to outsiders, highbrows. He had demonstrated to the people that school art was practical and acceptable. As a result of his strategy, the considerable attention he subsequently gave to the development of an art program met with local approval.

A School in a Wealthy Area
with Inspiring Local Subject Matter

On the seaboard of the northwestern part of the state of Washington, there is a thriving settlement of some 20,000 people. Here lumber and other wood products are produced in a number of large mills. The district is wealthy and no reasonable expense for the school system is refused. Art rooms are models of efficiency; supplies are abundant.

Miss A accepted a position in one of the large elementary schools in this town and was assigned to teach art in the fourth, fifth, and sixth grades.

Miss A is a competent painter whose work is sensitive, rather than powerful. She is, furthermore, an experienced art teacher and is thoroughly familiar with the contemporary movement in art education. Her home was formerly North Dakota—a complete contrast to northwest Washington.

In studying the art output of children under the guidance of her predecessor, she was disappointed to discover that the program had been extremely formal. Its nature was evidenced by still-life drawings of flower arrangements, exercises in perspective and in color theory, and a few illustrations based upon literary themes.

As she looked about her, Miss A was deeply impressed by her new environment. At her back rose the great mountains, before her was the sea, while in the distance the peaks of an island mountain range showed their caps of snow. At night she could hear the rumble of the mills and could watch the moving lights of the ships as they came and went with their cargoes. She saw some of the Indians of the local tribes and became familiar with the native art of these peoples.

Miss A discovered a mystery and a grandeur she had never before experienced. In short, she fell in love with her new surroundings. She felt deeply moved by all she saw and told herself that here was all manner of inspiration for art.

The people of the settlement went busily about their affairs, apparently giving little aesthetic attention to their environment. The children, as is often the case with the young, likewise seemed unaware of their surroundings. Miss A, however, had an enthusiasm. Somehow, she decided she must make the pupils really see and feel this place.

She began her program simply. She got the pupils to produce pictures which were based upon the usual happenings in their lives. Their first work was neither more nor less inspired than one would find in many other schools. Gradually, however, she introduced them to the strange folklore of the Indian coastal tribes. She showed them the artifacts of the Indians and admired with the children their strength and originality. She played music of the sea—not the tinkly kind, but powerful compositions, like Britten's "Sea Interludes" from his *Peter Grimes*, Mendelssohn's *Fingal's Cave*, and the majestic tonalities of Sibelius.

Occasionally, she read them excerpts from Conrad and Masefield. After the children had produced some pictures on sea themes, she showed them reproductions of works by Marin, Mattson, and Ryder, and a print of *The Great Wave* by Hokusai.

Following the motivation related to the sea, she introduced the subjects of the mountains and valleys, and later the forests and the lakes. In each case, she used related literary and musical interpretations of these subjects. Then she told her classes stories of the explorers of the West Coast. Finally, she turned to the mills and to the drama of heavy industry.

By this time the children's work was improving rapidly. Because Miss A introduced subjects for expression with deep personal feeling and enthusiasm, the children could not fail to respond. She spoke of what they knew, and their output grew in clarity and power.

As time passed, the art program expanded in many directions. Miss A discovered, for example, a local wood which was suitable for carving. Later she introduced various kinds of textile printing into her program and encouraged the children to use motifs based upon the local environment. She helped the children organize fist-puppet shows, for which they wrote original scripts about life, either past or present, on the West Coast.

In recognition of her success, the local school authorities placed her in charge of art in the junior and senior high schools, as well as in the elementary schools of the area. One of the most recent projects completed is a series of murals in oils to decorate the library of the Junior High School. Their subject is the impact of the white civilization upon the Coastal tribes. At the entrance to this library stands a carving in wood depicting a stylized bird with a wing spread of twelve feet. So excellent did the quality of the work become that finally a major art gallery displayed the drawings, painting, and sculpture of her senior pupils, not primarily as the product of an educational process, but rather as art worthy of some serious consideration.

In Miss A's program, the choice points arising from theme suggested either a continuation of a formal, "classic" type of subject matter or a utilization of the local scene. Choice of media, tools, and techniques offered unlimited scope and the problem was one of selection. The social setting and taste of the pupils raised few problems.

Miss A as an artist knew intimately the nature of art as a discipline. She possessed many artistic skills and her taste was impeccable. Her pupils also possessed some skills and a reasonably developed taste. Her strategy, then, was first to make the local scene acceptable to the pupils as a basis for expression; second, to get the pupils to use the abundance of two- and three-dimensional materials wisely in expressing reaction to their locality; and third, to make use of important historical facts having artistic significance.

She carried out her strategy naturally enough by exhibiting the work of artists and artisans who had lived in, and had been moved by, similar surroundings and by inspiring the pupils through a display of her own deep and commendable enthusiasm. It was she who was the chooser of the basic theme for expression and quite frequently the type of material which might most profitably be used, but knowing art and the need for freedom of those who practice it, she was able to avoid becoming harmfully dictatorial.

A School in a Depressed Area of a Large City

Mr. G is an art teacher in a school situated in an old section of an American east-coast metropolis. The buildings of the district are dirty and monotonous; housing conditions are poor; heavy trucks rumble continually to and from the adjacent docks. Four blocks distant is the glitter of the city's world-famous amusement area. There is neither a playground nor a public park within convenient reach of the school.

Mr. G enjoys his work because he senses a great need for it. His own classroom is a model of neatness, order, and attractiveness. He has sponsored the formation of a pupils' committee which is responsible for hanging attractive displays of art work in the halls of the school. Because the school board has painted the halls and classrooms in attractive colors, entering the building after leaving the drab street is a happy experience.

The program followed by Mr. G is in some respects similar to that which may be found in many other situations. The pupils make pictures related to their lives and intersperse this type of activity with some of the usual three-dimensional projects. If some of the pupils' output displays unhealthy interests resulting from a sordid environment, their expressions at least have the saving graces of honesty, clarity, and reasonably good design.

The one outstanding feature of the art program under Mr. G's guidance is the attention given to home and community planning. During his art periods, one may always observe some members of his class working at problems related to this theme. Perhaps a park is being designed, or an apartment. Sometimes a plan for a recreation center is engaging the children's attention. On one occasion, the pupils reconstructed in miniature the entire neighborhood. Some of the boys and girls have planned a "dream house" and other individuals have designed the bedroom or kitchen each would like to occupy. As frequently as possible, Mr. G takes the pupils on expeditions to see the layout of the city parks, new housing developments, or other building projects worthy of note.

Mr. G was faced with grave problems arising from the choice of theme and the social setting. Should the pupils continue to express sordid things, or turn to another type of subject matter remote from their present world? Other choice points contained few problems out of the ordinary. Fortunately Mr. G had sufficient insight into art to realize that expression must arise from what the pupils knew, even though what they knew was often far from socially desirable. To rely upon artificial subject matter, he knew, would probably serve only to affect adversely the pupils' artistic taste. Therefore, he made sure that the pupils had some socially commendable experiences upon which he could capitalize when the children employed these themes. The discipline of art was still operative, expression was still within the artistic tradition, but now it embraced a more healthy world. This was the objective of his strategy which he felt succeeded as far as was artistically expedient.

A School in a Settled
Rural Community

Miss L is the science and art teacher in a village school situated in a prosperous rural section of New Hampshire. Life in this peaceful and charming area jogs along in an unhurried manner. Miss L maintains the pace of her surroundings.

When Miss L first took up her duties, the ambitious principal, formerly from New York, was disturbed on two counts: first, Miss L never appeared to exert herself sufficiently; and second, she seemed incapable of planning her art lessons in advance. When asked at the beginning of the term what her intended art program might be, she admitted not being quite sure of what work would be accomplished.

During the science periods, the children began to collect some snakes and turtles which they enclosed in an open wire cage in the school grounds. Because these creatures "might be lonely," the children explained, an old tennis net was rigged above the cage and butterflies were added to the collection. Flowers were placed in the enclosure "to feed the butterflies." Some broken branches of small trees were placed in the cage under which the animals could hide.

As the collection grew the children made many sketches in crayon, tempera, and water color of the various objects they had gathered together. Some of the children made linoleum cuts based upon the themes in their graphic work. The drawings, paintings, and linoleum cuts displayed an infinite variety of observation and pictorial arrangement.

In the school was a spare classroom which was put to use for quiet games and reading on rainy days. Miss L suggested that curtains would improve the appearance of the room. Both the principal and the children agreed with the suggestion. Accordingly, textiles were decorated with linoleum block prints in two colors. Later, the children were interested in a collection of prints Miss L happened to find, among which they greatly admired some designs from California.

When the curtains had been hung, it was obvious that the room required some paintings. A small mural was developed and put in place together with several paintings produced by individual children. All themes were selected from the children's science collection.

Later, when the pupils were studying soil, some local clay was used to produce pottery. A sgraffito pattern derived from the rhythms of the local hills and valleys was employed to decorate the pottery. Eventually the pottery led the pupils to sculpture.

Miss L continues to develop an art program in a leisurely and natural fashion. The work of the children reflects the charm of the surrounding country. It displays an unmistakable character which arises from known and felt experience.

The principal is wise enough to let the art program develop in this fashion, and no longer worries over Miss L's apparent lack of planning. The art program goes along, now taking one direction and now another. Somehow, nevertheless, a commendable amount of work is completed each term, and the children never seem to be at a loss for ideas. The work is always noteworthy for its aesthetic quality and its charming individuality.

Miss L is a teacher who welcomes a multiplicity of choice points and builds her teaching upon many such points. She is sufficiently knowledgeable and skillful to feel capable of making personal choices, should the need arise, but she is reluctant to do so, preferring instead that the pupils choose. Moreover, she is never afraid to let the pupils experiment for fear that their work will become untidy or of a generally poor standard. She knows that gentle teaching at the right time will bring favorable results. What at first appears to be lack of planning and vigorous teaching in her program actually is a subtle strategy working with the utmost smoothness towards desirable educative results. By hint and mild suggestion, Miss L steers the program in this or that direction, always with tact, taste, and due regard for the pupils' readiness and the community setting, within and without the school.

It will be noted that the programs of the four teachers just described, while varying in detail, display several common characteristics. While each teacher reacted differently to the various choice points, they all were influenced by the five criteria of choice in an art program. Because artistic expression was never remote from the experiences of the children or from the community setting, the work produced was closely bound to artistic tradition and exhibited a vitality, coherence, and honesty which can arise only from personal reactions to familiar experiences. Each teacher, while stimulating and helping the pupils, allowed them sufficient freedom of expression and choice of activity within the framework of each theme. Finally, it must be pointed out that all the programs were successful because the teachers fully believed in their work and were sufficiently competent both in pedagogical and artistic matters to make each program effective.

ACTIVITIES FOR THE READER

1. Describe in some detail the significant "choice points" which might arise in an art program being developed in the following situations:

   (a) A sixth-grade classroom in a new, wealthy, materialistic, suburban district near a large city.

   (b) A third-grade classroom in a temporary school for the children of construction workers in an isolated part of North Carolina.

   (c) A mixed-grade classroom (first to fourth grades) in a mission school for Indians situated in New Mexico.

2. Describe how you would constructively handle a situation in which your principal was more interested in having an art program based upon a rigid form of Neo-Impressionism than upon a contemporary, creative approach.

3. If a fellow teacher in your school gave evidence of atrociously bad taste in the kind of art work he admired, and one day he asked you for an honest appraisal of his efforts, describe what you would say or do.

4. You are elected chairman of an eight-man *ad hoc* committee in a city system to submit ideas to a central authority for the improvement of the art program. You are expected, furthermore, to select the eight members of the committee. State the kinds of people you would choose. Tell what agenda you would draw up for the first hour-long meeting.

5. You as a teacher want your fifth-grade pupils to become active in helping you to develop an art program, but the pupils do not appear interested. What might be wrong? Describe what you might do to improve matters.

6. Describe how you would proceed in developing an art program in your new teaching position in which the former teacher had for two years taught nothing to fourth-, fifth-, and sixth-grade pupils except the copying either of comic strips or of colored postcards.

Arranging and Equipping

a Classroom for Art Activities

In kindergartens and in the first six grades of elementary schools, it is general practice for the classroom teacher to be responsible for his own art program and for the children to perform art activities in their own home rooms.

The generally accepted practice of teaching art in the children's regular classroom, while not entirely convenient in all situations, has much in its favor. Any schoolroom especially provided for art is usually shared by many teachers, and, as a result, each class must occupy it according to a prearranged schedule. Art activities in the elementary school, however, should in general take place immediately following a stimulus. This is especially true in the lower grade levels. In a situation where a special art room is provided, children, particularly the younger ones, may often be ready to express themselves through art but are denied the opportunity because the special room is occupied by another class. When the regular classroom is used for art work, on the other hand, expression may occur as the occasion demands. By using his own classroom, moreover, the teacher tends to have greater control of the supplies and equipment required for work in art.

In order to conduct an art program successfully, the teacher must often plan alterations and additions to the basic classroom accommodation with which he is provided. Accordingly, this chapter will discuss some of the ways and means by which the layout, first, of a kindergarten and, next, of regular classrooms may be modified to accommodate pupils engaged in art work. Some attention will be given also to the planning of an art room, in case a teacher may at some time or another find himself in a position in which such a room is to be established.

Many of the problems which arise from the task of reorganizing a room for art are peculiar to the situation. The size and shape of a room, the number of children in a class, the type of activities in the program, and so on will modify the arrangements to be made. The making of suitable physical arrangements for art, therefore, presents the teacher with a personal challenge which in the long run only he can satisfactorily meet.

It might be noted here that this chapter deals only with the physical equipment and functional arrangements for art activities in different types of rooms. Suggestions about display and added general attractiveness of the classroom are to be found in Chapter 13. Furthermore, this chapter is concerned only with art education. While the general classroom might well contain a vivarium, an aquarium, charts, maps, a library corner, and the like, it is beyond the scope of the book to recommend particular placement of most of these items, since certain scientific specifications which sometimes must take precedence over artistic considerations are involved.[1]

A classroom, and especially an art room, is a workshop, and its design must be governed primarily by functional considerations. Fortunately, however, if functional demands remain strictly paramount in all classroom arrangements, the setting will then tend to be sympathetic for whatever display techniques are subsequently employed. There is little or no reason, in other words, for a functional classroom to be anything but attractive.

General Operations in a Classroom Arranged for Art

Since the physical arrangements in a classroom for any particular subject depend upon the operations to be carried out, it is necessary at this time to analyze the various important operations which occur when art is taught.

Before an art session takes place, the teacher must usually make some preparations. As every experienced art teacher is aware, a class of eager children descends upon art supplies like a flock of starlings in a cherry orchard. Things disappear fast! Unless the teacher has made adequate preparations so that the supplies are abundant and easily obtainable, much confusion and subsequent dissipation of energies which should be channeled into expressive work may occur. The teacher must often select the supplies which

---

[1] For example, the placement of an aquarium will depend upon the type of fish it contains, the geographical position of the school, and the like.

the children require from a storage area. Because many supplies come in bulk, he frequently has to arrange them in convenient units before putting them in a position where the children can most easily reach them.

Now the children enter the picture. After knowing what to obtain and where to obtain it, and how to move so that they do not get in each other's way (all of which they learn through discussion with the teacher and subsequent practice), they must have suitable places in which to work.

Art supplies and processes raise special accommodation problems. Papers for drawing and painting are usually much larger than those for writing, so that surfaces to accommodate them must be larger than some school desks. Then certain activities such as wood sculpture or linoleum block printing demand a special surface where the materials may be cut. Through use, this surface will become rough and hence unsuitable for drawing and painting and some other activities. Two different surfaces—a work board and a drawing board—are therefore necessary.

After the children have worked, their semicomplete and complete output will create more special problems. The semicomplete work may be wet and a place must be found where it can be dried before being stored away. Both drying space and storage space must therefore be provided. The finished work—two- as well as three-dimensional—must be put on display. Hence display boards and shelves must also be available.

In summary, a classroom in which art is taught requires physical provisions for the following operations: storing bulk equipment and supplies; preparing current supplies for the class; setting out supplies for the current work; working delicately as in drawing and painting, or robustly as in cutting and hammering; drying semicompleted or completed work; storing semicompleted work; displaying work.

29 *Children in class selecting supplies. Simple arrangements based on the cafeteria system are practical.*

Brigdens

Basic Supplies and Equipment

Each type of art activity demands particular tools and equipment and sometimes special arrangement of furniture. Sometimes also, the developmental level of the pupils or the grade level at which the work is being performed will influence the choice of items. Subsequent chapters will discuss in detail the tools, media, and other special features of teaching particular art subjects at the various developmental levels. For the present these topics will be mentioned only in general.

No matter what special subjects are contemplated in art, the accompanying alphabetical list of general tools and supplies appears to be basic to nearly any art program.

1. brushes	painting, flat, hog bristle, one inch to one-quarter inch wide
	painting, pointed, sable, large (size 6 or 7)
	paste
2. chalk	soft, 10 or 12 colors, black, white
3. crayons	wax, soft, 10 or 12 colors, black, white
4. drawing boards	about 18″ × 24″, soft plywood at least "B C" grade (i.e., clear of knots on at least one side)
5. erasers	Artgum type
6. inks	ordinary blue-black fountain pen
	black India, 2-oz. bottles
7. paint	poster, liquid in pints or powder in pounds (white, black, yellow, blue, brown, green, red, as basic; magenta, purple, turquoise as luxuries; probably twice the quantity of black, white, and yellow as of other colors chosen)
	water colors in boxes of 8 colors (sometimes useful but not entirely necessary if funds are low)
8. paper	roll of kraft (i.e., brown wrapping), about 36″ wide, or "project roll," 36″ wide
	manila, 18″ × 24″, cream and gray
	colored construction, 12″ × 18″ (red, yellow, blue, light green, dark green, black, gray, and perhaps some in-between colors like blue-green, red-orange; some 40 colors are obtainable)
	newsprint, natural, 18″ × 24″

9. paint tins	muffin tins, with at least 6 depressions
10. paste	school, in quarts
11. pencils	black, drawing, soft, about 5B
12. work boards	plywood (3-ply) 18″ × 24″ (old drawing boards are suitable)

Miscellaneous supplies and equipment such as scissors, thumbtacks, and paper cutter (18-inch cut minimum) are not listed since they are part of general equipment for other subjects.[2]

In order that the supplies may be handled efficiently and the work proceed in an orderly fashion, the following supplementary furniture is needed:

1. A storage cupboard with some adjustable shelves, the latter at least 8 inches wide for small items and other shelves at least 18 inches wide for larger items. The outside dimensions of the cupboard will, of course, be determined by the floor and wall space available.

2. Two tables, preferably at least 5 feet long and 30 inches wide, one to be used largely by the teacher in arranging and displaying supplies and the other for children's group work.

3. A sink, or a stand for pails of water, the details of which will be discussed later.

4. A drying shelf or battery of shelves near a radiator or other source of heat. The shelf should be about 12 inches wide and as long as space permits.

5. Some extra display facilities to be discussed later in this chapter.[3]

Some Particular Arrangements

Having listed the basic tools, supplies, and equipment for any art program, we may now consider some special physical arrangements for art. To illustrate the manner in which arrangements for art are influenced by the age level of the pupils and local educational conditions, four situations will be discussed; the kindergarten, the unequipped standard classroom, the modern general classroom, and the art room.

---

[2] Exhaustive lists of supplies and equipment can be found in such state publications as *A Course of Study in Art Education* (Harrisburg, Pa.: Department of Public Instruction, 1951), pp. 64–67, and *Art and Youth* (Richmond, Va.: Commonwealth of Virginia, 1955), pp. 127–42. See Appendix 5 for further listing.

[3] Also in Chapter 13.

Jack Engeman Studio

30 *Kindergarten children working at art. The floor is a safe place for painting in the kindergarten.*

A Kindergarten

The problems in arranging the kindergarten arise largely from the stage of physiological development of the pupils. Because kindergarten-age youngsters use the large muscles in drawing, painting, and three-dimensional work, they need generous working spaces. They also require relatively large tools and bulky media which create storage problems.

The teacher's preparation of art materials for kindergarten children is often quite different from that in the higher grades. Older children can usually select art materials for themselves, but in kindergarten, the teacher must, at last at the beginning of the school term, arrange sets or "kits" of materials. These vary greatly in number of items contained. For example, for crayon drawing the youngster needs merely six crayons and a sheet of manila paper. For painting requires perhaps an apron, a sheet of newspaper or oil cloth to protect a painting surface, two brushes, a sheet of newsprint, and a paint cloth, not to mention some liquid colors.

From a necessarily large and convenient storage space the teacher selects items to make up the "kits" and places them on a long table, "cafeteria" style. She may place the six crayons on a paper plate and set this on a sheet of paper. The painting kit may be assembled on a metal or plastic tray, or on a wooden work board. Note that the paint is not included in the list at this point, because of accidents which may occur if the children transport it to a place where the painting is done. The paint or any other "dangerous" material is placed in the working area ahead of time.

The following suggestions may be helpful in preparing tools and supplies for distribution:

1. Brushes and pencils should be placed in glass jars, with bristles and points up (see Fig. 31). Blocks of wood with holes bored in them, each hole large enough to hold one item, are another convenient way of arranging this type of tool.

31 *Brushes, pencils, or crayons are easily stored in glass jars or in a block of wood with holes bored in it.*

2. Crayons should be separated according to colors. Each container, which might be a paper plate or a small cardboard box, should hold only one color.

3. Moistened clay should be rolled in balls and placed in a large earthenware jar or a tin container, either of which should have a lid to keep in the moisture.

4. Paper should be cut to size and arranged on a shelf in piles according to size and color.

5. Paper scraps should be separated according to color and saved in small cartons.

6. Paste should be kept in glass jars (or, if dry, in the bulk packages). The teacher should place paste on disposable paper plates or simply on cardboard after it has been mixed for use.

Fortunately, the furniture in most kindergartens is movable; when it is, the floor provides an excellent work area for art. If the floor is covered with heavy linoleum or linoleum tile, it is necessary to set down only a thin protective covering such as oilcloth or wrapping paper before work begins. If the floor is in any way rough, cardboard mats may be put over the areas where the activities are to take place.

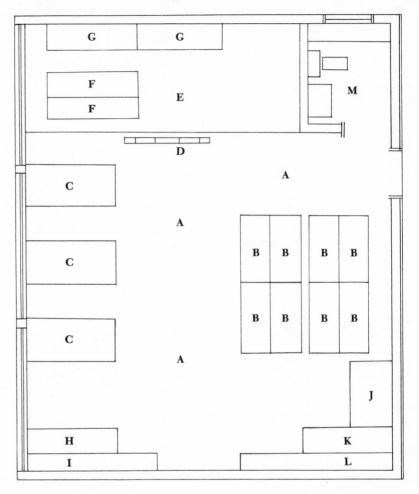

A—Painting area of floor
B—Tables for working with paper, card-
  board, wood, clay, etc.
C—Drawing and painting tables
D—Easels
E—Platform for puppets, etc.
F—Tables for working on puppets
G—Storage for puppet supplies
H—Table for drawing and painting sup-
  plies in use.

I—Cupboard for drawing and painting
  supplies.
J—Paper-cutting tools and supplies, etc.
K—Paper supplies in use (including
  cardboard, boxes, and perhaps wood)
L—Cupboard for supplies
M—Washroom

The type of work being done, whether delicate or robust, will also often determine the kind of floor or table covering to be set down. It is usually necessary for the teacher to have available the following types of protective covers:

1. A smooth piece of thick cardboard or 3-ply wood, about 18 inches by 24 inches, not necessarily thick, for drawing and painting.

2. A heavy piece of cardboard or 3-ply wood, about 18 inches by 24 inches, for hammering, cutting, etc.

3. A piece of waterproof oilcloth, about 18 inches by 24 inches, for clay work, finger painting, etc.

Any of these coverings may be put with the "kits," although many teachers prefer to put them in place either themselves or with the help of the more advanced children.

Some teachers like to hang paintings to be dried on a clothesline with spring clothespins. Tables are often used for drying three-dimensional projects. The floor, of course, if part of it can be conveniently reserved, is an excellent place for drying all types of work. Not much semicompleted work requiring storage is produced in the kindergarten, most projects being completed in one art session.

It is desirable, of course, for all children eventually to learn how to procure and replace equipment and supplies for themselves. Even in the kindergarten, children must be taught to do this. Attention, therefore, must be given to the arrangement of the room so that the children themselves may obtain and replace materials and tools. In the kindergarten, as elsewhere in the art program, the cafeteria system mentioned above may be used.

It will be realized that to obtain and to replace art materials demands considerable ability. Obviously, children must develop the ability according to a plan which they, themselves, help to determine. The teacher should discuss with the children why they must learn these skills, because skill of any kind can be developed most effectively in conjunction with an understanding of its purpose. However, in the kindergarten the children will usually follow plans willingly and treat the routine as a game.

An Unequipped Standard Classroom

Often a beginning teacher is discouraged by the classroom in which he is placed. With every good intention of sponsoring a reasonably liberal program of art, he may find that literally no conveniences for this work have been provided. Let us assume that he is confronted with the worst of conditions and then see what steps for improvement may be taken.

Before improvements can be made, the teacher should ascertain what funds are available and how to go about getting permission to spend some. Furthermore, he must be able, with the assistance of the pupils, to do rough carpentry or find someone else who can. The following discussion assumes that both someone who can do simple carpentry and a modest sum of money are available.

Here is a classroom in which no arrangements have previously been made to conduct a program of art. On one side wall are windows, on the front wall and other side wall are blackboards, while the rear wall is simply plaster. The room has no sink and no cupboards, and to the floor are permanently fixed thirty-five small school desks of a standard pattern so that very little space may be found for tables or art desks. In this room extra storage space must be made for supplies and semicompleted work; places must be found for current art supplies; sufficiently large work areas must be provided for drawing, painting, and some three-dimensional work; drying areas must be planned; and display places must be established.

Since the surfaces of the desks are too small for most art work, the teacher's first task is to provide convenient working surfaces. To this end, various devices may be used. Drawing boards will provide surfaces for individual work. For group activities, especially those in three dimensions, heavy (5-ply) plywood may be cut in strips about 24 inches wide and four feet long and rested on the tops of rows of desks as shown in Fig. 33. To keep the plywood in place, strips of wood should be fixed on the under surface to form a lip along the edges of the desks. While working, the children, of course, stand in the aisles between the desks. Large sheets of thinner (3-ply)

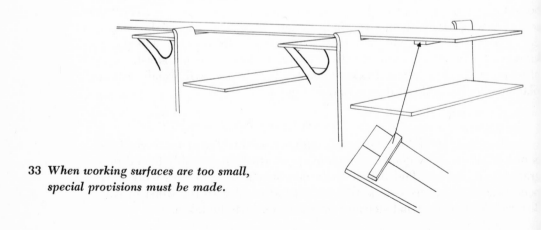

33 *When working surfaces are too small, special provisions must be made.*

plywood may be cut to fit over the blackboards and kept in place when required for painting by means of wooden buttons. Under the chalk rails may be fitted shelves which swing upward and have collapsible legs.

To provide adequate cupboard space is another equally important problem. Unless radiators block the way, a long cupboard about 30 to 32 inches high may be constructed below the windows. The top of this cupboard can be covered with a hard building board so that its surface can be used for work with some three-dimensional materials. The width of the cupboard must be sufficient to take care of paper and tools, as well as partly finished two- and three-dimensional projects. Twenty-four inches is probably sufficient, although available space will govern the dimension. To provide storage space for small items of equipment, such as pencils and paint brushes, one can cut a number of blocks of wood similar to those suggested for kindergartens and in these bore holes in which the pieces of equipment may be placed end up. This arrangement, while taking very little space, allows a self-service system to operate readily and a quick-check survey to be made for mislaid articles.

In a classroom such as this, careful plans must be made, especially for the distribution and handling of paint. Along the rear wall of the room an open double shelf may be built, with the lower shelf wider than the top one. On the top shelf should be placed the paint currently in use. Both this shelf and the wall behind it should be protected with oilcloth or linoleum. A spoon or a wooden paddle should be placed next to each color. It is a good plan to put both jars and paddles on scrap paper, so that the cleaning-up routine may be easier. On the top shelf also may be placed two pails, one for clean water and the other for dirty water.

The second shelf has several uses. In the first place, it catches drops of paint and for this reason should be covered with linoleum or oilcloth. It also serves as a resting place for paint tins and brushes when the children are selecting the colors they desire. The shelf may also be used as a storage place for paint containers, such as eight-section muffin tins, when they are not in use.

To provide some display space is the next problem. The end wall behind the paint shelves can be covered with a soft plywood (3-ply pine), buttoned into place (see Fig. 34). The area above the blackboards can also be faced with the same materials. Along the top of the blackboards, a shelf can be constructed upon which to display three-dimensional work. This shelf, however, is rather high and should be used only for fifth- and sixth-grade classrooms and then only if no other space is available. For hanging paintings to dry, the clothesline system mentioned in connection with the kindergarten is also practical for this classroom. Batteries of drying shelves can be con-

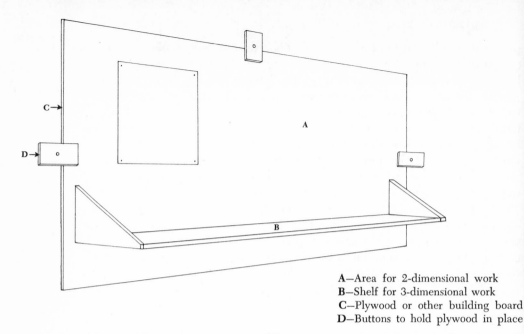

A—Area for 2-dimensional work
B—Shelf for 3-dimensional work
C—Plywood or other building board
D—Buttons to hold plywood in place

34 *A simple arrangement for displaying two- and three-dimensional art.*

structed above radiators or other heat outlets, and some library shelves for art books and periodicals could be built in a corner.

If floor space is available, the teacher will find long tables convenient for sorting and displaying supplies and equipment, for drying purposes, for group activities, and even for displaying completed work.

A classroom of this kind will probably be crowded and particular attention must therefore be paid to system, order, and cleanliness. Every child should feel he is responsible for the good appearance of the room and should have a specific job in this connection. Cooperative planning should help decide the division of labor. Some pupils should see that all paint is wiped from the desks, some should keep the paint shelves in good condition, others should look after the displays, and so on. The attractive condition of the room will be recognized by all as most rewarding, and any normal group of youngsters will take pride in these surroundings. There is always something satisfying in building from practically nothing, and the classroom which presents a real challenge often brings the greatest pleasure to those who improve upon it.

In the next section additional, but more expensive, suggestions will be found which can be added gradually to the room, as the funds allow.

A Modern General Classroom

Not all conditions are as challenging as those described in the previous section. In many contemporary school plans, considerable thought is being given to suitable accommodation for art activities in general classrooms. While the classrooms in question are, of course, designed for conducting learning in all branches of the school curriculum, many of them include special provisions for art. A description of these is offered here primarily for those teachers who are provided with a reasonably liberal budget for the modernization of the art facilities in their classroom.

In the majority of classrooms being constructed today, the desks are not fixed to the floor but, rather, are readily movable and can be arranged to suit the studies in progress. Movable desks are a great convenience for drawing and painting since they allow a pupil to use a drawing board without interfering with other children. With movable furniture, furthermore, convenient clusters of desks may be arranged so that large flat areas of working space are available for group activities.

In some contemporary classrooms, the entire end wall is provided with fixtures to facilitate the teaching of art, as shown in Fig. 35. A counter covered with linoleum or some other suitably processed material is built from wall to wall. This counter houses probably the most important single convenience for art activities—a large sink which is supplied with hot and cold water. Below this counter are several storage cupboards equipped with adjustable shelves and swinging doors where all expendable supplies may be stored with reasonable convenience. About twelve inches above the counter, a second row of cupboards is suspended. This, likewise, has adjustable shelves, but the doors are of the sliding variety so that pupils will not bump their heads on them when open. In these cupboards, either additional supplies or the unfinished work of the pupils may be kept. Electrical outlets are frequently provided at convenient intervals along the counter. This whole assembly, which resembles to a considerable extent a work unit in a modern kitchen, occupies relatively little floor space. Sometimes in these contemporary classrooms, an additional work counter is provided along part of the window wall; below this counter, cupboards are frequently built.

Because a teacher in a general classroom requires a relatively large expanse of chalkboard, it is sometimes difficult to find sufficient space for art display purposes. This is often provided, however, on the side wall to the rear of the room, while on two walls above the chalkboards a wide strip of tackboard is fastened. But since even these areas are usually insufficient for display purposes, many new schools are being equipped with display boards and cases in the main halls of the building.

35 *End wall fixture for art activities in a general classroom*
(sketch based on original design
by Ontario Department of Education)

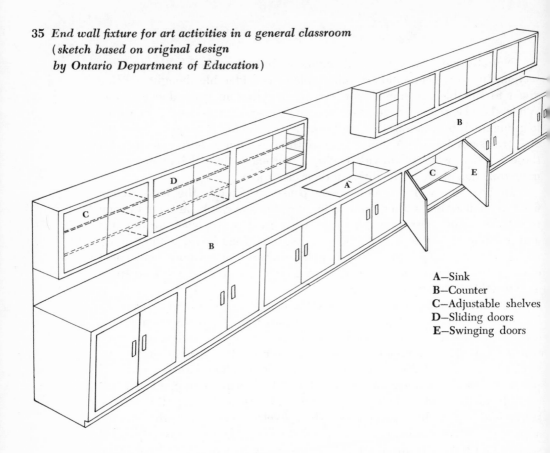

A—Sink
B—Counter
C—Adjustable shelves
D—Sliding doors
E—Swinging doors

Teachers who are fortunate enough to occupy modern classrooms of the type described seem to experience little difficulty in conducting a reasonably broad and effective program. This is particularly the case in buildings provided with what is known as an "art service" room.

An "Art Service" Room

In certain elementary school systems in the United States—notably in the city of Baltimore—the "art service" room has been developed for the use of the teachers. As shown in Fig. 36, this is a room for schools where art is taught in regular classrooms, rather than in an art room. One should note that the art service room is not restricted to new buildings but can be provided in any school building where space can be found.

The art service room serves several important purposes. It provides a place outside of their own classrooms for teachers to experiment with art materials and equipment. Here, lessons involving the use of new materials may be planned away from the gaze of youngsters, which on some occasions may be embarrassing.

From a stock of tools and materials in the art service room, the teachers may conveniently prepare whatever they need for art work in their own classrooms. In the service rooms are "art service carts," which resemble tea wagons with several trays and may be easily wheeled to the classrooms when loaded with the appropriate supplies. It is maintained that a considerable outlay of money, which would otherwise be spent in duplicating supplies in several classrooms, is saved by this means. This is particularly true of block printing, weaving, and woodcarving equipment which is not used frequently in any one classroom during a term.

The art service rooms are equipped not only with storage shelves and cupboards for expendable material but also with shelves for work in progress. Consequently, teachers may send such items as costumes and properties in various stages of preparation for school plays to be stored safely until needed. Clay objects may also be kept safe there before firing, while objects made from papier-mâché may be set out for drying. Classrooms are thus kept free of half-finished objects which might come to some harm if they remained in the room.

Finally, the art service rooms serve as a depot for storing, sorting, and

36 *An art service room showing wagon onto which the teacher at the left is loading supplies. Children are helping Baltimore teachers to obtain art supplies and equipment.*

Jack Engeman Studio

preparing current exhibitions of school work. Teachers may bring to the rooms such pieces of work as they consider suitable for exhibitions. Art shows thus may be coordinated and carefully arranged and hence may be more representative of the school.

It will be observed therefore that the art service room serves many useful purposes and tends to eliminate many of the difficulties associated with teaching art in home rooms.

An Art Room

Let us now consider a fourth situation in classroom accommodation. Here, let us suppose we are asked to give advice in planning an art room in a new school. Let us also make two further rather farfetched suppositions: first, that no expense is to be spared and, second, that whatever the art teacher proposes will be acted upon (see Fig. 37).[4] In the real educational world, budgets are not always large enough for our needs, and the wishes of art teachers are not always respected. However, there is no harm in hoping for the best, and if not all the ideas set forth in this section can be adopted, perhaps some of them may be employed as the teacher gradually improves the working conditions in his school.

An art room should be placed on the main floor of a school building near a service entrance, for convenience in delivering supplies and equipment. The room should face north so that the natural light will be as constant as possible. It is preferable also to have the room situated reasonably close to home economics rooms and industrial arts shops in order that pupils may conveniently transfer from one room to another when the use of special equipment is required. It is further recommended that the art room be not too far distant from the auditorium, since puppetry and stagecraft sometimes demand ready access to the stage.

The room should be large, with about 30 feet by 60 feet as a minimum floor space. The floor should be laid in heavy linoleum or rubber tile. Mastic tile may also be used, but this is rather more tiring to walk on than are other types of tile.

Lighting in an art room is of the greatest importance. Artificial lighting should have an all-over intensity of 80 to 100 foot-candles and should be so arranged as to cast no pronounced shadows. Preferably lights should be set flush with the ceiling with the exception of spotlights to be beamed on important displays. Unless the teacher has a daylight screen, blackout curtains for the windows should be provided for the showing of films and filmstrips.

---

[4] Elaborate plans may be found in the Virginia *Art and Youth* and the Pennsylvania *Course of Study in Art Education.*

37 *Comprehensive plan for all-purpose art room (sketch based on design produced by the Department of Public Instruction, Commonwealth of Pennsylvania).*

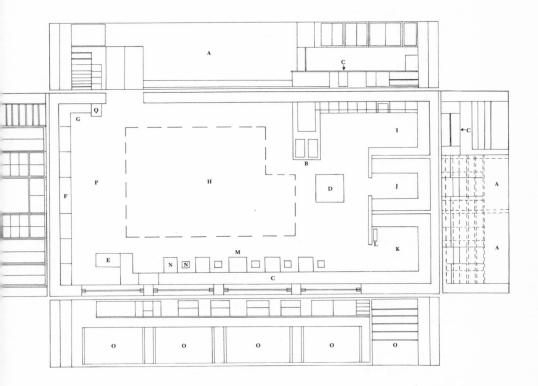

A —Tackboard	**J** —Storage area: expendable art material
B —Sinks	**K** —Storage area: work in progress
C —Work counters	**L** —Step ladder
D —Heavy work bench	**M** —Area for 3-dimensional work
E —Teacher's desk	**N** —Solid desks for 3-dimensional work
F —Cabinets and display cases	and individual stool for each desk
G —Library corner	**O** —Windows
H —Central space for tables and seats	**P** —Area for easels, posing models, etc.
I —Clay working area	**Q** —Filing cabinet

In all matters pertaining to both natural and artificial lighting, one should consult architects and lighting engineers. Many excellent materials and arrangements are available, including directional glass bricks, opaque louvers, clerestory lighting, and various types of blinds.

We may now consider the use of space around the walls. Along one of the shorter walls, storage rooms jutting into the room might be planned. Two storage rooms are desirable, one housing a stock of expendable art materials and the other, the unfinished pieces of pupils' work. Each storage room should be fitted with as many adjustable shelves as convenient. Since the shelves may be built up the walls to a considerable height, it would be well to have at least one light stepladder available which might be stored in either one of the rooms. The "outside" walls of these rooms, facing the main classroom, can be faced with tackboard.

The sinks can be located opposite the windows on the long side of the room as illustrated in Fig. 37. Their position should be reasonably central, and they should be accessible from at least three directions. They can be placed in a separate piece of furniture so that the pupils can approach them from all directions, or they may be placed at the end of a counter running at right angles from the wall towards the center of the room. However arranged, the sinks should be large, deep, and acid-resistant, and each should be equipped with hot and cold water taps. Clean-out traps should be fitted, and all plumbing leading from them should also be acid-resistant.

Along the entire wall at the end of the room opposite the storage rooms, storage cupboards might alternate with glass-enclosed display cases. These cases should be provided with adjustable glass shelves and illuminated with hidden or indirect lights.

Beneath the windows, a work counter might run almost the full length of the room. Below the counter, storage cupboards could be constructed, or the space be left open to house tools. Jutting out at right angles might be a series of small counters for delicate work. Each small counter, which might be collapsible, should be provided with a stool of convenient height. At the extreme end of this wall, an area might be set aside for the teacher's desk and files. This area would be quieter and more dust-free if it were enclosed in glass.

The remaining wall area, which is opposite the windows, should for the most part be faced with tackboard running from about 30 inches above the floor to the ceiling. An area of about 20 square feet, however, should be reserved for a blackboard. Whatever space is left might be fitted with counters and cupboards.

Once the preliminary plans for the walls are complete, attention may be given to the matter of electrical outlets. This is a problem for an expert who understands electrical loads, but the teacher must be sure that outlets are placed in correct positions. As well as providing for kilns, pottery wheels, and service outlets in general, there should be an outlet for an electric clock. A clock is an important piece of equipment in an art room; it should be located so that the pupils are always aware of how much time is available to begin certain phases of their work, or to start cleaning up towards the end of the art period.

Certain items of special equipment should be provided and placed conveniently in relation to the arrangements around the walls. These might include an electric kiln with a firing area of not less than 3000 cubic inches, a storage bin of the pull-out type for clay, a storage box for keeping clay damp, and a spray booth. The clay-working area should be located near a sink. A corner of the room should also be set aside for the display of art books and periodicals. A filing cabinet is another important piece of equipment.

Furniture for the art room must be chosen with care. Suitable art desks come in a variety of designs and may be studied in catalogues. A type of desk with low shelves on which the pupils may place school books is worthy of consideration. Desks with movable tops, by which the slope of the working surface may be regulated, have not proved to be particularly serviceable because they tend to get out of order. For seating, either chairs, stools, or benches have proved practical. As well as desks for drawing and painting, the room should be provided with one or two carpenter's benches. These should be supplied with vises and have storage space beneath them for tools and other equipment.

The colors used to decorate the art room must be carefully planned. Bright colors are generally to be avoided since they rebound and confuse a painter. Neutral colors—pale grays or umbers—are to be recommended for the walls and ceiling. The ceiling should be lighter in tone than the walls. The floor should also be neutral, although mottled. Chalkboards need not be black but may be bought in pale greens or ivory. Natural or limed wood finishes on cupboards and doors are attractive and serviceable. In general, color in an art room must not interfere with the color work in progress, and it must serve as a background for the displays of children's work.

Before an elaborate art room of the type described can be planned successfully, much study must be given to the problem and many experts consulted. Not only should plans of the room be drawn, but a model should also be made. Particular attention should be given to the grouping of furniture and equipment so that overcrowding in any one part of the room is avoided, while everything necessary for any one type of work is conveniently located in one area. Obviously, an art room entails costly construction, and whatever arrangements are made, good or bad, are likely to be in use for a long time.

1.   Everyone who teaches art efficiently develops a number of good ideas for the distribution and collection of supplies. Start a notebook and in it make brief notes of any ideas you observe being put to use by art teachers.

2.   Visit a number of art rooms used by children in various grades. Make notes on the manner in which "traffic" is regulated when supplies are being distributed and again when they are being returned.

3.   Discuss with a group of children what might be the best ways of (a) preparing supplies; (b) distributing supplies; (c) keeping supplies in good order while work is in progress; (d) returning supplies; (e) cleaning up room after work.

4.   Discuss with children some of the best ways of keeping tools in good condition.

5.   Organize teams of children to look after tools, supplies, and the classroom in general. Have the children appraise the results of their work.

6.   Make a cardboard or wooden model, to scale, of the art room in which you would like to work. Use 25 or 30 symbols (such as red squares of wood or buttons, to represent the pupils) and push them around your model to indicate the positions of the pupils during any given time in an art session. Make a note of "traffic jams" and rearrange the system to eliminate congestion of pupils.

The Development

of Children's Art

Expression in art relies upon both the unique personal qualities of its creator and the experiences he has had in life. Since children neither possess identical personalities nor react in wholly similar fashion to experience, their output in art must of necessity vary. Nevertheless, at certain periods of their general development, children tend to pass through several stages of artistic production and consequently to adopt recognizable modes of artistic expression.[1] It is highly desirable that a teacher be familiar with the developmental stages of artistic production and with the accompanying modes of expression. Often the stage of expression which a child has reached will give clues not only to the type of subject matter which may interest him, but also to the tools, materials, and activities with which he may cope successfully. Knowing his stage of expression, furthermore, will help the teacher to determine what kind of stimulation, assistance, and general educational treatment he requires. This chapter will concentrate upon a description of the stages and modes of children's artistic expression.

While discussing primarily the stages and attendant modes, or "form concepts," of expression, including the peculiarities of design, found in chil-

---

[1] The terms "mode," "schema," "scheme," "form concept," and "formula" have all been used synonymously by various writers. The words denote the all-over means by which a child tries to make clear to us his artistic intention.

dren's art work, the chapter will also comment upon some ways in which well-known writers have categorized the artistic output of children.

In describing children's artistic development, it is difficult to indicate definitely at which grade level or age each stage occurs. Lowenfeld attempts to state specific ages at which developmental stages may be found, but he warns that "it is self-evident that human development differs and that teachers must flexibly deal with such average expectancies." [2] Some writers, probably in attempting to steer away from too rigid a classification of developmental stages, present so general a list of "expectancies" that their statements tend to become meaningless.[3] In this chapter, every attempt will be made to be as definite as possible in describing the developmental stages and modes of expression. The reader should understand, nevertheless, that human behavior, perhaps especially in art, is more often unique than it is uniform.

Developmental Stages and Modes of Expression in Children's Art

Scholarly interest in the art of children has been manifest for a surprisingly long period. Read indicates that it probably began with John Ruskin in his book *The Elements of Drawing,* which appeared in 1857.[4] In the years 1885 and 1886, Read continues, were published the "first documents in a long and increasingly complicated process of research." These were articles written by an English school teacher, Ebenezer Cooke, for the *Journal of Education* (London).[5]

Read then lists at least a dozen writers, from James Sully in the 1890's, who defined some of the stages of development in terms similar to those we

---

[2] Viktor Lowenfeld, *Creative and Mental Growth* (N.Y.: Macmillan, 1952), p. 42.

[3] Erdt, for example, when listing the "expected outcomes" in various grades, sometimes appears to overgeneralize. To state that in the first and second grades the child "becomes aware of his environment" and "finds an acceptable outlet for nervous tension," or in the third and fourth grades, "gains skill in using plastic and three-dimensional material," and "is able to use repetition and a rhythmic line"; or in the fifth and sixth grades, "develops greater manual dexterity" in craft work, is true enough, but the statements could refer, of course, to almost any grade level. See Margaret Hamilton Erdt, *Teaching Art in the Elementary School* (N.Y.: Rinehart, 1954), in particular Chapter 9. The quotations are from pp. 218–20.

[4] Herbert Read, *Education Through Art* (N.Y.: Pantheon, 1945) p. 115.

[5] Read says, "These articles . . . are . . . remarkable as an anticipation of subsequent theories." *Ibid.*, p. 116; extracts of the articles may be found in an appendix on pp. 167–68.

use today,[6] to Helga Eng,[7] who in the 1930's made a searching analysis of the modes of expression, or *schemata*,[8] to be found in children's drawings.

Scientific interest in the nature of children's artistic production and a desire to classify it has apparently grown with the years. Today numerous classifications are to be found, but basically they all agree upon the existence of at least three main stages which occur before adolescence.

First appears the stage in which the child manipulates materials, at first in an apparently exploratory and random fashion. Later in this stage the manipulation becomes increasingly organized until the child gives a title to the marks he makes. During the next stage the child develops a series of distinct marks or symbols which stand for objects in his experience. These symbols are eventually related to an environment. Finally comes a preadolescent stage at which the child begins to become critical of his work and expresses himself in a more self-conscious manner. The fact that these stages appear in the work of most children in no way detracts from the unique qualities of each child's work. Indeed, within the framework of the recognized artistic stages and modes of expression, the individuality of children shines more clearly.

The Stage of Manipulation
(Up to Kindergarten and First Grade)

The first stage of artistic production—that of manipulation—may begin earlier in life than many people realize. When a child is little more than a year old he may reach for something which will make a mark such as a pencil or a crayon, grasp it in his fist, and make a few hesitant scratches. This is the beginning of the manipulative stage and, indeed, is the start of all artistic expression. The infant Michelangelo probably began in just this way the career which included the painting of the Sistine Chapel.

The period for producing scratches lasts several days, weeks, or months, depending upon the child's muscular development, intelligence, general health, and the time devoted to practice. As time goes on, the scratches are increasingly controlled; they become more purposeful and rhythmic, as may

---

[6] James Sully, *Studies of Childhood*, (New York: Appleton, 1896).

[7] Helga Eng, *The Psychology of Children's Drawing*, trans. by H. Stafford Hatfield (N.Y.: Harcourt, Brace, 1931).

[8] According to Read, the word "schema" (pl. "schemata") was first used by Sully and later given great significance by the German psychologists (*Education Through Art*, p. 120). It is interesting to note the contemporary revival of the word, largely as a result of Lowenfeld's writings. See, for example, the latter's frequent use of the word in *Creative and Mental Growth*.

38 *First scribbles. The scribbles of this 15-month-old girl quickly became organized into large circular forms. Heavy, soft pencil is the medium.*

be seen in Fig. 38. Eventually many children tend to resolve their marks into large circular patterns, and they learn to vary their lines, to make them sweeping, rippling, delicate, bold, and so on.

When the child is given paint, in kindergarten if not before, further changes are to be seen in his output. Usually, he begins by handling the brush as he does the crayon; that is to say, he produces lines rather than areas of color. Later, particularly if he is given a broad flat brush, he is likely to paint masses of color, and sometimes he may outline these masses with lines of a contrasting color. Many children become fascinated with the various effects to be achieved with a brush, and attempt stippling, "dry-brush" painting, and sometimes even a controlled splashing of paint as a result of shaking the brush. Someone has said that children at this stage should be permitted to paint only in a bathtub.

If the child from about two to kindergarten age is given three-dimensional materials he goes through a similar process of manipulation. Clay may at first be squeezed through the fingers in a relatively uncontrolled fashion. Later the clay may be rolled into thin lengths or pummeled and otherwise shaped into balls. In box sculpture, the units may be stacked, knocked down, and restacked into arrangements which display little order. In time, however, the child may develop a system of stacking so that the larger boxes are used as a base for the smaller ones. When scraps of wood are used for sculpture, the same process is often observed.[9]

After perhaps five or six weeks of work with several art media, most children gain sufficient skill to repeat shapes, either in line or in mass, with paint, clay, boxes, or scraps of materials. The painting may, for example, take the shape of an oblong which reminds one of a window, or boxes may be crudely arranged to resemble, say, a bridge. Clay may be rolled to appear snakelike.

Up to this point the child has neither established a theme of expression nor given a title to his work. There comes a day, however, when the pupil lifts his eyes from his work and says: "It's me," or "It's a window," or even "That's Daddy driving his car." The manipulative process has at last reached the place where the product may be given a title. This development very often occurs within the first month of the child's school life.

The nature of the thinking which goes on during the naming of the manipulated material we do not exactly know. It usually appears, however, that the child does not begin work with a theme in mind but, rather, that the naming occurs after the material has taken shape. The child rolls clay, for example, mainly for the pleasure of rolling it. When the clay reminds him of some object, the appropriate title, which is always related to an experience, is attached to it.

Sometimes a title appears to arise from manipulative work because of kinesthetic or muscular associations. In such cases a child may pick up a brush loaded with paint, proceed to make rhythmic marks, say "choo, choo, choo," and subsequently inform his teacher that the paint marks represent a "ride in a train." Here, the movement of the arm has reminded him of motion in the train. Unless he is present when the painting is being produced, the teacher will no doubt experience difficulty in seeing the connection between the title and the marks set down.

As we have seen, the manipulative period in artistic expression includes three overlapping but recognizable phases: (1) random manipulation, (2) controlled manipulation, and (3) named manipulation. Although it is impossible to assign any stage of expression to any age group, or to predict how long each learner will take to pass from one stage to the next, certain generalities can be made about rates of development. Much depends upon the child's preschool or nursery school experience with art media and upon his muscular development. If the child is provided with materials and encouragement, he may begin random manipulation during his second year and

---

[9] All these media, together with large crayons and large soft pencils, are most suitable at this stage. Chapters 7 to 10 will comment in detail on the subject of suitable media at different stages.

reach the stage of relating symbols to an environment before he enters kindergarten. Another child, who has been given no practice in using art media, may be capable only of random manipulation when he enters kindergarten. A child with poor muscular coordination may spend a year or more learning to control his manipulation of art media, whereas another better developed child may pass through the whole manipulative stage and enter the symbol-making stage within a few weeks of beginning kindergarten or first grade.

Thus the teacher of the early elementary grades must be prepared to find pupils at many stages of development and must be equally prepared to have his pupils progress at different rates. In the case of most normal children, however, the teacher might expect satisfactory progress through the three phases of the manipulative period to take about six weeks to two months. At the end of this period most children will be entering, or ready to enter, the symbol stage.

Actually, no one leaves the manipulative stage entirely. Confronted with an unfamiliar substance or a new tool, we are likely to perform some manipulation before we begin to work in earnest. After buying a new pen, for example, we will probably scribble a few marks with it before settling down to write a letter. The artist who purchases a new kind of paint will in all likelihood experiment with it before he paints seriously.

The teacher should realize that manipulation is not a waste of educational time and materials but, rather, a highly educative process. By means of manipulation the child gains skill in the use of tools and materials, so that he may be ready for further developments in artistic expression.

The Stage of Symbols
(Approximately First to Third Grades)

THE EMERGENCE AND DEVELOPMENT OF SYMBOLS: The control of tools and materials which the child gains through manipulation allows him to enter the symbol phase of expression. To produce symbols, the child must be able to give his marks or shapes desired characteristics and must be able to reproduce these forms at will. Compared with manipulation, the production of symbols demands a relatively high degree of precision, because a symbol, unlike most of the results of manipulation, is a precise statement of a fact or event in experience.

Before a symbol proper appears in a child's work, he has usually produced many consistently similar marks or shapes. Circular shapes may have appeared in paint or clay, for example, or an elongated, enclosed form may have been invented and repeated in paper sculpture. Some children may produce dozens or hundreds of marks or shapes having a family resemblance. Eventually, as was noted above, the child relates the result of this

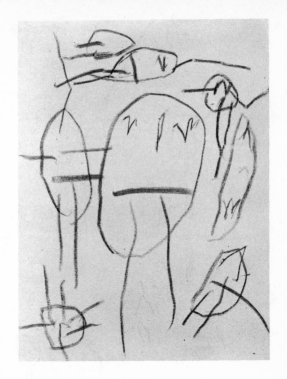

39 *The little girl (three years and nine months old) who drew these symbols gave each the name of a friend. The drawing is done in wax crayon.*

manipulation to a specific object. Pointing to a circular mark in paint, he may say: "That is a man." A symbol has then been established. We have no precise knowledge as to how he arrives at this pictorial-verbal statement. We have suggested that the shapes he has been producing in his controlled manipulations remind him of objects in his environment. On the other hand, the dawning realization that marks or shapes can convey meaning, together with a newly acquired skill to produce them at will, may prompt him to plan symbols. Perhaps the symbol appears as a result of both mental processes, varying in degree according to the personality of its author. Whatever the process may be, one important fact is incontrovertible: the ability to produce symbols constitutes an enormous advance in the child's educational career. The kindergarten child has now developed a new means of expression and communication with his associates which is definitive, personal, flexible, and artistically effective.

The first symbols to appear in a child's output vary from one child to another. The objects in the pupil's experience that have most forcibly impressed him appear to determine the subject matter of his symbols. Among the objects represented may be flowers, animals, furniture, or people, but the symbol which appears most frequently depicts "man."

Once a child has arrived at a symbol, he works hard with it, producing

40a, b, and c

Diagrams showing some symbols which represent man, tree, and house. All diagrams, from simple to complex, are copied from the work of kindergarten children.

many others in the same category. To a casual observer, each symbol may appear to be a mere repetition of its predecessor. Such, however, is not usually the case. As the child works, he apparently thinks about the objects he is delineating, so that the symbol becomes increasingly recognizable in form (see Figs. 40a, b, and c). For example, the first symbols for a human being are crude. To an elliptical or circular shape may be attached one or two appendages denoting legs. Later, marks may be included to indicate arms, while circular shapes may be added to stand for buttons or eyes. Still later perhaps, marks are added for hair or some other feature common to human beings. Little by little, with each addition giving clarity to the statement, the symbol takes form. After much thought and labor, the symbol becomes unmistakably human and cannot be confused with symbols for other objects.

Differentiation of the symbol progresses further. Once the symbol for, say, *man* is firmly established, the categories within the human race begin to appear. The marks or forms for hair may be lengthened, and thus *woman* is depicted. Emphasis may be placed upon items of clothing to portray particular people. In time, the child can produce to his satisfaction, not only a human symbol but one to depict any particular person he has in mind.

Children do not usually concentrate upon the full development of any one category of symbol. Many diverse objects receive their attention simultaneously and are developed in symbolic form at a rate which is governed by their knowledge of and interest in the objects depicted, together with their skill in portraying these objects. Usually before the child has finished kindergarten, and generally before he is seven years old, two or more symbols delineating different categories of objects will appear in his output. This development may sometimes be found almost simultaneously with the appearance of the first symbols, although it may occur some days, or even weeks, later. When the development occurs, however, the child has made an advance into a second phase of symbolic expression.

RELATING SYMBOLS TO AN ENVIRONMENT: Whenever a pupil produces in the same composition two or more symbols related in thought, he has demonstrated an advance in visual communication. When the diverse marks or three-dimensional forms he has evolved no longer exist as objects apart from an environment but instead become related to some other items of expression, he has realized that a relationship of objects and events exists in the world. Once this realization occurs, he is in a position to make further rapid progress in visual communication. The problems which now confront him revolve around a search for a personal means of expression in which are depicted satisfactory relationships between symbols and their environment. In striving for such a means of expression, he is engaged in the main task of all artists.

By a natural and inevitable development, the child has arrived at the traditional core of artistic endeavor. Normally he does so by the time he is about seven years old.

It should be noted at this point that the development described so far can occur only if educational conditions are right. Unfortunately, during these delicate developmental stages, more havoc may be perpetrated by adults than during any other stages in the child's artistic life. The child's work up to now exhibits to the eye of the uninitiated an untidiness, a disorder, and, often, an unintelligible appearance. Hence certain "devices" are sometimes used to make children's work neater or clearer. These devices include the coloring of outlines of objects drawn by adults, the copying and tracing the work of others, the forming of shapes of men, birds, and the like from circles, squares, and triangles supplied in kits. All these activities, often designed by well-meaning people, have been proved beyond doubt to interfere with the developmental processes mentioned earlier.[10] In performing them, the child begins to rely upon them and ceases to exert himself in a search for adequate modes of personal expression.

Let us return, however, to the normal pattern of development as a result of creative effort. The child may begin relating a symbol to its environment by simple means. He may depict with paint, clay, or some other suitable medium two similar symbols for human beings to which he gives the title "Me and My Mother." Soon he begins to put together symbols for diverse objects which have a relationship in his thought (see Fig. 41). Thus, his work may be given such titles as the following:

> Me and my brother
> Our house has windows
> My dog is in the sun
> I am riding on my wagon
> Daddy's car bringing me to school
> The postman bringing me a valentine

If children have been greatly interested in some vicarious form of experience, they will sometimes include this in their pictures. Expression based upon stories told or read to them or events they have seen on the television or the cinema screen may appear in their output, with such titles as:

> These are the bears and this is Goldilocks
> Here is a wolf going to blow a house down
> This is a little mouse who lives in a house
> The Indians are running

---

[10] For further discussion, see, for example, C. D. and M. R. Gaitskell, *Art Education in the Kindergarten* (Peoria, Ill.: Bennett, 1952), pp. 13–14.

41 *"Our Family"—a painting in tempera by a six-year-old boy. Notice how important Father is, as indicated by his size. Duchess the dog is included, as is Baby David who is in the basket on the left. Note also the sky line.*

It is interesting to note that even in these early years some difference in preference for subject matter, dependent, of course, upon experience but associated with the child's sex, is to be found. Boys, for example, produce three times as many symbols for mechanical objects as do girls. Boys also depict animals more often, while girls use a larger number of symbols of human beings.

Although children may first depict nothing but the objects they mention in the titles of their output, they soon begin to provide a setting or background. There are some indications that certain children in an early symbolic stage consider the paper on which a drawing or painting is being made as an environment for the symbols being delineated. To emphasize this idea and thus define the limits of the environment, children have been observed to paint a border around the edges of the paper on which a symbol is placed and to give the resulting work a title such as "I am in a room" or "I am in a garden." Quite frequently the child uses this convention before he produces the more generally recognized symbol called a "base line" (see

42 *"My tooth is frozen. He put a needle in my gum." A girl,*
five and one half years old, uses a diversity of symbols
in a tempera painting. Note the balance of the work.

Fig. 42).[11] Sooner or later, however, most children use the base line as an
indication of a floor or ground upon which another symbol may stand. The
base line may be placed remote from a symbol, or it may touch the symbol.
It may take the form of a line drawn from edge to edge of the paper, or it
may be painted in a mass. Sometimes children paint several base lines when
they wish to depict two sides of a street or different events in a story which
are closely connected in thought but remote in space. The child may extend
the meaning of the base line by using it to depict such items as steps, hills,
sidewalks, or railway tracks (see Plate IIa).

Another symbol arising from the environment is that of the sky line.
Sky is usually indicated at first by a line drawn across the upper portion of
a working surface, as may be observed in Fig. 41. Often accompanying this
symbol is that of a sun which is depicted as a circular shape with radiating
lines. Starlike shapes are sometimes added as a further indication of sky.
These symbols often persist for many years, and the sky does not appear as

[11] Lowenfeld, in *Creative and Mental Growth,* has made some penetrating observations
of this and other schematic representations. See in particular his Chapter 4, "The
Achievement of a Form Concept."

a solid mass of color touching the earth until the pupil has developed greater maturity of expression, probably some time between his eighth and tenth year.

As the child's use of symbols broadens and his expression consequently grows in complexity, he is confronted with an increasingly difficult task of finding adequate modes of expression to make his meanings clear. His usual strong desire to express himself with clarity leads him to adopt many curious artistic conventions. The ingenuity exhibited by the child in overcoming a lack of knowledge of technical devices, such as linear perspective, and in substituting acceptable and expressive devices of his own is nearly always interesting and, indeed, is sometimes little short of miraculous.

Let us consider some of the means which a child may adopt to make his artistic expression clear. One of the most obvious devices is to vary the relative sizes of the symbols used in his work. A symbol having emotional or intellectual importance to the pupil may be made larger than others related to it. "Mother," for example, may be depicted as being larger than a house,

43 *"I am skipping." Approaching the age of seven, the girl painter has added many details to her symbols. Notice that she makes herself much larger than her playmates.*

or, perhaps more frequently, the child, who is generally egocentric at this stage, will delineate himself as towering over his associates. The child will employ this device in connection with all the familiar art materials, but it is especially noticeable in his painting, as illustrated in Fig. 43. When he uses paint, he not only gives a greater size to the object which appeals most to him but also may paint it in a favorite color. Thus we may say that color is often chosen for its emotional appeal, rather than for its resemblance to a natural object. Soon, of course, the child's observation of the world affects his choice of color—sky becomes blue and grass green. When this happens, often when the child is seven years of age, his paintings tend to lose some of their naïveté.

Even though the young child lacks a technical ability to express himself through visual forms, he is extraordinarily inventive in devising relatively complicated modes of composition in which to present his emotional and intellectual reactions to life. The young painter, for example, has no hesitation in combining interiors and exteriors of buildings in order to tell a complete story. Frequently he weaves into one composition events which occur at various times. In a sense, he may treat a painting subject in a manner similar to that of a written composition. As an example, in a painting entitled "Shopping with Mother," he may show himself and his mother driving to a shopping center, making various purchases, and finally unpacking the parcels at home. Here we have, as it were, a story in three paragraphs with all of the items placed upon the one painting surface. Some of these compositions may be arranged aesthetically, while in others the items may tend to be pictorially unrelated. If not always related aesthetically, however, the items are at least related in thought.

Another interesting device adopted by many children passing through the "symbol-and-environment" phase of visual expression frequently arises from their inability to use linear perspective (see Plate IIa). In a picture of a hockey game or of people seated around a table, for example, some of the participants may appear to be lying flat or to be standing on their heads. The many children who produce compositions of this type usually do so by moving their picture in a circular fashion as they delineate objects related to the theme. Thus, a child may draw a table and place Mother or Father at the head of it. Then, by turning the paper slightly, the child may place Brother in the now upright position. This process continues until all are shown seated at the table. As an alternative to moving the drawing or painting surface, the child may walk around his work, drawing as he goes.

The preceding examples illustrate not only that the child is highly inventive when he is moved to express himself artistically, but also that he tends to use reason in solving his problems. A careful study of the composi-

44 *This painting, the altarpiece* Maestà *by Duccio (1255–1319), illustrates an enlargement of the important figures. Compare the use of this convention with that found in Figure 43.*

tions of children at this developmental stage usually reveals a logic as well as an aesthetic quality.

To the uninitiated, children's art may appear unrelated to traditional artistic expression. A careful study of their work, however, reveals the interesting fact that many of the devices employed by the very young resemble expressive modes to be found in some highly esteemed professional output. The child's treatment of sky areas, for example, has its counterpart in some Oriental paintings. The flat painting of children finds its sophisticated echo in Braque, who believes that the flatness of a painting surface should be retained. The enlargement of important figures in painting and sculpture, while resulting in part from an edict of the Church during the early Renaissance, has been used expressively by many great artists, for example by Duccio in his majestic alterpiece designed for the cathedral of Siena (see Fig. 44). Again, the "X-ray" type of picture so common in the work of young children is to be found over and over again in professional work, not only in painting but also in the theater. As a means of depicting movement, space, and time, the Futurists, whose work can be illustrated by Duchamp's well-known *Nude Descending the Staircase*, produced a type of art form reminiscent of the space-time compositions developed intuitively by children.

45 *"Our Class in the Gym." Tempera painting by an eight-and-one-half-year-old girl. Notice the rhythmic delineation, the complete background, and the careful detail.*

The Preadolescent Stage
(Approximately Third to Sixth Grades)

Since all artistic expression is a reflection of the personality, one may expect to discover further developments as the pupils grow out of early childhood in about their eighth to ninth years and into the stage of life recognized by the broad term "preadolescence," or later childhood, at about their eleventh to thirteenth years.

The approach of the older child to expression in art is different from that of the young child. While the older child is still naturally inquisitive and creative, he has learned to be more cautious in what he does. The little child goes about his work in art with a fine, free abandon; he "tries anything once," often regardless of consequences. To him practically every experience in art is a new one, and he revels in the excitement of working on unfamiliar ground. The older child, on the other hand, has lived long enough to learn that one is, to some extent at least, held responsible for one's actions, and whatever one does will probably affect other people. The older child, in other words, is beginning to learn what we all must realize as we pass through life; namely, that we live in an organized society which has little room for completely egocentric behavior. The older child's approach to his art activities, then, is relatively more cautious and studied. His work, moreover, tends to be more complete in statement. Central objects are depicted with increasing reality so that details of feature and clothing appear. Backgrounds are given greater attention, sometimes to such an extent that they become confused with the main objects in the composition. Light and shade and textural effects are employed, not so much for aesthetic ends as to give the work greater authenticity or "reality." In the same way, color, while becoming more refined through the use of tints and shades, tends to approximate the hues actually to be found in the objects depicted. Instead of presenting a flat appearance, the output of older children often is given depth. This effect is achieved by means of an overlapping of objects, of toned color, and of linear perspective, all of which devices are taught to the children as their need and readiness become apparent.

Later childhood is a period in which youth often bands together into groups composed of individuals of the same sex. In our culture, this is the only period in life when the sexes willingly and consciously draw apart, and the division immediately precedes the marked commingling of the sexes during adolescence. Expression in art is affected by activities and interests arising from the group and peculiar to the sex of the child. Boys may emphasize the activities of athletic teams, while girls may place more emphasis upon social events. Both boys and girls, however, are often attracted to adventurous situations. The following are representative titles of work produced by this developmental group (see Plate V):

> Camping out
> My first party dress
> The "Tigers" beating the "Hawks"
> Our school concert
> Going to the art gallery
> Climbing the mountain
> The fight for the middleweight crown

As with former age groups, vicarious experience, particularly that of an adventurous nature, affects the older child. Thus, titles such as the following may appear:

> Conquering Mount Everest
> At the North Pole
> Mardi Gras
> Lost in Death Valley
> Take-off for the moon

Hero-worship derived from song and story not infrequently may stimulate expression. Real or fictitious characters including presidents, space cadets, pugilists, explorers, warriors, actresses, and so on may receive attention. No one can deny the catholic taste of the preadolescent.

As adolescence draws closer, a few pupils exhibit some further developments. Sometimes an interest may be shown in design for its own sake. In such cases, the pupil may welcome activities which allow his insight to grow in this direction. Portraiture and life drawing may also have appeal. In some drawings produced by pupils at this stage, one may find that considerable attention has been given to anatomical detail. This overabundance of detail, or the attempt to delineate objects with photographic realism, tends to affect adversely the aesthetic values of the work.

The advanced preadolescent has many distinct problems which demand sympathetic and skillful teaching practices from the art teacher.[12] Few pupils, however, reach this stage within the first six grades of the elementary school.

Developments in Children's Design

As with professional art, the design output of children is inseparably linked with their general expressiveness. Thus the physical, mental, emotional, and social development of the learner, which of course influences the subject matter of his expression, governs also the design he produces. Although reference has occasionally been made previously to the designs found in children's work, such reference has been largely incidental. The rest of this section will describe a relatively consistent development which occurs in children's work.

We noted earlier that what amounts to designing comes naturally to little children, and at a surprisingly early age. We observed that some children will grasp a crayon and make marks with it before they are fifteen months old. These marks are at first scratchy and uncertain, but it is not long before lines become pleasingly rhythmic. Why the child has this ability we can only surmise. Perhaps the pleasing quality of the lines may be ascribed to the fact that the little child normally possesses a naturally beautiful and efficient body, the movements of which, when recorded in crayon, cannot fail to have aesthetic merit. The fact is that the bodily movements of all young creatures are mass movements, and these result in broad rhyth-

---

[12] The characteristics of preadolescence and early adolescence have been described in some detail in C. D. and M. R. Gaitskell, *Art Education During Adolescence* (N.Y.: Harcourt, Brace, 1954).

mic action.[13] When a very young child paints, he does so from his finger tips to the end of his toes. Not until he grows older and gains control of the smaller muscles do his muscular actions in art become localized to the arm and hand.

Even up to the age of nine or ten, children design almost entirely intuitively. As far as one may observe, little conscious thought is given to aesthetic structure until the child enters preadolescence. The work, nevertheless, is often pleasant to look at and presents a naïve, uninhibited appearance of great charm.

As well as exhibiting an ability to design in two dimensions, children often learn to produce three-dimensional designs before they come to school. By the time some children have reached the age of three, they have experimented with sand, and—sometimes to their parents' horror—mud. Some have joined together scraps of wood and cardboard boxes or used building blocks in such a way as to bring about the semblance of an organized three-dimensional form.

Upon entering kindergarten at the age of four or five, those children who have had practice at home with art materials and who have produced pleasing designs tend to lose the ability to design in a natural and charming manner. Sometimes their work becomes deficient in visual unity because of a lack of balance and rhythm. Often children at this level show little feeling for space as an element of composition. Variety in the use of the elements and particularly in line may eventually reach a condition of confusion.

The causes of these conditions are not hard to find. In the first place, the children are passing through a period of adjustment in a strange social setting. Many of the children are for the first time remote from the protection of their mothers and their homes. Unfamiliar faces and situations surround them, and a new and powerful adult in the form of a teacher must sometimes be placated. The confused condition of their art is simply a reflection of a slightly upset little personality. A second reason for the deterioration of their design at this period is the fact that many are passing through a new phase of artistic development. From the scribble or manipulative stage they are progressing into that of symbols. As mentioned earlier, in this latter stage marks can no longer be placed at random upon a sheet of paper but rather must be set down with greatly increased precision. In their attempt to achieve greater command of symbols, the children tend to lose control of design. Not until the young learners feel more at home in their new environment and gain mastery over their new expressive forms does the quality of their design improve.

---

[13] See the interesting study by G. E. Coghill, *Anatomy and the Problem of Behavior* (Cambridge, Eng.: The University Press, 1929).

ꓘ A two-year study of the designs produced by kindergarten children, who had been enrolled in class long enough to have become accustomed to their new environment, revealed some interesting facts about their artistic production.[14] Through experience in handling media and organizing ideas and through the normal progress of orientation in the classroom, the children's designs rapidly became more coherent. The aesthetic qualities of their output developed naturally and improved rapidly.

Kindergarten children usually produce designs displaying a considerable degree of unity. The means most frequently used to achieve this is the establishment of a center, or centers, of interest. Of the pictures studied, about 57 percent had one clearly defined center of interest, about 42 percent had none, while the remainder had more than one. The majority of the children usually developed their centers of interest by making their central symbols large, or by embellishing a central figure with copious detail.

Also, in the establishment of a unity of design, the children made use of series of rhythms and of balances. Distinct rhythms appeared in 52 percent of the pictures and were produced largely by means of line or by a series

---

[14] Research sponsored by the Ontario Department of Education, 1949–1952. Some 9000 children enrolled in 425 kindergartens were studied. See C. D. and M. R. Gaitskell, *Art Education in the Kindergarten.*

46 "Me and My Friends in the Hospital." A rhythmic treatment of subject matter by a first-grade girl, age six years.

of color masses or dots of pigment. Obvious balances appeared in 66 percent of the work.

Kindergarten children seem to have greater difficulty in maintaining a variety in their designs than they have in developing a unity. The large brushes and the standard size of crayons used seemed to prevent the children studied from varying the thicknesses of line. Their method of working with full pressure of the brush, as well as their marked preference for delineation of objects in solid outline, also tended to interfere with the variety in their designs. Some variety, however, was achieved by the changing directions of the lines drawn. Even the youngest children apparently have the ability to produce lines which change from straight to curved and from rippling to flowing. Since many of the young children, however, were attempting to find security in the development of newly discovered symbols, they were more likely to resort to a repetition of elements, rather than to a variation of them. In color, nevertheless, they found scope for variety, and many used color to a degree of chaos unless the teacher restricted in some manner their choice of pigments.

Regressions in ability occur with each child, of course, from time to time and may be observed at any level of development. Absence from school, illness, or temporary emotional upsets are clearly reflected in the design output of any child in the elementary school. The quality of design deteriorates, furthermore, if the child is subjected to dictatorial teaching techniques, related not only to design itself but also, as indicated earlier, to the symbols of expression and to any other general ideas being stated. Regressions may also occur whenever the child is attempting to solve a new problem such as, for example, the delineation of an object which he has never before attempted or the most effective uses to which a new medium may be put. It is of interest to note that immature children are more subject to regression in these respects than are the more advanced pupils.

The period of most marked regression in the design ability of children between the stage in which symbols are first developed and adolescence may be found during preadolescence. This regression can occur in the third, fourth, fifth, or sixth grades but is most common in the sixth grade. At this time some children tend to become intellectually critical of their artistic efforts, and consequently their output begins to lose some of the naïve properties of a young child's production. The mental attitudes of the period are a forerunner of adolescence, when the critical abilities of young people often develop far in advance of their productive capabilities in art. Some children in the last years of their elementary education seem obsessed with the desire to draw and paint in a factual manner. They do so at the expense of the design qualities of their work. The photographic delineation of objects is often accompanied by a self-critical, self-conscious, and, hence, inhibited approach to art work which takes its toll of design. Lines, for example, which in former years were produced with a joyful rhythmic freedom, now may become broken and hesitant; color which was once gay may grow muddy; spaces may lose their interest because of backgrounds crowded with detail; and so on. The plunge into adolescence is beginning.

Perhaps the most outstanding general impression one may gain from the art production of children is the honesty and directness of their designing. These attributes are apparent in both two- and three-dimensional output. Materials are treated with respect and for logical purposes, while compositions are usually developed with economy and clarity. Unfortunately, some children are not always encouraged to design in this fashion. Some so-called art teachers, as well as certain teachers of industrial arts and home economics, have grossly interfered with the development of honest and forthright designing. Instead of helping children to think clearly about the function of objects and the proper use of materials, teachers have supplied them with vulgar and inappropriate patterns to copy. Needle cases to resemble sun bonnets, tie racks in which a clown's nose or a dog's tail is extended to hold ties, lamps made to resemble pumps, ashtray holders in the form of well-known cartoon characters are but a few of the horrors of design which have been foisted upon unsuspecting children in the name of art and crafts. No wonder that some children have grown to adulthood with warped ideas of the nature of design. The most unfortunate aspect of this type of teaching, moreover, is the fact that it is contrary to the original innate approach of children to design problems.

Under suitable educational conditions in the elementary school, however, children may make steady progress in design. Despite certain ups and downs and with a minimum of the right kind of assistance, most children may progress favorably in design from kindergarten to the end of the sixth grade.

Classifying Children According to Art Produced

Certain writers have classified children into personality types largely according to the art work they produce. Perhaps the best known of these authors are Herbert Read and Viktor Lowenfeld. In view of the wide interest their writings on these subjects have aroused and because of the influence their theories—especially those of Lowenfeld—appear to have exerted upon art education in the United States, it seems necessary to discuss them at this point.

Read finds that children's drawings can be classified into eight categories. In compiling his list of types, Read describes how he was influenced in particular by two writers, Edward Bullough and C. G. Jung.[15] Read also expresses admiration for the work of Lowenfeld.[16]

After a preliminary analysis of children's drawings, Read found that he was left tentatively with twelve categories. Bullough, however, after investigations related to the perception of single colors, had listed four "types of aesthetic appreciation," while Jung described eight "psychological types." By an extraordinary feat of intellectual gymnastics, which nevertheless does not fail to be logical, Read reduces his original twelve types to eight, so that he may both relate them readily to the categories listed by Bullough and Jung and support Lowenfeld's ideas. After this he demonstrates a parallel between their classifications and his own.[17]

Lowenfeld is concerned with a reduced number of categories. He says: "We can now clearly distinguish two types both by the end products of their artistic activities and by their attitude toward their own experiences." [18] These types he calls "visual" and "haptic." [19] The visual type, says this author, is an observer and "usually approaches things from their appearance," [20] while "the main intermediary for the haptic type of individual is the *body-self*—muscular sensations, kinesthetic experiences, touch impressions, and all experiences which place the self in value relationship to the outside world." [21] Of the people he studied, Lowenfeld says, "forty-seven percent tested were clearly visual, twenty-three percent were haptic, and thirty percent . . . were . . . not definable." [22]

Many teachers who work intimately with children may regret the apparent static quality of personality which the classifications of Read and in particular of Lowenfeld, seem to imply. Barkan points out that while Read's "interpretation is somewhat more fluid than Lowenfeld's . . . his effort to categorize individual creations according to personality types seems to con-

---

[15] Bullough published a number of articles pertaining to psychology and aesthetics in the *British Journal of Psychology* during roughly the first two decades of this century. Of Jung's books, Read finds his *Psychological Types, or the Psychology of Individuation* (N.Y.: Harcourt, Brace, 1923) of exceptional significance in relation to the art of children.

[16] See in particular Read, *Education Through Art,* pp. 132–34, where he mentions Viktor Lowenfeld's *The Nature of Creative Activity* (N.Y.: Harcourt, Brace, 1939).

[17] Read's classifications are as follows: "Organic, Empathetic, Rhythmical Pattern, Structural Form, Enumerative, Haptic, Decorative, and Imaginative." *Education Through Art,* pp. 141 ff.

[18] Lowenfeld, *Creative and Mental Growth,* p. 231.

[19] "Haptic" derives from the Greek ἅπτειν, "to touch."

[20] Lowenfeld, p. 233.   [21] *Ibid.,* p. 234.   [22] *Ibid.,* p. 232.

fuse his primary emphasis on individual uniqueness." [23] Because Lowenfeld is much more rigid in defining static typological categories of personality, Barkan finds his ideas even less acceptable than those of Read. Lowenfeld's error, intimates Barkan, lies in his apparent failure to recognize the "potency of social experience as an agent for the development of personality." [24]

Can it be that experience—especially art education—has so little effect upon the basic personality that one who works at art may not exhibit a change in type? Actually, there exists no indisputable evidence that the personality remains static, and there is much evidence to indicate that personal change can result from experience. We are aware, of course, that psychiatry can change personality by planned experience. We know also that general experience may markedly alter a person's pattern of overt behavior. A solitary and apparently introverted child, for example, by attending a well-conducted summer camp, may learn to mingle freely with his fellows and seemingly enjoy their company.

Manifestations of inner personal development seem to occur not infrequently in the output of some eminent painters. While most painters may eventually develop work of a recognized type, many of them seem to pass through various expressive phases. Picasso's *Man in a Cap* which he painted in 1895 is very different from, say, his *Night Fishing at Antibes,* painted in 1939. Are not the early drawings of Van Gogh, in which he used genre subjects, different from the paintings which appear towards the close of his career? Could one not say that a like development occurred between the early and later expressions of El Greco, in which his work changed from relatively objective statement into one of personal, flamelike ecstasy? Do we not find in the portraits of Rembrandt an ever deepening realization and expression of self? So one might continue offering examples of apparently deep personal development in artist after artist.

Partly in order to learn the apparent effects of artistic activity upon the behavior and output of children, a study was begun in 1948 with a group of 70 pupils ranging in age from nine to fifteen years.[25] These pupils showed especial interest in art and some appeared to give promise of talent. The study is being continued and classes meet regularly outside of school hours. Each year, new children are enrolled, but 30 of the children have attended classes for a period of six years.

---

[23] Manuel Barkan, *A Foundation for Art Education* (N.Y.: Ronald, 1955), p. 168.

[24] *Ibid.,* p. 169.

[25] Ryerson Institute of Technology, Toronto, in art classes for children sponsored by the Ontario Department of Education. The staff is composed of educators and artists; consultations are arranged at irregular intervals between members of the staff and other types of specialists such as psychologists.

47a Peasant Woman at Twilight *is an early Van Gogh, indicating what seems to be rather a "visual" approach to subject matter.*

47b The Street Pavers *by Van Gogh is a later painting, illustrating the inner development of the painter through which he has become more personally involved with his subject.*

48a *"My Portrait"—the work of a fairly talented boy, twelve years old. This portrait in oils is said by some to show "haptic" characteristics of the painter.*

Because Lowenfeld, unlike Read,[26] gives clear indications of the difference in the work of visual and haptic people, the study found that it was not difficult to sort output according to his categories (see Figs. 48a and b).[27] While haptic, visual, and undetermined cases did not appear, in the opinion of the Ryerson staff, in percentages similar to those discovered by Lowenfeld, a working differentiation of types was achieved. As the children worked over a period of years, each piece of their output was typed as accurately as pos-

[26] Of his eight types, Read says: "It must be emphasized . . . that none of these types . . . is found in a pure state. . . ."—*Education Through Art,* p. 148. "What the child . . . draws, might best be described as an act of poetic intuition, and a mystery beyond logical analysis," *ibid.,* p. 209.

[27] Lowenfeld makes several differentiations in *Creative and Mental Growth,* pp. 233 ff. He uses pictures to support his text. Some of the differences of his two types may be further described as follows:

a. VISUAL—feels like a spectator; sees the general shape of an object, then details; usually begins work with outline of object, then adds details; "how a thing looks" is first reaction to an encounter with any object; uses correct proportions and measurements of drawn or modeled human figure; likewise, space is represented by linear perspective (true according to camera).

b. HAPTIC—"the self is projected as the true actor of the picture"; "sizes and spaces are determined by their emotional value in size and appearance"; "human figure is likewise represented in proportion only to the significance the parts have for the artist"; "haptic space is a perspective of values."

sible according to Lowenfeld's description of visual or haptic categories. By comparing the work of each child from one year to another, certain peculiarities became manifest:

1. Nearly every child produced work in each year which sometimes appeared haptic and at other times visual in conception.
2. The longer a child worked at artistic pursuits, the greater seemed his tendency to produce pieces having the characteristics reminiscent of Lowenfeld's haptic type.

The following deductions were accordingly made. It was felt that a child may, during a given period of time, produce various pieces of work, some of which have haptic characteristics and others visual. The difference arises largely from his varying responses to unlike experiences. If he feels personally involved with a subject so that his emotions and intellect are noticeably aroused, he may sometimes give expression to his subject in a seemingly haptic manner. If the subject does not excite him, and certainly not every subject is equal in its appeal, the work may appear more visual in character. However, as many of the children gained facility with the media and tools of

48b *"My Portrait While Skating"—the work of a twelve-year-old girl showing what some might call "visual" characteristics.*

expression, as they matured through adolescence, and as they became more selective in the choice of subject, they apparently tended to feel their way into the expressive acts engaging them. Hence, controlling their materials and developing their insight, they could give greater attention to the inner nature and meaning of their subject matter. Perhaps for this reason, some of their work seemed to swing towards the type of expression associated with Lowenfeld's haptic category.

The incomplete research described above does not, of course, invalidate the opinions of the writers who have seen fit to type art production and the children responsible for it. As far as the research goes, however, it does little to support the permanence of the categories under discussion.[28]

The danger, if one exists, arising from a typology such as that of Lowenfeld or even of Read lies in its possible effects upon teaching methods. By stretching the imagination, one can see the ultimate extreme in an art lesson by a mythical teacher entirely convinced of the existence of static types of children. Here would sit one-quarter of the class—the "haptics"—blindfolded and making drawings of abstract nouns. There would sit one-half of the children—the "visuals"—drawing the chalk boxes before them. In the middle would wait the others, hoping someone will decide what they are! Since children are capable of what might be called aesthetic growth, and because this growth has a potential in many directions, to restrict a child in any manner with regard to experience or mode of expression because one believes he fits a type, would in all probability cause havoc in his educational career. In the words of Barclay-Russell (who, incidentally, believes there are fourteen varieties of expression to be found in the art of adolescents): "It is probably much more important in practice for art teachers to use such comparisons as approximate guides rather than to think of children's art in terms of psychological labels which may well be only partially understood." [29] While it may be interesting for a teacher to study the opinions of those who wish to place children and their work into categories, to base a system of pedagogy upon such opinions might not be an altogether wise course of action. A sounder and more practical viewpoint in the business of art education is to consider each child as a dynamic individual, capable of personal growth and of unique artistic output.

We have now come to the close of Part One of this book. We have seen how art education has changed through the years and how today it is com-

[28] The research, which is continuing, includes a study of the effects of stimulus, media, and teaching methods upon artistic output. Also more time and further cases are required to clarify the problem of the effects of the pupil's physiological maturity upon his work.

[29] A. Barclay-Russell, "Art and the Adolescent," in *Education and Art* (Paris: UNESCO, 1954), p. 47.

patible not only with a traditional aesthetic and a contemporary psychology, but also with the democratic ideal. We have reviewed certain teaching methods, and here again we have become aware that a practical system of art teaching must adhere to principles of democratic freedom. A study of design, of the development of a program of art, of classroom arrangement, and of the work of children illustrates that art education today in every phase is concerned with the maximum development of the individual within his social setting. Knowledge, then, about art and art education must be used with caution. Any form of teaching based upon a belief that personality is in any manner static could be nothing but inhibiting. Successful art education of young children occurs when teachers recognize and encourage diversity of expression in an atmosphere of democratic freedom. It has invariably failed as an educative force when standardization and regimentation have been allowed to influence its guiding principles.

ACTIVITIES FOR THE READER

1. Collect a series of drawings and paintings from a kindergarten and a first-grade class which illustrate the three phases of the manipulative stage.

2. Collect some drawings and paintings, the work of one child in each case, to illustrate the development of a single symbol, such as that for "man" or "toy" or "animal."

3. Collect a series of drawings and paintings from several children enrolled from the first to the third grade which illustrate developments in symbolic expression.

4. Collect drawings and paintings from pupils enrolled in the third to the sixth grades to illustrate some of the major developments in the preadolescent stage.

5. Make one collection of drawings and paintings which are representative of artistic developments from kindergarten to the end of the sixth grade.

6. Collect work in three-dimensional materials such as clay or paper from the pupils in situations identical with, and for purposes similar to, those mentioned in the five activities above.

7. Make a collection of children's work to illustrate the normal developments in design from kindergarten to the end of the sixth grade.

8. Attempt to classify a number of sixth-grade drawings and paintings according to Lowenfeld's "haptic" and "visual" types.

9. Over a period of at least one school term collect drawings and paintings of individual children who have been subjected to many art experiences. At the end of the period analyze the work of each child according to Lowenfeld's categories. What, if any, evidences do you find of both categories in the work of any one child? Explain your findings.

10. Make a note of any art teaching you may observe which is based upon a typology (or strict classification of pupils according to personality type). Comment upon the effects which this type of teaching seems to have upon: (a) the attitudes of the pupils; (b) the work produced.

part two

TEACHING ART

In this section the emphasis changes from professional preparation to classroom activity. Several of the following chapters present a detailed description of work in both two- and three-dimensional media. The sample classroom activities outlined in detail in the coming chapters, especially Chapters 7 to 10, are presented primarily to give practical applications of the theory of art education discussed in this book and consequently have been selected with special goals in mind.

It will be observed that not every art activity is given equal or similar emphasis. Weaving, for example, while an excellent activity for some people, tends to be very repetitive. It is therefore described only in connection with the special pupils whom it might benefit most. Again, only little reference is made to the firing and glazing of pottery, since these activities often depend too much upon the efforts of the teacher and not enough upon the original thought and action of young children. Then, whole lists of activities have been omitted which keep children busy but which upon analysis do not come within the definition of art. These include, for example, the use of commercial transfers to be applied to wood or some other substance; the stringing of popcorn beads; the mechanical folding and cutting of paper doilies (often called snowflakes); the scribbling of lines in which by chance one must subsequently find and develop a "fantastic" fish or bird; the use of old spools, pine cones, or some other unlikely articles to make a "giraffe" or a "funny little man"; and a host of other similar "ideas" which deny the true nature of art and may very well lead to a degradation of taste. The only activities approaching busy work are some of those mentioned for slow learners. Even these activities, however, will not degrade taste and may very easily lead certain of the mentally handicapped into more creative endeavors.

Only those activities which demand of the normal child that he master a medium largely through his own efforts, and by which, in a reasonable time, he may express his reactions to his environment, will be suggested. Each activity described will also assist the child to gain insight into the nature of artistic acts. Moreover, these activities should help the child to learn some of the responsibilities and possibilities which accompany the freedom of thought and action in artistic acts. Many of them should bring the child into closer touch with his environment, and all of them should assist in the development of good taste. While most of the sample activities in these chapters are for children working more or less by themselves, group activities are also discussed in a chapter set aside for this topic.

Before the specific activities are discussed, one might for a moment consider the general sources of subject matter suitable for all types of work. It was shown in Chapter 6 that children can select suitable subject matter for any art process of which they are capable. We saw that the most natural procedure for most children who are confronted with unfamiliar processes is to try a kind of experimental play with the new materials. No matter in what stage of development the child may be, he will adopt experimental procedures until he has gained some familiarity with the techniques under consideration. In other words, he tends to revert to a stage of manipulation. By doing so he eliminates for the time being the difficulties of developing a suitable design from observation of the objective world. Instead, he turns to what one may describe as nonobjective design in which the elements are arranged without reference to experience in life. The processes to be described lend themselves readily to nonobjective subject matter. Indeed, some of them, such as certain forms of printing, appear to be more sympathetic to nonobjective design than they are to objective design.

It would be unfortunate, however, if children were to be restricted entirely to nonobjective design in relation to any processes. In time, it is natural for them to return to the traditional source of inspiration for all artistic expression, which is experience in life. Having gained some insight into the various techniques through the nonobjective, sufficiently mature children may then give attention to the usual occupations and events of childhood in which their interests lie or have been aroused through skillful motivation.

A source of subject matter eminently suitable for most processes lies in nature. Plants, fish, animals, and other natural forms may be conveniently translated into designs for sculpture, modeling, linoleum cutting, and stencil work not to mention drawing and painting.

Nature is available as a source of inspiration for design to children living in urban as well as rural communities. The child living in a city, although lacking many of the advantages of a natural environment, may still find evidences of nature from which to create his designs. Visits to the zoo and the aquarium, for example, will provide him with animal and fish forms, while birds such as sparrows and pigeons are usually overabundant in many large cities. Again, from time to time snowflakes fall on many of our large cities, and their delicate forms may easily be seen under a magnifying glass. The florist's windows display a great variety of flowers and leaves for study. Perhaps more natural forms than one may at first imagine are available to those city dwellers who are encouraged to use their eyes.

In their general environment, children will find suitable subject matter for both pictures and motifs. For the child living in the city, there are the crowds of people, the flickering of lights, the rows of buildings with their signs and awnings and television antennae on rooftops from which he can extract those small but significant details which make up a successful design. In rural areas, there are barns, farm machinery, groups of animals, and fence posts to be composed into suitable aesthetic arrangements. The child living in a seaport or a fishing village enjoys the glorious opportunity of turning to the boats, the nets, the fish, and other forms of sea life which surround him. From the occupations of the people in his vicinity, any alert pupil may discover those "intimate corners of experience" leading to personal and suitable themes for expression.

One may assert that there is no necessity, either from a technical standpoint or because of a lack of suitable subject matter, for children in this country to employ second-hand themes for any expressive purpose. By referring to their environment, they may produce original and attractive designs in either two or three dimensions.

The disciplines peculiar to the materials, tools, and techniques of any art form will, of course, influence the appearance of the children's work. We shall see these disciplines at work in paint, paper, clay, wood, wire, and other materials. The teacher should always be aware of the important relationships existing between a technique and a design which results from it.

The design of a painting by a child of any age depends not only upon the theme selected but also upon the brushes, paint, and paper he chooses. The painting may be relatively delicate in places where small brushes have been employed; textural effects may arise from the use of powdered color, while a wide range of tone may occur as a result of mixing color. In a linoleum cut, even one dealing with a theme similar to that depicted in a painting, the presentation must be completely different. The lines made by cutting tools are much coarser than those of brushes; the textures achieved with paint cannot be produced with the printing technique, while a range of color easily applied to the painting, could never be arranged in the print. In sum, in using an unfamiliar technique, the child must face a new set of circumstances leading to a new design form.

To what extent the new technique will affect his output, the child can discover only through direct experience with the unfamiliar tools and materials. Much of what he has learned about design in past art experiences will of course be valuable to him. He must discover, nevertheless, that what he could do formerly with paint and brushes, he cannot repeat with, say, cutting knives and linoleum or stencil paper. The subtle curves of the brush must give away to the bolder lines of the knife or gouge; the former tonalities of color must be replaced by arrangements of light and shade.

It goes without saying, then, that the teacher must encourage children to work directly with the unfamiliar materials. To teach a beginner to trace a successful still-life drawing upon a piece of linoleum and subsequently to suggest that he reproduce the drawing in the linoleum cut would merely serve to confuse him and to interfere with a successful outcome in the new material. Still life or any other kind of subject matter may well be rendered in several of the art processes, but the planning and execution of the design must occur in the closest possible relation to the materials and tools in use, and design must not be copied from work which evolved originally in a different medium.

Whatever the technique, therefore, both the deepest educational insight and the most striking artistic output will be achieved by the beginner only when subject matter and technique are developed from the most direct experience possible.

The ideas just discussed dominate most of the following chapters. Part Two opens with Chapter 7 dealing with drawing and painting. Working with paper, sculpture, and printing form the topics of the next three chapters. Group activities are discussed in Chapter 11. In Chapters 12 and 13 teaching art to exceptional children is discussed, the former devoted to slow learners and the latter to children who are talented in art. Relating art to other school subjects, displaying art, developing art appreciation, and appraising children's progress in art are the themes of Chapters 14, 15, 16, and 17, respectively.

The book ends with Chapter 18, which summarizes the ways and means of developing professionally as a teacher of art.

Drawing and Painting

This chapter will describe the tools and materials related to drawing and painting, with comment on their use at various developmental levels. Reference will be made to certain problems related to the teaching of drawing and painting, among them working with color and linear perspective; developing skill in drawing; producing figure, landscape, portrait, and still-life compositions; using mixed media; and, finally, improving pictorial composition.

As was pointed out in Part One, at one time drawing and painting in school referred to a manual activity demanding great dexterity "of hand and eye" but little personal expression. Children were taught the mechanics of drawing and painting, rather than encouraged to explore their potentialities as expressive activities. This was the era of map-drawing, of drawing chalk boxes and railway tracks, and of laying down water-color washes. Today, children produce drawings and paintings for the purpose of saying something about their reactions to experience. Because drawing and painting may be used effectively in this manner by nearly every child, many art educators are inclined to believe that these activities, often called picture-making, are perhaps the most important work in the entire art program. Certainly, drawing and painting, when taught effectively, are universally enjoyed and provide an extremely flexible and practical means of expression for the young at all stages of artistic development.

Drawing and Painting During
the Various Stages of Expression

The Manipulative Stage

(The chief purpose in encouraging beginners to draw and paint is to allow them, first, to become familiar with the materials associated with the making of pictures and, second, to help them develop sufficient skill so that they can produce symbols easily when they reach the symbol stage.[1])

MEDIA AND TECHNIQUES: In selecting media for children in the manipulative stage, one must keep in mind their working methods. Since the small child works with the large muscles and usually is not concerned with detail, the materials should have a strong "covering power." Paints or crayons should be easy to handle and should deposit a rich and satisfying sweep of color when the child applies them to a surface. When the medium is selected according to such criteria, the child works quickly and spontaneously according to his natural inclinations. For beginners, soft chalk and charcoal are rather too dusty and tend to smear too easily. These media are more acceptable when the child has progressed well into the symbol stage, about grade two.

Since little children tend to use large quantities of a medium, cost becomes of some importance. Certainly, a school system cannot be expected to provide expensive materials for the very young. Fortunately, media may be obtained which possess qualities suitable for the muscular and other requirements of the children and at the same time cost much less than materials which would satisfy more experienced painters.

When young children begin to draw, they seem to find wax crayons most convenient. These are sold in boxes containing from ten to a dozen sticks of various colors and should be firm enough to resist breaking but soft enough for the color to adhere to the paper without undue pressure. The paper to be used with wax crayons should be about nine by twelve inches in size. The effort involved to lay down color on surfaces much larger than this tends to be tiring for most young children. Manila paper is inexpensive and has sufficient "tooth" for the crayon. Some newsprint is also suitable but, while having the advantage of being even less costly than manila, has rather too smooth a texture and may be too thin.

Shortly after beginning to draw with wax crayon, a child should also work with paint, which is a splendid, exciting medium attractive to all children. The most suitable paint for the beginner, an opaque medium usually called "tempera," may be purchased in several forms, the most usual being liquid or powdered. The powdered variety is relatively less expensive than

---

[1] See the film, *Beginning of Picture Making*, Creative Hands Series, see Appendix 6.

49a *Kindergarten children working with finger paint.*

the liquid but must be mixed with water before it is used.[2] (With beginning pupils, the teacher must mix all the paint.) It has one advantage over the liquid paint in that its textural qualities may be varied as desired. The liquid paint tends to go on with a more uniform smoothness, while the powdered variety may be more conveniently applied with various degrees of roughness or smoothness depending upon how much water is mixed with it. The textural advantages of the powdered paint, however, are of more importance to children who are producing symbols than to those in the manipulative stages.

Since little children work naturally in a broad and sweeping fashion, which is even more noticeable with paint than with crayon, it is necessary to provide paper for painting measuring at least twelve by eighteen inches. Both newsprint and manila paper are suitable, as are the thicker papers called "sugar," "bogus," and "kraft."[3]

Brushes for painting should be broad, with long handles. Hog bristle brushes with handles about ten inches long are recommended. The brushes may be either round or flat, although the former seem for many children to be easier to handle. If flat, the brushes should measure about one-half inch

[2] Some brands tend to turn sour in time. This souring may be largely prevented by adding a few drops of oil of cloves to the mixture.

[3] Ask your supply firm to submit samples.

across the bristles. After use, the brushes should be washed in cold water and stored in jars with the bristles up.

A medium lending itself readily to manipulation but of decidedly limited artistic value is finger paint. Working with this paint one does not use brushes, but instead uses the fingers, knuckles, and the palm of the hand to create rhythmic patterns. Should a child wish to do so, he may quickly erase a pattern by smoothing the paint with the flat of the hand before proceeding to produce another pattern on the same prepared surface.

Finger paint may be readily prepared by mixing tempera paint with school paste. A little powdered soap may also be stirred into the mixture to make it smooth and to make the paint easier to wash off hands and clothing, but this addition, while perhaps sometimes desirable, is not necessary for successful results. Finger paint may also be purchased ready-mixed from school supply houses. Several spoonfuls of the paint should be placed by the teacher on a well dampened sheet of paper having a glazed surface. After the child has spread the paint over the dampened surface of the paper, finger painting may begin.

Children·must exercise some care with finger painting, so that the paint is not spilled upon their clothing or upon the desks and floor. Obviously the painters should wear aprons, and the painting surface should rest upon a protective covering such as oilcloth, cardboard, or absorbent paper. Newspapers

49b *Finger-paint pattern by a six-year-old boy in the first grade.*

make a good covering and because of adhesion resulting from excess paint, have the added advantage of keeping the sheets of finished work flat.

While finger painting is an acceptable medium for children in the manipulative stage, one may question its value for picture-making until the pupils are quite mature. The technique lends itself well to the making of repetitive patterns, such as shown in Fig. 49b, but young children in the symbol-making stage cannot adequately control it. To paint a picture with this medium, in fact, requires an extraordinarily high degree of ability.

TEACHING: (The very young child is usually anxious to experiment with the media which confront him and will often do so merely by finding crayons, paint, and paper within reach. His span of attention, however, is short, so that within five minutes or so he may exhaust his interest in this work and seek a new activity. The more a child experiments with art media, however, the longer his attention span becomes.)

When first the child uses paint, it is a wise practice to offer him only one color. Very soon, when he has gained some skill in the manipulation of the paint, two colors might be provided, then three, then four. He can learn to handle as many as eight colors by the end of one school year of painting. When supplying more than one color, the teacher should provide contrasting hues. The teacher should put the paint in small containers such as glass jars or baby-food cans, and to prevent accidents, these containers should subsequently be placed firmly in a wire basket or in a cardboard or wooden box. One brush should be supplied for each color, since the very young child cannot at first be expected to wash his equipment between changes of color.

From the beginning of the child's experience with paint, the teacher should attempt to enlarge the pupil's color vocabulary. This may be done naturally by naming colors as they are used. The use of "coloring drills," often seen in some kindergartens, seems unnatural and hence to be avoided. The child learns about color most effectively by using it and talking about it.

When the child has become familiar with crayons, paints, and brushes, the teacher may try a few simple teaching methods to encourage him and perhaps to help him improve his technique. Sometimes music played in the background helps a child improve the rhythm of his lines or color areas. Occasionally the teacher may suggest that a large area of color be established before lines are added to the composition so that a center of interest may be developed. When certain children in the group make discoveries, such as stipple or dry-brush effects, the teacher might draw the attention of the class to these discoveries. The teacher should also, in a general way, praise each child's industry or some other broad aspects of his endeavor. Actually, the work he produces has little meaning for the young child since it is in the activity itself where he finds delight. When the child reaches the phase of named manipulation, the teacher should encourage him to talk about the subject matter of his painting. In so doing, the pupil tends to clarify ideas and thus progresses into further stages of development. One must remember, however, that whatever learning takes place at the stage of manipulation depends largely upon the child. The teacher, in other words, has little actually to teach, but must simply be encouraging. To a certain extent this principle applies to all art teaching, but it is particularly true at the manipulative stage. A pleasant working environment and one in which suitable materials are readily at hand are the main ingredients of a successful program during this stage of expression. The teacher must give much thought to preparing and distributing supplies and equipment and work out satisfactory procedures for collecting work and cleaning up after each session. See Chapter 5.

The Symbol Stage

MEDIA AND TECHNIQUES: When the child begins to produce symbols in his work, the media and tools may remain the same as those used during the manipulative stages. As children add details to their symbols, however, they frequently require several types of brushes in various sizes. If rounded bristle brushes were first used, some of the flat type should also be made available. The sizes of flat brushes may vary from about one-eighth to one-half inch, while the rounded types should be offered in a corresponding range, as well as some large (sizes 6 to 10) sable hair brushes. A wider range of colors in tempera paint should also be provided.

In earlier art sessions little or no chalk has been employed, but now, with his newly acquired skills, the child will probably be ready to use soft chalk, or "pastels," as they are sometimes called, which may be purchased in sets of ten to twelve colors. Chalk may be used conveniently on manila and some newsprint papers, about twelve by eighteen inches in size. Charcoal is another medium which might be added to the list and which may be used on the paper mentioned above. A considerable variety may be developed in chalk drawings by using both the end and side of the drawing medium.

Transparent water color may provide a further medium for children at this stage. However, it has lost some of its popularity in recent years, owing largely to the fact that tempera paint, which has replaced it, is much easier to handle. Before the pats of water color are used, they should be softened with clean water. Beginners should be encouraged to use pure, rather than mixed color, since a mixture of hues often tends to become discouragingly muddy. Though its transparent quality makes corrections difficult, water color is pleasant and quite different in character from opaque tempera paint.

TEACHING: Once the symbol stage has been reached, drawings and paintings represent subject matter directly derived from the child's experiences in life. This being the case, the teacher may from time to time assist the children to recall the important facts and features of the depicted objects. For example, for those children developing symbols for "man," the teacher should draw attention to activities such as running, jumping, climbing, brushing teeth, wearing overshoes, combing hair, washing hands, and so on. The children should act out these activities so that the concept inherent in the symbol may be expressed more completely. Judicious questioning by the teacher concerning both the appearance of the symbol in the child's work and its actual appearance as observed by the child in his environment might also take place. In this way the child is encouraged to recall many of the objects with which he has been in contact.

These teaching methods, it should be noted, are not suggested for the purpose of producing "realistic" work, but rather to assist the child to concentrate upon an item of experience in order that his statement concerning it may grow more complete.

When two or more symbols appear in the child's output, the teacher will have to be particularly careful to ensure that children are inspired by topics which appear to them worthy of expression.[4] It is now that vicarious as well as actual experience may be used effectively. Besides discussing topics related to home, parents, school, companions, and the like, such stories as "The Three Bears," "Little Red Ridinghood," and "Jack and the Beanstalk" will provide children with opportunities to relate pictorially two or more symbols having differences in appearance.

When the child relates his symbols to an environment, his chief difficulty often arises from an inability to make the symbol sufficiently distinct from the background of a picture. In this case, the teacher may find it necessary to suggest a greater contrast of color between a symbol and its background or that the symbol be outlined or in some other way accented with a contrasting color. At times the child may depict background and figure in equal detail and must be shown that in order to achieve the necessary dominance, either figure or ground must be left relatively unadorned with detail. The problem of developing contrasts between figure and ground, especially in color, light and shade, and sometimes texture, is one of the most important which the pupil should be helped to solve at this time.

The Preadolescent Stage [5]

MEDIA AND TECHNIQUES: By the time a child reaches this stage, he will usually have enjoyed a considerable amount of experience with art media

---

[4] Review Chapter 6, in connection with this important topic.

[5] See the film *Picture-Making in the Gang Age,* Creative Hands Series, listed in Appendix 6.

50 *A variety of brushes suitable for preadolescents.*

and will have developed many skills in their use. Within reason, a brush or a crayon should now do for the child what he wants it to do.

An even wider variety of brushes should now be provided and should include a range from about size 4 to size 10 of the soft, pointed type made of sable or camel hair as seen in Fig. 50. The hog bristle type should also be available in long-flat, short-flat, and round types and in all sizes from one-eighth inch to one inch. Since the children at this stage will sooner or later use tints and shades of color, it is well to provide gray paper so that the tonalities of color may be more effective. Some pupils avoid pure white papers because of their confusing glare. Pupils in this stage will require not only the standard opaque and transparent paints, but also colored inks, crayons, pastels, and drawing pencils of reasonably good quality. Conté crayon, which is available in both black and sepia, makes an excellent drawing medium, and may be used effectively with white chalk on gray paper when a study of highlights and shadows is being produced. Crayons might have a range of some 20 colors. Lead pencils should range in weight from about 3B to 8B.

Developing facility with color: Children in the early preadolescent stage become increasingly concerned with the relationships of background to foreground. This concern, together with their interest in effects of light and shade, creates problems related to the tonalities of color. Up to this point, the teacher has probably been supplying most colors ready mixed, including some of the deviations from the standard hues. But when the teacher considers the pupils mature enough to do some color mixing on their own, he should lose no time in encouraging them to do so.

Most pupils can begin mixing some of the opaque pigments by the time they reach at least the third or fourth grades. Once it is decided that the mixing of color is to be performed by the pupils, the physical arrangements in the classroom for the distribution of pigments must again be carefully planned. The cafeteria system mentioned in Chapter 5 should be established, so that the pupils can select their colors from jars of powdered or liquid tempera and, using a spoon or wooden paddle, dip the desired quantity of each color into a muffin tin. The mixing of paint and water and mixing of colors can be done right in the tins. It should be noted that children tend to be wasteful of paint and they should be cautioned to help themselves only to a reasonable quantity of pigment to meet their requirements. When children mix two colors, they should again be cautioned not to mix too large a quantity. By adding a darker color to a lighter one, such as blue to yellow or red to white, rather than the reverse, a quantity of paint may often be saved.

Color may be altered from the standard in a variety of ways. To mix black with the standard tempera color results in a *shade*, while the addition of white produces a *tint*. If water color is used, the addition of black results in a shade, while water itself provides the tint. The ability to mix tints and shades and thus arrive at different values greatly broadens the pupils ability to use color. However, there is another means of changing color from the standard which children in the elementary school can master without undue difficulty: A standard hue is altered also when it is mixed with its complement. Hence, when green is added to red, the character of red alters; the more green added the greater the change in the red, until finally a gray results. Grays achieved by this means are various in character and distinct from those achieved by mixing black and white. When used in a composition, they give dramatic emphasis to the areas of bright color.

To help the child understand how to alter color by adding its complement, one may use a color wheel, shown in Fig. 51, in which a circle of standard hues, ranging from the reds to the oranges, the yellows, greens, blues, violets, and back again to the reds, is depicted. If a color wheel is to be made, the teacher is the person to make it, not the children. Moreover, it should be used only to point out which color is opposite another, not to force children into using some of the inhibiting standardized arrangements of color so frequently found in school art programs of former years.

By the time children have gained some ability to mix colors, they should have a reasonably broad range of standard hues with which to work. This

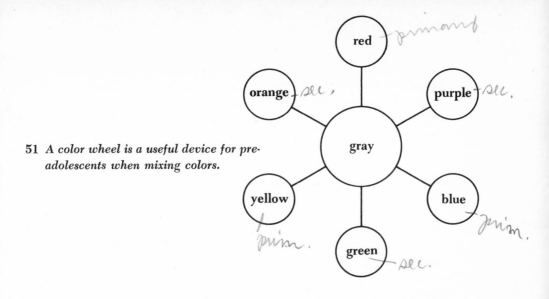

51 *A color wheel is a useful device for pre-adolescents when mixing colors.*

(handwritten annotations: "primary" by red; "sec." by orange; "sec." by purple; "prim." by yellow; "prim." by blue; "sec." by green)

range might include as many pigments as the following: black, white, red, yellow, blue, light and dark green, violet, orange, magenta, turquoise, light and dark brown. Because of this wide range, however, from time to time the teacher may find it necessary to caution the pupils against employing too broad a palette. Children will often attempt to use too many colors; in fact, they will sometimes try to use every color available in one painting, thus, of course, creating difficulties for themselves in building a unity of composition. The pupil should learn, by using varying amounts of white, black, and "opposite" colors, to extract from each hue a reasonably wide range of tonalities in order that the unity of his work may not be disrupted. At the same time, he must learn to use sufficient color both in strength and range to liven his work.

Developing facility with linear perspective: As well as using various tones of a color, some children in this stage, especially around the end of the fourth and beginning of the fifth grade, attempt to employ linear perspective in their work. The artistic convention of linear perspective is based upon the fact that in nature, objects appear to become smaller as they recede from the observer. Through the use of converging lines which reach vanishing points at the eye level on the horizon, an appearance of infinite depth and distance may be achieved.[6]

---

[6] Although found in paintings as old as those preserved on the walls of Pompeii, linear perspective is of relatively limited significance in art. It was not extensively developed in Western art until the early Renaissance in Italy. The prevailing artistic mode prior to the Renaissance—the Gothic tradition—largely ignored linear perspective, although it did appear from time to time, notably in the unique and powerful art of the Florentine Giotto (1276–1336). By the fifteenth century, or *quattrocento*, of the Italian

Not all pupils, however, turn to this mode of expression and there is no need for them all to do so. Pictorial expression may occur quite adequately without recourse to linear perspective. Even in professional art linear perspective is not employed by all painters. Some contemporary painters, recognizing what they consider to be limitations in this mode of delineation, either have eliminated depth in their work or have turned to other means to achieve this effect. Braque and his followers, for example, concentrate upon other elements of painting and tend to exclude volume and inward space from their work (see Fig. 52). Other painters use overlapping surfaces or planes and tonalities of color to achieve an effect of inward movement from the picture frame, without resorting to linear perspective.

Nevertheless, linear perspective appears in much contemporary painting, and, provided the artist does not allow the mechanics of the device to rule him, it is often used to good effect. Some preadolescent children, likewise, may employ linear perspective to good effect. The teacher can greatly assist the child who is trying to use perspective by teaching him some of its rudiments. For example, the teacher can demonstrate through observation the simple concepts that objects diminish in size as they recede from the observer, as shown in Fig. 53a. Something of the nature of vanishing points and their position in relation to the eye may be effectively demonstrated by a careful study of natural objects. By looking through a window at a receding row of objects, such as a line of telephone poles, the pupil can see that they appear to become smaller as they recede from the eye. By marking the glass with dots of soap to indicate the apparent position of the top and bottom of the poles, he can demonstrate to himself that the dots come closer together. The fact that lines below the eye level seem to rise while those above seem to fall may likewise be demonstrated by means of soap lines drawn on the window to conform with the lines under observation. Such simple but fundamental concepts seem to be sufficient for most pupils in the elementary school.

Also in connection with linear perspective, some children require assistance in understanding what is known as the ellipse. This is the apparent oval to be seen at the end of cylindrical objects as they occur above or below the eye level. The ellipse that the eye actually sees is a smoothly formed oval bulging slightly on the side toward the observer. In art, however, a distortion of this fact often leads to an interesting pattern. Many painters make no attempt to be governed by the actual appearance of the ellipse, but instead

---

Renaissance, many painters began to understand this artistic convention and to use it effectively. The experimenters, Masaccio (1401–1428), Uccello (1397–1475), and others, made marked advances in this direction, so that by the High Renaissance linear perspective had become the accepted device in Western painting which it is today.

indicate the top or bottom of a cylinder by a circle, a straight line, or an area coming to points (Fig. 54). The teacher can help children who wish to learn how to draw an ellipse by pointing out the characteristics of various objects in varying relationships to the eye level, as shown in Fig. 53b. The child will quickly observe the variations which appear in an ellipse when an object such as a tin can or teacup is raised and lowered across his eye level. Again, by looking at such objects as smoke stacks or gas storage tanks, both close at hand and in the distance, he may again observe the changes in appearance which occur at the extremities of cylindrical forms.

Under no circumstances should perspective be taught by such mechanical methods as drawing complicated diagrams of chalk boxes or cylinders in various positions. Indeed, the pupil should be fully aware that to follow the laws of linear perspective blindly, without due regard for aesthetic considerations, will inevitably tend to interfere with a successful outcome in picture-making.

In teaching perspective, as in teaching color, it is necessary to observe the fundamental principles of good pedagogy. Only when the child is ready for help and when he personally is aware of a need for help, should assistance be forthcoming. The teacher should keep in mind that successful painting may be produced without recourse to linear perspective. Should a child in the elementary school not exhibit any inclination to

52 *Braque's painting* The Table *almost completely lacks depth achieved through linear perspective.*

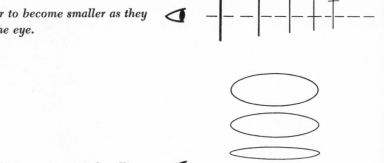

53a *Objects appear to become smaller as they recede from the eye.*

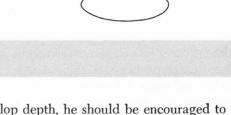

53b *Some facts of the ellipse.*

adopt this means of drawing to develop depth, he should be encouraged to master the alternate modes of composition such as the overlapping of planes and the toning of colors. Should the pupil, on the other hand, show an interest in this type of perspective, judicious teaching concerning it may allow his expression to grow in clarity and power.

Assisting in the development of drawing skills: In the later preadolescent period, especially in the fifth and sixth grades, many pupils develop a marked interest in drawing. That is to say, they wish to go beyond the symbol and to depict objects "that are real." Very few pupils, of course, are capable of developing the skill necessary to draw in a strictly photographic manner.[7]

---

[7] The photographic delineation of objects or, as one might say, photographic "realism," is old in art. It dominated Greek sculpture during the late fifth century B.C. and has occurred intermittently ever since that time. The sculptors of Rome depicted, as Cheney says, "every wrinkle, rib, and whisker"—*A New World History of Art* (N.Y.: Viking, 1956), p. 157. Many of the figures painted by the Florentine Masaccio, who died in 1428, are merely realistic delineations of nude bodies, as are the drawings of numerous uninspired painters of the late fifteenth century who followed him. In the portraits of

In spite of the long tradition of photographic realism in Western art, one may assert that artistic production invariably suffers when the artist becomes merely a copyist of nature. While craftsmanship and the ability to draw with the utmost skill may be desirable, art demands more of its producers. Is not art an expression of man's reaction to his environment, rather than an exact statement of the environment itself? In art we hope to find a human, personal document and not a mechanical photograph. Hence, it is the archaic sculpture of Greece we tend to admire today rather than much of the "realistic" output in the classic tradition of the fifth century. It is to the imagery of El Greco, Blake, and Cézanne we turn, rather than to the "natural-as-life" effects of, say, Ribera, Hunt, and David. In fact, from the expressions of primitive man to present-day abstract art, we find that the most distinguished artistic expression has in varying degrees tended to deviate from the natural appearance of the external world. In his attempt to arrive at a design suitable to convey his idea, the artist has more often than not departed from the exact camera view of his environment.

Is "realistic" drawing, then, always bad drawing? Not necessarily. If the artist finds in nature a pattern which serves to express his experiences, his pattern will have value. But the value is found chiefly in its form and not in its representational qualities. "The painter may . . . imitate what he sees," says L. A. Reid, in his attempt to find a place in art for "realistic" drawing, "but he imitates what he sees, because what he sees fulfills and satisfies his needs." [8] Good drawing must occur then, when the artist selects, interprets, and presents in a personal, aesthetically coherent composition those items of experiences which move him, whether or not the presentation is "realistic." Evidently, bad drawing occurs when the forms used are drawn merely to fill gaps in the pictorial surface, regardless of the unity of the pictorial composition as a whole. In performing the feat of organization most artists have found it necessary in varying degrees to depart from nature in the interest of design. Certainly, the most eminent painters appear to have done so.

This fact about the tradition of delineation has extraordinary significance for teachers of art. One is led to assert that there is little merit in encouraging children of any age to draw with consistent photographic accuracy. While some older pupils may tend toward this type of delineation, many will be disinclined to do so. Most pupils, in fact, find themselves uninspired in rendering in paint or pencil an object as it appears to the eye. While failing

the late sixteenth-century Venetian Moroni and his followers, we find again this exact "realism." After El Greco, most Spanish painting suffered from extreme photographic statement. Flemish art from 1400 helped to establish the "camera eye" as a kind of official European art which was largely dominant until the close of the nineteenth century.

[8] L. A. Reid, *A Study in Aesthetics* (N.Y.: Macmillan, 1931), p. 236.

54 Still Life with Newspaper *by Juan Gris. The subtle distortions of ellipses enhance the interest of the composition.*

to draw photographically, these same pupils often may display in their work certain aesthetic qualities arising from their use of the various elements of design. These qualities should be noted by the teacher and pointed out to their authors. Examples of professional work in which similar qualities are exhibited should be shown to the pupils. In this manner, the children may come to realize that "realism" is not necessarily a criterion of good art, a fact which many children at this stage of development often fail to grasp. When dealing with the few pupils who draw in a "photographic" manner, the teacher should show especial concern for their pictorial composition. Here the task is one of allowing the pupil to pursue his accomplishment while at the same time bringing to his attention the importance of developing an integrated pictorial arrangement.

Developing figure drawing, landscape, portraiture, and still life: It will be realized from what has been stated previously that good drawing depends in no small measure upon the producer's experience of the things drawn. Such experience, it should be noted, depends not only upon the eye, but upon a total reaction of the artist, involving, ideally, all the senses.

Often in the fifth and sixth grades, good drawing may be developed through the use of some of the time-honored subjects which demand a comprehensive reaction to experience. Life (or figure drawing) and landscape drawing as well as portraiture are among these means. For a few pupils in these grades even still-life work may be welcome and effective.

The majority of pupils in the preadolescent stage do not consider life, landscape, portraiture, and still life as ends in themselves.[9] They find it necessary to work in life, still life, and the like in order to produce pictures which satisfy them; see, for example, Fig. 55. Largely as a result of this condition of "need," the pupils readily turn to these artistic activities.[10]

As far as is practicable, the children should have responsibility for arrangements related to these fields of study. For example, they should have some control in posing the model for life drawing. The teacher, of course, will have to oversee the lighting and the setting of reasonable time limits for poses. Artificial lighting by one or more spotlights should be used, and these lights must be moved until anatomical details are clearly revealed and an interesting pattern of the elements, especially perhaps line and light and shade, is to be seen. Models must not be asked to pose after the holding of a position becomes painful (usually for a preadolescent youngster, five minutes is a lifetime). However, if poses are too short for completed drawings to be made, the teacher merely needs to remind the model to memorize his position so that he can return to it after a rest. The teacher, of course, should also remember the pose in case the pupil forgets it. Chalk marks to indicate the position of feet often help to establish a former position.

In producing both life drawings and portraits, the older pupils will be assisted by an elementary study of pertinent anatomy. The pupil who is maturing physiologically often shows his interest in the human body by drawing anatomical details in a rather pronounced manner, especially when females are depicted. Any emphasis beyond the requirements of aesthetics may be counteracted to some degree by a study of the human body. It will help the pupils to know something about the large surface muscles and to realize the nature of the mechanically independent body blocks: the head, the torso, and the pelvic girdle. The pupils may also make note of points of reference where bones come close to the surface. These points create interesting contrasts with the more fleshy parts of the body, and, since they are caused by the underlying skeleton, they provide the pupil with a kind of framework of thought for the body as a whole.[11]

[9] Review Chapter 6, for acceptable themes of expression.
[10] Review Chapter 2, concerning "readiness" and "need."
[11] A simplified study of anatomy for art students, school teachers, and some pupils is C. Earl Bradbury, *Anatomy and Construction of the Human Figure* (N.Y.: McGraw-Hill, 1949).

55 *"My New Skating Outfit."* An eleven-
year-old girl in the sixth grade creates
a self-portrait for expressive purposes.

In still-life work, the pupils should not only arrange their own group
of objects but should also be given opportunity to become thoroughly fa
miliar with each item. Before the final arrangement is made for drawing, the
pupils should be encouraged to handle the objects, so that they may experi
ence differences in their textures and their degrees of hardness and softness
All these experiences will tend to have an effect upon their drawing and
painting. To depend only upon the eye in art work may limit unnecessarily
the experience of the creating person.

The teacher must, of course, ensure the adequacy of still-life arrange
ments. They must have a challenging variety of objects, in which variou
types of contrasting surfaces (textures such as glass, fur, metal, cloth, and
wood) are to be found. Contrast in the shapes of objects (masses and spaces
must also be arresting. A sea shell and a piece of the root of a tree would
inspire the pupils more than, say, an old hat or a shoe. All the elements—
line, light and shade, and color—as well as those already mentioned should
be considered for the variety they display when brought into a still-life
arrangement. As the objects are assembled, however, an attempt must be
made to bring them into a unity of composition.[12] Even then, of course, the

[12] Review Chapter 3, for ideas about variety and unity.

pupils should be encouraged to improve upon the arrangement in their pictures.

In general, landscapes selected for outdoor painting or for preliminary studies to be finished in the classroom should have a reasonable number of things in them to be used as a basis for composition. Hence, a scene with a barn, some animals, a silo, and some farm machinery might be preferable to a sky and a wheat field, or a lake and a distant shore. By having many objects before him, the pupil may select the items which he considers will make an interesting composition. The wheat field or the lake may leave him at a loss for enough to draw.

The work in these activities need not be of long duration. Quick sketches occupy but a few minutes, and the speed of output is often stimulating and attractive to the pupils. However, some pupils may wish to produce a more finished type of work and, of course, should be encouraged to do so.

Developing methods of mixing media: While drawing or painting people and things, the pupils turn to many media. Children will mix media from an early age, so that by the time they reach the higher grades they may achieve some outstandingly successful results by this means. The use of repellents, for example, is practical for preadolescents and tends to maintain their interest in their work. Scratch-board technique may also be handled effectively by older pupils.

The technique illustrated in Plate VIIa of using repellents relies upon the fact that waxy media will shed liquid color provided the color is sufficiently thinned with water. A reasonably heavy paper or cardboard having a mat, or nonshiny, surface is required. Ordinary wax crayons are suitable and may be used with water color, thinned tempera paint, or colored inks. The last are particularly pleasant to use with this technique.

In producing a picture, the pupil first makes his drawing with wax crayon and then lays down his wash of color or colors. To provide accents in the work, thicker paint or India ink may be used. If ink is employed, it may be applied with either a pen or brush, or with both tools.

In using a scratch board, the pupil scratches away an all-over dark coating to expose selected parts of an under surface (see Fig. 56). Scratch board may be either purchased or made by the pupils. If it is to be made, the cardboard known as Bristol board is probably the most desirable to use. The surface is prepared by covering the Bristol board, or other glazed cardboard, with a heavy coat of wax. For this purpose a wax candle is convenient. The waxed surface should be powdered with talcum powder or chalk dust, so that a subsequent covering of paint will not form puddles. To the powdered coat, a coating of tempera paint or India ink sufficiently thick to hide the Bristol board should be applied and left to dry. Later, the drawing

56 *Scratch-board drawing by a ten-year-old boy, showing a
pleasant arrangement of black, white, and textured areas*

may be made with a variety of tools, including pen points, bobby-pins, scissors, and so on. It will be found that a careful handling of black, white, and textured areas will result in highly dramatic effects.

The techniques described above are basic and may be expanded in several ways. For example, white wax crayon may be used in the "resist" painting, and the pupil then relies upon paint to provide color. Again, colored wax crayon may be used as the first coat in preparing the scratch board.

One should not consider these techniques as merely "child's play." Many reputable artists have used them to produce significant drawings and paintings. Some of Henry Moore's sketches, for example, produced with wax and water color in the London air-raid shelters during World War II are particularly worthy of note.[13]

Developing Pictorial Composition in Children's Work

Few children in the elementary grades are ready for formal instruction in design. Some assistance in pictorial composition must occasionally be offered.

[13] See Henry Moore, *Shelter Sketch Book* (N.Y.: Wittenborn, 1946) and *Sculpture and Drawings*, with an introduction by Herbert Read (N.Y.: Valentin, 1949).

however, if they are to realize their goals of expression. This means that children should be helped towards an understanding of design and a feeling for it, largely in connection with their general picture-making. At this time the teacher will be particularly thankful for the understanding he has acquired about composition.[14]

One of the chief concerns of the teacher is to see that each child has a broad experience with all the elements of design. This experience, as noted below, is sometimes introduced most profitably in three-dimensional materials, before drawing and painting occur. Line presents few problems for the teacher, since children manipulate this element from their earliest years. Mass and space may be emphasized in the first few weeks of school through three-dimensional media such as paper, Plasticine, and scraps of wood. Color may be used at the beginning of the children's school career in the form of tempera paint, wax crayons, or finger paint. Light and shade may be brought to the attention of young children if the teacher mixes some tints and shades for use in conjunction with standard hues of tempera paint. Experience with textures offers some problems, since many materials having a great variety of textural qualities from rough to smooth must be supplied.

As children gain experience with the elements of design, they should be praised for any discoveries they make in their use, while any obvious advances might be discussed informally by the class. As time goes on, there is no reason why some professional work emphasizing certain elements of design should not be brought to the attention of pupils, even those who are still in the early symbol stage. The works of Picasso, Matisse, Gauguin, Klee, Chagall, and others may be viewed by children with much pleasure and considerable profit if related to their acts of expression.[15]

As time goes on, children tend to become more concerned over certain elements of design than others. Somewhere between the third and fifth grades, for example, preadolescents begin to incorporate shadow effects in their pictures and to pay some attention to details of background. It is then that they require assistance in arriving at suitable tonalities of color. Later, some children may wish to depict with greater accuracy textural appearances of materials such as fur or metal. They require assistance in their experimentation with the surface qualities being depicted, and in the exploration of such techniques as dry brush, wash, stipple, and the like to achieve various textural effects.

From time to time some children need help in arriving at a successful unity and variety of composition. In cases of this kind, the teacher must

---

[14] It may be advisable to review Chapter 3 at this time.
[15] See Chapter 15 for a detailed discussion of this topic.

resist the impulse to supply formulas for the designs of pictures. It would be a simple matter, for example, to tell children who are finding difficulty in creating a center of interest to draw a central object on a large scale. Children instructed to do this would without question establish a desirable focal point, but in so doing they would be following an ultimately stultifying formula. Instead, they should be exposed to or discover for themselves through carefully arranged activities all the various means of developing centers of interest. No single method should receive undue prominence.[16] What has been said about centers of interest applies equally to the establishment of rhythms and balances. Each child must arrive at satisfactory arrangements of his own devising.

To assist children to achieve a sufficient variety in their compositions a number of teaching devices can be used. In the first place, many different materials and many different tools to use with them can be put at the learners disposal. Secondly, the learners can be shown how to use two or more media in the same piece of art work—for example, wax crayon can be combined with colored inks applied with both brush and pen. Thirdly, the learners can be encouraged to explore the possibilities of different techniques and how to use them together in combination in one composition.

It was indicated above that a few pupils in the preadolescent stage develop an intellectual curiosity about formal design, although the majority do not until later in adolescence. Should the teacher discover some pupils with this curiosity, he would be wise to allow them to perform a few simple design activities of a formal character. Some of the activities mentioned in Chapter 3, in connection with design work for teachers to explore, will give clues to suitable experiments for these pupils.[17]

A most important task for the teacher is the development of a precise vocabulary of terms related to design. In all other subject areas, attention is paid to the exact meaning of words. This has not always been the case in art education, partly because the vocabulary of art in general has tended at times to be nebulous and partly because teachers have not always attempted to build for themselves a precise vocabulary of art terms. In the adult world of today there are many indications of untidy thinking about design and a related fear of "modern art." These manifestations probably arise from the fact that many people fail to develop an adequate understanding and knowledge of the use of words about art in general, and design in particular.

Some teachers have been eminently successful in assisting children to

---

[16] Review Chapter 3 for the means of developing centers of interest, rhythms, and balances.

[17] See also Chapter 5, C. D. and M. R. Gaitskell, *Art Education During Adolescence* (N.Y.: Harcourt, Brace, 1954).

use words about design with precise meaning. They have done so, of course, with due regard for the fact that art should not be studied verbally but rather should consist of experiences which are largely visual and tactile. When words such as those mentioned in Chapter 3 are used in a classroom, therefore, these teachers have made sure that eventually they are used with understanding and precision. Thus, although the teacher might at first compliment a child on the rhythmic flow of lines in his composition by saying that the quality of line was "like the blowing of the wind," later he would use the word "rhythm." In this incidental but natural manner, the vocabulary of even the youngest child may be developed. If there has been continual attention paid to such informal vocabulary-building, a pupil may leave the elementary school with a reasonably adequate command of art words which will enable him to participate later in a more formal program of composition. Such a command is, of course, highly desirable, because the child feels more at home with art as he becomes more familiar with the words related to it. By the time the pupil reaches adolescence, it is most necessary for him to have a working vocabulary in art. At that period in his development, the learner is often ready and in fact eager to approach design from a more formal and intellectual manner. Without at least a rudimentary vocabulary, he is handicapped in engaging in the type of art work his stage of development requires.

ACTIVITIES FOR THE READER

The teacher should make himself thoroughly familiar with the tools, media, and techniques which he will use in the classroom. The following activities are suggested so that he may gain this familiarity. Knowledge of the processes of art, in this instance, is more important than the art produced. Therefore the teacher should enter into these activities without feelings of inadequacy because of technical inabilities. Experience with art media is what counts at this stage.[18]

---

[18] See Munroe Wheeler and John Rewald, *Modern Drawings* (N.Y.: Museum of Modern Art, 1944), for a variety of drawing techniques; also for line work, see Wheeler's *Modern Painters and Sculptors as Illustrators* (N.Y.: Museum of Modern Art, 1946). Also interesting from the point of view of drawing is Thomas Craven, Ed., *A Treasury of American Prints* (N.Y.: Simon & Shuster, 1939). For landscape work, a good book for the beginner is Kenneth Clark, *Landscape Painting* (N.Y.: Scribner's, 1950).

For technical information about work with chalk, see L. Richmond and J. Littlejohns, *The Art of Painting in Pastel* (London: Pitman, 1918), and for information about water color, see their *Technique of Water Color Painting*, 2nd Ed. (N.Y.: Pitman, 1948).

An excellent study of masterly drawing and portraiture is John Rothenstein, *Augustus John* (N.Y.: Oxford Univ. Press, 1944).

1.   With a box of wax crayons of about 12 colors and some sheets of manila paper, draw nonobjective patterns with special regard for interesting variety in mass and space and color relationships.

2.   On construction paper of a dark hue, make a nonobjective pattern with about four colors of soft chalk. Try to develop interesting rhythms, to establish one center of interest, and to keep the work in balance.

3.   Using a large hog bristle brush for broad work, paint in tempera an interesting arrangement of color areas on a sheet of dark paper. Over some of these areas try to develop differing textural effects in the following ways:

a. BY USING DRY BRUSH

Dip the brush in paint and scrub it nearly dry on a piece of scrap paper. Then "dry-brush" an area where the new color will show (i.e., scrub lightly with the partially loaded brush).

b. BY STIPPLING

Dip the brush in paint and wipe off excess paint on scrap paper. Hold the brush upright so that the bristles strike the paper vertically. Stamp it lightly so that a stipple pattern of paint shows.

c. BY BRUSH DRAWING

Select a sable brush and load it with paint. Paint a pattern over a color area with wavy or crisscrossed lines, small drawn circles, or some other marks to give a rougher looking texture than is found in surrounding areas.

d. BY USING POWDERED PAINT

Apply powdered paint mixed with very little water heavily to your composition to obtain some actually rough areas (add sawdust or sand to liquid tempera if you have no powdered tempera).

4.   Select a small segment of the landscape you can see from a window and make a preliminary sketch of it with Conté crayon or 5B to 8B pencil on manila or better quality drawing paper. Keep working at your sketch, rearranging the positions of items until you think you have an interesting variety and unity of masses and spaces and light and shade. With water color or thin tempera, paint over parts of your drawing to form an interesting color pattern.

5.   Select some objects you think are interesting to see and feel—perhaps some silk, a leather-bound book, and three yellow apples. Arrange them for painting a still life. Sketch the arrangement with wax crayons, putting in areas of light bright color where you see the highlights at their brightest. Where you see the darkest shadow spots, use dark-colored crayons. Mix a middle tone of gray or brown water color or thin tempera and paint this quickly over the whole composition, using a broad sable hair or hog bristle brush.

6. Mix school paste with tempera and place some of the mixture on dampened, shiny surfaced paper. Smear it around with thumbs, fingers, and the flat of the hand to develop an interesting pattern. Wash your hands and then try again with two colors. The colors should be ones that harmonize, such as red and blue, yellow and blue, yellow and red. Black may also be used in the second painting. Later, smear one color all over another sheet of paper and wash your hands. Then dip your fingers or the side of your hand into a second color and begin creating a pattern. When thoroughly messy, wash your hands and look at the film *Finger Painting* to see how easy it is.[19]

7. Using heavy drawing pencil, try to make some of the following drawings in a strictly accurate, photographically correct manner. (Remember: lines below the eye level rise to this level; lines above fall to this level; all lines meet at the eye level.)

(a) A sidewalk or passageway as though you were standing in the center;

(b) A cup and saucer below your eye level on a table;

(c) A chimney stack, silo, or gas storage tank, the top of which is above your eye level.[20]

8. Sketch a house or collection of houses or other objects with crayon or heavy pencil, being guided by linear perspective. Rearrange in another drawing the drawn areas so formed, to improve the pattern of masses and spaces. Choose an area for a bright color and others for dull tones. (You are now practically a cubist!)

9. Have a friend pose for you. On at least 12-by-18-inch manila or newsprint paper, make an outline drawing in Conté crayon or heavy pencil. Draw quickly, not bothering much with anatomy or proportion and taking no longer than three to five minutes for each sketch. Do not erase mistakes; simply draw new lines. Make many drawings of this type based upon standing, seated, and reclining poses.[21]

Now begin to draw more carefully, thinking of places where bones come close to the surface and where flesh is thicker. Heavy pressure with the drawing medium will indicate the bony areas while the reverse will indicate fleshy parts. Think also of the torso, head, and pelvic regions as moving somewhat independently of each other. Begin to check proportions of body.

---

[19] See Appendix 6.

[20] At this point, study Ernest R. Norling, *Perspective Made Easy* (N.Y.: Macmillan, 1940). Good problems are to be found at the end of each chapter.

[21] At this stage, study the following: Bradbury, *Anatomy and Construction of the Human Figure,* or some other standard work on the subject, and Kimon Nicolaïdes, *The Natural Way to Draw* (Boston: Houghton Mifflin, 1941).

Later make drawings with India or other ink and a sable brush. Work quickly and fearlessly always.

10. Place yourself before a mirror to draw your own portrait. Study the different flat areas, or planes, of your face. Notice the position of prominent features (especially eyes, which are about half-way between the top of your head and the bottom of your chin). Draw quickly a life-size head in charcoal, crayon, or chalk. When you become used to yourself, try some other media, such as inks or paints.

11. Make scratch boards according to the directions given earlier and produce illustrations on them. In scratching out, be sure that you have a pleasant distribution of white, black, and half-tone (lined) areas. Practice scratching with many different implements, from razor blades to bobby-pins.

12. Now take time out for a few formal exercises. These express nothing, but are to help you develop technique. They are valueless for children but good for you at this stage. Here are some examples:

(a) Draw about a dozen 2-by-2-inch squares, one above the other. In the top square paint a standard hue; the bottom one leave white. Make a graduation of color areas, ranging from the standard hue to white, by progressively adding a little white to the standard hue. For the first area, just a little white should be added; for the second, more; for the third, even more; and so on. The "jumps" from one area to another should appear even.

(b) Repeat with some other hues. Use transparent water color as well as tempera paint for some exercises, adding water instead of white to the water-color pigment.

(c) Repeat by adding the complementary color on the color wheel, from the first one chosen. Now the graduations will go from standard to gray, rather than white.

(d) Add black progressively to a standard hue to obtain the twelve jumps from the standard to black.

(e) Try shading about six 3-inch-square areas with Conté crayon, charcoal, or heavy pencil so that you progress from very light gray to very dark gray.

(f) Try to draw textures in four 3-inch-square areas so that each becomes rougher than the next. Crisscrossed lines, wavy lines, circles, dots, and crosses are some of the devices to use. India ink and a writing pen are useful tools in this exercise.[22]

---

[22] Review Ralph L. Wickiser, *An Introduction to Art Activities* (N.Y.: Holt, 1947), at this time.

13. With insight gained into drawing and painting as a result of performing activities such as those suggested above, make the following plans for the classroom.[23]

(a) Draw plans for setting out materials for children in the grade or grades in which you are interested for the following: painting in tempera; painting in water color; working with a variety of media. Show arrows on your plan to indicate the flow of children.

(b) Draw plans complete with arrows to indicate how children would return supplies and equipment for each case above.

(c) If possible test these plans in a classroom. Make notes of overcrowding or any other difficulty which may arise. Revise your plans accordingly and test again.

14. Write a list of "art" words with which you think children should become familiar in each developmental level.

---

[23] Review Chapter 5.

Working with Paper

In recent years, paper and its derivations have become increasingly important as media of expression in art education. At one time used largely as a surface, sometimes called technically a "support" for paintings, paper is now employed in a variety of techniques. This chapter will present an outline of the manner in which paper and its derivatives may be used for expressive purposes. A description of the use of paper in picture-making, modeling, and general construction work, together with ways of using paper as a plastic medium, will be found in the following paragraphs.

In art education today, paper is employed as creatively as paint. While exact directions as to how to use paper to make specific objects might produce neat, precise work in the classroom, to suggest to children that they approach this medium in any but a creative fashion would be contrary to the nature of artistic activity. Whatever is produced in paper according to strict directions and prearranged designs is a kind of "handiwork" far removed from the contemporary program of art education.

When should work in paper appear on the art program? Should it come before or after drawing and painting? The answers to these questions depend upon circumstances.[1] Only the teacher who knows these circumstances can decide. Sometimes paper work will introduce art activities; sometimes it will supplement expression in paint; sometimes it will serve as the medium for

---

[1] Review Chapter 4.

major activities. No formula for its place in the art program can be offered.

Not all types of paper work are acceptable to children in all three stages of development. Picture-making with paper is practical at the manipulative, symbol, and preadolescent levels, but box sculpture loses much of its appeal as the child enters preadolescence. Other kinds of free-standing paper sculpture, on the other hand, are a welcome activity from the symbol stage to that of preadolescence. The use of molds is a relatively complicated technique suitable only for preadolescents, but papier-mâché may be successfully used at all stages. Forms in space may also be produced by children in all levels of development.

Picture-Making with Paper

MEDIA AND TECHNIQUES: Every child from kindergarten to the end of the sixth grade may profit from picture-making with paper. The paper provided for this purpose should be varied in color, texture, and weight and should be available in several shapes and sizes. Cartons containing odds and ends of paper, from newsprint to corrugated cardboard and including metallic as well as transparent papers, should be provided so that the children may select whatever type they may require for the work in hand. The very fact of being able to select from many types of paper is stimulating for those working in this medium, whether they are in the manipulative, the symbol, or the preadolescent stage.

Ordinary school paste, which may be purchased in either powdered or liquid form, may be used by all children for fixing the papers to the background. Liquid paste is the more popular. For the youngest children, the teacher will find it necessary to dip out small quantities of this paste from the main supply. Several children may share one small supply. Paste may be placed upon cardboard pie plates, saucers, or even upon a scrap of cardboard. Individual jars of paste fitted with a small brush in the lids may be purchased, but these cost more than paste purchased in bulk. When children are older and more experienced in using art materials, sticky substances may be provided in tubes. Rubber cements and various chemical plastics are pleasant to use and can be readily controlled. These substances are more expensive than paste and should be used only when a considerable degree of precision is required.

Children may spread the paste with tongue-depressors, which are washable. Some teachers like children to use strips of cardboard which can be discarded afterwards. Brushes, of course, may be used to spread paste, but one must remember that paste spoils a brush for further painting. The bristles stick together unpleasantly after being dipped in a sticky substance,

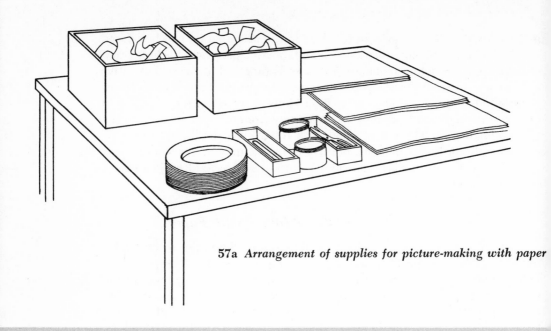

57a *Arrangement of supplies for picture-making with paper*

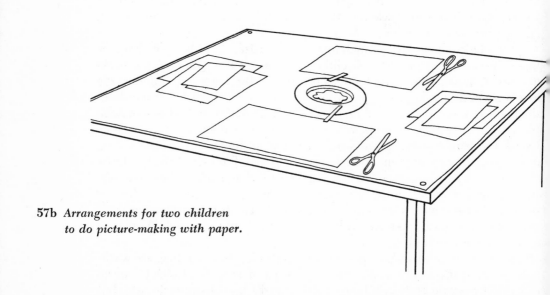

57b *Arrangements for two children to do picture-making with paper.*

58 *A picture made from cut paper by a five-and-a-half-year- old girl in kindergarten.*

and the hot water which must usually be used to remove the paste also takes away the "life" or spring of the bristles.

Children in the early manipulative stage can create pictures merely by tearing paper. Very soon, however, they will wish to use scissors, and these should be chosen with care. For the little children, the scissors should be short and light; for the more experienced pupils, they may be heavier and have longer cutting edges. Although their cutting edges may be kept sharp, the scissors should never have pointed tips; these may be much more convenient to use but they are dangerous. As well as being provided with scissors, the pupils in the preadolescent stage might also be allowed to use knives for cutting paper. These also have their dangers, but most pupils in about the third grade and up can learn to handle them safely.

The sources of subject matter for picture-making with paper are identical with those mentioned earlier for paint. The child in the early manipulative stage will experiment with the paper without attempting to produce a composition based upon a theme related to experience in life. This child will tear, cut, and subsequently paste paper to a support in an aesthetically uncontrolled manner. He is likely to use a wide variety of papers, smooth or rough, with shiny or mat finish, and in all colors available. As times goes on, the work of these young children tends, as with paint, to become more organized. Symbols such as shown in Fig. 58 then develop which are similar to those found in drawing and painting, and in due course the symbol-and-environment phase appears. Eventually the characteristics of preadolescent art are to be observed. Problems arising from more exact representation of objects, depth, tonality of color, and pictorial composition make themselves felt in paper work as they do in paint.

TEACHING: Children who work with paper to make pictures seem to find no insurmountable difficulties arising from the new medium and tools. The stimulation and counsel offered by the teacher will be like those given for drawing and painting. The use of paper, however, entails a few mechanical problems not found in painting.

Young children often use too much paste with the result that when pressure is applied, ridges of excess paste will form along the edges of the paper. The children must learn to be economical with paste and to apply it especially thinly along the outside edges of the paper. Beginners also frequently have difficulty in holding scissors in a cutting position. The teacher will have to use considerable judgment in determining whether or not the child possesses sufficient muscular coordination to use scissors. Just as there appears to be a condition called "reading readiness," so also it seems there is a time when a child is ready to use scissors.[2] Until that time arrives, the teacher should encourage the child to tear paper. At first, the pupil tears robustly and therefore with little control, but with practice he learns to be more exact.

Children's general abilities in designing noted in connection with drawing and painting are echoed in paper work. Teaching this medium will help the pupils expand their ideas about design. As a child in the manipulative stage becomes familiar with paper for picture-making, he finds it possible to develop many interesting effects peculiar to this medium. The teacher should encourage the children to play not only color against color, but also texture against texture, metallic surface against the usual paper surface, and mat against glazed finish. He might suggest that transparent papers be used to add more variety to the design, particularly when two or more transparent papers overlap both themselves and regular papers of varying hues.[3] The

---

[2] According to the Vineland Social Maturity Scale (Edgar A. Doll, Director of Research, The Training School at Vineland, New Jersey), ability to use scissors comes between the ages of two and three years. Observation in kindergartens leads one to believe that not until they are over five years of age are many children able to use scissors effectively.

[3] Some of the work of Bruno Munari is particularly worthy of note in this connection. Munari has designed Christmas cards by placing transparent papers in a transparent envelope. Instead of opening the envelope, one holds it to the light to receive the warm greeting of color.

children might be encouraged to make use of various textiles, string, and thin wood in addition to paper.

As time goes on, children, particularly those in the symbol stage, should be encouraged to build up their compositions in paper from the support, thus developing three-dimensional effects. In working on the theme, "My flower garden," for example, the child may first glue the paper flowers flat to the support. Later the teacher may demonstrate how petals may be curled by running the paper between thumb and scissors, and gluing only the center portion of the object. Three-dimensional effects may again be achieved by scoring, say, a center vein of leaves or petals. The child may be similarly encouraged to progress into other three-dimensional effects by bending, folding, twisting, cutting, and stretching.

Although the teacher will have to demonstrate these techniques, he should resort to these teaching devices with extreme caution. Demonstration is a necessary and effective practice, which wrongly used is very inhibiting to all children, but especially to those in the manipulative and symbol stages. Classes of children have been observed in which the paper work displayed an unfortunate similarity resulting directly from an overeffective lesson on "how to work with paper." The folds and cuts which the teacher made were observed by the class to be practical, and as a result, the children tended to rely upon the teacher's thinking, rather than upon their own. Since children often have the ability to arrive at suitable methods themselves, it seems a pity for them to cut short the struggle for mastery of the medium in order to arrive at quick results. Significant development in paper technique is made largely as a result of a personal conquest of the medium. Unless demonstrations are offered sparingly and with strict regard to the needs of the pupils, paper work may easily become stereotyped.

Actually, successful pictures in paper result from many teaching devices other than demonstrations. As we observed earlier, in the initial phases of manipulation, most children will stick the torn or cut paper to a background without much help or suggestion from the teacher. The bright paper and the natural curiosity of children suffice to start the production of pictures. Praise for being merely adventurous will encourage further experimentation. As children progress from manipulation to the production of symbols, the teacher's pleased and vocal recognition in the work of some individuals of well-established centers of interest, rhythms, and balances tends to help the class generally to improve design. When children exhaust their own ideas, the teacher may demonstrate some of the ways of treating paper mentioned previously. As preadolescence approaches, problems arising from the pupils' desire for more "realistic" statements will occur. Ranges in color of paper should then be expanded so that the pupils may employ tints and shades of

59 *Some ways of developing three-dimensional forms in paper: (a) folding and bending, (b) frilling, (c) pleating, (d) stretching, (e) scoring, and (f) twisting*

60 *Object made from cardboard boxes by a girl in the third grade.*

the various hues of paper for depth and emphasis. Likewise the teacher must see that papers having many different types of textures are readily available. Should the pupils appear to feel handicapped in relying entirely upon cutting and tearing, they should be allowed to draw or paint over some areas requiring detail, as a supplement to the basic technique. Judicious demonstration, verbal suggestion, and general encouragement usually are sufficient to keep picture-making in paper moving forward with commendable progress.

Free-Standing Forms

Box Sculpture

MEDIA AND TECHNIQUES: Activities involving the use of paper and cardboard to produce free-standing three-dimensional objects may be used in all stages of the child's development.

As a preliminary type of three-dimensional work to complement the picture-making discussed above, box sculpture is highly effective. Here the only supplies necessary are, first, an assortment of small cardboard containers, and, second, some school paste. Tempera paint and suitable brushes may also be supplied. The containers should vary in shape and should range in size from, say, one foot each way, down to about one inch as the largest dimension. If possible, cardboard tubes of different diameters and cut into various lengths should be available, while perhaps a few empty spools might also be provided.

61 *Through experimentation with paper, fifth-grade children evolved a cylindrical form as a basis for the figure of a clown.*

TEACHING: Little children take delight in pasting the containers together to build shapes at random, and later they like to paint them. As one might expect, they first build without apparent plan or subject matter in mind. Often in a matter of a week or so, however, the children begin to name their constructions. "This is a bridge," says five-year-old Peter to his classmates, describing an object faintly resembling such a structure. "This is my dad's factory," says Arthur who has placed a chimney-like object on top of a box. "I guess it's a castle," says Mary, describing a gaily painted construction.

Finally, the pupils begin to make some plans before beginning work. "I'd like to make a boat," decides John. "I'm going to make a house and paint it red and put a garden around it," says Ann. Thus children, when working in box sculpture, tend to progress through the usual stages of manipulation and symbolic expression. This, however, is about as far as they go in this type of work. The preadolescent usually loses interest in it and looks for another kind of paper work in three-dimensions. For those children in the manipulative stage little teaching is required apart from the usual general encouragement and attempt to keep the children reasonably free of paste and paint. In the symbol stage, the children should have ample opportunity to discuss their symbols with the teacher and with each other. In this way their work will grow in clarity and completeness. The teacher should encourage these children to add significant details in cut paper and in paint.

Other Free-standing Forms

MEDIA AND TECHNIQUES: On reaching the preadolescent stage, children find making other free-standing forms of paper sculpture both stimulating and challenging. The supplies required include the usual scissors, knife, construction paper and cardboard, odds and ends of colored paper, paste, and a vast array of miscellaneous articles such as drinking straws, toothpicks, and pins with colored heads.

The chief problem for the child in developing free-standing forms in paper lies in the necessity to develop a shape which will support the completed object. A tentlike form is perhaps the first such shape a child may devise. Later, he may fashion a paper tube or a paper cone with sufficient strength to support whatever details he plans to add. In constructing a figure of a clown, for example, the child might evolve a cylinder of paper for the head, body, and legs. The arms might be cut separately from flat paper and later glued to the sides of the cylinder. A hat could then be made in conical shape from more paper. Details of features and clothing might then be added, either with paint or more paper.[4]

For preadolescent children the technique of employing rolled paper to

---

[4] See the film *Paper Sculpture,* Creative Hands Series, listed in Appendix 6.

62 *Rolled paper animals made by fifth-grade pupils.*

Royal Studio

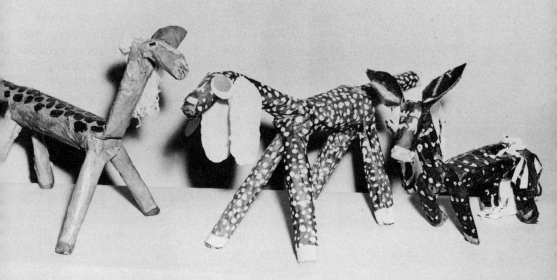

construct objects is also practical. Old newspapers may be used, together with paste, string, and sometimes wire. Before a child begins this work, he must obviously possess some ability to make plans in advance of production. He must have some idea as to the nature and size of the object he intends to fashion. Will it be a man or a bear, a chicken or a giraffe? While he need not plan the object in any detail, he must at least have reached decisions regarding its general shape, since this shape will largely govern its basic construction.

The underlying structure is easily developed.[5] Arms, legs, body, and head may all be produced from rolled newspapers. A chief component—say, the body—should be tied at several places by string, and to this component, others may be fastened, again with string. Should one part of the creation tend to be flimsy because of extreme length—perhaps the giraffe's neck—it can be reinforced by wire or strips of cardboard or wood.

When the main structure is complete, it is strengthened by the following means. One-inch-wide strips of newspapers are dipped in paste and then carefully wrapped around all parts of the object until it looks like an Egyptian mummy. While it is still wet, the pupil can add details such as ears, tails, and the like for which buttons, scraps of fur, and other odds and ends may be used. When dry, the creation may be painted, after which the paint may be covered with shellac or varnish.

Preadolescent children may also wish to fashion miniature buildings. Heavy construction paper or thin cardboard may be used for this purpose; also required are a ruler, scissors, a knife, and strong glue. In the kindergarten and perhaps the first grade, children also construct buildings, but these are very simple and symbolic in character. Only the façade may be produced which, in order to stand upright, must be supported by a small box to which it is glued. The preadolescent pupils wish to develop more realistic four-sided structures. After folding the four sides of a construction-paper house into a hollow square, the pupil will want to put on a roof, which at first may be flat but later will have a peak. Little by little the pupil improves on the structures he produces and in time learns to plan in advance even the details of cutting and folding (Fig. 63a-d). Tabs are left for gluing and peaks arranged for a pitched roof. Details such as windows, doors, and porches appear, painted on or cut from other paper and fixed in place. To the basic structure, furthermore, wings, garages, and so on will probably be added. Drinking straws, tongue depressors, swab sticks, wire, and string are among the items which the child may eventually use to enlarge upon his architectural ideas.[6]

---

[5] See the film *Animules*, listed in Appendix 6.

[6] See the film *Making Model Houses*, Creative Hands Series, listed in Appendix 6.

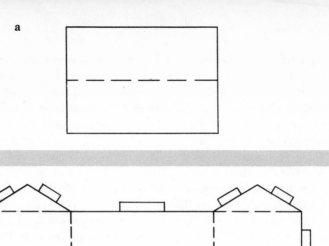

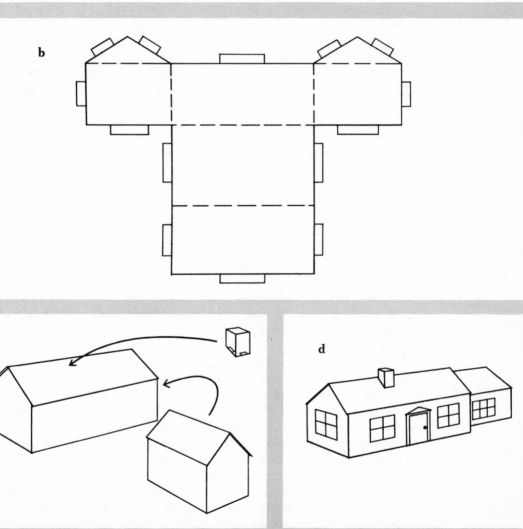

63 *A diagram of detailed plans for a cardboard house based upon the work of a sixth-grade boy. (a) Roof; (b) walls and base with tabs left; (c) structure with chimney and garage being added; (d) completed structure.*

TEACHING: The teacher will often find it necessary to resort to demonstrations of the techniques involved in general free-standing paper sculpture, rolled-paper sculpture, and miniature architectural work in paper. The difficulties which arise from demonstrations have been noted earlier and need not be repeated here. However, it may be said that in order to keep the work as creative as possible the stages and possibilities of construction in each of the three techniques should always be fully discussed with the pupils. Solutions to the problems arising from the discussion should, as far as possible and practicable, be suggested and acted upon by the pupils.

When basic forms are being produced to represent, say, a girl in paper sculpture, a horse in rolled paper, or a garage in folded paper, the teacher will find it necessary to keep a close eye on each pupil. He must be ready in time of need to make suggestions so that an otherwise impractical improvisation in a paper technique can be altered to result in success. For example, the pupil may have forgotten to leave sufficient paper to make tabs for fastening two pieces of paper together. Sticky tape might then be suggested.

A horse's head in rolled paper may be so heavy that it droops. Mention of a thin stick of wood, wired to the neck from body to head, may help solve the problem.

The teacher may find it necessary also, at least with the less experienced pupils, to offer many suggestions concerning the finishing of the articles. Studying a clown's figure in rolled paper—the work of a pupil—the teacher might suggest, for example, that absorbent cotton from the scrap box would make a good beard, or that small real buttons would add to the general effect if they were glued to the main paper figure.

As the pupils gain in experience, the teacher must emphasize the necessity of making reasonably detailed plans in advance. The pupils might make sketches of the basic shape of a figure so that it may be accurately cut, otherwise it may require considerable later alteration before being glued together. Even a sketch of a rolled-paper figure in which some indication of proportions and reinforcement points is given would help some pupils. In fact, the pupils and teacher together might well go through all the stages of using a medium in advance of individual construction.

Sometimes in architectural construction, even more detailed plans should be made. Every tab and fold, together with each component of the planned assembly, should be decided upon. However, all such details of a piece of paper work need not always be planned in advance. Much of the fun in this, as in other art work, comes from improvisation. Nor should perfection be expected in the child's work in this medium. The child must be permitted to develop both his thinking and his skills at his own pace. The preadolescent is usually no more ready to construct, say, a well-made model of a house than he is to produce a professional painting. His first architectural efforts, while possessing charm, will lack precision. Walls will lean, roofs will not fit, and chimneys will tumble. The same will be found in other early paper construction. Only time, experience, and effort will allow him to master the difficult feat of constructing in paper. The teacher must accept the learner's apparent deficiencies until such time as his skill grows more exact.

Paper in Plastic Forms

Two types of paper work in which the material is sufficiently plastic to be molded and modeled will be described in this section. The first is dampened paper; the second, mashed paper, or, as it is more commonly known, papier-mâché. Dampened paper is suitable for children in the advanced symbol stage and papier-mâché may be used by pupils in all stages.

MEDIA AND TECHNIQUES: For molded paper, old newspapers, school paste, tempera paint, shellac, perhaps some clay, scissors, and a willing pair of hands are the necessary items for production.

The technique consists of building a preliminary form over which strips of paper dampened thoroughly with school paste are laid and pressed into place. After drying, the paper strips, now forming a hard shell, are removed from the underlying form and usually finished with paint and shellac.

Model igloos, tunnels, mountains, and the like may be readily produced over different types of preliminary forms. These can be made with fine wire netting, clay, or balls or slightly dampened newspapers, pressed into the shape desired and then covered with the sticky strips of newsprint.

A life-size mask is slightly more difficult to construct. A detailed description of the process will suggest practicable ways of making not only the mask itself, but also the miniature objects mentioned above.

In producing a mask, newsprint is first used to establish a suitable size. The pupils should fold the paper into a strip about three or four inches wide, then fit the strip under his chin and over his head. When glued correctly, the oval of paper indicates the outside dimensions of the mask. The oval may then be stuffed with wads of slightly dampened newspaper until a mound is formed within the oval. Pinching the dampened newspaper will make a lump for a nose, while pressure in the right places will form eye sockets. Over this mound small pieces of wax paper should be placed in order that the next layers will not adhere to the mold just completed. The entire assembly should then be covered with strips of newsprint which have been dipped in paste. As each layer of paper is added, it should be laid down in an opposite direction from the preceding layer. The crossing of the strips adds strength to the construction. By using papers of different

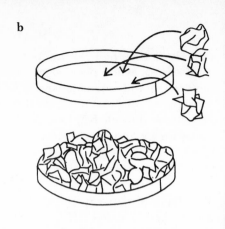

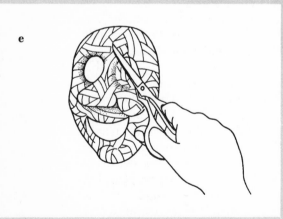

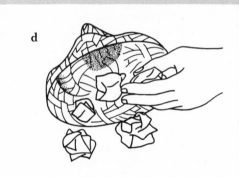

64 *Diagram of the steps in mask-making used by a fifth-grade girl: (a) measuring for size, (b) filling paper oval with balls of paper and molding feature, (c) sticking on lengths of paper, (d) removing base, (e) cutting features, and (f) adding trim.*

colors, the pupil can distinguish one layer from another. When the paper has dried into a hard shell, the wads of newsprint may be removed. Holes may then be cut for the eyes and nostrils. Features such as ears, hair, and nose may be developed further from paper or various scraps of materials. Paint and shellac give color to the finished product.[7]

Molded clay of which the surface has been thoroughly greased or covered with wax paper before the strips of paper are set down may also be employed as a base for much of this type of work.

Mashed paper, or papier-mâché, has been used as a modeling medium for centuries. Chinese soldiers of long ago are said to have made their armor with this material. Mashed paper is strong and may be put to many uses in school. To prepare this plastic medium, newsprint is torn into small pieces. Paper with a glazed surface should not be used. The torn paper is left to soak overnight in water and the next day is boiled for at least two hours. Then the excess water is drained off, leaving a pulp. The pulp is then wrung dry in a cotton cloth so that there is less likelihood of excess moisture deteriorating the paste which must next be used. About a cup full of school paste or wheat flour is well mixed with approximately five cups of pulp. The mash is then ready to be used as a modeling medium.

Children in the manipulative stage will roll it and pummel it; upon reaching the symbol stage they produce three-dimensional symbols with it. Preadolescent pupils learn to control it further and model interesting sculptured pieces. After the mashed paper has dried—a process which requires about a week—it may be worked with hand tools. The dry substance may be sandpapered, holes may be bored in it, it may be carved, and it will take paint.

TEACHING: The remarks made earlier about teaching in connection with other techniques involving paper will, of course, apply to molding and modeling in this medium. One additional teaching device, however, might be employed to good effect here. Because a kind of metamorphosis occurs in the medium between the beginning and end of modeling or molding, the pupils may be confused unless they have a clear picture in their minds of the entire process before work begins. It is recommended, therefore, that the teacher prepare in advance a step-by-step display of paper as it changes from a flimsy newspaper to a hard painted shell resulting from the molding technique or to a hard, solid object resulting from the papier-mâché process.

---

[7] See Matthew Baranski, *Mask Making* (Worcester, Mass.: Davis Press, 1954). The work described in this book is often too difficult for young children, but the techniques will be of interest to teachers. See also the film *Mask Making,* Creative Hands Series, listed in Appendix 6.

Forms in Space

MEDIA AND TECHNIQUES: The making of forms to be displayed in space, or "mobiles," either for their own sakes or to be used for certain practical purposes, such as Christmas tree ornaments, is a challenge to the children's ingenuity.

In general, the paper for this work should be of "construction" weight and available in black, white, and a full range of colors. The only tool necessary for children other than preadolescents is scissors. Older children capable of more precise output may wish to use a wooden or steel ruler as well as a razor-type knife and a paper punch. For fastening papers together, rubber cement, paste, glue, and a stapler or paper clips are required. As will be seen later, stiff wire or string in several colors is useful.

As Toni Hughes points out, forms in paper may be evolved by the following means: multiple folding or pleating; cutting strips of paper and joining them in various ways; using one continuous cut, say, a spiral, in a sheet of paper; folding and making related or repetitive cuts; cutting away parts of the paper (see Fig. 65a-f). Forms may be developed also by cutting slots into two or more pieces of paper and pushing the pieces together.[8] Which of these means of treating paper the pupils attempt will depend upon their stage of development. However, most children in the early manipulative stage make use of pleats and strips and soon learn to make a continuous cut. The ability to make related cuts and to produce forms by cutting slots in paper often follows before the close of the manipulative period. Likewise, pupils soon learn to cut away desired areas of paper before reaching the symbol stage. Children in all stages of development, even preadolescents, have much to gain from this work by approaching it in a spirit of experimental play.

TEACHING: To work from predeveloped plans might militate against a desirable experimental attitude towards the activity. Instead, the paper must be approached at all levels with the idea, "Let's see what happens!"

Since the type of paper work being discussed in this section ranges from the very simple to the complex, the problem of suggesting suitable teaching techniques is more than usually difficult. In an attempt to examine the duties of a teacher while forms in space are being produced and perhaps as a summary for teaching any type of paper work, let us observe some children at work.

It is Christmas time, and the children want to make paper ornaments

[8] See Toni Hughes, *How to Make Shapes in Space* (N.Y.: Dutton, 1955). This book will interest a teacher, although the activities are in general too advanced for elementary school children.

65 *Some ways of evolving forms in space from paper: (a) multiple folding,*
(b) cutting and joining strips, (c) continuous cutting, (d) repetitive cut-
ting (e) cutting away parts, and (f) slotting papers together.

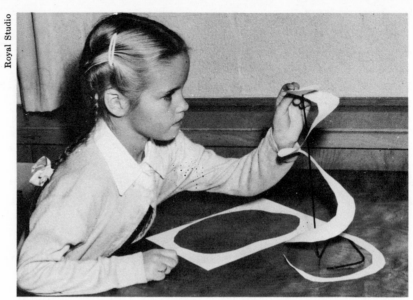

66 *Mary's work.*

67 *Arthur's work.*

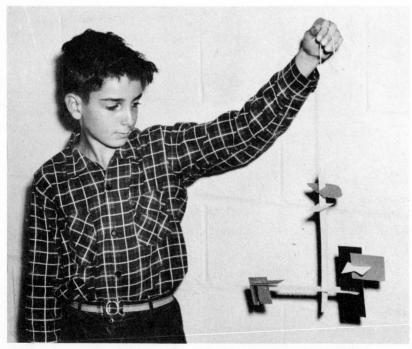

for the classroom tree. The teacher has placed some strips of paper about one inch wide and twenty inches long in front of them. Here is John, aged six, who is still in the manipulative stage. With no suggestion from anyone, he picks up a strip, makes a hoop with it, opens the hoop, twists the paper and makes a twisted hoop. At the teacher's suggestion, he pastes the ends of the hoop together. Repeating these maneuvers, he manages to place a second hoop inside the first. He repeats this process after being complimented by the teacher. The teacher gives him some colored string. Without hesitation he ties more hoops together and holds up his "mobile" Christmas tree ornament to be admired.

Mary, in the symbol stage, is seven. She has in her hands a seven-inch square of paper. "I wonder what we can make out of the paper," says the teacher. Using scissors, Mary starts to find out. First she trims the paper so that it is no longer square but irregular in shape, and then she starts on a trip with her scissors through the shaped paper. With encouragement from the teacher, she cuts, traveling in a circular fashion towards the center. Finally, she can cut no longer, so she picks up the paper and a "snake" ripples away from her fingers. Then having seen a classmate do likewise, she takes a piece of wire or cane. Experimenting, she thrusts it upwards through the dangling shape and at the teacher's suggestion fixes it by means of rubber cement to the top of the ornament.

Susan, a resourceful child, is twelve and in the preadolescent period. The teacher suggests the problem to her of devising a paper form in space. After the teacher advises her merely to experiment with folding followed by cutting, she folds in half a sheet of paper measuring about five inches by eight inches. Taking her scissors and still experimenting, she makes a cut from the folded edge and parallel to the short side. With a knife she slices down from the first cut and at right angles to it. These maneuvers she repeats several times to form similar cuts. Then she opens the paper and twists it to discover the various effects she may achieve by means of the repetitive cuts, until she is satisfied with the results.

Arthur is an intelligent boy of eleven in the preadolescent stage. He has seen a film called *Works of Calder* [9] and he wants to make a "mobile." The teacher tells him that he should try first fixing one piece of cardboard to another and build upon this technique. The teacher demonstrates and Arthur repeats the demonstration, cutting slits into two pieces of cardboard and pushing them together. He continues to build in this manner, later adding some curved shapes, and all the while watching the play of the various colors. Finally, he discovers a point of balance and ties his design with string so that when suspended, it will respond with movement to whatever air

[9]. Produced by Burgess Meredith (see Appendix 6). This is a poetic, stimulating film.

currents touch it. Arthur has thus constructed a simple "mobile" design. He continues to produce this type of art form and expand his ideas by employing pliers and wire to construct more complicated floating forms. Occasionally he goes to the teacher for help and advice. He learns that it is not a simple matter to arrange the physical balances necessary to make a satisfactory mobile. He also experiences difficulty in determining an aesthetic balance once the physical balances have been established. These problems he discusses with the teacher. The teacher criticizes his design and says that he must guard against a floating composition which is merely a muddle, instead of an aesthetic composition interesting to observe in its movements and in the relationships of its elements as they shift from one position to another.

Because Arthur is resourceful, he succeeds. Most pupils in the elementary grades may find the problems associated with the making of mobiles like this rather too advanced and must master the simpler cardboard constructions described earlier in this section. Others, however, will be able to progress into more complicated moving forms.

Where did the ideas for these techniques originate, once motivation had occurred? Obviously some of the children came across them entirely through experimentation. Other children, however, required timely suggestions from the teacher and demonstrations. Whatever the source of their inspiration and insight, the children all had the satisfaction of feeling that they were in command of the situation. To all intents and purposes, the discoveries they made were largely their own and no pattern for the design itself was emphasized. As a result the children developed paper work which possessed the stamp of originality.

ACTIVITIES FOR THE READER

1. Make some pictures with paper:

   (a) With a range of colored papers (including some light, dark, and middle grays, black, and white) and some rubber cement or paste make a nonobjective picture on a piece of heavy paper or cardboard no smaller than 18 by 24 inches. Perhaps you might like to start by developing a colorful center of interest out of an irregularly shaped area cut from a bright piece of paper. Thin strips of paper in contrasting colors would act as a contrast to this center and could be used to develop interesting and useful rhythms. Watch the balance of your composition as the background becomes covered with pieces glued to it. Stop before the work becomes cluttered.

   (b) Cut some pieces of paper from the colored, the half-tone, and the black-and-white pages of a magazine. Make a picture using these pieces but recutting them where necessary. Study in particular the differences in texture of the various scraps, and use these differences to good aesthetic effect. Your theme should be objective but could range from a study of flowers to that of a collection of old buildings.

(c) Set up a still life and base a paper picture on this arrangement. Be very careful of your tonalities of color and other aspects of general composition.

(d) Select a theme for a paper picture, such as a portrait of a tramp, an old man, or a teen-ager, and use some materials such as absorbent cotton, felt, printed cottons, as well as paper, in your work. Absorbent cotton might suggest hair or eyebrows, for example; felt or sand paper, a man's beard; printed cloth, a background for an elderly woman. Use a little paint for details if you wish. Try to be imaginative, but use some restraint from the point of view of the variety in your design.

2. Think back over the techniques you used in your paper-picture work, and list the ways in which you treated the paper. Prepare a chart showing paper that has been scored, twisted, frayed, stretched, curled, torn, and so on, until you have included all the ways you can remember of treating paper for picture-making.

3. Make a collection of papers to develop a graduated range of textures from roughest to smoothest.

4. Make a collection of gray papers and graduate them in tone. Do the same with a range of papers in one hue.[10]

5. Make a collection of cardboard boxes and wooden spools. Select a relatively large box for the body of some creature. Add smaller boxes or spools for legs, neck, and finally head. Add paper, felt, or cloth ears; a string or paper tail; paper, button, or large pin-head eyes. Paint with tempera color, and when dry, cover with one or two coats of varnish or shellac. A brush one inch wide is useful for applying the varnish or shellac. After shellacking, wash the brush in methyl alcohol (this is a poison). After using varnish, wash the brush in turpentine or a turpentine substitute (be careful of fire).

6. Make free-standing figures of animals or people based upon each of the following basic forms: (a) a tent made with one simple fold; (b) a cylinder; (c) a cone which may be cut to shape after twisting and gluing.

---

[10] At this point, the student should read Mary Grace Johnston, *Paper Sculpture* (Worcester, Mass.: Davis Press, 1952), and Minnie McLeish, *New Colour Cuts* (Peoria, Ill.: Bennett, 1954). This was originally a publication of the Dryad Press, Leicester, England. The work suggested is highly creative.

68 *A method for using rolled newspaper in the construction of objects.*

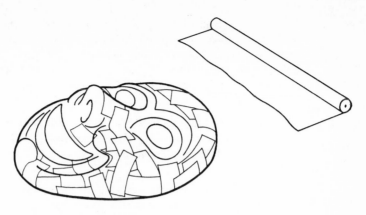

69 In making a mask with a clay base, small pieces of wax paper are placed over the base before pasted paper is applied.

Heads and legs should be devised by cutting and shaping paper and gluing it in place. Add features and details of clothing by gluing cut paper pieces to the basic shape.

7.   Make an object out of rolled newspaper. Roll the newspaper into a tight cylinder and tie it with string in three or four places. For arms and legs, tie thinner cylinders of newspaper as above. Tie the arms and legs to the body. Next the neck and head should be attached. Dip strips of newspaper or paper toweling about one inch wide into paste and wrap around figure. When the object is dry, add details with colored paper, scraps of fur, and so on. Finish with paint and shellac.

8.   Make a model building out of cardboard. Sketch your plan, working out the position of tabs. Draw plan accurately on cardboard. Cut away excess cardboard and score cardboard with back of scissors where the folds are to be made. Fold and glue. Add details such as drinking straws for veranda posts and cut paper for windows. Prepare a landscape for the model, perhaps using green and gray paper for lawns and paths, twigs with green paper leaves for trees, and paper in bright colors for banks of flowers.

9.   Make a mask over a clay base.[11] On a workboard, model a mold for the mask in clay. Leave clay to dry overnight; then cover with small pieces of wax paper.

11 Review the film *Mask Making.*

Dip one-inch strips of newspaper into paste and lay them over clay mold, pressing them gently to the wax paper covering the clay. Crisscross paper strips until four or more layers from the mask. When dry, lift away from mold, trim edge, cut holes for mouth and eyes, paint, shellac, and add other features from a "junk" collection, such as curtain rings for earrings, fur for hair, and so on.

10. Practice laying a shell of newspaper strips over a mold of wads of dampened newspaper. After doing (9), above, the reader will find the directions offered earlier in the chapter sufficient for this work.

11. Prepare papier-mâché according to the recipe offered earlier in the chapter. While it is wet, model some of this plastic medium on a workboard into a nonobjective form. With some more plastic, model an objective form. Be sure to keep these objects solid and "chunky," rather than spindly; the solid form will more readily stay in one piece as it dries. When the objects are dry, try making one of them smoother by rubbing lightly with fine sandpaper. Try painting both the smooth and the rough object with tempera paint to enhance the designs already created.

70 *Some techniques used in making mobile sculpture from wire.*

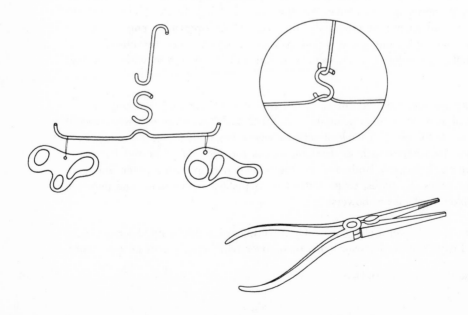

12.   Prepare an attractive and easily understood exhibit for display in a classroom, to show the whole papier-mâché process, from newsprint to finished object.[12]

13.   Make four simple paper or cardboard "mobiles," going through each of the processes described for John, Mary, Susan, and Arthur earlier in the chapter. Carry your exploration as far as you can until you have a satisfying moving form.

14.   Make a mobile with wire and cardboard such as that described earlier for Arthur. Obtain some wire of the weight and type found in coat hangers—coat hangers, themselves, will serve the purpose—and a pair of long-nosed pliers with a wire-cutter "built in." Snip off a piece of wire about four inches long and another about six to eight inches long. Curl up one end of the short piece, put a hump in the middle of the long piece, and join the first to the second with an S-shaped link. Squeeze the open part of the S together. Curl the ends of the long piece so that anything attached at either end will not slip off. At either end of the long piece of wire attach by means of thread some cardboard pieces of interesting shapes and colors. This is the first unit of a simple wire and cardboard mobile. Try making some more mobiles with additional units.[13]

---

[12] Now read Victoria Betts, *Exploring Papier-Mâché* (Worcester, Mass.: Davis Press, 1955).

[13] Now read John Lynch, *How to Make Mobiles* (N.Y.: Studio, 1953).

Sculpture and Modeling

Sculpture and modeling include the fashioning of three-dimensional art forms, either in relief or in the round. Although the definitions are not always strictly adhered to, in art education *sculpture* usually refers to a process by which a part of a material is removed to form the finished product, while *modeling* is performed by building up from a mass of material and often by adding even more material to that which is being formed. Thus to produce a piece of sculpture in wood, one whittles away the wood until the desired form appears. In modeling a piece of clay pottery, on the other hand, one shapes the object from the mass of clay and may later add handles to it.

Sculpture and modeling are activities in which raw materials from the earth and forest are directly manipulated by the artist. In modeling, the pupil may approach the clay with no tools other than his bare hands, while in wood and other types of sculpture, a tool as primitive as a knife allows him to pit his skill and strength against the material.

If the worker shows respect for the substance engaging his energies, the primary characteristics of the original material remain in the finished product. Wood remains wood, clay remains clay, and each substance clearly demonstrates its influence upon the art form into which it was fashioned.

This chapter will concentrate on sculpture in wood and in plaster of Paris and on modeling in clay. Pottery will also be mentioned, but the emphasis will be placed upon ways in which this craft may be performed by children without undue attention from their teacher. The chapter will close with a mention of what is generally called "wire sculpture." [1]

Children in all stages of development can work successfully in one form or another of wood sculpture. Likewise all children can do some modeling in clay. Only older preadolescents, however, are able to carve wood and plaster of Paris since the skills involved are beyond the ability of younger children and some of the tools required are dangerous for the little ones. Wire sculpture is a good activity for children in both the symbol and preadolescent stages but usually does not seem to appeal to those in the manipulative stage.

Sculpture in Wood

Using Scraps of Wood

MEDIA AND TECHNIQUES: Children in the manipulative and symbol stages work with wood much as they work with paper box sculpture. If the school has an industrial arts department in which wood work is taught, the teacher may obtain from this source scraps of wood varying in shape and size. These scraps of wood should be inspected to see that they have no dangerous splinters. In addition to scraps of wood, the children might be supplied with tongue depressors, swab sticks, wooden spools, and so on. To fix pieces of wood together, a particularly strong glue (sometimes called "strength glue"), which may be purchased from any hardware store, is necessary. The children put together pieces of wood much as they put together the boxes and tubes in box sculpture. Two pieces of wood are selected, both are smeared with glue along the edges to be stuck, and they are then pressed firmly together. The process is continued until several pieces of wood form one solid structure. A swab stick or a tongue depressor should be used to apply the glue. After assembling the pieces, the children often like to paint their structures. Although to cover wood with paint may not be the best art practice, children should be allowed to do so at this early stage. Young children have no thought of camouflaging the nature of the material with which they are working, but rather use the paint simply for decorative purposes. Tempera paint applied with a hog bristle brush is recommended.

---

[1] In connection with this chapter, start to study some of the following: Andrew Carnduff Ritchie, *Sculpture in the Twentieth Century* (Museum of Modern Art, 1952); Bernard Leach, *A Potter's Portfolio* (N.Y.: Pitman, 1951); New Educational Library (Lord Gorell, Advisory Ed.), *The Arts: Painting, the Graphic Arts, Sculpture and Architecture,* (London: Oldhams Press, 1948); James Johnson Sweeney, *Henry Moore* (N.Y.: Museum of Modern Art, 1947); Jacques Schnier, *Sculpture in Modern America* (Berkeley and Los Angeles: Univ. of California Press, 1948).

TEACHING: The teaching techniques recommended in connection with box sculpture are suitable here. An encouraging attitude at all times, recognition and praise of individual accomplishments, and making arrangements for plenty of suitable supplies are all part of the teacher's work.

The distribution of supplies causes few special problems. Scraps of wood may be placed in cartons and each child can help himself to a number of pieces. The glue is best distributed by the teacher, who should place a dab of it on paper or cardboard set before each child. Paint is handled in the usual manner described for picture-making.

Sculpture in the Round

MEDIA AND TECHNIQUES: Only older preadolescent children, usually in about the fifth and sixth grades, will be able to produce wood sculpture in the traditional manner. Traditional wood sculpture consists of carving bumps and hollows in a piece of wood which is suitable, or, as sculptors sometimes say, "sympathetic," for this purpose. Neither very hard woods like oak nor very soft woods like balsa are suitable for children. The hard woods, of course, demand of the workers a strength which they do not possess, while the soft woods fail to offer the resistance which the developing muscles of the young require.

Wherever possible, woods from the local environment should be selected. In using local wood, children explore their immediate environment and capitalize upon their own resources. Seasoned woods of some of the cedar and cypress families are excellent for sculpture because they cut cleanly without splintering and do not demand too much physical exertion. Old cedar fence rails are perhaps the most pleasant and practical of all the woods with which to work since they are well seasoned, carve conveniently, and take an excellent finish. Unfortunately, they have all but disappeared from most parts of our landscape. However, wood of the poplars, pines, birches, and many other varieties, when seasoned, has excellent qualities for sculpture. Lumber merchants often sell suitable scraps of these woods. If wood to be used for sculpture is damp, it should be stacked under cover out of doors until it dries. Wind dries the wood, while stacking prevents it from warping.

In cities, the children often have to depend upon scraps of wood from discarded objects such as old boxes or broken furniture. A friendly fruit dealer or building contractor is often a good man to know when one contemplates wood sculpture in a city school. If a source of discarded wood is not available, the school can usually, at reasonable cost, purchase sufficient wood for its needs.

Wood may be worked to a considerable degree of satisfaction merely

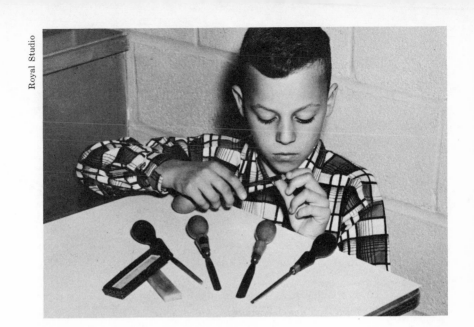

71 *A set of wood-carving tools and an oilstone.*

with a strong sharp pocketknife. Sets of carving tools may be bought, however, which allow the worker to produce a wide variety of cuts. These tools may be obtained in a number of shapes, including straight-edged knives, V-cutters, and U-gouges. All tools should be kept sharp by constant honing on fine oilstone. In addition, some files, rasps, and sandpaper, from coarse to fine grain, may be required.

While wood may be cut on a 5-ply workboard placed over a school desk, wood sculpture is best performed on an industrial arts (carpenter's) bench. These benches usually are fitted with vises which allow the worker to place both hands on the cutting tools. (Without a vise, the pupil must hold the wood with one hand which may easily be injured unless great care is exercised.) In general, the cutting should be done in a direction away from the body. If some rough two-by-four strips of wood are bolted to the side of the heavy work bench, the pupils who work without a vise may sit while doing much of their carving (see Fig. 72).

One method of working in wood which is often suggested in books for teachers is not recommended here. By this method, the pupils are supposed to cut with a saw, first, a side profile, and, second, an end profile of the subject in wood. The method recommended in this book, on the other hand, is that of "roughing-out" the subject from all sides. The wood is held in one hand and pressed against the bench, or is placed in the vise if one is avail-

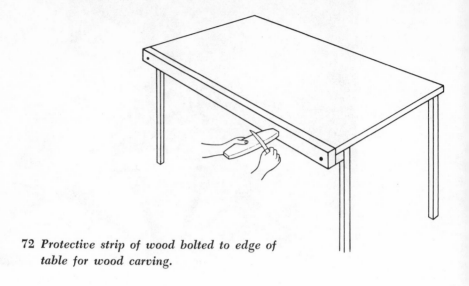

72 *Protective strip of wood bolted to edge of table for wood carving.*

table, while the carving tool is applied along the grain. Turning the piece and cutting, the pupil gets rid of excess wood until a desired shape begins to be formed. Rasps—very coarse files—may be used at the close of the roughing-out process if a vise is available. The in-the-round approach allows the pupil to create a solid, chunky piece of sculpture which is attractive in its "woodiness"—a desirable feature in this type of sculpture which is difficult to achieve by the other method.

The finishing of the article must be performed with some care so that neither the design nor the inherent quality of the wood is spoiled. Should the pupil want a smooth finish for his product, he can apply a rasp and then a file to its surface and later run sandpaper over it.

Wood usually requires the application of a preservative, perhaps the most acceptable being wax. A thin coat of solidified wax can be applied with a cloth and then polished vigorously (in spite of what the advertisements say about "no rubbing"). Successive coats should follow until the wood glows. Sometimes stains are used on wood. A thin oil stain might occasionally be employed to enhance the wood, but such preservative should be used with caution. For one thing, it is often difficult to maintain a desired uniformity of tone because of the effect of the grain of the wood. Also, a bright stain may distort the natural appearance of the wood. Too often one sees a fine white wood spoiled by the application of what is fondly called a "mahogany" stain. Other than wax, perhaps the safest and most satisfactory finishes for wood are clear varnish and colorless shellac, both of which may be applied with a brush. Even with these coverings, however, there is a danger of making the wood look like toffee. In short, nothing is better than the quality of wood itself. To maintain this quality, the pupil must learn to use good judgment in choosing a preservative for his sculpture.

TEACHING: Many opportunities for effective teaching arise through sculpture in wood. Discussion and demonstration are often necessary teaching devices. Wood provides the pupils with a medium having excellent qualities which must not be debased through clumsy and inappropriate working techniques. The teacher's first task is that of discussing with the class the interesting qualities of wood—its color, its texture (as shown in the grain), its response to various finishing techniques including sanding, waxing, and painting. Studies might well be made of some of the varied uses to which wood may be put and how man has often relied upon it to develop his civilization.[2] Included in this study might be examples of faulty as well as successful treatment of wood.

---

[2] See Lewis Mumford, *Technics and Civilization* (N.Y.: Harcourt, Brace, 1934), especially Chapter 3 and Plate V, "Technics of Wood," facing p. 148.

73 *Wood sculpture in the round by sixth-grade boys and girls.*

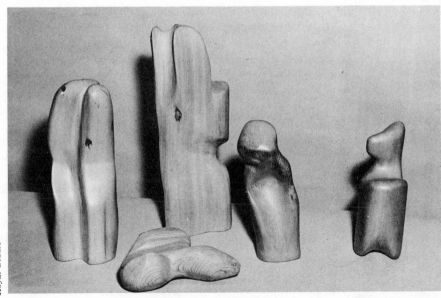

Royal Studio

74 The Avenger *by Barlach—an expressive sculptured form in wood.*

Since most of the tools for working with wood are dangerous, the teacher should demonstrate correct ways of handling them. Discussion about safety in using tools and how to give first-aid following a cut could very well be included among the topics which follow demonstrations of carving techniques. The teacher should also give lessons concerning the sharpening and care of tools and should emphasize the pride which a good workman has in the tools he uses. A class trip to a sculptor's studio would be very worthwhile at this time.

The teacher will also find it necessary to discuss the subject matter suitable for wood sculpture. Here the opportunity will arise to point out the need for original expression based upon experience. Reference to the work of some eminent sculptors (see Fig. 74), from Michelangelo to Barlach, will indicate to the pupils that sculpture is a form of expression equally as personal as painting.[3] In this way the teacher should help the pupils to avoid the clichés of the "Sleeping Mexican" or the "Noble Dog" to be found in

---

[3] See William Zorach, *Zorach Explains Sculpture* (N.Y.: American Artists Group, 1947); *Art in Our Time* (N.Y.: Museum of Modern Art, 1939); Reginald H. Wilenski, *The Meaning of Modern Sculpture* (London: Faber & Faber, 1932).

many craft books published for the use of teachers and pupils of two decades or so ago.

As well as suggesting expression based upon objective themes, the teacher might encourage the pupils to do some nonobjective work. In this way they can occasionally concentrate upon troublesome aspects of technique without being bothered over subject matter.

The child who works with wood in the round should learn that the "chunky" appearance of this sculpture is a natural outcome of the technique. The teacher should emphasize the fact that flimsy protuberances of any kind are not in keeping with wood sculpture and tend to affect the design adversely. The child should also be taught that any detail which is cut into the main contours must be developed with some restraint lest the strong wood quality of the piece be lost. Such insights into the technique will come, of course, to a great extent, through practice.

As the child works in wood, he should be taught that the bumps, hollows, and textures he has carved must be studied for the patterns of light and shade they produce. By holding the child's sculpture in a reasonably strong light coming from one source, the teacher can demonstrate how to study the high lights and shadows. As in other art, it is far more important for a pupil eventually to learn to judge the quality of sculpture from the point of view of design than from its "realistic" appearance.

In summary, a constant challenge to the teacher of sculpture is to select and employ only those teaching methods which develop the pupils' artistic integrity and taste. The search for excellence of craftsmanship will show clearly in wood sculpture as will the growing mastery of tools. Any subterfuge in the treatment of wood likewise soon becomes evident. For example, no pupil should be obliged to obliterate the tool marks from the surface of his work if he does not wish to do so. Tool marks may add greatly to the quality of design of a sculptured piece, particularly to its texture, and hence they are often to be treasured rather than eliminated. Again, wood finishes, as mentioned earlier, must be used with sensitivity to the qualities of this fine medium.

Carving in Relief

MEDIA AND TECHNIQUES: Relief carving in wood is a type of picture-making. Since the sharpness of the tools and the strength required to perform this work excludes the younger children, only those preadolescents in the fifth and sixth grades should occupy themselves with this activity.

The wood should be well-seasoned gumwood, pine, or any other fine-grained variety that cuts well. A piece for carving might measure about one inch thick and perhaps up to twelve and fifteen inches in its other dimensions.

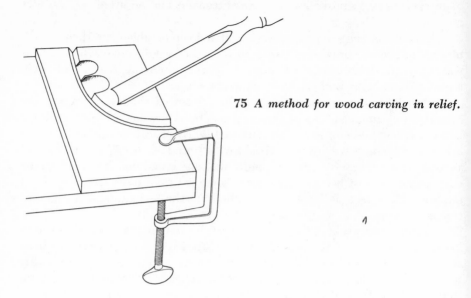

75 *A method for wood carving in relief.*

A C-clamp (a clamp so named because its design forms the letter of the alphabet) to hold the slab of wood in position while it is being cut will sometimes be convenient. The carving tools might range from a pocketknife to the sets of implements mentioned in connection with sculpture in the round. Their sharpness must be constantly maintained by periodic honing on a fine oilstone.

Provided the tools are sharp and the wood suitable, the actual carving in low relief is not too difficult. A straight cut is often made around the main masses of the composition, after which gouges are used to produce incisions meeting the deepest extremity of the straight cuts. Details in the main masses may be conveniently arranged with V-cuts. Since the design depends to a large extent upon light and shade, the pupil should learn to hold his work from time to time in the path of a source of light as he would when working in the round. In this way, he will be helped to develop contrasting effects, such as sharp edges and rounded contours, together with deep and shallow hollows, in order to exploit the elements of light and shade.

The remarks concerning preservatives and finishes for wood offered in connection with sculpture in the round apply also in relief work. Care must be taken, however, not to clog delicate cuts with wax. In this connection, using a toothbrush to apply thin coats of wax to some parts of the carving will be found to be more effective than rubbing on the wax with a cloth.

TEACHING: Because low relief carving is a kind of picture-making, the nature of its subject matter will therefore resemble that found in the children's drawings and paintings. Following a demonstration of the technique of cutting in low relief, the teacher should discuss with the pupils suitable subject matter for the work. The pupils should then make sketches which they believe to be suitable.

It must be remembered that although a close relationship exists between relief carving in wood and drawing, the fact that wood and steel tools are being employed instead of paper, crayon, and pencil will materially affect the design. While sketches help to plot the main areas of the proposed design much of the work should be composed directly upon the wood rather than on paper. Very often lines drawn with a pencil or crayon cannot be duplicated with a steel tool, while the actual depressions, protrusions, and textures, easily developed in wood but impossible in painting, add dimensions and problems which can be attached only in the wood itself.

In order to assist the pupils to realize the difference existing between carving and drawing and at the same time to teach them the valuable lesson that tools and materials affect technique, the teacher should encourage them to manipulate the surface of some scrap wood with a chisel and a gouge. This process should be considered a kind of game, and pupils might profitably discuss with each other new effects as they are discovered. The teacher should also let the class know about new discoveries by individuals as they appear. Short dips and longer scoops with the gouges, straight V-cuts or crossed cuts with the straight chisel, and so on, will lead to many interesting effects. The pupils should study their sketches in the light of their experiences with the new process.

The comments made earlier about tools and materials in connection with teaching sculpture in the round, of course, apply also to sculture in relief.

Sculpture in Plaster of Paris

MEDIA AND TECHNIQUES: For most children in the preadolescent stage a suitable medium for sculpture is plaster of Paris. A child who is capable of using any kind of cutting tool safely may be successful with this material. Sculptured pieces displaying satisfying qualities in either relief or in the round can be produced with it.

The plaster is usually bought in sacks. It should be mixed in small quantities by adding water and "puddling it in" with a spoon until the mixture reaches the consistency of thick cream. A pail is a good container for mixing. If the plaster tends to dry too quickly, the rate of drying may be retarded by adding about a teaspoonful of salt to two cups of plaster.

After being mixed with water, the plaster must be poured quickly into a mold to dry and harden. Children will find that small cardboard containers make suitable molds. The container is selected according to the type of work intended; a shoe box, for example, might have the right length and height for a plaque on which a relief carving is to be inscribed, while a carton which held a large tube of toothpaste would serve to mold plaster to be carved in the round. When the plaster dries, which it does with extraordinary rapidity, it contracts slightly so that the cardboard is easily peeled away.

Molds may also be made from wood. A smooth board or sheet of thick plywood can be used as a support for strips of wood which are tacked to it to form a box. The strips of wood act as the walls of a vat to contain the plaster. This type of mold allows the pupil greater control over the dimensions of the articles to be made. Whatever kind of mold is used, the plaster should be poured to a depth of at least three-quarters of an inch to one inch for satisfactory results.

Almost any cutting tool may be used on plaster—pocketknives, woodworking tools, or linoleum cutters. Some people even use worn-out tools which they obtain from their dentist. No special accommodation is necessary for this work. Cutting should be done on a board—say, an old drawing board—and some care must be exercised not to litter the floor with cut-off pieces, since when crushed by the pupil's feet, the plaster is difficult to sweep up. The technique of cutting plaster is rather less robust than that used with wood. When cutting is satisfactorily completed, the plaster should be lightly

76 *Examples of sculpture in plaster of Paris by fifth- and sixth-grade boys and girls.*

Royal Studio

rubbed with fine sandpaper to obtain smooth surfaces where they are desired. A preservative finish is not necessary and would spoil the attractive appearance of the medium.

TEACHING: The duties of the teacher include some demonstration, although, because this medium is less difficult than wood to cut, demonstration need occupy relatively little time. Pupils often require more assistance in preparing the plaster than they do in working with it. The teacher should be sure that every child knows what his subject matter and technique are to be before he molds his plaster. Low relief requires a flat slab, while in the round requires a block of plaster. Obviously once the plaster is molded, the child is committed to work which suits the shape of his material. More than this need not be said about teaching children to carve plaster of Paris, since the suggestions made earlier in connection with the teaching of wood carving are generally applicable to the problems which arise from working with this substance.

Modeling with Clay

Modeling is another activity in which school children in all stages of development may participate. Clay has been a standard modeling medium in the schools for many years, while comparatively recently asbestos powder has come to be fairly popular. Special quick-drying clay for school use is also on the market.

Three-Dimensional Modeling in Clay

MEDIA AND TECHNIQUES: Clay may be purchased or it may be found in the ground in some localities, especially along lakes, bays, or small creeks. Any slippery, soapy earth having a red, blue, or whitish tinge and adhering tenaciously to the hands is probably clay. If in doubt, one can send a specimen of the earth to a government agricultural agency for analysis. Working with the earth, however, will soon reveal whether or not it is suitable for modeling. Natural clay must usually be refined before it can be used as a modeling medium. If dry, it should be powdered and put through a sieve to remove lumps, pebbles, and other foreign matter. If wet, one must roll and knead it on a porous slab or "bat," breaking lumps with the hands and removing foreign substances as they come to the surface. A suitable porous bat consists of plaster of Paris prepared in the manner outlined previously.

When purchased, dry standard clay is usually packaged in fifty- or one-hundred-pound bags. To prepare this clay for use, water should be poured over about half a pail of clay and mixed in with a spoon. It takes about five quarts of warm water to soak thoroughly twenty-five pounds of dry clay. A tablespoon of vinegar added to the water will neutralize any alkaline con-

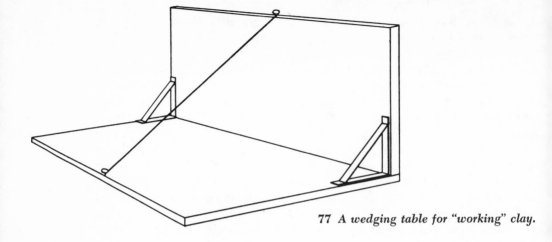

77 *A wedging table for "working" clay.*

tent and make it easier on the hands. After the clay has settled overnight, any excess water can be poured off. Some firms now sell wet clay in large cans or plastic bags, which both eliminates the need to dampen and overcomes some storage difficulties.

Before modeling can be successfully performed, the refined and dampened clay should be kneaded and rolled on the porous surface until it is almost rubbery. When a coil of it can be twisted and bent so that it neither breaks readily nor adheres unpleasantly to the hands, it is ready for modeling. To assist in "working" the clay to this necessary condition, a piece of apparatus called a "wedging table," illustrated in Fig. 77, is useful. The wedging table consists merely of two boards about one-half an inch thick, or five-ply wood, fixed at right angles to each other with screws. Brackets strengthen this assembly. The measurements of each board should be at least 18 by 24 inches. A length of strong but fine wire should be attached from the top center of the upright board to about the outside center of the lower board.

Wedging is done to make the clay uniformly moist and free from air bubbles. A lump of clay is cut by pressing it into the wire. The resulting two pieces are then thrown with force onto the surface of the wedging table or slapped together. This process is continued until no tiny bubble holes are to be seen in the cut clay.

A reasonably large quantity of clay for modeling may be prepared in advance and stored for a short time in airtight tins or earthenware containers. Indeed, this storing tends to make it more workable. Small pieces of clay for each pupil may subsequently be cut away by means of a wire.

Used clay can often be reclaimed by soaking it in water for about 48 hours. When the clay appears workable again it may be put back in the covered container.

The youngest children are incapable of preparing the clay for modeling, so that this task must be performed by the teacher. For this reason some teachers have turned to asbestos powder or the commercially prepared oil clays (such as Plasticine). While these substances can be substituted, actually nothing can entirely replace natural, water-based clay as a modeling medium.

Before the children work with clay or other modeling materials, the working surfaces should be protected with newspapers, sheets of cardboard, or oilcloth. The children will find it convenient to model the clay on a board placed on the protective covering. While working on the board, the children can turn it to view the sculpture from all sides.

No tools of any kind are necessary for modeling. Modeling in clay and other materials is essentially an activity for the fingers. However, sets of tools are available which assist more experienced children to produce details in their pieces. A small pointed stick, the size of a lollypop stick, is also handy at times. A damp sponge or cloth is useful to moisten the fingers and partially to clean them at the close of the activity.

The child's stage of development in pictorial work will be reflected in his output in clay as seen in Fig. 78a and b. The youngest and most inexperienced children will be satisfied with a short period of manipulation, after which the clay is left in a shape resembling nothing in particular. Later, the children may give a name to shapes of this kind. Still later, the symbols associated with drawing and painting may appear in the clay in three-dimensional form. Finally, the preadolescent refines a symbol in contour and detail and may relate it to another or others in the same composition.

There is no one manner recommended for modeling. Children begin to model naturally with considerable energy, enthusiasm, and, usually, dexterity. Given a piece of clay weighing from one-half a pound for kindergarten and first-grade pupils to two pounds for those in higher grades, the child will squeeze, stroke, pinch, punch, and pat it until he is satisfied with the results.

The younger children tend to "draw out" from a central mass of clay to form features, such as legs, arms, and head of an object they are representing. As they gain experience, one notices the tendency in them to add pieces to the central mass.[4]

---

[4] Viktor Lowenfeld, *Creative and Mental Growth* (N.Y.: Macmillan, 1952), p. 308, discusses such differences of approach. He suggests that they depend largely upon the mental type of the worker. One cannot help feeling that perhaps Lowenfeld tends to neglect the influence upon technique of the characteristics of the material being used and of the personal changes in the pupil as a result of maturation.

78a *Symbols in clay by first-grade pupils.*

The finished product in clay must be a solid, compact composition. If the child, as he gains confidence in the medium, attempts to form slender protuberances, they usually fall off and he quickly learns not to draw out the clay too far from the central mass. He may add little pellets of clay for, say, eyes and buttons, but even these must be kept reasonably flat if they are to adhere to the main body of the clay. The use of watery clay, or "slip," may help him to fix these extra pieces. Slip is prepared by mixing some of the clay used in the modeling with water until the mixture has the consistency of thick cream. The worker "scores," or roughens, the two surfaces to be stuck together with the teeth of a comb, a knitting needle, or a pointed stick and then paints or dabs on slip with the fingers before pressing the pieces together.

If worked on too long, the clay becomes too dry to manipulate. In order to keep the clay sufficiently moist, it should first be wrapped in a damp cloth over which is wrapped a rubber or plastic sheet, and, if possible, the whole should be placed in a covered tin until it is to be worked again. When the work is finished and left on a shelf to dry, it should be dampened from time to time with water applied with a paint brush. By this means the small protuberences will be prevented from drying before the main body of the work and hence have less tendency to crack or drop off.

In some forms of advanced modeling, malleable wires called "armatures" are sometimes fixed to a base and then twisted into the general outline of the object as it is conceived in the mind of the artist. These devices are a convenience to the experienced person because once they have been arranged, the clay can be built up around them to form a more delicate open type of work. For most elementary school children, however, the use of armatures is too difficult. It is wise in the elementary school to model without armatures, except in cases where the child exhibits a marked ability in clay work. The simple, solid mass of unsupported clay is challenging enough for most young children and results in a wide variety of significant output. However, a small pointed stick can be thrust up from the base of the partially completed object to assist in keeping, say, a head erect.

TEACHING: The teacher must concern himself especially with the preparation of the clay, the physical arrangements for handling it in the classroom, and the subject matter selected by the children. Preparation of the clay must be done entirely correctly if the work is to be successful. The directions given earlier must, therefore, be carefully observed. Next, unless physical arrangements in the classroom are carefully planned, the classroom will be-

78b *Preadolescents' clay work which has been glazed and fired.*

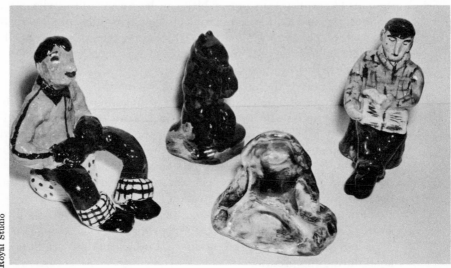

Royal Studio

come impossibly messy. Third, only certain types of subject matter can be handled with success with this medium. If the children choose unsuitable subject matter, their work cannot possibly be successful. When clay work is being done, the teacher's duties thus are onerous. However, these extra-heavy duties are worthwhile. Children have much to gain from a manipulation of clay, provided that the teacher is well prepared professionally for the activity.

For the youngest children, the teacher must prepare the clay himself. For the older children, he should give step-by step instructions, followed by carefully supervised activity on the preparation of the medium.

The room and its furnishings must be adequately protected from clay dust and particles. The teacher should ask each child to spread newspaper on the floor under the place where he works. Desks or tables on which the work is performed should be covered with oilcloth, rubber, or plastic sheeting, or with more paper. Many cleaning cloths dampened with water should be readily at hand, and the pupils should be taught to use them when the work is in progress and when it is finished. The pupils must also learn to pick up the protective coverings, both newsprint and oilcloth, carefully so that clay particles are not left on desks or floor. The teacher can scarcely overemphasize neatness when clay is being used in the classroom.

Subject matter for modeling in clay is somewhat restricted. Usually it involves one person or thing, or at the most two persons or things resolved into a closely knit composition. Only objects or shapes which are "chunky" and solid can be successfully rendered. Thus the human figure and certain animals like squirrels or pigs, which can be successfully stylized into a solid composition, are more suitable subjects than naturally spindly creatures such as giraffes, spiders, and flamingos. Discussion regarding the need to select a subject in keeping with the character of clay must take place in the classroom before the pupils begin work.

Often, before the actual modeling occurs, the teacher will be obliged to demonstrate some of the techniques of handling clay, especially for preadolescent pupils, who wish to arrive at a more exact representation of the objects they are fashioning. Included among the demonstrations will be the two chief methods of modeling; namely, pulling out from a central mass and shaping or welding, in which prepared pieces such as arms and legs are scored and treated with slip. The use of some modeling tools to produce details may also require demonstration.

Finally, good teachers will see that adequate shelves are provided for storing clay work. They should carefully supervise each child as he stores his work and make sure that the products of other children are in no way damaged during the process.

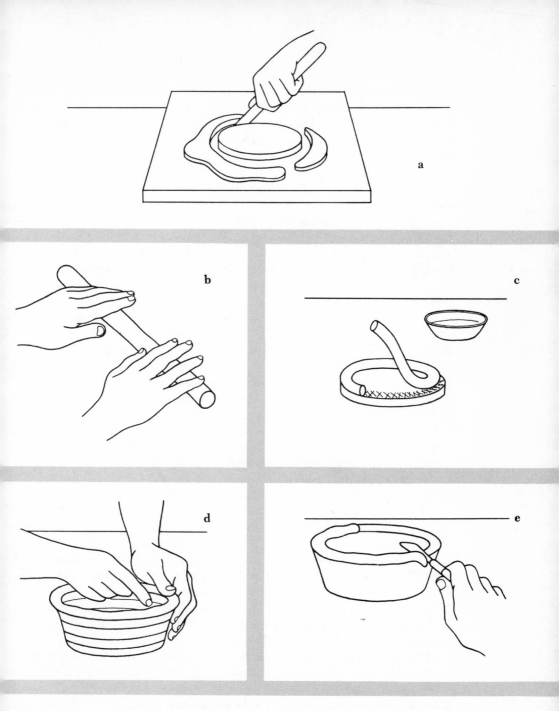

79 *The coil method of pottery showing* (*a*) *trimming the base,* (*b*) *rolling the coil,* (*c*) *applying the coil,* (*d*) *smoothing the coil, and* (*e*) *trimming the lip.*

Pottery

MEDIA AND TECHNIQUES: Pottery is a form of clay modeling in which the children in the symbol stage will make play "dishes" by hollowing a solid lump of clay. Preadolescents are capable of what are called the "coil" and "slab" methods. Using the potter's wheel is usually beyond the capabilities of most children in the elementary school.

In producing coil pottery (see Fig. 79a-e), the child will find it most convenient to work on a bat of plaster. A ball of clay is flattened to the bat until it is about half an inch thick. Then it is trimmed with a knife to the desired size, usually about three to five inches in diameter. A coil of clay about half an inch in diameter is next produced by rolling the medium between the hands. The coil is then applied to the edge of the base, which should be scored and dampened with slip so that adhesion between base and coil is assured. The coil should then be pinched to the base. A second coil is then built upon the first, in the same way. No more than three coils should be made in one day lest the assembly collapse under its own weight. After letting it dry for a day, the pupil may add another three coils. This goes on each day until the bowl has reached a required height.

The position of the coils will determine the shape of the bowl. By placing a coil slightly on the outside of the one beneath it, the pupil may flare the bowl. By placing it towards the inside, he will diminish the bowl in diameter. While a perfectly uniform bowl is not expected, nor indeed altogether desirable, it is necessary to examine the rising edges from all angles to see that the shape of the object is reasonably symmetrical. A template, or contour, cut in cardboard may be applied to the side of the bowl, but this technique is frowned upon by many people for the very good reason that it is mechanical and rather extraneous to the process of coil pottery.

When the outlines of the bowl are formed, the pupil should smooth both its inside and its outside with his fingers. Dipping the fingers in slip while the smoothing is taking place is often helpful. The lip of the bowl should be flattened or tapered and perhaps trimmed with a wire tool or knife. The bowl should then be cut away from the slab by means of a wire. Its edges may then be gently smoothed with the fingers.

The slab method, as shown in Fig. 80a-d, involves the assembly of a number of flat pieces of clay to form a box. Well-prepared clay is rolled flat, like pastry, with a bottle or rolling pin which rests upon wooden guides. The base of the object being made is then cut to size, as are sides and ends. A coil of clay is prepared after the ends of the sides and edges of the base are scored and dabbed with slip where they are to be joined. A side is put in place and reinforced on the inside by the coil which has also been pre-

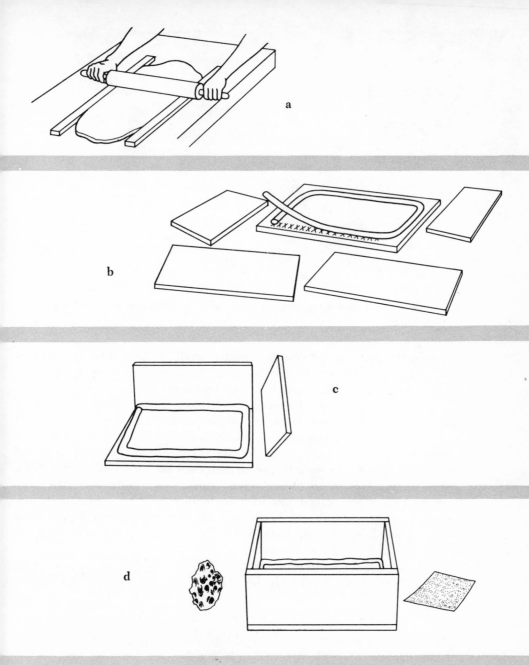

80 *The slab method of making pottery, showing (a) the preparation of the clay, (b) placement of the supporting coil, (c) application of the sides, and (d) sponge and sandpaper for smoothing the sides.*

81 *Some ways of making designs in clay, using a comb, a spoon, and a piece of fire-brick.*

pared with slip. This process is repeated until all four sides are pressed firmly in place in an upright position. Fine sandpaper or a damp sponge may be used to make the sides smoother once the object is dry.

TEACHING: Little further need be said about the teaching necessary for the production of pottery. However, two important demonstrations peculiar to the slab method of construction will be necessary. First is the method of rolling clay flat. The teacher should take a ball of well-prepared clay and flatten it to about three-quarters of an inch thick on a piece of rubber sheeting or plastic. Two pieces of wood about one-quarter to three-eighths of an inch thick should be placed parallel to each other along two opposite boundaries of the flattened clay. A bottle or rolling pin should travel over these pieces of wood until the thickness of the clay has been rolled to a thickness equal to that of the strips of wood.

The second demonstration involves sticking the sides of the box to its base. This process has already been described and requires no further comment.

Finishing Clay Objects

MEDIA AND TECHNIQUES: Several techniques may be used to decorate objects made of clay. These include glazing, incising, painting with engobe (colored slip), and pressing with various objects. A combined technique known as "sgraffito" is also used. Painting clay with tempera or water color and shellac is also done.

To glaze clay successfully, many steps must be taken which demand the exercise of skill based upon experience. First, the raw clay must be especially carefully wedged to remove air bubbles. Next, after the modeling is done, the object must be dried thoroughly, often in artificially heated cabinets. Then a kiln or oven must be skillfully stacked with the pieces for what is called the "biscuit," or preliminary firing, during which varying temperatures must be maintained before, during, and after the firing. The first firing successfully completed, one must then apply the glazes, of which there are at least five distinct types, stack the kiln in such a way as to prevent the glaze on one object from interfering with that on another, and go through a second process of firing and cooling. While producing lovely results, glazing is a formidable process and few people can learn how to do it merely by reading a book on the subject. To learn how to glaze competently, one should enroll in a workshop under the guidance of a ceramics expert. Under such conditions, glazing is not too difficult to master in a reasonably short period. A month's course at night school or at a summer school allows ample time for a mature student to become reasonably proficient at this fascinating craft.

Incising merely involves the scoring of marks in the clay with a knitting needle, sharp hard pencil, or some other object. The clay must be partly

82 *Some examples of the sgraffito technique by sixth-grade pupils.*

Royal Studio

dried before incising can take place. Any one of a number of objects ranging from nails to pieces of comb and keys can be repeatedly pressed into fairly moist clay to make an interesting pattern, particularly after the second firing.

Engobe, or colored slip, is underglaze pigment, a teaspoonful of which is added to twice that quantity of finely powdered dry clay. The same clay used in the model must be used in engobe. After the dry pigment and clay have been well mixed, water is added until the mixture resembles a thick cream. A few drops of glycerine makes the engobe flow readily. Commercially prepared engobe is available from school supply houses. Painting is done with a sable brush on fairly dry clay. When the painted clay is dry, it must be fired twice as described earlier.

Sgraffito involves both incising and painting with engobe. Engobe in a color contrasting with the clay on which it is being applied is painted onto the partly dried object. Two coats are applied, the first by brushing constantly in one direction, the second by brushing constantly in another direction. When the engobe coats have dried, lines are incised through them—usually with a stick—to the clay before firing the object.

Painting with tempera or water-color on clay must be done when it is dry. When the paint is dry, it is covered with shellac.

TEACHING: The finishing of clay objects produced by elementary school children places the teacher in an educational and artistic dilemma. As D'Amico says in speaking of pottery, glazing is the "crowning experience" of the craft.[5] More than that, glazing is the only really acceptable finish for clay. While clay will take paint, which may in turn be covered with shellac or varnish to give it a shine, such a finish does not incorporate itself with clay and tends to make the best of work look cheap and tawdry. On the other hand, while children can paint clay easily enough, most of them cannot successfully fire it without help from the teacher. So much help is required, in fact, that the children must usually surrender their control of this activity to an adult.

Teachers have attempted to solve the dilemma arising from the finishing of clay products in several ways. Some tell the children that it is impossible for them to fire and glaze their work at the present time, but that they might try pressing a design into it or incising one. The decorated object is then preserved in its natural form. Often teachers glaze for each child one or two examples on which he has used an engobe, sgraffito, or other technique which the teacher has demonstrated. Others show the children how to coat

---

[5] Victor D'Amico, *Creative Teaching in Art,* Rev. Ed. (Scranton, Pa.: International Textbook, 1953), p. 140. This book contains, among others, excellent chapters on sculpture and pottery, but largely for teachers and older students.

83 *A wire sculpture in a wooden base by a
sixth-grade boy.*

the work with shellac and explain that this is merely a makeshift; this fact
may be emphasized by calling the children's attention to some well-glazed
pieces. Still other teachers, having explained that not all the steps in glazing
can be taken by the children themselves, go ahead with glazing but take
every opportunity to let the children do whatever lies within their competence. Thus a young child might at first only paint his bowl with engobe but
later might help to stack the kiln. None of these alternatives is wholly satisfactory, but, owing to the nature of the problem which the finishing of clay
presents, one would apparently be wrong to condemn any of them.

Wire Sculpture

MEDIA AND TECHNIQUES: Sculpture in wire, shown in Fig. 83, is a practical activity for all but children in the manipulative stage. Wire lends itself
to the creation of a composition which depends largely upon a continuous line.

The wire should be malleable, that is to say, when bent into any position, it should stay there. Copper or aluminum wire, or wires made of alloys
of these elements, is suitable. The tools necessary include snips to cut the

wire, long-nosed pliers to manipulate it, and a drill to bore holes in a base for the sculpture to stand in.

TEACHING: No very great difficulties are encountered in teaching this work and children should be strongly encouraged to approach the activity experimentally. A teacher might demonstrate with a length of wire how it can be bent and then generally leave the children to continue making their own discoveries. The first bends may be made with the hands, while later the details might be added with pliers. When the desired shape appears, the teacher might suggest that either one or both ends of the wire be placed in a base sufficiently heavy to support the sculpture. At first, the children might be encouraged to use clay for a base, but the suggestion could be made to the older pupils that a more satisfactory base and a pleasant contrast to the wire is a piece of wood in which holes have been drilled. By polishing the wire with an appropriate metal cleaner and the wood with wax, the pupils learn to finish the sculpture so that it shines in an attractive fashion.

After further experimentation, children may use two separate pieces of wire effectively. They might also discover interesting ways of adding some other pieces of wood to the assembly, together with fine copper wire screening.

This craft is a relatively delicate one. It requires no special equipment and it makes little mess, except perhaps in the preparation of the wooden bases. The teacher meets no outstanding problems in arranging the classroom for the work involved.

Some Substitute Materials

As mentioned earlier, there is no actual substitute for natural clay. Quick-hardening clay may be used, however, and while only approximating the natural substance, has the advantage of hardening without firing. This clay may be purchased from supply houses, together with special paints to coat finished work. These paints, in the opinion of most people, are very much a second-best when compared with a true glaze.

Plasticine, the previously mentioned mixture of oil and clay, is always rather sticky and is considered unsanitary if one piece is used by several children. It cannot take any kind of finish but it models reasonably well.

Asbestos powder, which is different from clay, is a practical medium for modeling. The dry powder may be purchased in sacks from hardware stores at a reasonable cost. Before being used, it must be mixed with school paste in the proportion of five parts of powder to one of paste. When the mixture is dampened to the point where it is like dough, it may be modeled in a manner similar to that used with clay. After drying, the objects produced in this medium may be painted with tempera and later coated with shellac.

As a substitute carving material, some schools make use of soap. While some interesting sculpture may be produced in this substance, it is not to be highly recommended. Because of the sizes in which soap is available, subjects must be worked in miniature. Furthermore, it tends to break. It would seem that soap should be used for sculpture only if the better materials previously discussed are impossible to obtain, and then only by more mature pupils. The most satisfactory soap for carving is the soft laundry type, rather than brittle toilet soap.

ACTIVITIES FOR THE READER

1. Survey the district around your school for materials suitable for sculpture and modeling. Is there any clay, wood, or wire to be had? Test the materials according to the suggestions found in this chapter under the subheadings "Media and techniques."

2. Make a point of getting to know an efficient industrial arts teacher. If he knows his business, he will be only too happy to talk about wood. Ask him questions about the types of woods and their various properties, seasoning wood, hand and power tools for woodworking, the care of tools (including sharpening), and finishes for wood.

Ask for demonstrations of some of the processes associated with woodworking. Seek advice about brands of tools and types of sharpening stones.

Paint a picture for him as a bribe and then ask him for scraps of wood. He may "sand" them smooth for you.

3. Go to a good furniture store and make a note of the different types of finishes. Speak to the industrial arts man if you do not understand some of them.

4. Glue scraps of wood together to form a piece of sculpture. Smooth the surfaces of the sculpture with medium, then fine sandpaper. Wax the sculpture and then polish it with a soft cloth to a point where it glows. Ordinary solid floor wax is suitable.

5. Experiment with various kinds of wood by cutting them with a heavy pocket-knife. (Keep the knife sharp by rubbing it gently over a fine oilstone.) When you find wood which you like to cut, plan either in your mind's eye, or in a pencil sketch on paper first and then on the wood, a nonobjective design which you intend to cut. Start cutting, turning the wood from time to time so that you cut

from all angles. Cut away from you and keep your other hand behind the cutting edge. Study the developing design for unity and variety of the elements. If you would like to put some holes in the wood (like Henry Moore) to get three-dimensional effects, you will have to use a large drill or brace-and-bit. (Ask your industrial arts friend.) When the carving more or less satisfies you, put it gently in a vise and start filing it smooth. Sometimes sculptors protect their work from the jaws of the vise by placing pieces of wood between the sculpture and the jaws. Let the file "bite" by pushing it away from you. Finish with medium and fine sandpaper and, finally, polish with about a dozen coats of wax.

6. Do some wood sculpture, this time using a set of wood-carving tools and an objective theme such as a human torso, a head, or a full figure. Keep the tools sharp, the work "chunky," and continue to be careful of your noncutting hand.[6]

7. Select a flat piece of solid gumwood or pine. Practice with carving tools by making some V-cuts with two strokes of a knife, making a vertical cut and removing pieces of wood by gouging towards the first cut, gouging a circular depression, creating many different textural effects by cutting, chipping, and gouging.

8. After performing (7), above, plan an objective composition—say, a group of three human figures, or some leaves or flowers of your locality. Sketch the main outline of your composition upon a piece of wood no smaller than about 6 by 8 inches. Try for interesting textures. Finish with wax.

9. Cast a plaque about 6 by 9 inches in plaster of Paris. Carve a nonobjective design in the plaque based upon overlapping oblongs and squares. In some areas devise textural effects by cutting or gouging. Tint some areas with water color.

10. Cast a block of plaster of Paris about 2 by 2 by 8 inches. Plan an objective subject (a torso is excellent) and carve it out of the block.

11. Model a nonobjective shape in clay; model an objective form in clay.

12. Enroll in a clay workshop under the guidance of an expert in ceramics. Learn something about pottery of various kinds, decorating pottery, firing, and glazing.[7]

---

[6] See Ruth Green Harris, *Techniques of Sculpture* (N.Y.: Harper, 1942).

[7] See Julia Hamlin Duncan and Victor D'Amico, *How to Make Pottery and Ceramic Sculpture* (N.Y.: Museum of Modern Art, 1947).

13.   Go to a hardware store and ask to see samples of malleable wire. Buy a few feet of different sizes and types. Using only the hands, bend some of the kinds of wire into nonobjective shapes. Then, with pliers, try to fashion the outline of some objects in wire such as flowers, leaves, or animals. Watch your rhythms.

14.   Plan a piece of nonobjective wire sculpture in which you use some fine copper wire screen as well as at least two types and sizes of wire—say, heavy copper and fine aluminum wire. Work out the main rhythms with the wire. Then add some screen areas to the composition. The screen pieces may be cut with shears or heavy scissors and finally fixed in place with a clear plastic cement or by weaving the wire through the screen. Watch for variety of rhythms and screen areas. Be careful of your centers of interest.

10

Printing

This chapter concentrates largely upon the printing processes in which a paint or a dye is spread upon a prepared surface which in turn is pressed upon another surface. Printing includes the production of pictures and patterns of various types which are developed by a repetition of design unit or motifs.

The printing processes exert especially strong influences upon printing design, and the treatment of subject matter often requires considerable modification to suit the technique. Compared with printing, drawing and painting, paper work, and sculpture and modeling are largely direct activities. Printing is indirect, in the sense that one does something to one substance in order to produce an effect upon another substance. Between the child and the finished printed product, in other words, lies a whole series of moves with intermediary materials which must be completed successfully before the product itself appears.

Printing is, therefore, a relatively complicated art process for the young and raises a number of questions about the selection of subject matter and the influences of technique upon design. However, printing techniques have been invented which lie within the capabilities of most school children. These include monoprinting and vegetable and "stick" printing which children at all stages can do successfully. Even the intricacies of linoleum-block printing can be mastered by the preadolescent from the fourth grade up.

84 *"The Loon"—a monoprint by a sixth-grade boy, showing excellent treatment of white, textured, and dark areas.*

This chapter will include a description of all these types of printing. In addition, stenciling will be discussed since, although this is not strictly a form of printing, it is closely allied to it and makes use of many of the materials required to produce printed art forms. Most preadolescents are capable of stenciling.

Monoprinting

MEDIA AND TECHNIQUES: The printing technique most closely related to drawing and painting and to which any child may transfer some of his abilities in picture-making is called monoprinting, illustrated in Fig. 85. The supplies required are a sheet of glass with the edges taped to avoid the danger of cutting the hands. As an alternative to glass, a piece of linoleum may be used measuring about six by eight inches and preferably glued to a slab of wood. Also required are a rubber roller about two inches to six inches in length called a "brayer," some water-soluble ink in a range perhaps of brown, blue, white, and black, and finally newsprint or other reasonably ab-

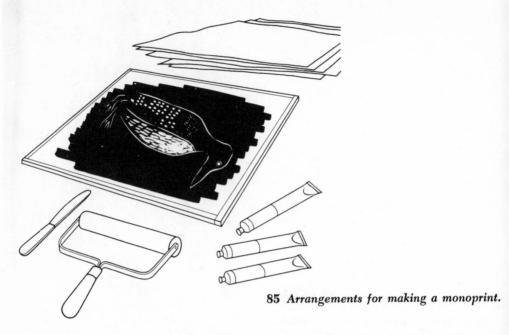

sorbent paper. Brayers and water-soluble inks made especially for this work are sold by several school supply firms.

The ink is squeezed from its tube upon the surface of the glass or linoleum and then rolled evenly over the surface. More than one color may be used if desired. If two colors are used, for example, they may be dabbed onto the glass and then blended lightly with the brayer. Another method is to mix the colors lightly with a palette knife before rolling. Each technique produces its own effect.

The drawing can be produced with almost any implement capable of making a strong mark in ink. The eraser end of a pencil, a piece of cardboard and a broad pen point are but a few of the suitable tools. The drawing, which is made directly in the ink, must be kept bold because the inked surfaces are not sympathetic to fine details. Obviously, only the ink remaining upon the surface will be recorded in the final printing (see Fig. 84).

For the printing, a sheet of paper should be placed gently over the prepared inky surface and pressed to it with the tips of the fingers, unless an inexpensive press for this purpose is available. A clean brayer rolled evenly over the paper also produces a good print. The completed print may then be gently peeled away. Sometimes two or three impressions may be taken from one drawing. By using papers with varying textures an interesting variety of prints will be achieved.

Another method of monoprinting is as follows. The glass is covered with ink in the usual manner. The paper is then placed gently over the inked glass. Next the pupil draws with a pencil on the upper side of the paper. The resulting print is a composition of dark lines with some imprint of ink on the background areas.

Monoprinting may also be done by arranging objects such as string, a piece of wire screen, burlap, or scraps of cardboard with a reasonably pronounced texture on a clean glass. Newsprint is placed over the arrangement and an inked brayer is run over the paper to obtain a print.

TEACHING: Three main tasks confront the teacher of monoprinting. The first is to arrange furniture, tools, and supplies so that printing may be done conveniently; the second is to see that the ink does not get all over the children and the room; and the third is to give stimulating demonstrations and continued encouragement.

Printing should be done on a long table covered with newspapers or oilcloth. At one end of the table, the teacher should arrange the glass, brayers, and inks. Several such stations for printing might be set up and a definite order of pupils to print established. Since it would be uneconomical for each pupil to have a set of printing equipment, the pupils who are not printing should know what other activities are available for them. As each pupil is doing his printing, the teacher should direct him to place the prints carefully on the remaining table space. When the printing is complete, the teacher should encourage the children to select those which they consider most interesting. When dry, these prints should be taken away for pressing between the leaves of a heavy book or with a warm iron.

As can be imagined, a large amount of ink comes off on the children's hands. Therefore the teacher must insist that each pupil either wash his hands continually or at least wipe them on a damp cloth. This means that unless the classroom has a sink, the teacher must make sure that pails of water, soap, and towels or damp cloths are handy.

The teacher should demonstrate efficiently all methods of monoprinting. While the techniques are simple enough, he would be wise to practice before the lesson since monoprinting can be very messy unless one has had some previous experience with the work. If the teacher appears clumsy during the demonstration, he may anticipate having a very inky classroom once the children begin to experiment. Neatness, on the other hand, seems to beget neatness.

The selection of subject matter creates no special problems for the teacher. When the children draw on the glass or the paper, as indicated in

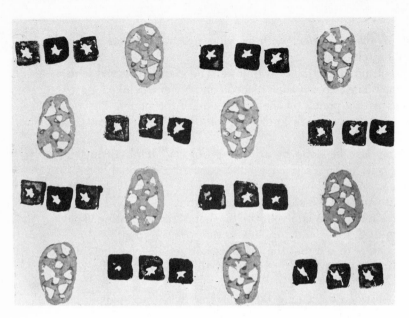

86 *Potato printing by a fourth-grade boy. Two colors were used.*

the first two methods, the kinds of subjects they use will be the same as those associated with ordinary picture-making. When objects are placed on the glass, as in the last method, the work will usually be nonobjective.

Pupils find monoprinting challenging and stimulating. Once they know how to begin, they are eager to discover all the possibilities of this technique. It is a valuable activity not only because it demands spontaneous work, but also because it gives children a reasonably accurate idea of the printing process in general.

Vegetable and Stick Printing

MEDIA AND TECHNIQUES: All children can produce work in the technique called vegetable printing, while nearly every child once he reaches the symbol stage can print with sticks (see Figs. 86 and 87).

First, the beginner should select a piece of a vegetable such as cabbage, carrot, potato, or celery. The piece should be large enough for the young child to grasp easily and should be cut flat on one side or end. All the child does is dip the flat side of the vegetable into water color, tempera paint, or colored ink and dab it on a sheet of newsprint. The child in the manipulative stage at first dabs at random, but later he controls the pattern until he develops a rhythmic order of units. Fruit rinds or sponges of various kinds may also be used in printing.

The next step in technique is to control the design by cutting into the end of the vegetable. The best vegetable for this purpose is a crisp potato, but carrots are also suitable. The potato should be sliced in half and the design cut into it with a knife. If a different shape design is wanted, the printing surface can be trimmed into a square. Water or tempera color may then be painted over the designed end, after which printing on paper may begin.

Organized all-over patterns may be produced by means of vegetable printing. If precision of pattern is desired, it is usually necessary to rule the surface to to be printed with guide lines.

Sticks to be used for printing should be selected from any soft wood such as pine and should measure from one-half inch to two inches square at the end by six inches long. The beginners will use only the uncut stick. When children can prepare sticks for themselves, sometimes in the first grade and usually in the second grade, they should do so. The design for the printing end of the stick may be made with a pocketknife or a three-sided file. (A file is a safer tool than a knife for first-graders.) The end of the stick may be left

87 Stick printing by a fifth-grade boy. Two colors were used. The cuts were made with a knife.

square, of course, or may be made round. These end shapes may be altered by filing either the sides adjacent to the end or the end of the stick itself or by cutting grooves in them with a knife (see Fig. 88a).

The technique of printing is similar to that used with vegetable printing and may be done on paper or textile. Newprint is suitably absorbent and will react favorably to tempera or water color. The stick may be charged with color by dipping the end in paint, or the paint may be applied to it with a brush. Some experimenting may have to be done before the right consistency of paint is found. Usually tempera paint must be thinner for stick printing than for picture-making.

Printer's ink, which may be purchased from school supply firms, may be used if designs are printed on cloth, but since the ink is not soluble in water, only more experienced preadolescent children should use it. (A textile printed with this ink may be washed in soap and water.) If necessary, the printer's ink may be thinned with copal varnish or a thinning medium such as turpentine. Turpentine must also be used to clean the sticks periodically during and after the printing. Before printing on textile takes place, it is advisable to lay the fabric over a soft surface such as felt or many layers of paper so that the color readily penetrates the textile.

TEACHING: If only printing on paper is planned, the teacher will not be faced with the problem of providing special accommodation. Printing on textile with sticks, however, will necessitate the preparation of a printing surface. A suitable surface would be a table covered with felt. The edge of the covering should be tacked on the underside of the table to prevent it from slipping. If papers are used, they might be covered with cotton sheeting, also tacked like the felt (see Fig. 88b).

If printer's ink is used, the turpentine needed with it is most safely stored in, and dispensed from, tins. A little turpentine for washing sticks should be put into another tin can, perhaps the standard type which is used for vegetables or fruit. Cloths must be plentiful but should always be placed in a tin container after use. Since they are highly inflammable, the school caretaker should be warned of their presence so that he may dispose of them at the close of the day.

Because the techniques involved in vegetable and stick printing are interesting, the teacher will probably have no problems associated with motivation. His chief task is to encourage every child to explore the numerous possibilities of the process. The children should be encouraged to find and use many vegetables and other objects suitable for printing. When controlled cutting is used, the teacher could suggest that not merely a knife, but spoons, forks, and other implements may also be used to cut the ends of vegetables so that different designs may result. The teacher should also suggest that

88a Sticks for stick printing: plain, cut, and filed.

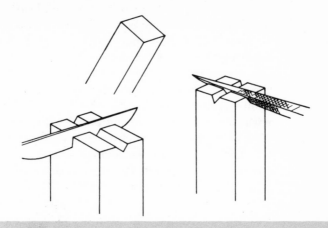

88b Arrangements for stick printing on textile with printer's ink.

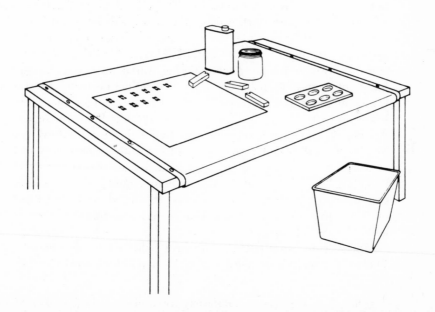

background papers for these types of printing can be especially prepared with thin color laid down with a wide brush. Also, the teacher should note that backgrounds may be prepared with a large vegetable such as a cabbage sliced in half, as described earlier, over which the potato with the controlled cut may be used for printing in a contrasting color.

Stick printing should be made equally challenging. The pupils should use several sticks having different designs upon one printing surface. Also, combinations of colors should be tested. Backgrounds should be painted with thin water color or patterned with vegetables, sponges, or even crumpled balls of paper which have been dipped in thin paint.

Few, if any, problems will arise over subject matter since only nonobjective or highly abstract patterns can result from this work and since the techniques lend themselves to repeated patterns rather than to picture-making.

Linoleum Cutting and Printing

MEDIA AND TECHNIQUES: A linoleum print, as shown in Fig. 89, results when linoleum has had pieces cut out of it, has been inked, and, finally, has been pressed to a suitably absorbent surface. The parts not cut away create the pattern. The technique involves the use of sharp tools, some physical strength particularly in the fingers, and an ability to perform several operations of a relatively delicate nature. Only the more mature preadolescents in the fourth, fifth and sixth grades, therefore, will be capable of this work.

The usual heavy floor covering with a burlap backing is suitable for linoleum printing. It may be purchased from furniture and hardware stores or from firms which lay floor covering. Linoleum comes in large sizes, but scraps of it may often be obtained at a reduction from the standard price. Conveniently small pieces may be cut from a larger piece by scoring the linoleum with a knife and then bending it.[1] The linoleum snaps apart where it is scored and then it remains only to cut through the burlap with a knife. The pupils will find it convenient but not entirely necessary to fix the piece of linoleum to be carved to a block of five-ply wood the exact size of the linoleum. The burlap side of the linoleum should be smeared with a strong carpenter's glue, then pressed against the wood, and held firmly in a press until the glue is dry. Linoleum blocks may also be purchased with the linoleum already affixed to the wood.

Sets of linoleum cutters and short holders for them may be purchased. These sets consist of straight knives, V-shaped tools, and U-gouges of varying

---

[1] At first, 3″ x 4″ pieces are satisfactory; later, pieces as large as 6″ x 8″ can be used; and in sixth grade, pieces can be even larger.

89 *"The Big Tree"—a linoleum print by a sixth-grade boy.*

sizes. The knife and gouges are perhaps the most effective tools, although the V-tool is capable of producing some highly sensitive lines and interesting textural effects. A sharp pocketknife is also a handy tool to use in this work. It is especially important to keep the tools sharp, and for this purpose a specially shaped oilstone may be bought.

The ink for linoleum printing on paper may be water-soluble. Almost any reasonably absorbent paper will be suitable, from inexpensive newsprint to the costly but delightful Japanese printing paper. Even the paper tissues used for blowing one's nose take a good impression from the linoleum. For printing on textiles, an oil-base or printer's ink is necessary. Many textiles, including cottons, linens, and silks, will be found practical for printing provided their textures are not rough.

A few other supplies are also necessary—rubber rollers or brayers, a sheet of plate glass for a palette, and, for printing on textiles, a mallet. A small printing press, while not necessary, is always a welcome luxury for printing on paper.

In cutting the linoleum, many people use the V-tool to make a preliminary outline of the main areas of the composition. When using this tool, one will discover that it is often more convenient to move the block against the

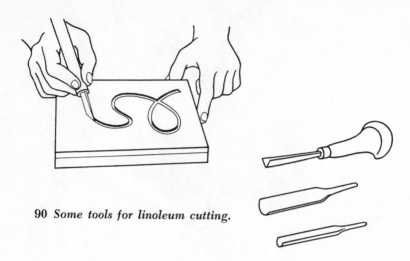

90 *Some tools for linoleum cutting.*

tool than the reverse. A straight knife is also an efficient tool for making the preliminary outlines, but if a knife is used, two cuts to form a V must usually be made. After the outlines have been inscribed, the white areas in the composition may then be conveniently cleared away with gouges. If any textural effects are required in these areas, the linoleum should be cut so that some ridges are left. If, however, the worker wishes the areas to print pure white, the linoleum should be gouged out almost to the burlap backing. Various kinds of "gray" or textured areas may be made by carving parallel lines, crosshatching lines, or removing "pecks" of linoleum with the V-tool.

The pupil may sometimes find it convenient to take rubbings of his work from time to time to appraise his progress. To do this, he should place a thin sheet of paper over the linoleum and, holding it firmly, should scribble with a soft pencil across the treated surface.

While no formula may be offered here, or to the pupils, regarding a successful linoleum cut, it may be observed that a composition which displays some white, some black, and some gray or textured areas will prove to be particularly interesting.

When the pupil finds the linoleum cut satisfactory, he will wish to pull an impression of it. Before printing on paper takes place, it is wise to dampen all but the softest tissues with a sponge. After the paper has been dampened, it should be placed between blotting paper so that excess moisture is taken away. Then, using the brayer, the pupil coats the brayer by rolling water-soluble ink evenly over the glass palette. After this, with long sweeps of the

91 *One way to mount a linoleum print.*

brayer and working in several directions, he should coat the linoleum evenly with ink. The dampened paper, or dry tissue, should then be placed over the linoleum and this in turn covered with a sheet of blotting paper. Then the covering paper should be pressed and rubbed gently with the hands until contact between the block and the paper is satisfactory. The back of a large spoon rubbed carefully over the paper assists in this process. The print may then be peeled away from the block, and to prevent it from wrinkling, it should be tacked to a drawing board and allowed to dry before it is removed and perhaps mounted.

A mount for the print may be constructed as illustrated in Fig. 91, by folding in half a sheet of paper of appropriate size and color and then cutting a "window" in one of the halves through which to display the print. The print may then be fixed in place behind the window by means of rubber cement or sticky tape. If the paper on which the print is taken is translucent, as in the case of certain tissues, an interesting effect may be obtained by fixing colored papers behind it.

When printing is to be done on textile, the cloth should be spread over felt or newspapers. The block should be inked in the manner just described for paper, except that, as mentioned previously, an ink with an oil base should be used. This ink may be thinned with turpentine. Printing can be done with the hands, although one must exert strong pressure. A small wooden mallet is the most effective tool for this job. The block should be tapped smartly, first in the center and then on each corner. Each time the block is used it should be freshly and uniformly inked.

TEACHING: The chief problems in teaching linoleum cutting and printing concern the selection of suitable subject matter and the development of skill in cutting. Organization of the classroom, of course, raises problems, but these are similar to the organizational problems found in stick printing.

Linoleum cutting has often given rise to some unfortunate teaching methods concerning the selection of subject matter. Even some teachers who have emphasized the importance of developing original subject matter in the direct processes have allowed pupils to copy designs for linoleum work so that they may concentrate upon technique. Such a teaching practice, however, proves in the long run to be as ineffective when applied to linoleum cutting as it does when applied to other types of art. No matter what the art form being produced, subject matter and technique must develop in close relationship to each other.

The suggestion was made earlier that sculpture in wood might begin with an experimental play procedure. The teacher will find this method practical for linoleum work as well. At first the child should work directly with linoleum. Rather than attempting to follow a drawing, he should explore the many ways of chopping and slicing out pieces of the linoleum. After becoming acquainted with the cutting methods, he can follow the teacher's suggestion of making some preliminary sketches with India ink and a brush. By that time, he will have insight into the limitations of the medium and will realize to what extent a plan may help him in this work.

The discussions about the selection of subject matter in both the Introduction to Part Two and in Chapter 7 have particular reference to crafts such as linoleum cutting. This is a craft which lends itself to picture-making as well as pattern-making, so that the problems arising from the selection and treatment of subject matter are varied. The teacher must, of course, help the children to select suitable items from their experience in the ways indicated in the earlier sections of this book. After that he will find that the work produced is modified both by the child's artistic level and by the technique itself. The child's output in linoleum cutting, in other words, while strongly reminiscent of his picture-making, is not identical with it because of differences in the media and tools. Nevertheless, whatever emerges must, of course, be a child's personal expression. Often a display of the entire process of making a cut is helpful in getting linoleum cutting away to a good start. After that, further demonstrations of technique may be necessary from time to time. These, however, should be kept to a minimum so that children can develop their own methods of working. Linoleum, unlike some other substances, is a medium which allows many variations of approach which may be discovered through experience.

The possibilities for exploration of linoleum cutting and printing are

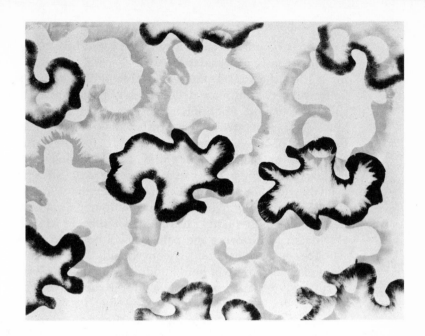

92 *Stencil design for textile by a fifth-grade boy.*

endless.[2] The various types of cuts, the selection of different papers, the uses of two or more colors upon the same block, the placing of units upon the textile, and, for the sixth-grade pupils, even the use of two or more blocks to form a pattern may all challenge the pupils engaged in this art.

Stenciling

MEDIA AND TECHNIQUE: Stenciling is a technique which allows the child to print repeated units of design with considerable control (see Fig. 92). The technique demands a reasonably high degree of skill and an ability to plan in some detail in advance of production, and, hence, it may be performed only by the more mature preadolescents. In stenciling, holes are cut in special paper, after which paint is applied to a surface covered by this paper. Only where holes have been cut will paint appear on the under surface, and, thus, a controlled design is established. The pieces removed by cutting may also be used as "masks" in the stencil process, as shown in Fig. 93c.

Strong waterproofed or special stenciling paper should be used. Such

[2] See Robin Tanner, *Children's Work in Block Printing* (Peoria, Ill.: Bennett, 1936).

paper may be purchased or may be prepared by coating a heavy paper with shellac, varnish, or wax, later smoothed with a hot iron. Knives are required for cutting the stencil paper, and although a sharp pocket- or razor-blade knife will serve, for more detailed work special knives made for the purpose should be bought. For applying the paint, hog bristle brushes may be used, but since inexpensive stencil brushes may be obtained, it is recommended that some of these be made available. If stenciling is to be done on paper, water color or tempera color will be suitable, while for stenciling on textiles, ordinary oil colors in tubes may be used. Special stencil paints, however, are available and are very satisfactory to use. Almost any surface will receive a stenciled pattern, provided it is not too rough. Evenly woven cotton cloth is perhaps the most suitable textile for children to use, and almost any available paper for drawing and painting will be found serviceable.

To cut the final stencils conveniently, the paper should be laid over plate glass or a piece of hard building board. Care must be taken to be exact in cutting, so that a cut stops where it is supposed to stop and joins exactly with another cut. The worker must leave "ties" or narrow bands of paper to hold parts of the design together. Hence the design must be simple. To perform this relatively delicate cutting some people find it convenient to push the knife away from themselves in the Japanese manner, while others prefer to draw it towards the body.

When paper is to be stenciled, it should be pinned to a drawing board. Textile, on the other hand, must be stretched tight over newsprint or blotting paper and then pinned firmly in place. The paper underneath the textile will absorb any excess paint which might otherwise run and spoil the work.

Paint should be thick enough not to run, yet not so thick as to form an unpleasantly heavy coating upon the surface being printed. Tempera paint for printing on paper can be placed in a muffin tin. After being dipped into the paint, the brush should be scrubbed slightly on scrap paper to rid it of excess paint. Oil paints for textiles should be squeezed from the tube to a palette which might be a piece of glass. The amount of paint picked up by the brush can then be conveniently controlled by gently dabbing the brush on the palette.

Paint should be applied to the holes in the stencil with some care, for if the brush is used too vigorously, the stencil may be damaged. If color is desired evenly over the entire cut-out area, it may be applied with a dabbing motion. If a shaded effect is required, stroking from the edge of the stencil into the cut-out area may be used.

TEACHING: The teacher's most important task in stenciling is to insist on cleanliness of tools and equipment while the pupils are using the process.

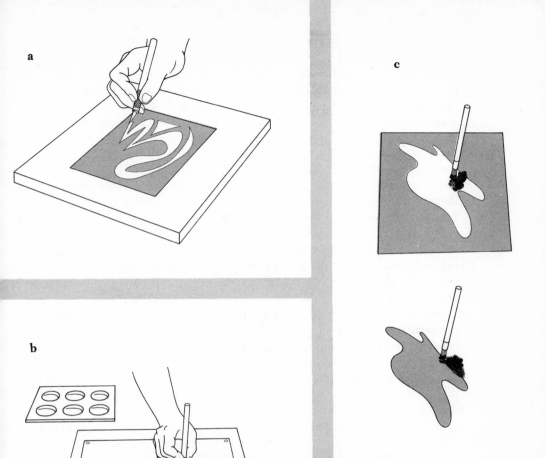

a

c

b

93 *Techniques for (a) cutting stencil and (b) applying color. (c) Both the hole
and piece cut out may be used to create a stencil pattern.*

It is particularly necessary in stenciling to keep all equipment clean if smooth work is to result. He must insist that brushes be kept scrupulously clean. While cool water will suffice to wash brushes used with tempera paint, turpentine is the solvent for oil-base colors. After a brush is cleaned in turpentine, the teacher must see that the pupil washes it again in a cool solution of soap and water. After the brushes have been washed, they should be placed in a container with the bristles up. It scarcely needs to be added that the pupils should be taught to clean palettes after they have been used. Should the pupils wish to preserve the stencils from one day to another, the teacher should direct them to wash the stencils carefully with water or turpentine, depending upon the type of paint used, after which they can be suspended from a line strung in a storage cupboard for the purpose.

A second task for the teacher is to assist the pupils to become familiar with the stenciling technique as a means of personal expression. As in the case of linoleum cutting, it is advisable to encourage the pupils at first to create the design directly on the paper, rather than to attempt to trace a previously drawn and painted unit. Children should therefore be given ample opportunity to experiment with the stencil technique. Preliminary practicing may be done on ordinary paper or cardboard. Following the teacher's demonstration and after practice in cutting, the children will discover how to leave the "ties" or small parts to hold parts of the design together. Largely through practice accompanied by the teacher's comments, they will learn that a stencil design must be kept simple and that intricate shapes are generally to be avoided.

Finally, the teacher should encourage experimentation, for which stenciling provides many opportunities. Various colors may be used both separately and blended together. The stencil may be moved slightly with some charming effects when a second color is to be used. Furthermore, two or more stencils may be employed on the same surface. Many experimental arrangements may also be explored while placing the units of design upon textile or paper.

ACTIVITIES FOR THE READER

1. Produce a monoprint in nonobjective design, first, by using one color and drawing directly in the color after you have applied it to a sheet of glass. Repeat, using two colors lightly blended with the brayer.

2. Produce a monoprint in nonobjective design by drawing on the paper which is laid down first over the inky glass. Experiment by using concurrently several colors of ink.

3. Repeat (1) and (2), above, using objective subject matter. Be careful of the design of your work.

4. Produce a monoprint in nonobjective design by laying down an orderly arrangement of string, burlap, and cut cardboard on the inky surface before applying the paper on which the monoprint is to be impressed.

5. Experiment with a number of vegetables, suitably cut, to produce various printed textural effects on paper. Over these effects, print an orderly design with a potato or carrot into which you have cut a pattern with a knife.

6. **a.** Experiment with a potato, scoring it not only with a knife but also with a fork or a spoon. Try printing a sheet of paper with an all-over pattern in which the unit is repeated exactly.

   b. Prepare two potatoes with different designs, calling one "a" and the other "b" and print the units as follows:

a,	b,	a,	b,	a,
a,	b,	a,	b,	a,
a,	b,	a,	b,	a,
a,	b,	a,	b,	a, etc.

   c. Now print as follows:

a,	b,	b,	a,
b,	a,	a,	b,
a,	b,	b,	a,
b,	a,	a,	b, etc.

   d. Print, turning "a" or "b" upside down.
   e. Print, overlapping "a" and "b."
   f. Print with a space between the "a" 's and "b" 's:

a	a	a
	b	b
a	a	a

   g. Create some different arrangements, perhaps eventually using three and four motifs or units. In all cases, they should be repeated exactly.[3]

   h. Combine some of your printed arrangements with interesting backgrounds prepared experimentally.

7. Cut sticks so that they will print a unit and experiment on paper as indicated in (6a–h), above.

8. Select the arrangement you like best and print it on textile.

[3] See R. R. Tomlinson, *Picture and Pattern Making by Children* (N.Y.: Studio, 1950).

9. Experiment with a piece of linoleum, making a nonobjective design to obtain many different types of textures. Take several "rubbings" of your work as you progress. Finally, print it on paper.

10. Cut a 2-inch square of linoleum and glue it to a block. Make a nonobjective unit from this piece of linoleum. Print on paper in the manner indicated in (6a–h), above.

11. Print the pattern produced according to (10), above, on textile rather than paper.

12. Make an objective linoleum print. From a landscape, still life, life drawing, or some other objective work you have produced, plan a picture to be cut in linoleum. In India ink, make a drawing the exact size you intend your cut to be, say 5 inches by 8 inches. Cover your linoleum with a thin coat of white tempera paint and then redraw your sketch on the linoleum. Start cutting, taking as many "rubbings" as you require and later some test prints to give you an idea of your progress. Finally, print in several single colors. Then try printing with two colors simultaneously. Select the prints you like best and mount them.

13. Cut a stencil using a nonobjective design no smaller than 3 inches square and print it on paper. Experiment on paper as indicated in (6a–h), above.

14. Print the pattern from (13), above, on textile.[4]

---

[4] One of the best books for the teacher to read at this time is H. Woolner, *Teaching Fabric Printing in Schools* (London: Evans, n. d.). Much of the work suggested is too difficult for children, but the ideas are excellent for any teacher. Tanner, *Children's Work in Block Printing*, is also excellent.

11

Group Activities in Art

In the opening chapter of this book reference was made to art and the democratic ideal. It was asserted that artistic endeavor is compatible with the democratic credo, while "the totalitarian state does not tolerate individual expression of individual experience." [1] The statement was made furthermore, that among the aims of the art program is the development in the pupils of greater insight into the nature of the democratic ideal. It is the purpose of this chapter to enlarge upon some of these ideas. First we shall consider some of the outstanding characteristics of a democratic group; next we shall discuss how such a group functions; and finally we shall study some artistic activities which are especially suitable for the development of the children's democratic insight. Among these activities are various forms of puppetry and mural-making.

The Democratic Group

In his book *Democracy as a Way of Life*, Bode says that "teaching democracy in the abstract is on a par with teaching swimming by correspondence." [2] This is why he feels that "the school must undertake to exemplify in its or-

---

[1] Hellmut Lehmann-Haupt, *Art Under a Dictatorship* (N.Y.: Oxford Univ. Press, 1954), p. 238. See especially the conclusion, "The Challenge to Democracy."

[2] *Democracy as a Way of Life* (N.Y.: Macmillan, 1937), p. 75.

ganization and procedures its conception of democratic living." [3] Bode then attempts the difficult task of defining the nature of a democratic community. In such a community, he says, there is provision for each person to have a share in the common life according to his interests and his capacities. A democratic school promotes the doctrine that men are "free and equal" by taking proper account of individual differences and by reliance on the principle of community living.[4] Such a school neither excuses the individual from a responsibility to the group nor replaces one set of fixed ideas about living with another equally static set. The child in a democratic school enjoys a free play of intelligence, and he emerges from this school with his own set of conclusions. The child, asserts Bode, must acquire something "other than a docile acceptance of a point of view." This something is a "quality of mind and heart," [5] according to which life is accepted pragmatically as a continuous reorganization and renewed outlook, but with the faith that, in the long run, the most acceptable conditions of life will be reached through democracy.

Less poetic and more detailed, but agreeing with Bode's statement, is Hollingshead's summary of the nature of democracy.[6] Democracy, he states, has as its sole objective the development of the individual. The individual in a democracy has equality of rights and enjoys both freedom and fraternal relations with others in the same society.

In a democracy, he says further, individual and group welfare are interdependent and common goals are reached through the cooperative activities of its members. The method of government, therefore, is indeed "of the people, by the people, for the people."

The democratic group must function according to certain conditions, continues Hollingshead. The members must have a strong feeling of being part of the group. Everyone must work for the personal development of each fellow member and goals must be reached through the efforts of all. The group must possess a workable organization and must have leadership which offers guidance, not dictatorship.[7]

In the classroom it is the task of the teacher not only to provide democratic leadership, but also to make provisions for certain of the pupils who appear to possess this ability, to assume some of the duties of leadership themselves.

---

[3] *Ibid.*, p. 77.   [4] *Ibid.*, p. 82.   [5] *Ibid.*, p. 103.

[6] Arthur D. Hollingshead, *Guidance in Democratic Living* (N.Y.: Appleton-Century, 1941). See Chapter 2, "Nature of Democracy," for a discussion of these and other "principles of democracy."

[7] *Ibid.* See Chapter 3, where these and other conditions are discussed in detail.

The Role of the Teacher
in a Democratic Group Activity

While realizing the desirability of including group activities in an art program, the teacher may find certain questions arising in his mind concerning the mechanics of this technique. How does the group activity work? How should the activity be chosen? What should be its scope? What is the role of the teacher?

A number of years ago, Kilpatrick outlined the typical steps in what he called a "purposeful activity." These steps, which have stood the test of time, he called *purposing, planning, executing,* and *judging.*[8] A group activity must begin with a wholehearted purpose. This, Kilpatrick says, supplies the drive to the project. Moreover, it is the children who must do the "purposing." The teacher, of course, may make suggestions, but before these suggestions can be effective, the children must accept them wholeheartedly. Likewise both the "planning" and the "executing," which are outcomes of the purposing, must be controlled by members of the working group. Finally, the children themselves must ask the general and the specific questions concerning the outcome of the activity. Did they do what they planned? What was learned in the doing? What mistakes were made? How could the activity be done better next time? "Purposeful activity of this type," says Kilpatrick, "is the very essence of thoughtful living; it must become the essence of intelligent learning."[9]

The functions of the teacher in a group activity in art are parallel with those associated with individual learning.[10]

The methods of motivation, isolating and defining themes, establishing artistic goals, and selecting media and tools of expression now must be applied to those pupils, whether few or many, who make up the art group.[11]

In the corporate life of the school or classroom, the occasion invariably arises in which the need for group effort in art is apparent if goals are to be reached. "Let's have a play," the children say, "Let's run a puppet show. . . . Let's make a big picture to go in the hallway. . . . Let's decorate our Christ-

[8] W. H. Kilpatrick, *Foundations of Method* (N.Y.: Macmillan, 1925), pp. 203 ff. See also Frances Pauline Hilliard, *Improving Social Learnings in the Elementary School* (N.Y.: Teachers College, 1954), p. 68, in which this writer discusses "the process of cooperative planning and working." Her ideas will be clearly seen to be an elaboration of those of Kilpatrick.

[9] W. H. Kilpatrick, *Remaking the Curriculum* (N.Y.: Newson, 1936), p. 25.

[10] See Hollingshead, *Guidance in Democratic Living*, p. 120, for the necessary "personal qualifications" of a successful teacher in a group activity. Another recommended reference is Lavone A. Hanna, Gladys L. Potter, and Neva Hagaman, *Unit Teaching in the Elementary School* (N.Y.: Rinehart, 1955).

[11] Review Chapter 2.

mas tree." Very little suggestion need come from the teacher to set in motion a desirable group project. The children themselves, who are usually quick to realize when working together will get desired results, will often be the first to suggest to a sympathetic teacher that an enterprise of this kind be considered.

As Kilpatrick suggested for general learning, every group activity in art should arise from a natural situation in which the children clearly see the need for cooperative effort. To force group work where none is desired or necessary can lead not only to undesirable social learnings, but also to bad art.

The teacher must keep in mind that no matter how desirable it may be to encourage children to work cooperatively, art is a matter of individual concern and will always remain so. An art form should never be produced by a group unless the size and scope of the work is such that an individual could not possibly master it. Only when a work requires for its successful completion a diversity of skills, a fund of energy, and a span of attention exceeding those of any one child, is the need for group endeavor indicated.

Before encouraging children to proceed with a group project, the teacher must judge not only whether it is sufficiently challenging to occupy the attention of several people, but also whether it may be too large for successful completion. In their enthusiasm over art, children in school are sometimes willing to plunge into a task which they could never complete. Once fired with the idea of a mural, for example, a group of fifth-graders might cheerfully embark upon the enormous task of designing murals for all four walls of a school gymnasium. While one or even two murals might be made successfully, to produce many more would exhaust the pupils. For a group activity in art to come to a wavering halt because the children have lost interest or lack competence to complete it, is of course a reflection, not only upon the group techniques but upon the teacher's judgment. When failure looms, the teacher must help the pupils to alter their plans so that they can achieve success.

With his greater maturity and insight into democratic processes, the teacher must fill the role of counselor with tact, sympathy, and skill. As soon as the need for group work in art is apparent, he must see that the children elect leaders and establish necessary committees so that "purposing, planning, executing, and judging" may occur. In the paragraphs that follow we shall see how these stages of group work occur in relation to specific art activities, so further detailed comments concerning them need not be offered now. In general, however, it must be said that the teacher should see that as far as is practical the children must control these steps. Although having the power of veto, the teacher should be reluctant to use this power. If at times he senses that the children's decisions are wrong, he should nevertheless allow them to proceed in the manner of their choice, only provided that their chosen course of action would not lead to overwhelmingly disastrous results. It is part of the democratic process for people to make mistakes and, profiting from them, subsequently to rectify them.

To one aspect of counseling the teacher must give his special attention. Since democratic group procedures depend for success largely upon the maximum contribution of each participant, he must see that every child in the group, regardless of intelligence and ability, is given a fair opportunity to make a suitable contribution to the project.[12]

Group Activities
for Beginners at School

MEDIA AND TECHNIQUES: Often beginners at school, either kindergarten or first-grade children, are insufficiently mature to participate fully in a group enterprise. Nevertheless, a beginning may be made early in their school career. This takes the form of a quasi-group activity in which children pool work originally completed as a result of individual effort.

The activity requires little or no group planning and does not appear as cooperative endeavor until its close. Teachers make use of the quasi-group activity even with children who have not reached the symbol stage but are still in the stage of manipulation. In one kindergarten enrolling children at this stage, for example, a small Christmas tree was successfully decorated. Each little child twisted and curled colored paper into a gay decoration, which later he hung upon a branch of the tree.

The quasi-group activity may be based upon any theme within the interest of young pupils and may make use of any medium and technique which the children are capable of handling. If a kindergarten class happens to be talking about the subject of spring, for example, each child who has reached the symbol stage may select one item of the season to illustrate. The children may draw and paint symbols of lambs, flowers, birds, trees, and other spring-like manifestations. After drawing or painting each item, the children cut away the unused paper around the symbol. Then the drawings and paintings are assembled on a tackboard.

Many other suitable topics could be treated in a similar fashion. Among them might be included the following:

> 1. "Shopping with Mother," in which the various stores may
> be drawn and painted, together with people and automobiles.

---

[12] See Chapter 12, in part of which the relationship of slow learners to group activities is discussed. Chapter 13 deals with the same topic in relation to gifted pupils.

This subject could also be handled as an interior scene in which the articles on display in a "super-market" are depicted.

2. "Our House," in which the houses are eventually assembled to form a street.

3. "My Friends," in which the outlines of boys and girls are assembled to form a crowd of children.

Three-dimensional output such as is seen in Fig. 134 also lends itself to this quasi-group activity. For example, the children can assemble upon a table modeling and paper constructions, depicting scenes such as "The Farm" with barns, cows, and so forth, and "The Circus" with clowns, elephants, and the rest.

TEACHING: The teacher begins the group activity in the usual fashion associated with individual picture-making or three-dimensional work. Motivation and teaching occur as they are required. Eventually, when the children have produced their work, the teacher, who has reserved a display space in the room, asks each child to bring his work to the board and pin it in place. At first, a rather disorganized arrangement may be seen. A short discussion with the class, however, will bring forth a few suggestions for improving the

94 *"A Trip to High Park"—a poster resulting from quasi-group activity in the kindergarten.*

Brigdens

placement of the individual drawings. Some of the largest and brightest work can be located near the center of the panel while lambs or some other symbol drawn by several children might be grouped or arranged in a rhythmic line. The finished composition will, of course, have a pattern with many small areas of interest reminiscent of some of the output of Grandma Moses and other so-called Primitive artists. The teacher should not attempt to improve the layout by adding any of her own work. If she is tempted to provide a fence or road in perspective, or even a horizon line, the temptation should be resisted on the grounds, first, that only a muddle could result if adult work (however naïve) and children's work were assembled upon the one panel, and, second, that the children should learn to depend upon themselves in developing a group activity.

The main aim of conducting the quasi-group activity is to lead children to the point where they can control Kilpatrick's four steps. Therefore, even in this beginning stage, all the teacher's actions must be governed by this aim. The teacher should solicit themes from the children so that "purposing" may develop. Later she should urge the children to decide as a group which items of any class of objects each child should draw. For example, at first all children might draw lambs for the spring picture, but later the group might decide that certain children should draw chickens, ducklings, and so on, instead. This would lead to better "planning." Then group decisions about, say, media or centers of interest might begin to improve design. Finally, such a simple question as "Could we have made the picture better?" could begin the stage of "judging" even in these early years.

Group Activities for More Mature Children

When, following practice in quasi-group work, children exhibit an inclination to band together and work with even a minimum of cooperation, they are ready for group activities proper. According to most writers, group development should be fostered at some point in the kindergarten and should occupy more and more school time as the child matures through the grades.[13]

To encourage group work becomes much easier for the teacher as the child's age increases, especially in the third- or fourth-grade levels, when he becomes interested in associating with groups of his age-mates. Interests in the "gang," as explained in an earlier chapter, show in the children's drawings and paintings. The teacher may capitalize upon this interest in the group to promote such activities in art as may lead to a greater social maturity of

---

[13] See the chart, for example, in Hollingshead, *Guidance in Democratic Living*, p. 137.

the young participants. Among the group activities suitable for this purpose and selected for the major part of the discussion here are puppetry and mural-making.

Puppetry

Perhaps some of the most effective group activities lie within the several fields of puppetry. To produce a successful puppet play, the group as a whole must reach decisions, while each member of the group, although maintaining his personal identity, must give full cooperation if the enterprise is to succeed. Puppets range in technical difficulty from the very simple to the very complicated, so that groups of children at any particular stage of development may select techniques compatible with their capabilities. The three major types of puppets which elementary school children in one stage or another may select are fist puppets, string puppets or marionettes, and shadow puppets. Each type will be described in some detail in the following pages.

MEDIA AND TECHNIQUES FOR FIST PUPPETS: Simple "fist" puppets—the type operated directly with one hand—may be produced in a variety of ways. The beginner can draw a figure on cardboard and later cut away the excess background. The cut-out figure is then attached to a stick. (This kind of puppet is also known as a stick puppet.) In place of a cut-out figure, the pupil can use a bag stuffed with paper or absorbent cotton, decorated with paint or cut paper, and tied to the stick.

A paper bag may also be used for a puppet which moves its head, as follows: a string is tied about the middle of a paper bag, leaving just enough room for inserting the index finger. A face is painted on the closed upper portion of the bag. To operate the puppet, the hand is thrust into the bag up to the neck and the index finger pushed through the neck to articulate the head.

An old stocking, appropriately decorated with buttons for eyes and pieces of cloth or paper for hair, ears, and other features also makes an effective puppet when slipped over the hand and arm.

Animals such as snakes or dragons may be formed by this means and become especially fearsome if a mouth is constructed by cutting the toe of a sock and stitching cloth to form a lining to the throat so formed. Both top and bottom jaws should be stuffed with a material such as absorbent cotton. The jaws are worked by inserting the fingers in the upper section and the thumb in the lower. The attractiveness of this creation can be enhanced by making a lining of a color contrasting with the sock, or by adding teeth or a tongue made from bright materials.

More complicated fist puppets can be constructed from a wide variety

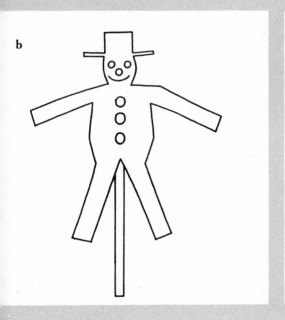

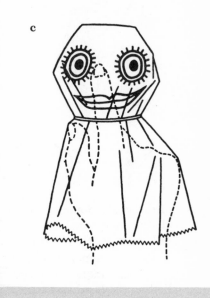

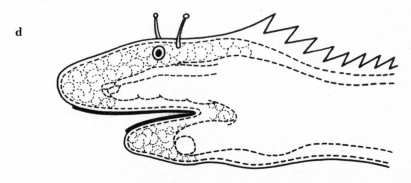

95 *Diagrams of stick puppets (a and b), a puppet made from a paper bag (c), and a puppet made from an old stocking (d).*

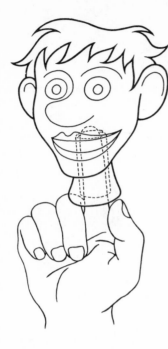

96 *A puppet head modeled over a cardboard fingerstall.*

of materials. Some of the modeling media mentioned in earlier chapters including papier-mâché and asbestos powder are suitable for the construction of heads; plastic wood may also be used. The bodies of the puppets may be made from remnants of most textiles.

These more advanced fist puppets should be capable of articulation both in the head and arms. The thumb and little finger are usually employed to create movement in the arms, while the index finger moves a modeled head.

To model a head, the pupil should first cut and glue together a stiff cylinder of cardboard (preferably light Bristol board) large enough in diameter to fit his index finger loosely. The modeling medium, which tends to shrink the cylinder slightly, is then worked directly around the cardboard until the head, including all features, and neck are formed. The neck of the puppet modeled over the lower part of the cylinder, or "fingerstall" as it is called, should be increased slightly in diameter in its base to hold in place the clothes which are attached by a drawstring. When the modeling medium is dry, it should be smoothed with sandpaper and then decorated with poster paint. An attractive glisten can be added to eyes, lips, or teeth by coating them with shellac or, better still, clear nail polish. In character dolls, attention can be drawn to outstanding features by the same means. Most puppets tend to be more appealing if the eyes are considerably enlarged and made conspicuous with a shiny coating. Hair, eyebrows, and beards can be made from absorbent cotton, yarn, cut paper, or scraps of fur pasted or glued in place.

The clothing covers the operator's hand and arm and forms the body of the puppet. The outside dimensions of the clothing are determined by the size of the operator's hand. His hand should be laid flat upon a desk with the thumb and index and little fingers extended. The approximate length of the puppet's arms will be indicated by the tips of the thumb and little finger, while the neckline should come halfway up the index finger. To produce clothing, one folds a single piece of cloth, makes a cut in the center of the fold for the neck and then sews the sides, leaving openings for the fingers. Small mitts may be attached to cover the finger tips, if this is desired. If the pupil wishes his puppet to have interchangeable costumes, a drawstring can be used to tie the clothing to the neck. If he plans on designing only one costume for his puppet, the pupil can glue it into place, as well as tying it, for extra security.

Puppet costumes can be made gay with bright textiles; men's old ties are valuable for this purpose. The lining of the ties should first be removed and the material ironed flat, before being folded over and sewn to make a garment. Buttons and so on may be added, of course, as they are required.

When a child makes a puppet he expects to use it in a stage production. In presenting a fist-puppet show, the operators work beneath the set. This means that the stage must be elevated so that the puppeteers can stand or

97 *Clothing for a fist puppet.*

98 *Simple fist puppet stage made from large carton.*

crouch under it while the show goes on. A simple stage can be constructed from a large topless cardboard carton with a hole cut in its base and one side removed. The carton is then placed upon a table with the hole facing the audience. The operators stand or crouch behind the table and are concealed from the audience by a curtain around the table legs.

Pupils in about the fifth and sixth grades may wish to construct a more elaborate stage from dressed one-by-two-inch lumber. A good general plan is a three-panel screen covered with wrapping paper or cloth, with an opening for the stage at the top of the center panel. The frames for the three panels of the screen are formed from one-by-two-inch lumber, each panel measuring about three feet by five feet. Each panel is braced by crossbars of the lumber; the center panel is made so that the crossbars do not interfere with the stage opening, which measures about two feet by three feet. The panels are assembled with screws (not nails) so that they can be dismantled easily and are joined by three hinges each. A wire is strung above the stage opening for the curtain. The three panels except for the stage opening are covered with kraft paper or old sheets dyed a dark color or a similar textile. When the screen is set in place for a stage production, the wings of the assembly are held in place by a piece of the one-by-two lumber screwed to the top members (see Fig. 99a and b).

The stage settings should be simple yet effective. A backdrop can be painted in a color which contrasts with that of the puppets. Because the stage has no floor, the background is held or fixed in position from below. On it may be pinned significant items such as windows and doors. Separate backdrops may be prepared for each scene. Likewise, stage properties—tables, chairs, and the like—must be designed in two dimensions. Spotlights are useful to bring out features of the presentation.

To operate fist puppets is not difficult; the pupils can teach themselves the technique merely by practice. One should remember, however, that when one puppet, accompanied by other puppets, is "speaking" on stage, some part of it should be in continual movement, so that the audience may know exactly which puppet is the speaker. The other puppets should be still.

MEDIA AND TECHNIQUES FOR STRING PUPPETS, OR MARIONETTES: A more flexible puppet, but one which is relatively more difficult to make and operate is the string puppet, or marionette. This type of puppet moves by means of strings and, if desired, every member may be articulated. Some puppets constructed by professionals may move even mouths, eyes, and eyebrows to the great delight and astonishment of a youthful audience.

Children in the elementary school, of course, could not even start to

99 (a) *Elaborate fist puppet stage (front view), showing the wood frame covered with cloth and draw curtain.*
(b) *Elaborate fist puppet stage (rear view).*

Royal Studio

a b

construct such puppets, let alone manipulate them. Nevertheless, they are able to make and manipulate marionettes which can walk, wave their arms, sit down, shake their heads, and perform a whole series of other interesting maneuvers.

Children in the symbol stage, but no younger, can produce a simple string puppet. A stuffed paper bag, wtih a head formed by tying the top of the bag with string and features drawn or painted or glued on, forms the main part of the puppet. Arms and legs can be cut out of heavy paper or cardboard and pasted to the body. Only two strings, attached from each end of a six-inch crossbar of wood (called the "control"; see below) to each shoulder, are required. Small screw eyes put in the ends of the control and adhesive tape stuck on the paper body serve as anchors for the strings.

An equally simple marionette may be fashioned in a similar manner from a stuffed sock or stocking.

After the children learn to control these simple puppets, they can modify them so that more strings can be added. For example, arms can be constructed of two pieces of cardboard with a paper-fastener joining the two pieces at the elbow and then strings attached to the hands. The child now has to control the shoulder strings and the arm strings, which he holds in his hands. More strings may be added as the operator's skill grows.

Preadolescents in about the fourth, fifth, and sixth grades who have practiced puppetry earlier will be able to make a much more elaborate marionette. Perhaps the most practical of these puppets has a modeled head and moving arms and legs made from cloth.

The head of the string marionette is modeled and finished in a manner similar to that described for fist puppets, with the exception that the fingerstall is replaced by a solid piece of wood of a similar size. The body is constructed upon a different principle.

A convenient material for making the body is cloth. Two cut-outs of the puppet's body—one for the back and the other for the front—are made from the cloth. The two pieces are then sewn together, leaving a small opening at the bottom through which to insert the filler. Absorbent cotton provides a good filler, although paper may also be used. Before the body is filled, a weight should be sewn inside the body at the base of the spine. Lead fishing sinkers are convenient to use, especially those that have loops at either end. Two-ounce sinkers are sufficiently heavy. When the body is weighted and firmly stuffed, an oval of cloth should be fitted over the bottom opening to provide an area to support the puppet when it assumes a sitting position (see Fig. 100).

The arms and legs are then made from rectangular pieces of cloth, which, like the body, are sewn, weighted, and stuffed. The weights should

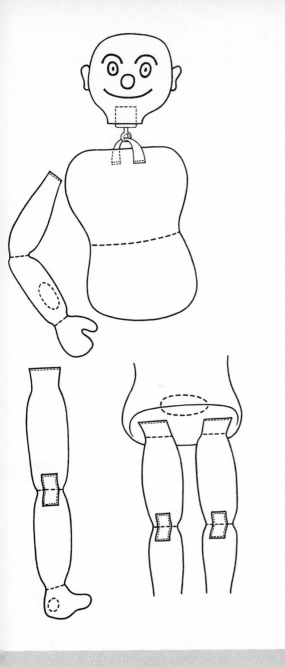

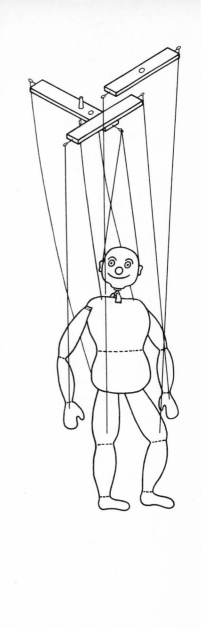

100 *Head, body, leg, and control assemblies of a string puppet.*

be placed on the bottom sides of the forearms just above the hands, while for the legs, the weights should go near the heel. At this time, joints must be made at elbows, wrists, knees, and ankles. These may be made merely by working a "channel" in the stuffing with the fingers and then stitching the channel. When the thumbs are up, the joints at elbows and wrists should be vertical. At the knees and ankles, the joints should be horizontal. The arms are joined to the shoulders by sewing. To make them flexible, it is a good plan to gather the cloth with a thread before it is fixed to the shoulder.

In order that their movement may be more readily controlled, the legs should be pressed flat at the hip so that their full width may be attached with a horizontal join to the base of the body. So that the legs will not bend in the wrong direction at the knees, one should sew a cloth hinge behind the knees on the outside of the leg at points slightly above and below the joint. The completed body, in which a joint may be put at the waistline, should be attached to the head assembly by a cotton tape. The wooden neck should be rounded at the end and have a screw eye fastened there. The tape is sewn to the puppet's body and runs from the chest through the screw eye to the back of the puppet where it is again sewn. This arrangement provides unlimited articulation for the head assembly (see Fig. 100).

As with the simple marionette described earlier, strings attached to certain parts of the marionette and leading to a control give movement to the puppet. The control is made of wood, and the strings are cut from fine fishing line or heavy linen thread. Ordinary string is not suitable because it tangles. Strings should be tacked to the puppet's ears, and should be sewn securely to the shoulders, the wrists, the tops of the knees, and the base of the spine. A total of nine strings can be used, which is about the maximum number an elementary school pupil can control with any degree of efficiency.

A simple control for this puppet consists of three pieces of wood as thin as one-quarter of an inch and about one inch wide. The main control is about six inches long, and to this, at one end, the first crossbar measuring about four inches should be tacked. The strings leading from the ears should then be fixed to a screw eye or tack placed at the crossbar end of the main control. The length of these strings, which determines that of all others, should allow the puppet's feet to touch the floor when the operator holds his arms horizontally with his elbows resting in their normal position close to his body. Now the strings from the puppet's wrists should be tied to screw eyes in the extremities of the crossbar and should be long enough to allow the arms to fall downward at almost, but not quite, full length. Then the strings from the shoulders should be tied to screw eyes placed on the main control just behind the crossbar. Next, the string from the base of the spine should be fixed to the main control at the end opposite the crossbar.

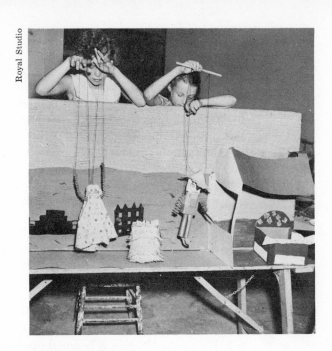

101 *A simple string puppet stage arranged by fourth-grade pupils, using a table and cardboard.*

Only the strings to the tops of the knees remain to be attached to a control. Since these strings are used for walking movements, they must be fastened to an independent crossbar which the operator may hold in advance of the main control. When the leg control is not in use, it can be rested on the main control on the point of a nail; for this, a hole is bored through the leg control so that it fits loosely over the nail. If the leg control is about two inches longer than the crossbar, it can be identified quickly when it is needed during a performance (see Fig. 100).

Once having strung the puppet, the pupil will then find it necessary to practice manipulating it. The technique of manipulation becomes personal, so that one may recognize the operator by the way he moves his puppets. Pupils are fascinated by this aspect of puppetry and will practice during any spare moment. The infinite numbers of basic movements of which the nine-string marionettes are capable may be discovered only through practice and no further comments about them need be offered here.

After making a human figure for a puppet, the children may like to experiment with bird and animal forms. The controls for birds whose wings merely replace arms will be similar to those used for humans. Animals, however, require controls to operate four legs, and these are usually made with two fixed crossbars attached at either end of the main bar.

When not in use, puppets should be carefully protected lest their strings become tangled. A tape placed behind the fixed crossbar is useful for hanging up the puppet. When the puppet is stored, however, the strings must be carefully gathered together and twined around the crossbar.

A simple puppet stage, as shown in Fig. 101, more for practice than for finished performances, may consist only of a sheet of cardboard, or even paper, with a hole cut in it for a stage opening, propped upon a large table. The pupils stand on the table while manipulating the puppets.

For a finished performance, it is more satisfactory to have a carpenter build a real puppet stage, such as that illustrated in Fig. 102. This stage consists of a framework of two-by-four-inch finished wood, strong enough to support the weight of the operators who lean against it. The stage opening, which must be tall enough to exhibit the puppets, is located at about two to three feet above the floor of the classroom. Above the stage opening, the wall of the stage usually extends high enough to hide the operators. Some stages, however, allow the audience to see these people, but unless suitably strong lighting is beamed upon the stage, the antics of the operators will greatly distract from those of the puppets. Directly behind the backdrop of the puppet stage floor is a platform on which the pupils stand. They are separated from the stage proper by a partition supporting the backdrop decorations over which they lean to animate the marionettes. Steps leading up to this platform are often a convenience. Stage curtains and at least two spotlights to be beamed on the stage are also refinements which may add to the effectiveness of a production. Costuming and décor may be arranged similar to the ways described for fist puppets. Since the marionette stage has a floor, which the fist puppet stage has not, properties are usually three-dimensional and may be constructed from cardboard suitably decorated with poster paint.

MEDIA AND TECHNIQUES FOR SHADOW PUPPETS: While shadow puppets are not difficult to make, to operate them successfully demands some finesse. In this technique, a silk or nylon screen is set up between the operators and the audience. Strong spotlights on the operators' side are then beamed upon the screen (see Fig. 103). The puppets are usually cut out of cardboard [14] and then tacked to a thin control stick. The puppet is held close to the screen in the direct path of the light, thus casting a shadow upon the screen. The puppet appears to the audience as a shadow silhouette, and since it takes this form, the figure needs no painting or decorating. The technique

---

[14] The Javanese, who are expert at this type of puppetry, use leather.

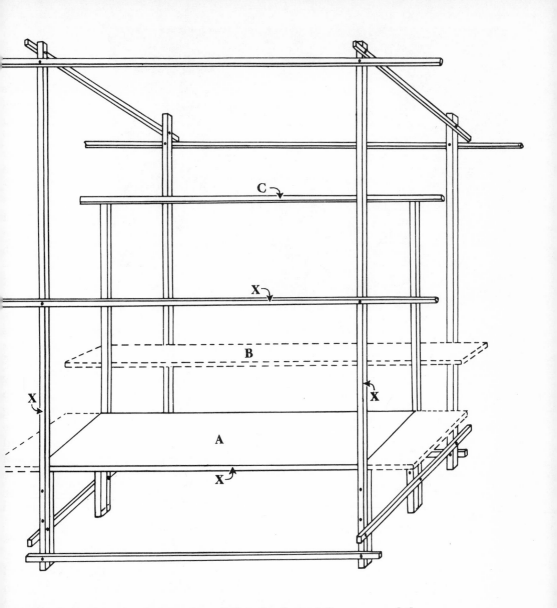

102 *The frame for a marionette stage. "A" is the floor of the stage, and the area
enclosed by the beams marked "X" is the stage opening. The board marked
"B" is the bridge, on which the performers stand; they lean over the beam
marked "C" to work their puppets. All parts of the frame, except the stage
opening, should be covered by cloth or wood. The area between "C" and the
back of "A" contains the backdrop.*

103 *Fourth-grade pupils practicing a shadow puppet play.*

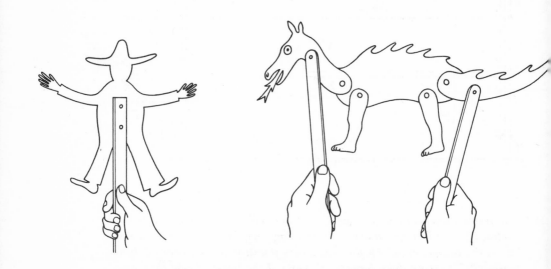

104 *A simple shadow puppet of a human figure and another of a dragon with moving head and tail.*

of operating is similar to that associated with fist puppets, so that the stage for the latter may also be used for shadow puppets.

Children in the earliest phases of the symbol stage can be taught to make a shadow puppet. The puppet can be made simply by cutting out a figure drawn on thin cardboard and gluing it to a stick. As the children develop their ability to produce symbols and as their skill to use cutting tools improves, they can make much more elaborate puppets. Outlines will become more subtle so that such features as shaggy hair, heavy eyebrows, or turned-up noses can be suggested in the silhouette. By punching holes or cutting inside the puppet, the pupil can depict, say, buttons, eyes, and frilly clothing.

Still more experienced pupils can make shadow puppets with some articulation. To make a dragon, for example, a number of small sections of cardboard are joined with paper-fasteners. Two sticks are attached to the assembly. Practice will result in an ability to make this creature wiggle in a highly satisfactory manner (see Fig. 104).

All properties, from tables to houses, must be cut from cardboard, placed on sticks, and also shown in silhouette.[15]

TEACHING ALL TYPES OF PUPPETRY: As indicated earlier, it is not difficult for a teacher to arouse pupils' interest in puppetry to the point where they desire to produce a play. Most children today are familiar with puppets from viewing them on the television screen. Some puppets have even gained national interest and affection.

Short educational films are available which show puppets in action.[16] The screening of such a film in the classroom is often enough to launch a puppetry project. A demonstration by the teacher is another effective way of stimulating interest in puppets.

Cooperative planning of the project is more difficult. Many teachers begin by holding a general discussion of the problems involved. Children are often shown a film and asked to analyze the various tasks which must be done before a show can be successfully produced. Eventually the main items of work are listed, and these include the following: selecting or writing the play; making the puppets; making the stage scenery and properties

---

15 It is recommended that some of the following be studied at this time:
    Marjorie Batchelder, *The Puppet Theater Handbook* (N.Y.: Harper, 1947). Winifred H. Mills and Louise M. Dunn, *Marionettes, Masks and Shadows* (N.Y.: Doubleday Doran, 1927); this contains an excellent section on shadow puppets. Joseph S. Kennard, *Masks and Marionettes* (N.Y.: Macmillan, 1935). F. J. McIsaac, *The Tony Sarg Marionette Book* (N.Y.: Viking, 1930). Waldo S. Lanchester, *Hand Puppets and String Puppets* (Leicester, Eng.: Dryad Press, 1948).
16 *How to Make a Puppet* (see Appendix 6).

(sometimes making a stage if one is not available); lighting the stage; practicing manipulation and general stagecraft.

The next move occurs when elections of committee chairmen take place. Because the children must be well acquainted before they can elect chairmen of necessary committees, a puppet show can be produced only after the term is well advanced and the children have gained knowledge of each other's qualities. Prior to the election, the committees are listed, together with the work each must do. The teacher cautions the children to choose chairmen whom they think have abilities and qualities which would help them be successful as head of each group. Chairmen are elected to head up committees such as the following: a selecting committee for the play with the duty of recommending suitable plays to the general group; a coordinating committee of production, or stage committee, to recommend suitable stage properties and backdrops for each scene, the general size of the puppets, and the costumes; a stage-building committee (if required).

Often the chairmen of the committees are elected with the understanding that they will form a "cabinet" with the duty of over-all coordination of the project. Either the members of the cabinet or all the children elect a head chairman, or president, of puppeteers from among the cabinet members. His duty is to report from time to time to the children about progress and to seek suggestions for improvement.

What the teacher does while all these proceedings are taking place is seeing that elections take place smoothly. His work intensifies later when the "executing" stage is reached. Often he must give demonstrations, short lessons, informal advice, and the like, in the manner associated with good democratic teachers. He must be particularly careful to keep in constant touch with the chairmen, often through the president, so that they may succeed in their efforts. Exactly what a teacher does at this stage, however, would be difficult to define for all cases.[17] Each situation brings its own problems and suggests its own procedures. The wise teacher will continually analyze his behavior in terms of the characteristics of a democratic group set down at the beginning of this chapter.

It is most important that group evaluation or "judging" take place both as the production proceeds and after the show is finished. Probably with the head chairman presiding, questions should be brought forward for discussion. Each chairman's report should be analyzed and suggestions for improvement made, should such be thought advisable. At the close of the performance, the time-honored question must be raised: "How could we improve the show next time?"

---

[17] See an amplification of this statement in Hollingshead, *Guidance in Democratic Living*, especially Chapter 7.

Mural-Making

MEDIA AND TECHNIQUES: The term "mural" in its strictest sense refers to a painting made directly on a wall. In many schools, however, it has come to denote any large picture, and this is the meaning of the word as it is used in the following paragraphs.

Before we go further into the question of mural-making it will be useful to consider some of the technical requirements of this art. While the youngest pupils may not understand the significance of all these requirements, the teacher should know about them and, when advisable, teach them.

The first technical requirement arises from the architectural quality of a wall. A plain, undecorated wall possesses some fundamental architectural characteristics which it should retain. It is obviously solid and flat, rather than undulating. In a mural, a wide diversity of depths achieved by linear perspective or an extreme range of colors tends to interfere with the basic characteristics of the wall. This condition most people find unpleasant. The design of the mural, therefore, must be kept reasonably "flat" if the wall is to maintain its architectural qualities.

A mural should be considered as part of a scheme of interior decoration and should be integrated with it. The color relationships already established in the interior in which the mural is placed should find their echo in the new work. Furthermore, since door and window openings set up a design in a room, the mural should be placed so that it does not violate the architectural arrangement of these features, but rather tends to maintain the existing plan or even to improve upon it.

A further consideration regarding the design of murals should be mentioned. This concerns the relationship between the concept of a mural and the purpose to which an interior is put. It is obvious that where gay events occur, the subject and treatment of the mural might also be gay. Where the events are more decorous, the mural could be expected to be in a more sober vein.

In spite of the technicalities which are required for the successful production of a mural, most children in about the fifth and sixth grades find that the activity is generally within their capabilities, and the experience of mural-making is a happy and rewarding one for them. Indeed, children from kindergarten to the sixth grade who are able to paint pictures individually and who have reached a stage of social maturity which allows them to work with some degree of cooperation, should find little difficulty in making some kind of mural.

The subjects selected will be similar to those found in individual picture-making. In other words, they will be derived from the children's own experiences. However, whatever subject is chosen must be sufficiently broad in scope to allow several pupils to elaborate upon it. To base a mural upon a still-life composition would not be particularly appropriate. A topic in which there are many objects of related but differing appearance, such as houses, factory buildings, or crowds of people, would be more suited to the nature of the activity. The following are examples of themes which elementary school pupils have successfully developed:

> Our school party
> A day at school
> Our school playground
> A trip to a market place
> What we saw at the experimental farm
> A carnival that came to town
> Playing outside during the winter
> Shopping at Christmas [18]

Most of the picture-making media are also useful for the production of murals.[19] The paper should be of a reasonably heavy, tough quality to support the weight of the finished product. "Kraft" paper, heavy brown wrapping paper which comes in large rolls, is suitable. Many school-supply houses offer a gray mural paper which is pleasant to use. The most effective coloring medium for young children is tempera paint. This should be applied with the usual wide range of the brushes of different types suggested for picture-making. Some especially wide brushes, however, should be available for painting the larger areas of the mural. Chalk can also be employed, but it is inclined to be dusty and to smudge badly when several children are working at one time. Colored paper is another medium by which effective results can be achieved. Wax crayons, however, are not suitable since they require too much effort to cover large areas. But crayons may be used in some areas as a "resist" with thin tempera.

The technique of planning and executing the mural varies with a child's social and artistic stage of development. The kindergarten child may begin by working side-by-side with his fellows on the same long strip of paper. Although all the children paint on the same topic suggested by the teacher and use the same medium, actually each child creates his own composition without much reference to the work of his fellows. Not until they reach the

---

[18] See Chapter 14 for a discussion of topics selected from other areas of learning in school.

[19] See Chapter 7.

third or fourth grade are some children able to plan the mural cooperatively. When they develop this ability, they may begin by making sketches lightly in chalk or pencil upon the area arranged for the mural. Considerable discussion and many alterations may occur before the design satisfies all participants. By the time they reach the fifth or sixth grades, many pupils are ready to plan a mural on a conveniently reduced scale before developing the work itself. They prepare sketches on paper whose dimensions are in proportion to the mural. These sketches are made in outline and in color. Later, when the mural paper has been laid over a large table or pinned to tackboard reserved for this purpose, the final sketch is enlarged upon the mural surface. Usually this is done freely, but sometimes teachers suggest that the squaring method of enlargement be used. By this method the sketch and the mural surface are divided into corresponding squares. What a pupil finds in a specific area of the sketch he redraws in the corresponding area of the mural.[20] Such a procedure, while common practice with professional

[20] A mural-making technique based on a method of enlarging has been developed by Vige Langevin and Jean Lombard, *Peintures et Déssins Collectifs des Enfants* (Paris: Éditions du Scarabée, 1950). The members of the class produce small paintings. One painting is selected and divided into squares which are numbered. Each child in the class is assigned one square which he copies on a large scale on another piece of paper. Eventually the large squares are assembled to form a very large picture. Although the children are encouraged to develop details in their copied area, one feels that the necessary emphasis upon copying is unfortunate. Considerable work of this kind may

105 *"Visit of the Bookmobile"—a mural in tempera paint by fifth-grade pupils.*

Royal Studio

muralists, may easily become inhibiting with elementary school children and should be used with caution. Only the most mature children are capable of benefiting from this technique.

After the drawing (or "cartoon" as it is sometimes called) has been satisfactorily transferred to the mural surface, the colors are applied. If tempera paint is to be used, it is usually mixed in advance in a relatively limited number of hues. Tints and shades of the hues are also mixed in advance. All colors are prepared in sufficient quantity to complete all areas in the mural where they are to be set down. In this way, time and paint are saved, while the unity of the mural created in the sketch is retained in the larger work.

If colored chalk or cut paper is used, the problem of running out of a color is not likely to occur.

When pupils use cut paper, the technique for producing a mural is less formal than when paint or chalk is used. With a large sheet of paper for the mural laid flat on the floor or a table, the pupils can push areas of the colored paper around to find the most satisfying effects. Thus plans may undergo even major revisions up to the final moment when the colored paper is stuck to the surface, a freedom which media such as paint and crayon restrict.

In carrying out the plan of a mural, the pupils quickly discover that they must solve other problems of design peculiar to this work. Because the length of a mural in relation to its height is usually much greater than in paintings, the technical problem arises of establishing a satisfactory center of interest. While one center of interest may be developed, it must not be so strong that the observer finds it necessary to ignore portions of the work at the extremities of the composition. On the other hand, if a series of centers of interest are placed along the full length of the composition, the observer may consider the result to be too jumpy and spotty. The solution in both cases, of course, is for the pupils to be particularly careful about the rhythms they establish so that no part of the mural is either neglected or unduly emphasized. The balances in a mural made by children, furthermore, have a tendency to get out of hand. Not infrequently the painters become intrigued with subject matter in one section of the work, with the result that they may give it too much attention and neglect other sections. Profuse detail may appear in the favored part, while other areas are overlooked.

One problem of design which rarely occurs in mural-making is lack of variety. Indeed, with many people working on the same surface, the prob-

be seen in some of the schools of Paris, and anyone who sees it cannot fail to be impressed with its bright charm.

lem is usually too much variety. Once they become aware of this difficulty, however, children are able to remedy the defect.[21]

TEACHING: Mural-making involves a number of group problems different from those found in puppetry. In puppetry, there is often enough work to be done to permit every member of the class to participate in the one endeavor. This is not so in mural-making. While all the pupils may discuss the making of murals, including the various media, the most suitable subjects, and the probable locations in which the work might be placed, eventually the pupils must divide into small groups, probably not again to reunite until the final evaluation period occurs. In the elementary school, these groups can conveniently comprise about three to ten pupils each, depending upon the size of the mural. The choosing of groups and leaders is therefore multiplied in this type of enterprise.

As with puppetry, it is not difficult to interest children in making murals. Showing a film or going to see a mural in a public building are two fairly practical ways of arousing the interest of some children in this work. Perhaps the most effective method is to discuss with the class the needs and benefits of making murals as decoration for specified areas of the school, such as the classroom, the halls, the cafeteria, or the auditorium.

The development of techniques for the planning of murals is reminiscent of that described for puppetry. With children in the symbol stage, only a general discussion of topic and then of medium need first take place. Then the teacher must assign each pupil to a work station at the mural and, while encouraging discussion, must assume the major share of leadership. After the children have had some experience, the teacher may choose teams of five or six pupils each to work on a mural; each team may elect its chairman, or captain, who will preside over discussions, though he often must rely upon the teacher for advice and encouragement. Eventually, however, as preadolescents, the children will be able to organize their own mural-making.

First, all the pupils in a class interested in mural-making assemble to discuss theme, media, and so on. With the pupils' suggested list of possible aspects of the main theme written on the blackboard, each pupil selects the aspect which most appeals to him. All pupils interested in the same aspect form a team to work on that particular mural. If too many pupils elect one aspect, two teams can then be created each to work separately upon the same subject. The teams are finally arranged and each elects its chairman.

---

[21] At this point refer to Arne W. Randall, *Murals for Schools* (Worcester, Mass.: Davis Press, 1956).

A good filmstrip is *Making a Mural* (listed in Appendix 6).

Discussion now takes place within each team concerning the size and shape of their particular mural, medium, and, sometimes, possible techniques. Sketches are then prepared, sometimes cooperatively, sometimes individually. Some teams will choose the individual sketch most liked by all, and others will prepare a composite picture, using the best ideas from the several sketches. The cartoon is then drawn, usually with the chairman supervising to see that the chosen sketch is being reproduced reasonably accurately. Then the color is added. From time to time the chairman may find it necessary to hold a team consultation to appraise the work so that some of the pitfalls of design in mural-making are avoided. This process goes on until each team's mural is completed, and the working area tidied.

At last under a general chairman, all the mural-makers meet to review their work and to discuss the usual topics arising from the "judging" stage.

All this while, the teacher has acted as a consultant. If the pupils have made individual pictures, the teacher will have few demonstrations to give. Apart from seeing that a working area [22] and suitable materials are available, doing the preliminary motivation, outlining some of the technical requirements of a mural, and illustrating the "squaring" method of enlarging if it is to be used, he will probably find himself free to enjoy observing the social and artistic growth which accompanies this excellent activity.

Other Group Activities

Some other art activities lend themselves to group endeavor. Any of the topics suggested earlier for murals could be produced in three dimensions. For example, "The Carnival Came to Town" could be developed in paper as suggested earlier in Chapter 7.[23] The tents and side shows could be developed from box sculpture or from folded, cut, and painted cardboard. Animals and people could be made from paper in plastic forms.

Again, pupils could produce a classroom play. Although this activity is somewhat outside the scope of this book, a few comments may be offered about play production in school. Most children in the elementary school cannot be expected to produce stage plays with large sets and elaborate costumes. A classroom play, however, can be offered with simple materials. Cotton sheets or large areas of wrapping paper strung on a wire make appropriate stage curtains and costumes can be created from odds and ends of materials brought from home. A child does not require much encourage-

---

[22] To find space in the classroom for mural work is often a difficult problem. See Chapter 5 for some possible solutions.

[23] See the film, *Paper Sculpture,* Creative Hands Series, listed in Appendix 6.

ment to place an old hat sideways on his head, loop some metal rings over his ears, wrap a scarlet sash around his waist, and announce that he is a pirate, a gypsy, or whatever character is wanted. If scenery is desired, a simple painted backdrop can be attached to the blackboard frame upstage. What are called "ground rows," or cut-out pieces of scenery, can be painted on stiff cardboard supported from the rear by as readily available an object as a chair. Lighting arrangements should be kept to a minimum and perhaps consist only of two spotlights. Most of the fun of costuming and staging in the classroom comes from improvisation. Probably children acquire greater insight into many aspects of the theater arts by these simple means than by participating in a full-blown auditorium play in which much of the effort for production has been assumed by adults or a few senior students.[24]

In conclusion, it must be pointed out that any art activity may develop into a group activity. Whenever a common problem arises in the minds of the pupils, the basis of group work is laid. How can color be mixed? What is texture? How can rhythms be established? Is Michelangelo more important as a painter or as a sculptor? All these questions might lead to a group activity developing both democratic and artistic insight, provided that the teaching methods are selected with these purposes fixed clearly in mind.

ACTIVITIES FOR THE READER

1. Study a group activity in a classroom, analyzing it according to Kilpatrick's four stages.

2. Define what you consider to be the ten most important duties of a teacher in a democracy.

3. Describe three quasi-group activities not mentioned in this chapter.

4. Make three fist puppets; a simple stick puppet; a more complicated paper-bag puppet; and, finally, a cloth puppet of an animal whose jaws will move.

5. Practice manipulating each of your puppets. When skillful, show your friends.

---

24 Victor D'Amico, *Creative Teaching in Art*, Rev. Ed. (Scranton, Pa.: International Textbook, 1953), has some good material for the teacher who wishes to produce a classroom play. See also Natalie Robinson Cole, *The Arts in the Classroom* (N.Y.: John Day, 1940). A complete technical manual and reference is John Gassner and Philip Barber, *Producing the Play*: with *New Scene Technician's Handbook*, Rev. Ed. (N.Y.: Dryden, 1953). A good, short, actor's manual is S. Rosenstein, L. Haydon, and W. Sparrow, *Modern Acting* (N.Y.: Samuel French, 1947).

6. Make three string puppets: the first from a paper bag, with two strings; the second from cloth, with three strings; the third from cloth, with a modeled head and a minimum of seven strings.

7. Practice manipulating your string puppets, eventually giving your friends a treat.

8. Try to form a puppet group in your locality.

9. Study any professional murals in your locality. Make a note of their subject matter in relation to their position, their design, and the media used.

10. Design a mural on a small scale which you think might be suitable for the interior of your local post office, the foyer of a local theater, or the entrance of the local high school. Choose subject matter of local interest.

11. Try to work with, or study, a group of children or adults who are working democratically on puppetry, mural-making, or a community activity in general. Note both the democratic and, if they exist, undemocratic practices. Write an analysis demonstrating how improvements in the technique of group working could be achieved.

Art Activities

for Slow Learners

Every modern educational system takes pride in the attention it gives to individual pupils. In comparatively recent years, many special programs have been developed for abnormal and atypical children, and the teacher in a general classroom, therefore, is unlikely to find extreme cases under his charge. Children, for example, with well-marked behavior difficulties arising from the more serious mental and nervous disorders, the definitely feeble-minded, or the obviously delinquent will in all probability be cared for elsewhere by specially trained personnel. It is well that this should be so, because a classroom teacher who lacks special training in treating these exceptional children will find himself in difficulties. With many handicapped children, art activities are used in highly specialized ways for specific and, in an artistic sense, narrow ends. Art is frequently employed, for example, as a device by which the child reveals his difficulties to a therapist, not primarily as a means of artistic expression. Whatever progress is made by these children, furthermore, occurs as a direct result of highly skilled diagnoses and subsequent clinical treatment, not necessarily because of participation in art activities *per se*.[1]

Although extremely atypical children will probably be educated elsewhere, the general teacher may very well find himself responsible for chil-

[1] See for example, Emery I. Gondor, *Art and Play Therapy* (N.Y.: Random House, 1954), a booklet written in simple language by a sensitive clinician.

dren displaying some deviation from the normal. The two largest groups of these children are usually called "slow learners" and "gifted children," and it is these two groups that the following two chapters will discuss. Because the majority of individuals in them participate in art activities primarily for expressive reasons, they constitute legitimate subject matter for this book.

This chapter will concentrate upon a program of art education for slow learners.[2] By "slow learners," one means here simply those pupils who consistently make considerably lower than average scores on intelligence tests and who progress in the academic subjects at a pace which is manifestly slower than that displayed by the majority of their fellows. It must be further understood that slow learners in general are almost inevitably slow learners in art. There is no evidence that children of retarded mental development are compensated by artistic gifts for their deficiency in intelligence.[3]

Some Characteristics
of the Art of Slow Learners

In order to participate at all in a program of art education, a child apparently must possess a certain minimum level of intelligence.[4] Children with I.Q.'s lower than 40 and M.A.'s (mental ages) lower than 3 appear to derive little or no profit from art activities. Those between about I.Q.'s of 40 and 50 and M.A.'s of 3 to 4 can manipulate certain materials and after considerable practice can improve slightly on the designs which result from this manipu-

---

[2] For a detailed analysis of the intellectual characteristics of mentally retarded children, the reader is referred to Karl C. Garrison, *The Psychology of Exceptional Children* Rev. Ed., (N.Y.: Ronald, 1950), in particular Chapter 12.

The reader is also directed towards the following at this time: Hollis L. Caswell, ed., "Teaching the Slow Learner," *Practical Suggestions for Teaching*, Rev. Ed. (N.Y.: Teachers College, 1951). Christine P. Ingram, *Education of the Slow-Learning Child* (N.Y.: Ronald, 1953). Arch Heck, *The Education of Exceptional Children*, 2nd Ed. (N.Y.: McGraw-Hill, 1953), Chapters 23–25. Florence L. Goodenough and L. M. Rynkiewicz, *Exceptional Children* (N.Y.: Appleton-Century Crofts, 1956), especially Part III, "The Intellectually Inadequate."

The reader should be warned that not one of these authors mentions art education for children of low mentality. However, they give a good general background for the subject. Art education for slow learners so far seems to be a neglected area, if one may judge from the lack of worthwhile literature on the subject.

[3] Much of the subject matter of this chapter is condensed from the statements made in C. D. and M. R. Gaitskell, *Art Education for Slow Learners* (Toronto: The Ryerson Press, and Peoria, Ill.: Bennett, 1953), by special permission.

[4] *Ibid.* The following statements are based largely upon a study of 44 child inmates of a mental hospital. These inmates were all in the low mentality group but apparently did not suffer, to any marked degree, from other types of mental difficulty. The intelligence range was from idiocy to an I.Q. of 56 and the chronological age (C.A.) range was 6 to 12 years.

106 *"My Brother and Me Playing Golf"—a crayon drawing by a boy C.A. 12, I.Q. 56.*

lation. Eventually some of these children can produce crude symbols. Those with I.Q.'s in the middle 50's and M.A.'s of 5 to 6 seem to be able to express by means of related symbols some ideas which are probably connected with their experiences. In other words, a child with an I.Q. of at least 50 and an M.A. of at least 5 apparently can participate, to a limited extent, in art activities. Since it is unlikely that a teacher of regular classes will find in his group a pupil who scores lower than, or even as low as 50 on an intelligence test, he may anticipate that every child under his care is capable of engaging in art work.

The slow learner enrolled in a regular classroom, like a normal child, begins his artistic career by manipulating art materials, rather than by drawing or modeling recognizable objects.[5] He is sometimes slower than a normal child to play with the materials given to him and may not explore their possibilities fully. Having been given a box of twelve wax crayons of various colors, for example, he might use only one color. Once he has begun manipulating a medium he is often reluctant to branch out into the use of symbols.

[5] *Ibid.* The study on which this and the following statements are largely based included 514 cases enrolled in 55 schools. The I.Q. range of these children was 50 to 89, with a median I.Q. of 70 and a C.A. range of 7 years, 6 months, to 16 years; they produced 3,674 pieces of art for analysis.

107 *"A Big Fish"—a tempera painting by a girl C.A. 9, I.Q. 60.*

If given a second type of material, he frequently prefers to manipulate the original medium, in the use of which he apparently feels more secure. In some cases, he seems to be content to watch other children play with the new materials. If familiar toys are available in the classroom, furthermore, he will often prefer to play with them, rather than to work with art materials.

Whereas a normal five-year-old child may arrive at the symbol stage in a period of time ranging from three weeks to six months, the five-year-old slow learner who has an I.Q. around 70 may not reach this stage for a year or more. In time, however, the slow learner arrives at the symbol stage in a manner which resembles that of the normal child. Once the symbol stage has been reached, several symbols may appear in his output in quick succession.

The mentally retarded child, because of his greater chronological age, often possesses powers of physical coordination superior to those of normal children of the same mental age. These, of course, help him to master drawing skills more readily and allow him to repeat a recently developed symbol without much practice. Repetition which requires little thought suits the slow learner and often gives his work a characteristic rhythmic quality.

His tendency to repeat a discovery interferes with his creation of new symbols and at the same time retards his development of the symbols already discovered. In other words, he is as slow to make progress in the stage of symbols as he is to pass through the period of manipulation. Nevertheless, a slow learner, like normal children, will sometimes surprise a teacher with a burst of progress.

As noted in an earlier chapter, reversion from the symbol stage to that of manipulation will sometimes occur in the work of all children as a result of such factors as fatigue, ill health, temporary emotional disturbances, periods of intense concentration, interruptions of various kinds, absence from school, or faulty teaching methods. Reversion of this kind occurs more frequently with mentally retarded children than with normal children.

Gradually, the slow learner begins to spend more time on his work and thus gives detail to his symbols. Sometimes he may learn to relate his symbols. The progress he makes depends largely, of course, upon the attention

108 *"The Telephone Men"—a crayon drawing by a boy C.A. 10, I.Q. 68. Note the lack of uniformity of development in the delineation of symbols.*

he is willing to give to his work. The slow learner's span of attention tends to increase with both his chronological age and his mental age. Of 342 mentally retarded children studied for their retention of interest in making a picture, some lost interest in their work within a few minutes, while others worked as long as an hour and a half. With some exceptions, the older children tended to work longer than the younger. Moreover, many of the older children were willing to return to the same picture for days on end.

The forms used by slow learners to extend the meaning of their symbols have some peculiar characteristics. The length of limbs in a human symbol may be greatly exaggerated, for example, if the child feels such distortion is necessary to tell his story. Although this type of distortion may be seen in the work of normal children, it seems to be more pronounced in that of slow learners. Again, details added to the symbols may fail to show uniform development. An otherwise crude symbol of a human being might include a most detailed and relatively accurate delineation of the features of the face or of certain small particulars of clothing which have special significance for the child. At the same time, because of his concentration upon details which hold his interest, the slow learner, with his limited powers of concentration, may omit some items which the normal child would probably include in his symbols.

A type of symbol, or mark, used more frequently by slow learners than by normal children of the same mental or chronological age, is an artificial, conventionalized notation like that found in professional cartoons. Lines, for example, may be employed to show noise emanating from a particular source—a flow of music from a radio or a rush of air from a window. Sometimes feelings of excitement or happiness ascribed to a symbol of a human being are also represented by this type of notation. As well as making frequent use of these marks, slow learners will sometimes employ writing with their symbols in an attempt to clarify their pictorial statement.

A few observations must be made concerning the general composition and aesthetic qualities of the pictorial output of slow learners. These children often use the usual childlike conventions, like "X-ray," "series," and "fold-over" pictures, but they adopt these relatively complicated conventions only after much practice of art. Very few slow learners ever use linear perspective. While the overlapping of objects to give pictorial depth may be seen in some of their work, relatively little use is made of this device. Even when the retarded child uses one of the above conventions, he does not, as a rule, use it throughout his composition, but applies it only to some selected point of emphasis.

Slow learners often fail to achieve unity in their compositions. The rhythms they adopt become monotonous; centers of interest which may appear as they begin work are later destroyed, and almost half of the work they produce lacks a center of interest entirely; and they fail to establish a reasonable balance in almost two-thirds of their work. Slow learners, however, are usually successful in achieving variety, if not unity, although the variety in their use of the elements of design is rarely as interesting as that found in the work of normal children. They appear to have most success in their use of color, although they make relatively little use of tints and shades, and rely, instead, upon standard hues. In fact, rarely will light and shade in any form be found in their output. Some slow learners use line quite successfully. In some instances the lines they produce may be either vigorous or delicate enough to be very interesting. Textural effects achieved by means of drawing occur extremely infrequently in any of their work.

It may be said, then, that the general appearance of the work of mentally retarded children is relatively uninteresting aesthetically. Occasionally a child may produce work which has some extremely attractive detail. On even rarer occasions, a slow learner may develop a composition which is both charming and original either in its pattern or in its subject matter, or in both. Perhaps largely because of its deviation from normal expression, such work may exhibit a strangeness which makes it significant as art. Work of this description is not usually to be seen, however, nor should one expect it to be. Since the insight of the mentally handicapped child into the meaning of his life is usually neither subtle nor deep, manifestly his art cannot, in an absolute sense, be significant. It is significant only in relation to the child who produces it. In spite of its deficiencies, however, and because both its content and its design are not infrequently expressive and creative, the output of many mentally retarded children participating in a program of art education may easily be included within the definition of art.

Subject Matter
Selected by Slow Learners

As indicated earlier, all children who have the intelligence to do so pass through the normal stages of pictorial expression mentioned in Chapter 6; the manipulation, symbol, and preadolescent stages. While the child with a mental age of around three and a chronological age of six will never go beyond manipulating materials, the child with the same chronological age and whose mental age is four or better may begin to enter the symbol stage. If his mental age is five, he will even place symbols within their environment.

Like normal children, once they progress beyond the stage of manipulation, slow learners discover subject matter for expression in their own experiences. Many of the titles which they give to their work are little different from those selected by normal children. The titles describe events which occur at home, at school, at play, or in the community. The following are representative.

> We are working in the garden
> Our class went to visit a farm
> I saw a big fire
> I helped my Dad wash the car

Titles such as these are usually selected by those slow learners in the late symbol or preadolescent stages of expression who are closest to normal intelligence. The titles are concise and in most of them the children have identified themselves with their environment. The less intelligent the slow learner, the less inclined he is to relate himself to the world in which he lives. In other words, an ability to identify oneself with environment seems to vary directly with intelligence.

The themes with which many slow learners deal are often closely connected with little intimate events in life. A normal child might overlook them, or, having touched upon them once or twice, would then find other interests. Many slow learners, on the other hand, seem to find constant interest in pictures of this nature. Some representative titles are as follows:

> I sat on our steps
> The birds are in the trees
> I am walking to school

In some of their titles, slow learners seem to place an abnormal emphasis upon authoritarian actions, either their own or those of others, which may indicate the child's personal desire to assume command, or an admiration of those in authority in a world in which he finds few opportunities to be a leader. Examples of such an apparent compensatory attitude may be found in the following titles:

> The guard is telling those boys when they can cross the street
>
> The soldiers are keeping the kids back as the parade goes by
>
> Dad only lets me decorate the Christmas tree
>
> There were two children in our tree; I told them to come down or I would fight them

Frequently, the several objects or actions depicted in the work of the slow learner have little or no clear and logical connection. His titles may illustrate his general inability to organize thought or to cope with some strong emotional experience. When the child shows deep concern about the

109 *"Robin Hood"—a chalk drawing by a boy C.A. 11 years 4 months, I.Q. 65.*

subject matter included in this type of expression, the teacher must take the work especially seriously. The following titles are illustrative of this class of expression:

> The car went bang and I was eating candy and then I cried
>
> I wish I had a doll and maybe Lucy is coming over to my house and I guess she is mad

In some of their titles, slow learners anticipate future consequences of the actions depicted in their illustrations. Here, the statements are usually logical and serve to complete a little story begun in the picture itself. These titles sometimes appear to illustrate the child's confusion between present and future action. The following indicate this form of anticipatory statement:

> This boy is going to be hit by a car
>
> This is my uncle; he has a big farm and I am going to visit him
>
> Our school is playing hockey and we are going to win

The mentally retarded, as well as the normal, child frequently likes to depict his reactions to vicarious experience, even though he is more attracted to actual experience. Dramatized versions of familiar stories and events shown upon the moving picture or television screen may excite him towards visual expression.

The adolescent slow learner, who shows a score in an intelligence test of around 70 or better, no matter what his grade level, tends to use some of the subject matter found in the art work of a normal adolescent. This often exhibits a growing interest in social events in which both sexes are present. Boys, especially, make pictures about sports and sporting contests, deeds of daring, and many kinds of mechanical objects. Where human beings are shown in pictures, considerable attention is often given to anatomical detail. These characteristic adolescent statements occur less frequently with adolescents whose scores on an intelligence test fall much below 70.

In summary, one may see that although most slow learners will not accept the full challenge which art presents, the sources of subject matter for their expression are very similar to those of normal children.

Methods of Teaching
Slow Learners

The fact that mental retardation, to a greater or lesser extent, usually affects the whole personality makes the task of the teacher of slow learners difficult. Often as the result of external pressures, a mentally retarded child suffers from emotional disturbances. Thus each slow learner, not only because of his mental handicap but also because of unfortunate accompaniments, may exhibit behavior which makes extraordinary demands upon the teacher's understanding.

To teach slow learners one must possess a number of commendable personal qualities and professional abilities. Since these children progress slowly in their work, the teacher must, in particular, be a patient person. He must be prepared to endure exasperations and discouragements which would make the life of any but a patient teacher unbearable. The teacher of slow learners must, furthermore, be able to challenge these children so that they are kept as mentally alert as is possible and practical. At the same time, however, he must refrain from hurrying them into work beyond their ability. Finally, the teacher must treat every slow learner as a unique being and not think of him as the possessor of some sort of standard type of personality. The fact that all such pupils suffer from a similar handicap does not mean that they lose identity as individuals. A study of their output in art offers a striking illustration of the fact that the personalities of slow learners differ widely.

If the teacher finds in his otherwise normal class one or two particularly slow learners in art requiring special attention, this should cause him little embarrassment. Obviously the teacher should in no way indicate to other members of the class the deficiencies of their mentally retarded classmates. Since all successful teaching in art rests upon a methodology which demands that the teacher treat all pupils as individuals, the fact that the slow learners are afforded certain special attentions in no sense should make them unique in the eyes of their fellows. Every child in the class, whether handicapped, normal, or gifted, will require individual treatment.

Again, if the teacher is placed in charge of a whole class of slow learners, the same educational principles apply. Although every member of the group is a slow learner, no two children will react in an identical manner to art. Here, as elsewhere, every child must be offered an educational program tailored to his individual needs and capacities.

As indicated earlier, no matter how efficient the teaching practices may be, mentally retarded children will make slower progress and produce a lower standard of art than normal children. Such being the case, some teachers of these children have been tempted to obtain more skillful-looking results by mechanical busy work. Exercises in tracing, copying, and coloring the work of others constitute one such type of work. Activities involving the chance techniques constitute another type. Tending to become busy work are activities which are taught step by step.

As stated earlier, the educational values of copying, even for normal children, are dubious, and, therefore, such work is not recommended. Copying also interferes with the ability of mentally retarded children to participate in a creative art program. Indeed, research has indicated that undesirable as this busy work may be with normal children, it appears to have even more inhibiting effects upon less robust minds.[6]

Busy work which produces results that are original but derived by chance, rather than by planning, poses a different educational problem.[7] The uncontrolled spilling of paint upon a dampened sheet of paper, for example, often produces pleasing effects. Such an exercise scarcely falls within our definition of art, however, since by art we imply a controlled

---

[6] Some of the harmful effects of "busy work" upon normal children are outlined in Viktor Lowenfeld (Ed.), "Workbooks and Art Education." *Research Bulletin,* 1952–53, Eastern Arts Association, Kutztown, Pa.

For a report on similar effects of this work upon slow learners, see C. D. and M. R. Gaitskell, *Art Education for Slow Learners,* pp. 32–34.

See Carl Reed, *Early Adolescent Art Education* (Peoria, Ill.: Bennett, 1957), which emphasizes chance methods. The same applies to large sections of *A Guide for the Teaching of Art,* San Francisco Unified School District, 1956.

reaction to experience. To include much of this work in the art program for normal children could not be recommended because it fails to provide the challenge inherent in real art work. For slow learners, however, these activities may be of some value. Since the mentally handicapped child cannot profit from certain of the more difficult activities found in the art program of normal pupils, his program may lack variety unless there is recourse to some chance activities. Some teachers, it must be admitted, are not able to agree with this point of view, and certainly the point is debatable. Since the work is not art, why should it be included in an art program, they ask? One may reply that although activities which depend upon chance are not originally art, they may well become so, *if* the pupil gains control of them through experimentation. If the limitations of this kind of work are recognized, it may profitably be included in the art program for slow learners, as a means of broadening it. Indeed, chance activities might be occasionally included in the art work of normal pupils, provided they are only a minor part of the program.

Finally, step-by-step teaching practices, while rarely of value to normal pupils because they present no real challenge, may often give the slow learner a valuable and necessary sense of achievement. Frequently this teaching method, if used wisely, may lead slow learners into more creative endeavors.

It may be said in summary that the approved methods now used with normal children are to a large extent also practical and effective when used with slow learners. The handicapped children, however, require more individual attention than their normal mental counterparts, and the pace of teaching often has to be slowed. Motivation, classroom arrangements, and appraisal of the effectiveness of the program in progress, nevertheless, require little or no modification in principle when applied to retarded pupils.

Art Activities Especially Suitable for Slow Learners

Having discussed the characteristics of slow learners, together with effective methods of teaching them, we may now consider in detail some art activities for them. Fortunately, most of the basic types of art activities have proved to be sufficiently flexible to be used with slow learners either in special classes or in regular classrooms. These activities include some types of drawing and painting, some forms of paper and cardboard work, a certain amount of sculpture and pottery, and some types of printing, all of which have been described earlier and hence require only brief mention here. Little additional comment about teaching these activities will be offered since the

110 *Work in box sculpture by pupils ranging in C.A. from 9 to 12 years 5 months and in I.Q. from 60 to 75.*

Royal Studio

reader may refer to other chapters where teaching methods were discussed at some length.

Some further activities, including certain kinds of weaving, embroidery, and bookcraft, are particularly valuable for slow learners, and these together with methods of teaching them will be described in some detail in the following paragraphs.

Basic Activities

MEDIA AND TECHNIQUES: In drawing and painting, slow learners may use the standard tools and equipment recommended for other pupils. Hence, wax crayons, tempera paint, the usual types of brushes and papers, and so on may be employed. Nearly all slow learners are capable of producing reasonably creative paper work. Most of these pupils achieve greatest success when cut paper is used as a medium for two-dimensional pictures. Some of the more intelligent pupils, however, may begin to build their pictures into three dimensions. Nearly all these children enjoy box sculpture, and many of them seem capable of doing some paper sculpture which is free-standing. Only the most intelligent, on the other hand, seem to be able to create forms in space. Many slow learners can use molds to make simple masks, while nearly all of them can work successfully with papier-mâché if it is prepared in advance for them.

Carving in wood and other substances cannot be recommended for most slow learners. The tools required in much of this work are too dangerous for them, and the technique is beyond their ability. Simple forms of modeling and pottery, however, may be recommended. The direct nature of modeling pleases these pupils, while the repetitive character of most pottery makes this craft highly suitable. In printing, both stick and vegetable printing are useful techniques, again, largely because they are repetitive. Stencil and linoleum work, however, are usually too difficult, except for preadolescent pupils scoring close to normal on I.Q. tests.

TEACHING: With all the basic activities mentioned above, the teacher of slow learners must modify his classroom techniques to suit the lesser creative abilities of these pupils. Often a step-by-step approach becomes necessary, not only in the work itself but also in the selection of tools and media. If their I.Q. scores fall below about 70, preadolescent slow learners usually experience difficulty when confronted by a wide range of color or by the problems of mixing tints, shades, and even secondary hues, such as orange from a blend of red and yellow. The teacher will, therefore, often find it necessary to supply all colors ready-mixed. Chalk and charcoal substitutes also create difficulties for many of these slow learners, as does the mixing of media.

When three-dimensional work such as pottery or box sculpture is being considered for slow learners, the teacher would be wise to analyze for himself the process from start to finish in terms of separate operations. Then, before the pupils begin work, they should be shown a finished object so that they know what to expect at the end of their labors. After that, however, demonstrations and general teaching should be performed only in relation to any one operation. The pupils should select the tools only for the one operation, complete the operation, and then return the tools. This process should then be repeated until all the necessary operations have been mastered.

The length of each operation will depend upon the class. Pupils of lower intelligence will be able to master only very short and simple operations. Perhaps the greatest challenge facing the teacher of slow learners is to judge correctly the length and complexity of a unit of work so that each pupil is challenged, but not confused. An example of a step-by-step analysis of work will be found in the "card-loom weaving" section which follows immediately.

Card-Loom Weaving

MEDIA AND TECHNIQUES: To replace some activities which are denied slow learners because the work is too difficult for them to master, one may readily turn to certain weaving techniques. This statement does not imply that weaving is recommended only for the mentally handicapped. Highly

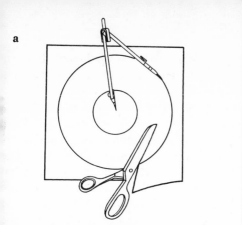

a

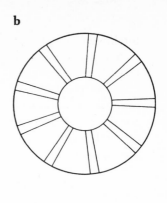

b

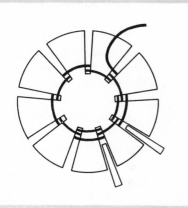

c

d

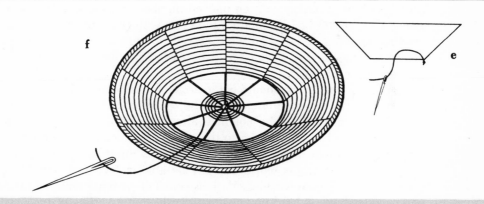

f

e

111 *Processes in card-loom weaving: (a) drawing and cutting the cardboard base, (b) marking the spokes, (c) weaving, and (d) finishing the rim of the basket, (e) sewing in strips of material for weaving base, (f) weaving the base.*

intelligent people, of course, engage in this work. Nevertheless, because weaving is an extremely flexible technique and depends largely upon a repetition of movement, it is especially suitable for slow learners.

The process called "card-loom weaving" allows children to produce a number of practical articles such as mats or baskets without too much mental concentration. To make a container, for example, one should draw on fairly heavy cardboard a circle having a radius from three to six inches and inside the larger circle, a smaller circle having about one-half that radius. Spokes about three-quarters to one inch wide should be drawn from the circumference of the smaller circle to the circumference of the larger circle. A space about one-eighth of an inch wide should be left between the spokes. It is recommended that an uneven number of spokes be drawn at first. The space between the spokes should be cut out and the spokes should then be bent upward (see Fig. 111).

Weaving may now begin with wool, string, or raffia—a grasslike substance having a long fiber. Starting from the base circle, the weaving material is simply taken over one spoke and under the next until each is entirely covered except for about one-quarter of an inch of cardboard at the outside extremity of the spokes. This may be doubled over from the inside to the outside to form an edge to the container. Any ends of weaving material that are sticking out should be cut off.

To finish the base of the article, one may glue felt to the center, both on the inside and the outside. The base may also be woven. First, with a large needle, one takes one strip of weaving material from the inside extremity of each spoke to the center of the base, after which over-and-under weaving may be done with the needle. This technique may be used, of course, only in a basket with an uneven number of spokes. The rim of the article may be finished by binding the edge with the same material as was used for weaving. If holes are first pierced through the edge of the spokes before binding begins, the task will be easier. Binding is done by sewing over and over.

To make a mat, one should cut a circle of cardboard of convenient size and then cut out a small circle from the center of the cardboard. The rim of the cardboard should be notched, after which the weaving material is looped repeatedly from the rim to the center of the cardboard. Binding the edge in the manner mentioned above completes the mat.

Many slow learners will eventually be able to try some simple experiments with card-loom weaving. Various colors of weaving material may first be introduced, while later perhaps material having a variety of both texture and color might be used. Again, the shape of the cardboard might be altered; an oval may be used instead of a circle. Later again, an even number of spokes may be used; and in this case two weaving materials of different colors can be used simultaneously to produce an interesting design. Handles for objects can be made by running a strand of weaving material over and under three long strands of the same material. Such handles may be attached merely by sewing.

TEACHING: Let us suppose that the teacher plans to have a class of very slow-learning pupils make woven containers.[8] To arouse interest and to make sure that all members of the class realize what the finished object may look like, he exhibits and talks about three containers. These objects are finished identically at the edges and centers but are made in different colors. The following operations and demonstrations are considered to be necessary with this group of children.

OPERATION A. *Preparing the cards*

Demonstration 1. Obtain cards, scissors, and compasses
2. Describe inner and outer circles; cut away excess cardboard
3. Draw spokes
4. Cut away cardboard between spokes

OPERATION B. *Weaving*

Demonstration 1. Select weaving material
2. Begin weaving
3. Weave
4. Finish weaving

OPERATION C. *Finishing center*

Demonstration 1. Obtain felt and glue jar containing brush
2. Measure center with compasses, transferring measurements to paper; cut out paper as guide for cutting felt; cut felt
3. Glue cut felt to center
4. Return scissors and compasses

OPERATION D. *Finishing edge*

Demonstration 1. Obtain large needle and binding material
2. Pierce cardboard
3. Over-and-over sewing
4. Sew between spokes, through weaving material
5. Finish binding, knotting, and cutting material

OPERATION E. *Returning all tools*

(no demonstration but verbal reminder to be orderly)

_____
[8] This lesson was planned for a class of boys, I.Q. range 50 to 70, C.A. range 11 to 15 years 5 months.

OPERATION F. *Picking up scraps and general tidying up*

(no demonstration but verbal request to do a good job)

In another class the teacher might combine some operations, should the intelligence of pupils allow this. Also, he might allow more choice in materials and techniques.

Box-Loom Weaving

MEDIA AND TECHNIQUES: The more intelligent of the preadolescent slow learners—usually those who score over 70 on an I.Q. test—are able to weave successfully on a simple "cradle" or "box" loom, as shown in Fig. 112. The loom is of such simple construction that the pupils may easily make it themselves. It consists of what look like two sets of miniature goal posts, joined by four dowel rods which can be made from old broom handles. At one end of the apparatus, slots should be made in the posts for a tension bar (see Fig. 113).

Three items of equipment are required before weaving can begin. The first of these is what is called a "heddle." This is a frame of metal about the

112 *Weaving on a box loom.*

Royal Studio

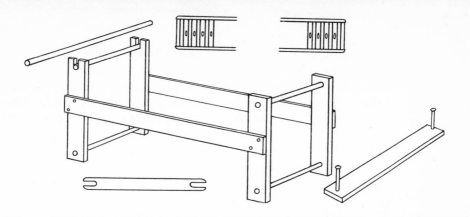

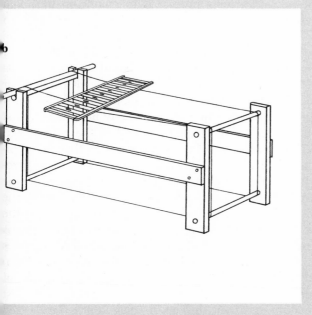

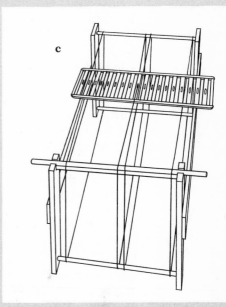

113 (*a*) *The equipment needed for box-loom weaving: the loom itself, showing
the tension bar separate, the heddle, the warping frame, the shuttle.*
(*b*) *The loom with the tension bar in place and the heddle resting on
the supporting threads.* (*c*) *The first two warp threads in place.*
(*d*) *The shuttle passing through the warp threads.*

same width as the loom, containing bars pierced by holes. The heddle is the mechanism which allows the cross threads to be put through the warp threads. Since heddles are made with considerable precision, they must be bought rather than made by the pupils. Most school supply firms sell heddles of various sizes, with differing numbers of bars to the inch. The number of bars determines the texture of the woven cloth. The second item is called a "shuttle." This is a flat piece of wood with notches cut at each end to hold the weaving material which is wound lengthwise around it. Pupils will find it a simple matter to make shuttles. The third item is known as a "warping frame." This is a piece of wood at the ends of which are two nails. It is used to measure yarn, and can be made by the pupils.

The first step in the actual weaving process is to mount on the loom the threads running lengthwise (called the "warp") and at the same time to thread the heddle.[9] To obtain warp threads, the pupil must first tie the weaving material to one nail on the warping frame and wind several turns around both nails. Then with a pair of scissors, he should cut the threads where they meet one of the nails, and thus provide himself with a number of warp threads of equal and correct length. The mounting of the warp threads and the simultaneous threading of the heddle may now begin. First the tension bar should be placed in the slots at one end of the loom. Next, two strings should be tied from the ends of the top dowels, so that the pupil has somewhere to rest the heddle. Next, taking one warp thread already prepared on the warping frame, the pupil passes it through the center hole of the heddle and around all the dowel rods and the tension bar of the loom. The ends of this encircling warp thread should be tied together at the top dowel rod opposite the end supporting the tension bar. This process must be repeated with another warp thread, except that this thread passes through the adjoining space on the heddle instead of the hole. The pupil must continue to thread the loom in this fashion, working on each side of the center of the heddle and passing the warp threads alternately, first through a hole in the heddle and then through a space, until the desired width of the material to be woven is reached. The function of the heddle will now be clear. By either pulling up or depressing the heddle, the pupil will observe that "sheds" are made, through which he may thrust the shuttle with the cross weaver or "weft" thread (see Fig. 113).

To perform the weaving, the pupil should first wind the yarn around the shuttle. Then he should raise the heddle and pass the shuttle through the shed on the near side of the heddle. With the heddle, the weft thread should then be pressed to the end of the loom toward the operator. Next, the pupil

[9] These and other weaving processes on the box loom are clearly illustrated in the film *Loom Weaving*, listed in Creative Hands Series, Appendix 6.

must press the heddle down and again pass the shuttle through the shed. This process is continued with the sheds being formed by the alternate raising and lowering of the heddle, the shuttle going from side to side, until the desired length of cloth is produced.

A certain degree of skill is necessary, of course, to perform well on a loom. The weft threads must be placed at equal distances from each other. If they are beaten too vigorously with the heddle, the weaving will be bulky. If not pressed closely enough, the cloth will be flimsy in places. Again, skill is required to keep the edges of the woven material straight and tidy. If the pupil pulls the weft thread too tight, the edge will have a wave; if he fails to pull it tight enough he may find the edge displaying unsightly little loops. However, difficult though the skill of weaving may appear to the beginner, actually the technique may soon be mastered satisfactorily on the loom described above.

Once the slow learner has developed an ability to use this loom, he will no doubt become very fond of weaving, and may wish to make articles such as scarves or a series of place mats requiring the full length of the warp thread. In such cases, he must learn to move the weaving around the loom so that he may continue to use the heddle in its normal place. To move the weaving, he needs merely to remove the tension bar, and then, using the heddle, to ease the weaving around the dowel rods until only warp threads are visible. After he has replaced the tension bar, he may continue weaving as described previously.

To finish the edges of an article after he has cut it from the loom, the pupil may knot together the warp threads by twos and then trim the strands to form a fringe. To make the edge more secure, he may also sew the last two or three strands of weft to the warp threads.

Experimentation in weaving is within the capabilities of many slow learners. Although four-ply wool is perhaps the best material with which to learn weaving, various types of both warp and weft material may eventually be used. Interesting patterns may be developed by using materials of different colors and textures.

TEACHING: Before slow learners are taught to weave on a loom the teacher should analyze the operations and list the demonstrations as was done above for card-weaving.

Loom-weaving creates storage problems, since both the loom and the wool are bulky. These may be partially solved by having collapsible looms which may be dismantled when not in use. Another solution to the difficulty, of course, is to have only a few looms and to have the pupils use them on a rotation basis.

Good weaving depends upon the tension on the strands. One learns to control tension largely through "feeling" in the same way that one learns to skate or ride a bicycle. Therefore, before teaching is done, the teacher should practice until he can maintain an even tension almost automatically. Since each type of loom has its own peculiarities the teacher should practice on the type of loom which the pupils will use.

As each step of setting up the loom is taught, the teacher should inspect the assembly of every pupil. The warp threads should be tapped with the palm of the hand to see that each strand is secure and that tension is right. The tension should be such that tapping the threads causes a vigorous rebound of the hand.

When everything is ready for weaving, the teacher can often help a slow learner by standing behind him, lightly holding his hands, and going through the motions of using heddle and shuttle until the pupil can follow the correct rhythm of motion.[10]

Embroidery

MEDIA AND TECHNIQUES: Another activity which need not be confined to slow learners but which is especially suitable for them because of its repetitious character is embroidery. This need not mean commercially stamped products depicting old-fashioned ladies or forget-me-nots, for embroidery can be as stimulating and original as many other contemporary art forms.

Cotton and burlap are very good materials on which to embroider. Needles may be purchased in almost any "five-and-ten-cent" store together with embroidery cottons in many colors. Wools in different weights and colors add variety to the work.

Many stitches are used in embroidery, among them the simple running stitch and more complicated stitches such as the blanket, buttonhole, chain, daisy, outline, and feather stitches. The use of several stitches in one design gives variety to the work (see Fig. 114).[11]

The design, which can be planned in advance or created on the cloth, is outlined with a simple stitch, and areas are given texture with the more complicated stitches.

TEACHING: The most practical way to teach embroidery is to treat it as a form of picture-making. With the simple embroidery materials mentioned above, even a mentally retarded child may immediately set to work. Fortunately there is no need at first to show him a number of complicated

---

[10] Recommended references for weaving are Harriet J. Brown, *Handweaving: For Pleasure and Profit* (N.Y.: Harper, 1952); Mary Kirby, *Designing on the Loom* (N.Y.: Studio, 1955).

[11] A good introductory booklet on embroidery is Mildred Ryan, *Needlecraft Handbook* (N.Y.: Arco, 1954).

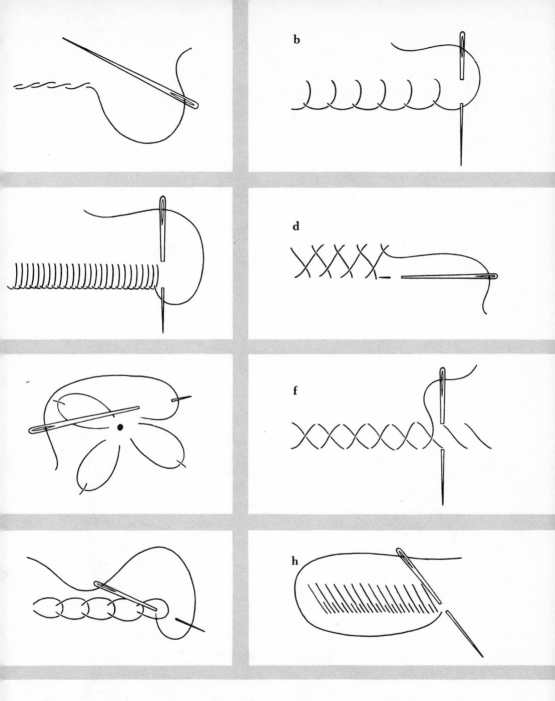

114 *Diagrams of some embroidery stitches: (a) one kind of running stitch,*
(b) blanket stitch, (c) buttonhole stitch, (d) feather stitch, (e) daisy stitch,
(f) cross stitch, (g) chain stitch, (h) long and short stitch.

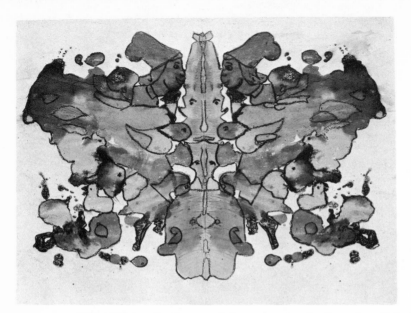

115a *"Chance" effect work in tempera paint by a boy C.A. 12, I.Q. 80. Paper is folded immediately after receiving paint. The pupil did some outlining when the paint dried.*

115b *"Chance" effect work in tempera paint, by a girl C.A. 12, I.Q. 70, in which paint is dripped onto paper. Blowing the wet paint helps to spread it.*

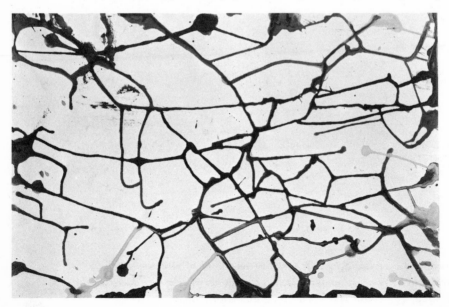

stitches, because what is known as the "running stitch" comes quite naturally to him. Mariska Karasz says:

> If you have ever held a needle in your hand you know how to do this stitch without being told. It . . . consists simply of running the needle in and out through the fabric at fairly regular intervals. It is the simplest kind of stitch with which to draw a line or outline a shape. But you will be missing its best use if you don't try it also as a filler.[12]

Thus, the child may use the needle directly as a means of expression. Selecting his cotton or burlap background material, he may start working upon it without drawing lines. Having gained experience in the technique, he might later sketch some ideas in pencil before he begins embroidering. After this he may be taught the more complicated stitches, some of which are nevertheless easy to learn.

Since embroidery depends upon easily learned skills, it is an especially useful field in which the slow learner can be creative. Using threads and background of varying colors, weights, and textures, exploring the potentialities of a newly discovered stitch, and the like, these pupils will find an exciting challenge in this occupation.

[12] "Creative Arts of the Needle," *House Beautiful,* January, 1952, p. 85.

115c *"Chance" effect work, by a girl C.A. 11, I.Q. 75, using string dipped in paint and pulled across paper.*

Bookcraft

MEDIA AND TECHNIQUES: Most slow learners can learn to make booklets, which can be used as attractive scrapbooks or notebooks, with decorated covers and end pages. Much of this work appeals to slow learners largely because the techniques used to decorate the booklets are simple and yet result in quite spectacular designs.

First, the pupil decorates the cover paper front and back. This may be done by stick or vegetable printing, finger painting, or some "chance" effects. Some of the techniques depending on chance, which are also suitable for producing gift wrapping papers or for backgrounds for various forms of printing, are as follows:

a) Paper is dampened with water, after which tempera colors are splashed over the damp surface. The colors will run and blend in a pleasing manner.

b) Into a shallow pan containing water are placed a few drops of thin oil paint of various colors. By gently blowing on the surface of the water, a pupil develops a swirling pattern of color. Paper should then be slipped into the water at one end of the pan, submerged completely, and then raised gently. The oil paint will adhere to the paper to form a unique pattern.

c) A toothbrush loaded with tempera paint is held over a sheet of paper. Taking a scraper, such as a knife, the pupil draws the blade towards him over the toothbrush, thereby spraying the paper. The use of several colors may result in a pleasant harmony. This technique may be controlled by using a "mask," or covering paper, to block off areas where the spray is not desired.

d) A length of string is dropped at random on paper, after which the pupil traces around the string with a pencil. The areas so formed can then be colored.

e) Tempera paint in two or more colors is placed thickly on paper. The sheet is folded in half with the painted surface inside. When drawn apart, the paper displays a bisymmetrical pattern.

To make the cover of the booklet, the pupil places the prepared cover paper on the desk. Next he cuts a sheet of stiff cardboard slightly smaller than the cover sheet. He then cuts the cardboard into two pieces of equal size and lays the two pieces side-by-side over the cover paper, leaving a small gap between them to form the spine of the booklet. He then folds

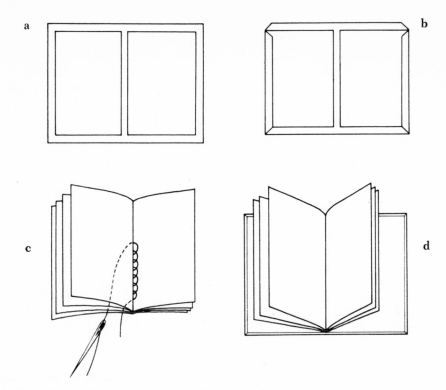

116 *Processes in making a simple booklet: (a) placing cardboard covers on treated cover paper, (b) mitering and folding cover paper, (c) and sewing the page inserts. The finished booklet is shown in (d).*

the edges of the cover paper over the cardboard. The cardboard and cover paper are pasted together; the corners are carefully folded and, if the pupil is capable of doing so, mitered (see Fig. 116).

To prepare the inside of the booklet, sheets of paper about one-quarter inch smaller than the cover are folded to form pages. These are lightly stitched together with a needle and thread along their spine. The front and back pages of this assembly are then pasted and pressed to the covers. To complete the booklet the pupil may shellac the cover.

There are, of course, many other types of bookcraft, but most of them are too exacting to be considered for slow learners.[13]

---

[13] The following references are recommended:
Chris Groneman, *General Bookbinding* (Bloomington, Ill.: McKnight & McKnight, 1941); Lawrence Town, *Bookbinding by Hand* (N.Y: Pitman, 1952); Douglas Cockerall, *Bookbinding and the Care of Books*, 5th Ed. (N. Y.: Pitman, 1954).

TEACHING: While the exact steps of making the booklet must be taught to slow learners, the teacher can employ a creative approach both in the "chance" effects of decorating paper and to some extent in the actual making of the booklet. The techniques leading to a chance pattern should be demonstrated one at a time so that the pupils will not become confused by a multiplicity of materials and ways of using them. While he should set maximum and minimum limits of size for the booklet, the teacher need not establish definite dimensions but rather leave them to be decided by the pupils.

Group Activities for Slow Learners

Whether in special classes comprised only of slow learners, or in classes in which only one or two slow learners are found, the mentally retarded require thoughtful consideration when group activities take place.

Most members of special classes for retarded pupils experience difficulty in participating in class or group activities in art. The difficulties arise largely from the differences in intelligence and in chronological age to be found in most groups. As indicated in an earlier chapter, group activity presents many difficulties even for normal people; for the mentally retarded, who have usually suffered to some extent from frustrations in life and hence are often emotionally volatile, the group activity must be particularly carefully chosen and supervised if it is to succeed.

One of the most highly recommended group activities for classes of slow learners is puppetry. This activity allows the child to work both as an individual and as a member of a group. Only the simplest of puppets described in Chapter 11 need be made for a highly successful group performance. The stick and fist type of puppets are suitable for most slow learners; string puppets are beyond their ability to build or to manipulate. The child's own symbols, cut in cardboard and tacked to sticks, or doll-like creatures made from old socks or paper bags and manipulated with the fingers, will form suitable characters for a play. A large cardboard carton, as described earlier, will provide a simple stage. As with normal children, the spoken lines and the action of the play may be derived from a well-liked story or based upon some experience in the children's lives.

Since mural-making demands group cooperation and organization at a high level, this activity is not generally recommended for slow learners. The quasi-group activity, however, in which the general plan is discussed and decided upon by a group but in which each child works by himself on his own section of the display, is more practical for slow learners, as it is for young children. Many partly cooperative activities of this type may be carried out in clay or in other modeling or building materials, including empty boxes and odd pieces of wood. A service station, a farm, a village, or a playground are among the subjects which slow learners might be interested in developing.

When only one or two noticeably slow learners are found in a class of normal children, the difficulties arising from group work are greater since these pupils must participate and attempt to hold their own with their classmates. The problem of having these pupils purposefully occupied is not too great when the whole class is engaged in a group activity such as puppetry. There are always some necessary jobs to be done, such as assembling the stage or hemming curtains, to which a slow worker can contribute his abilities if given some leadership. In the more technically difficult activities involving only a few pupils such as, say, mural-making, the slow learner's relative lack of ability tends to become conspicuous. Obviously he cannot be asked to do only such menial jobs as washing brushes or cleaning paint tins. He must be given a more important job if he is to retain his self-respect.

A solution some teachers have found is to arrange privately with one of the more intelligent and sympathetic class members who have been chosen as leaders, to elect a slow learner to his team. Once he chooses the slow learner, this leader takes it upon himself to provide him with some aspect of the drawing and painting and coaches and supervises him carefully. Thus the slow learner may fill in areas of color or outline certain painted areas with the knowledge that he is contributing materially to the activity.

Actually there is no adequate solution for the problems which arise from extreme variations in intelligence between classmates. The teacher can only make the best of a difficult educational situation.

In conclusion, one must reiterate that slow learners will reflect their deficiencies in intelligence in the slowness of their artistic development and the lower standard of their artistic production. Nevertheless, wherever possible they must be challenged by work of a creative nature, rather than lulled by copy work. Most art activities are sufficiently flexible to engage their attention profitably.

It is evident that art education may have considerable significance in the general program of education of most slow learners. There is wide agreement that a child who is adversely affected in one area of his personality is likely to be adversely affected in other areas. It is reasonable to suppose that this process could operate in reverse, and that a slow learner who profits from art activities might undergo desirable changes in his personality. Whatever progress in art is made by slow learners depends primarily upon the patience and sympathetic understanding of their teacher.

ACTIVITIES FOR THE READER

1. Collect drawings and paintings of slow learners in various grades and with various I.Q.'s. Compare the work of each group of slow learners with that of a group of normal children (a) in corresponding grades and (b) having corresponding chronological ages. List the differences between the work of slow learners and that of normal pupils in each instance.

2. Compare the work habits of the slow learners with those of the normal pupils in (1 a and b), above.

3. From a collection of work by slow learners in each grade, select pieces of art having some aesthetic qualities. How would the number of pieces selected compare with the number obtained from a collection of equal size comprising the work of normal children in corresponding grades? List some of the chief characteristics of the slow learners' work chosen.

4. Make a list of some curious titles which slow learners give to their drawings and paintings. Can you give any explanations for the peculiarities of the titles?

5. Describe the personal characteristics of a teacher of slow learners whom you know well.

6. In preparing to teach a class of slow-learning boys and girls (I.Q. range 50 to 70; C.A. range 11 to 15), analyze the *operations* and *demonstrations* considered necessary for successful outcome of each of the following activities: (a) making a rolled paper animal; (b) making a small clay bowl by the coil method; (c) making a painting in tempera of "We have fun in the school yard."

7. Build a small box loom as described in this chapter and, using heavy weaving material, weave two place mats.

8. Learning how to do advanced weaving through reading is difficult. Try to enroll in a night class or summer session where an expert teaches weaving. Reading about the work will then be more valuable.

9. On a piece of burlap or cotton about 12 inches square, create a nonobjective design in embroidery. First, using a lightweight cotton and embroidery needle

with a running stitch, make an interesting line arrangement which has a variety of enclosed areas. Using wools, cottons, and yarns in different weights and colors, create texture effects in some of the areas formerly outlined. If you are satisfied with your work, frame it under glass, like a drawing.

10. Using materials similar to those suggested in (9), make an objective picture in embroidery. Choose subject matter from life, still-life, or landscape studies which you may produce before beginning work on the cloth.

11. Splash paint around trying every one of the "chance" effects described in this chapter. Try combining some of the techniques. Select the result you like best. Use it for the cover of a booklet.

12. Observe an art class containing one or two slow learners at work on group activities. Note the techniques used to assist the slow learners. Describe any opportunities missed to help the handicapped children. Suggest practical steps which might have been taken to assist them.

Art Activities

for Gifted Children

$\mathbf{I}$n considering the gifted or talented child,[1] we are confronted with something of an educational mystery. Strangely enough for a society which looks to the gifted for its leaders, the gifted child is perhaps the most neglected of all types in North American school systems.[2] While we make heroic efforts to bring the mentally retarded up to the highest possible educational levels, we often allow the talented to shift for themselves. Such an emphasis, although seemingly commendable upon humanitarian grounds, can scarcely be justified for its educational efficiency. Obviously, it is the gifted who can return the highest rewards to the society prepared to provide them with adequate educational care. The neglect of gifted children cannot be ex-

---

[1] In some educational writing, "gifted" refers to children with a high general intelligence, while "talented" refers to a special capability in one field of endeavor. This differentiation of meaning is by no means universal and has not been adopted here. In this chapter, the words are used interchangeably.

[2] For evidence, see the following:

Byron S. Hollingshead, "Who Should Go to College in America," *College Board Review*, XVI (February 1952), 248–53. Leo T. Phearman, "Comparisons of High-School Graduates Who Go to College with Those Who Do Not," *Journal of Educational Psychology*, XL (November 1949), 405–15. C. Gilbert Wrenn, "Potential Research Talent in the Sciences Based on Intelligence Quotients of Ph.D.'s," *Educational Record*, XXX (January 1949), 5–22. W. Drayton Lewis, "Some Characteristics of Very Superior Children," *Journal of Genetic Psychology*, LXII (June 1943), 301–09.

cused, furthermore, on the grounds that they can make satisfactory progress without help. On the contrary, there is much evidence that cases of failure, delinquency, laziness, and general maladjustment easily occur among gifted children as a result of educational neglect.[3]

Since the preceding remarks refer to gifted children in general, they necessarily have reference also to those who are talented in art. At the present time we have no means of estimating the numbers of artistically gifted children who are not getting an adequate art education. Judging from the lack of educational provisions for the gifted in general, however, one is led to believe that the waste of artistic talent must be considerable. It would seem that in art education today our "problem children" are not so much the slow learners as the talented.

The remainder of this chapter will deal with three main topics: how to identify the gifted child; how best to educate him; and what art experiences he should have. Each of these topics contains problems for which we lack complete answers. However, some recent research offers at least partial answers for them.[4] The educational and artistic importance of arriving at a satisfactory solution to these problems will be realized when one considers that upon this solution probably depends the blossoming of much talent which otherwise might never be developed.

Identifying the Gifted Child

It is apparently more difficult to identify the artistically gifted child than the generally gifted. With the latter, investigators can rely to a very large extent upon the scores which the pupils make upon I.Q. tests.[5] The determination of artistic talent is not so simple. While the results of one study indicate that every child who seems to be gifted in art also scores above average in I.Q. tests, not every child who scores high in I.Q. tests possesses

---

[3] An excellent general reference to read at this time is The American Association for Gifted Children, Paul Witty (Ed.), *The Gifted Child* (Boston: Heath, 1953).

[4] These topics have been given systematic attention in Ontario during the past eight years, and the investigation is still in progress in the Classes for Gifted Children sponsored by the Provincial Department of Education. For some researches in the U.S., see Robert J. Havighurst, Eugene Stivers, and Robert F. DeHaan, *A Survey of the Education of Gifted Children* (Chicago: Univ. of Chicago Press, 1955).

[5] Among psychologists, L. M. Terman applied the term "gifted" to all those with I.Q.'s of 140 or over; L. S. Hollingworth suggested 130; H. H. Goddard, 120.

    Karl C. Garrison, *The Psychology of Exceptional Children*, Rev. Ed. (N.Y.: Ronald, 1950), presents a summary of the characteristics of "bright" children, p. 65. In Chapter 10, pp. 139–51, he outlines some suggestions concerning special educational arrangements for the gifted.

artistic talent.[6] Some, indeed, with exceptionally high I.Q.'s appear to be lacking in even normal artistic skills and sensibilities.[7]

One of the greatest difficulties in discovering artistic talent arises from the fact that no reliable measures exist to judge either art production or appreciation. As will be shown in a later chapter, whatever beliefs we may hold about a particular child's abilities in art are necessarily based upon our personal appraisal rather than upon data gathered objectively.[8] Most experts hold that subjective appraisals are not so important in such academic fields as reading, spelling, numberwork, and the like, where certain fundamental abilities may evidently be measured fairly accurately and, as a consequence, talent in them identified. But one suspects that the expressive and appreciative aspects of even these fields are no more amenable to measurement than they are in art.

Since, therefore, we must depend upon purely subjective means to identify our artistically talented youngsters, we can rely only with reservations upon our present estimate of their artistic future. Nevertheless, the pooled opinion of informed people has frequently led to surprisingly accurate judgments concerning artistic talent.

Some strong indications of the nature of talent may sometimes be found in case histories of artistically gifted people, but it is often difficult to unearth actual evidence of their early work. A child's art is usually lost, and both parents and teachers are generally unable to recall accurately the child's early behavior. Of some cases, however, we have reasonably detailed and apparently accurate data. Among these are the histories of two girls from upper-middle-class homes, Susan McF and Mary M,[9] who are now both 17

---

[6] In the classes sponsored by Ontario Department of Education, the lowest I.Q. among the children gifted in art was 112; the lowest C.A. was nine years, three months.

[7] Adding a further difficulty, some writers maintain that artistic talent appears to have a slower rate of maturation than other talents, particularly musical talent. See Florence L. Goodenough and L. M. Rynkiewicz, *Exceptional Children* (N.Y.: Appleton-Century-Crofts, 1956), p. 165. These authors cite Catherine Morris Cox, *Genetic Studies of Genius: The Early Mental Traits of Three Hundred Geniuses.* (Stanford, Cal.: Stanford Univ. Press, 1926), Vol. II, which discusses 13 great artists and intimates that their early work could not compare in stature with that of young musicians of similar chronological age. The differences in rate of maturation in the two artistic fields might be questioned, as Goodenough rightly suggests, on the grounds that we do not possess suitable measuring devices for artistic talent.

[8] See Chapter 17. In commenting upon Beatrice Lantz, *Easel Age Scale* (Los Angeles, Cal.: California Test Bureau, 1955), L. M. Terman suggested that "children [artistically] gifted may be recognized through the Easel Age Scale while still very young." In view of the nature of artistic talent, this statement appears highly extravagant.

[9] Because each girl has highly educated parents who are especially interested in art and enjoy a knowledge of both child psychology and pedagogy, records were preserved. The parents systematically filed the children's work after writing comments

years old. These girls have for many years given promise of talent in art. A study of their carefully preserved production shows that both of them began manipulating media just before they were a year old and that they had passed beyond the stage of manipulation before their second birthday. Around 15 months Susan was naming the marks she was producing in crayon. Mary did the same when she was 16 months old. Around this age, Mary began to use some spoken words clearly, but Susan was slower to learn to speak and instead was producing sounds such as "rrrrr," which consistently stood for "automobile," and "goong" for "duck." When, by the use of symbols, she depicted such objects in her paintings, she named them in this peculiar vocabulary. When she was 25 months old, Susan produced an attractive montage with sticky tape and colored paper. Around 27 months of age, both little girls could delineate many different symbols and give them some relationship in the same composition.

Both children led normal, active lives and during fine hot weather neglected their art for outdoor games. A study of their work (which their parents carefully dated) reveals, however, that inactivity in art did not seem to interfere with their continuous development. By the time both children were three years old, they were overlapping objects in their drawing and paintings, and at four Mary, in particular, seemed to recognize texture as an expressive element of design. By six, they were painting like veterans, toning colors, devising textural effects, and inventing outstandingly interesting compositions in general. Before she was seven, Mary even gave hints of linear perspective in her work. It is important to note that both girls attended schools which apparently provided progressive and highly commendable art programs.

By the time Susan was ten years old and Mary ten years and eight months, their work had lost most of its childlike qualities. Each girl passed through a realistic stage in which objects were rendered rather photographically. Then Susan's work became distinctly mannered in its rhythms, while Mary's output became reminiscent of that of several artists. In quick succession, she went through an Aubrey Beardsley period, followed by one reflecting Degas and later Matisse. When they were twelve years old, the girls first met and became friends. They attended the same art classes in high school, and produced paintings in a style obviously derived from that of the Impressionists. Fortunately their secondary school art program proved to be almost as efficient as that of their elementary schooling. After a time their work became noticeably more personal. Eventually both girls attended

___

about each piece on its reverse side. Both children eventually enrolled in the Ontario classes for gifted children, at which time the parents disclosed the girls' records. The girls' I.Q.'s are as follows: Mary, 120; Susan, 130.

special Ontario classes for children with artistic talent, where they remained for four years. Here they produced some sensitive paintings and sculpture in forms which continued to be recognizably personal. Both girls are now attending a college of art where, according to their teachers, they give evidence of outstanding artistic ability.

There seems to be little doubt that Mary and Susan are talented young people. What characteristics common to them both might identify them as such? First, we are struck by their almost lifelong preoccupation with art. Although at times their interest in art was intermittent, the production of art forms by both girls was generally uninterrupted. Second, both girls came from cultured homes in which the parents enjoy artistic interests. This second point raises questions concerning the extent to which environment creates talent. Since "like tends to beget like," talent no doubt depends to a significant extent upon biological inheritance. However, since the children of artistic parents are likely to live in artistically stimulating surroundings, they tend to have the double advantage of artistic "nature" and artistic "nurture" often denied the children of parents who lack these interests and abilities.[10]

Third, the progress of Mary and Susan throughout the phases of their childlike expression was both richer and more rapid than normal. Although both girls developed a skill in handling tools and materials which was obviously above normal, neither allowed her skill to assume paramount importance in her output. Again, at one period, the girls apparently became dominated by technique, and the work of other artists whom they admired strongly influenced their output. Fortunately, however, they possessed insight into artistic processes, personal integrity, intellectual vigor, and vision sufficient to overcome these powerful influences, which can be so seductive to the gifted young person who seeks a satisfying means of artistic expression.

Witty says that "perhaps it is desirable . . . to consider any child gifted whose performance, in a potentially valuable line of human activity, is con-

---

[10] It is interesting to observe that the classes for gifted children of the Ontario Department of Education, even though situated in a "low-income" section of Toronto, enroll over twice as many children from distant "high-income" areas than from the surrounding district, in spite of the fact that every effort is made to select the talented from any level of society in which they may occur.

See Paul Witty (Ed.), *The Gifted Child*, in which he discusses the "importance of home background" of the gifted, pp. 271–72. He quotes Lewis M. Terman and Melita H. Oden, "Correlates of Adult Achievement in the California Gifted Group," *Thirty-Ninth Yearbook of the National Society for the Study of Education* (Bloomington, Ill.: Public School Publishing Co., 1940), pp. 74–89. Terman and Oden state that talented pupils have generally "the more satisfactory family background in terms of occupational status . . . parental education . . . home instruction and mental stock."

117 *"Washday"—a painting in tempera by a gifted girl*
   C.A. 9, I.Q. 130.

sistently remarkable." [11] This statement can be accepted in relation to a creative field such as art only if the phrase "consistently remarkable" is interpreted broadly. Because the person employed in art is continually expending his energies in new fields of exploration, he cannot be expected always to produce work of a consistently high quality. Sometimes his researches may fail and then his efforts, however commendable, will probably result in bad art. In the careers of both Susan and Mary one can see ups and downs. "Consistently remarkable" must therefore allow for gallant failures as well as successes.

There is no denying, however, that "gifted is as gifted does." The child whose performance in art more often than not is "remarkable," may be suspected of being gifted. Such a child will almost inevitably possess a better than average intelligence, display skill beyond the ordinary, give noticeable evidence of sensitivity in organizing the elements of design, and have the capability of producing work which bears the stamp of a distinguished personality.

Because the data used in the evaluation of talent must be subjective,

---

[11] Paul Witty, "The Gifted Child," *Exceptional Children*, Vol. 19, (April 1953), 255.

judgment cannot be made either lightly or hastily.[12] The teacher who suspects a child of possessing unusual artistic talent might be wise to enlist from time to time the opinions of others, including artists and art teachers. Opinions of such well-informed people, furthermore, might well be sought over a relatively long period of time. A sudden appearance of talent may later prove to be merely a remarkable but temporary development of skill. Again, what may appear to be artistic talent in early years may disappear as the child develops other interests into which his energies and abilities are channeled.

In the Ontario experiment, the system of identification which is based on both time and the opinion of many specialists seems to function with

---

[12] A discussion of objective art tests will be found in Chapter 17.

118 *"At the Waterfront"—a painting in tempera by a gifted boy CA. 12, I.Q. 120.*

reasonable efficiency.[13] Pupils who, in the opinion of their classroom teachers and art consultants, have talent are recommended to attend special art classes. Recommendations are based not only upon their ability in art, but also upon their intelligence rating and success in other areas of school life. After a pupil has attended the special classes for eight months, the staff passes judgment upon his progress. If, in the unanimous opinion of the staff members, the pupil has failed to show an outstanding talent, he is usually removed from the classes so that room is made for another more promising pupil. By these procedures the staff seems to be able to select only the most gifted children with whom to do research.

Some Special Arrangements in Art for Gifted Children

When gifted children have been identified, the problem concerning suitable educational treatment for them immediately arises. There appear to be three main types of general educational arrangements designed for the gifted child. First, an "enriched program" may be offered by which the pupil is given advanced work in his regular classroom by his regular teacher. Research seems to indicate that such enrichment of the general program for gifted children is successful only when the teacher is outstanding.[14] A second arrangement for helping the gifted is the "special class," which educators believe provides the best solution to the problem.[15] A third method, called

---

[13] For a description of two other systems of selection, see Havighurst and others, *A Survey of the Education of Gifted Children*, p. 9. Neither the Quincy nor the Portland test described in this publication seems to be wholly acceptable. The Quincy test apparently includes such items as the drawing of "stick men," for example, which can scarcely be described as art activity in any sense. The Portland test appears to rely to some degree either upon a *laissez-faire* technique in which the pupils are given "free choice" of subject matter or upon assigned subjects in which, as far as one can ascertain from the account, the pupils may have little or no real interest.

For further discussion about "identifying the child talented in art," see Witty, "The Gifted Child," pp. 250–52. What this author says seems to be borne out in the performances of Susan and Mary.

[14] Miriam C. Pritchard, in *The Gifted Child* (Paul Witty, Ed.), pp. 52 ff. See also Arch Heck, *The Education of Exceptional Children*, 2nd Ed. (N.Y.: McGraw-Hill, 1953), pp. 396–97, who summarizes the "traits that aid the teacher." He says that the teacher should have unusual professional ability, should "be honest in her claims of ability," should be original enough "to recognize worth in spite of the fact that the product has not been shaped in customary molds." Drive, initiative, qualities of social leadership, and an attractive personality are further traits. The last curious but significant trait, perhaps especially in art, Heck says, is freedom "from jealousy of the gifted child."

[15] Schools in Fort Wayne, Indiana, Kansas City, Kansas, and Cleveland, Ohio, for example, have demonstrated how effective the special class may be. The Cleveland classes which enroll pupils in both elementary and secondary schools have been in

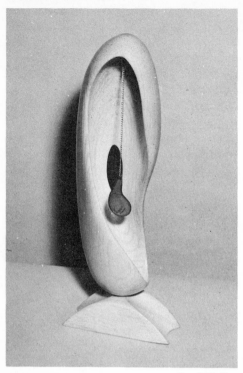

119 *Sculpture in wood by a gifted girl*
C.A. 13, I.Q. 120.

Royal Studio

"acceleration," which usually refers to grade-skipping, is also sometimes used. At one time general educators tended to condemn this method roundly, mainly because they believed it to be socially harmful to the child. This position has, however, changed somewhat in recent years.[16]

As has been mentioned many times earlier, the only practical means of conducting any class in art is to allow each child to work at his own speed and in such activities as arouse his interest. Indeed, to attempt to conduct a class by keeping all members in a lock-step program would be not only impractical, but, with the contemporary art program what it is, well-nigh impossible. The teacher who fails to provide for what are called "individual differences" can scarcely be said to teach art. In other words, the method called "enrichment" in general education is taken for granted in the well-

continuous operation since 1921. Baltimore reports success with special classes in art for secondary school pupils. See Havighurst and others, *A Survey of the Education of the Gifted,* for accounts of other special classes.

[16] Lewis M. Terman and Melita H. Oden, *The Gifted Child Grows Up* (Stanford, Cal.: Stanford Univ. Press, 1947), p. 448.

conducted art class. This procedure, moreover, does not place as great a strain upon the classroom teacher as one might anticipate. Since progress in art depends to a very large extent upon the pupil's personal effort, even a noticeably gifted child in the elementary school stands to gain from his studies in art in an ordinary classroom.

The plan of providing special art classes for the gifted, nevertheless, has much to recommend it. These classes are particularly effective because teachers can be engaged who possess capabilities in special artistic fields. Much as a sympathetic teacher of general subjects may help a gifted child in art, a specialist may provide even more assistance. In these special classes, in which none but the talented are enrolled, the need to provide for individual differences will be even more apparent.

The third arrangement for the gifted, "grade-skipping," which is sometimes used in the general educational program, has little meaning in art education. Progress in art occurs no matter in what grade the pupil is enrolled. Subject matter in art cannot conveniently be assigned to any particular grade level. Hence, to remove a child from one grade and place him in a higher one in the hope that in the higher level he may gain more advanced learning in art is not logical practice.

Whatever special arrangements are made for the child with artistic talent, two considerations of paramount importance to the child's future development must be kept in mind. In the first place, on no account must the child's artistic development be unduly hastened into adult forms of expression. In the elementary school, the talented youngster is still a youngster, and his artistic growth must occur with due regard for this fact. "Overstimulation, growing from the drive of eager adults . . . has often killed the child's urge for artistic expression." [17] In the second place, however, every talented child must be provided with sufficient challenge so that he will work to capacity. Unless this condition prevails, the gifted pupil may lose interest in the work, and his considerable energies and abilities may be dissipated in less worthwhile ways.

Under what circumstances will talent flourish? To begin with, the home should, at best, encourage an interest in art and, at worst, not discourage it. While it may be true in some cases that "genius will out" no matter what the circumstances, it nevertheless seems that a sympathetic home environment is extremely stimulating. The home which provides suitable art media, a library of art books, and a convenient place to work, together with loving and intelligent parents to admire the work being produced and to encourage further production, will aid materially in fostering talent. Next, the elemen-

---

[17] Viktor Lowenfeld, *Your Child and His Art* (N.Y.: Macmillan, 1954), p. 176.

tary and secondary schools which the gifted pupil attends should provide a sufficiently stimulating and challenging art program. Finally, somewhere along the line of his artistic progress, the gifted pupil should have special opportunities for the cultivation of his talent.

The unique and precious artistic gifts, which under existing conditions are being lost, may yet be retrieved by the cooperative efforts of parents, teachers, artists, and departments of education. After all, "talents ask little—the opportunity to show and know themselves, a little space and light and air to grow in, a little leisure to bloom." [18]

Art Activities Especially Suitable for Gifted Children

General Activities

Gifted children demonstrate a number of peculiarities in their selection of art activities. Their interests in such basic types of work as life, still life, landscape, portraiture, and sculpture develop early, and they appear to find a greater challenge and a deeper satisfaction in these than they do in some of the relatively minor fields such as weaving and paper construction. While they may occasionally turn to these crafts for their novelty, they return with renewed interest to what one might describe (for want of better words) as the more classic, or traditional, forms of art.

The mastery of any of the basic techniques of sculpture or modeling takes years to achieve. For those gifted pupils who are attracted to traditional forms of sculpture, a continual challenge will be found in the manipulation of clay and wood. Others will find delight in the more recently developed forms, such as wire sculpture and mobiles.

Not infrequently, however, certain of the printing techniques mentioned earlier also attract talented pupils. Linoleum cutting and printing in which several colors are used to produce one unit of design, more intricate forms of stencil work, and the like will keep some of the gifted children working at capacity.

The gifted child usually prefers to work at art by himself, rather than to participate in group endeavor. While as a group the gifted are socially inclined, at the same time they seem to recognize in art a subject which demands individual deliberation and effort. They are not entirely averse to participating in puppet shows, mural-making, and other art forms demanding a pooled effort, but most are happiest when they are submerging themselves as individuals in artistic problems.

---

[18] Donalda Dickie, *The Enterprise in Theory and Practice* (Toronto: Gage, 1940), p. 86.

Although gifted children should find a ready challenge in the usual media and activities suggested for normal children, a few special materials and techniques are especially suitable for them. The expense and technical difficulties associated with these materials and processes forbid their being widely used in the general art program for elementary school children, but they are to be especially recommended for the gifted enrolled in special classes. Since in the heterogeneous classroom no hard and fast divisions can be maintained between an art program for normal children and one for the gifted, teachers might also occasionally apply some of the following suggestions to general classes.

Painting in Oils

Painting in oils is a good example of a special activity suitable for the gifted, and by the time they reach preadolescence, they should have had an opportunity of working with it. Oil painting, however, is a relatively difficult medium to handle, and, until they have had experiences with many other types of paint, not even the most gifted children can use it effectively. There are many ways of using oil paint and a mention of them all would require a disproportionate amount of space here.[19]

The surface on which the oil paint is applied, usually called the "support," is traditionally made of wood or canvas. However, pupils can use shellacked paper tacked to a drawing board—an impermanent support—on which to practice. Later they can buy commercially prepared canvas boards or stretched canvas. They can also make their supports simply by coating a strong building board or one-quarter-inch plywood with either thick oil-ground titanium white or zinc white. After about a week of drying,[20] these prepared boards may be rubbed with sandpaper if their surfaces are too rough.

Oil colors have many peculiar characteristics. Some fade in light and are called "fugitive"; others do not fade and are called "permanent." Some can be mixed together safely and are called "compatible"; others set up chemical reactions when mixed and are called "incompatible." The cost of

---

[19] See Ralph Mayer, *The Painter's Craft* (N.Y.: Van Nostrand, 1948); Frederick Taubes, *The Technique of Oil Painting* (N.Y.: Dodd Mead, 1941); Max Doerner, *The Materials of the Artist*, Rev. Ed., trans. by Eugene Neuhaus (N.Y.: Harcourt, Brace, 1934); W. G. Constable, *The Painter's Workshop* (N.Y.: Oxford Univ. Press, 1954).

These publications are clearly written and cover the subject in sufficient detail. Before a teacher holds classes in oil painting, he should not only be able to paint, but also be familiar with at least one of these books.

[20] For absolute permanence, six months are usually required for drying. This, of course, is not necessary when young children are using the boards.

120 *Painting in oils made in a special art class by a gifted child C.A. 12.*

colors varies widely because of differences in manufacturing processes and in the raw products used.

The cheapest colors, called "students' quality," are not reliable because they are fugitive. They are suitable for practice, however, so that pupils might use them while learning to paint. To use inferior art materials for any length of time does not seem to be wise, and it is recommended that paints and supports of a better quality be supplied as soon as the pupils master some of the basic techniques of oil painting.

Every painter develops his own "palette," or range of colors, which he usually considers indispensable. Taubes recommends 17 pigments which he says "are all permanent . . . and most of them are compatible with each other." The following list is adapted from Taubes.[21]

[21] Taubes, *The Technique of Oil Painting*, p. 25.

White	1. Zinc or titanium white
Blue	2. Prussian blue
	3. Ultramarine
Green	4. Chrome oxide green (transparent)
Yellow	5. Yellow ochre
	6. Naples yellow
	7. Cadmium yellow light
	8. Cadmium yellow medium
	9. Cadmium orange
Red	10. Cadmium red
	11. Venetian red
	12. Indian red (or Mars violet)
	13. Alizarin crimson
Brown	14. Burnt sienna
	15. Raw umber, or
	16. Burnt umber
Black	17. Ivory black

For a beginner, this list is rather extensive, and he should not use it in its entirety until he learns how to paint. A basic palette for a young pupil might consist of the following pigments in Taubes' list: 1, 3, 4, 5, 7, 10, 16, 17. Each pigment is bought already ground in oil and in tubes. The 12-ounce, or "studio," size is economical for all but white, which should be bought in one-pound tubes.

Before one begins painting, small amounts of paint should be squeezed from the tubes to a palette, which may be a sheet of glass resting upon a table. If the glass is placed over a sheet of light gray or white paper, the colors will show clearly, especially when mixed. Another type of palette is the traditional, romantic-looking wooden board which is held in the painter's hand. This is also a convenient piece of apparatus, especially for out-of-doors painting. There is no one way recommended for arranging colors on the palette. Each pupil should develop a system of his own which he follows consistently until the selection of pigments during painting becomes automatic. Any painter should be able to reach for the desired color on a palette as automatically as one selects a control on the instrument panel of an automobile. One convenient method of arranging colors is to place black and white side by side at the far edge of the palette, and then to place the yellows, browns, and reds on the white side and on the black side, the blues and greens (see Fig. 121).

Painting tools consist of flat bristle brushes, from about size 6 up, and a palette knife. Easels are a convenience but not entirely necessary. Before he begins painting, the pupil should outline his subject upon the canvas with a pointed brush dipped in oil color diluted with turpentine. This outline

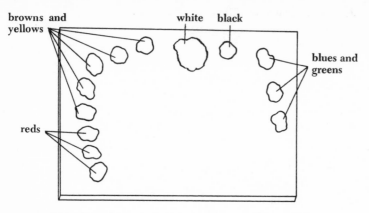

browns and yellows **white** **black** **blues and greens** **reds**

121 *An arrangement for a palette of oil colors.*

will often show after a painting is finished. Some painters use scarlet so that the outline will materially affect the design. Others use neutrals or near neutrals—grays or earth colors—so that the outline will not become prominent.

The safest and most convenient method of painting for children is called *alla prima.* In this method one paints spontaneously, trying for the final effect from the start.[22] If corrections are made later, the first coat of paint must be scraped off, rather than covered when dry with another coat. Usually the pigments as squeezed from the tube are of suitable consistency for application on the support, and need no oil or turpentine added to them. Indeed, it is an unwise practice for beginners to dilute their paint, except for outlining the subject. Painting should generally be done with the largest possible brush for the area being covered. As a general rule paint should not be used sparingly but laid on with reasonable thickness. Many painters like to keep the paint thinner in areas of shade and thicker where light is depicted, but this is a matter of personal choice. The palette knife can be used to load paint onto the support where a bold thick covering of pigment is desired. The wrong end of the brush may be used to draw lines through the wet paint to the support.

When the pupil has finished painting, he should thoroughly clean his brushes, palette knife, and palette. Turpentine can be used as a cleaning agent, although some of the commercially prepared cleaning fluids are easier

---

[22] Other methods involve the development of underpainting and, later, the application of glazes.

on the bristles of the brushes. Brushes should be washed in a solution of mild soap and warm water after they have been rinsed in the cleaning fluid.

Other Media for Drawing and Painting

Gifted pupils in the preadolescent stage will find several other media challenging. Some of the more expensive colored drawing inks, for example, might be used in conjunction with work in India ink or in some of the "mixed-media" techniques mentioned in Chapter 7. Work with steel pens as well as pointed brushes might be explored. Charcoal and Conté crayon in black and brown can also be used fairly extensively, either in quick sketching or in more deliberate drawing. Some of this line drawing might lead to a consideration of etching and other graphic processes such as those of dry-point, aquatint, and mezzotint.[23]

Some gifted children in the preadolescent stage become proficient in the use of various types of water colors. In the opinion of many painters, transparent water color is one of the most subtle and difficult of media. It must be used with precision and speed, and its "wetness," or watery character, should be reflected in the finished work. Good water-color paints, brushes, and, in particular, papers are relatively expensive. The pigments in tubes are more convenient to use than those in cake form. When a gifted pupil begins to paint seriously in water colors, he should be provided with materials of a higher quality than is usually found in school. In addition to transparent water colors, some pupils may be interested in trying opaque water colors.[24]

Silk-Screen Printing

An example of a craft suitable for the gifted is silk-screen printing, the results of which are shown in Fig. 122. Although not particularly difficult, it involves considerable quantities of oily textile ink which might create difficulties in a crowded regular classroom. This activity, however, seems to challenge gifted pupils sufficiently to produce some interesting results.

In this technique, ink is squeezed through a prepared screen so that a design is left upon a paper or textile surface. A light wooden frame, measuring approximately one foot square, is covered with silk-screen bolting cloth, nylon, or a good grade of organdy. The cloth is stretched tightly and tacked

---

23 See D'Amico, *Creative Teaching in Art*, Rev. Ed. (Scranton, Pa.: International Textbook, 1953), pp. 151–83, for a description of these processes. Before a teacher exposes gifted children to any of these processes, he should, of course, be skilled in the use of all tools and materials associated with them. Furthermore, he should have a well-equipped room in which the children can explore the processes.

24 See Ralph Mayer, *The Painter's Craft*, Chapter 7, pp. 153 ff., "Aqueous Paints," for a discussion of transparent and other types of water color.

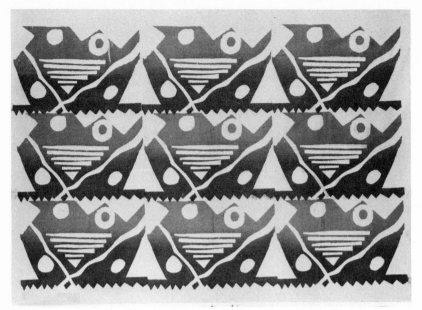

122 *Silk-screen printing by a girl C.A. 12, I.Q. 120. Masking tape was used for the design.*

123 *Sixth-grade pupils printing a silk-screen design based on pine needles and cones. Tusche was used to make the design.*

o the outside of the frame with carpet tacks. It must then be treated in uch a way as to prevent paint from passing through some areas of the creen and to allow it to pass through other areas (see Figs. 123 and 124).

Any of three methods of preparing the design on the screen might be considered for classroom use. The simplest of them is to put masking tape on the reverse, or downward, side of the screen. Another is to glue waxed paper on the screen.

A more complicated method, but at the same time one which leads to more controlled results, makes use of what is called "tusche"—a heavy black liquid. Using tusche, the pupil paints a design on the upper side of the screen. Next, to prevent paint from running under the frame, paper tape is stuck around the inside of the screen where the screen meets the frame. After this, a mixture of one-half ordinary glue and one-half water is spread thinly with a piece of cardboard over the entire screen, covering tusche and all, so that not even pinpoint openings are left. When this glue solution is dry, the tusche and the glue covering it are washed out with turpentine. To do this, the pupil should place the screen upside down on newspaper and pour turpentine over it. Gentle rubbing with a cloth will remove the tusche, leaving areas in the screen through which color will pass.

In all three processes, printing from the screen is done on a long table covered thickly and evenly with newspapers. To do the printing, textile ink is first poured into the screen. Then a rubber-edged scraper, or "squee-gee," about as long as the inside width of the printing frame, is drawn across the screen, pulling and squeezing the ink as it moves. The ink passing through the unglued areas makes a design on the paper or textile beneath. Before printing on textile, the pupils should try printing on paper.

Many experiments may be performed in silk-screen printing. The screen can be placed in various positions on the textile to form different types of all-over patterns; two or more colors can be used; more than one technique of preparing the screen can be used to give different effects; two or more screens can be prepared for use on one printing project.

Teaching the Gifted

The young gifted child will, of course, make use of the usual materials and perform the basic activities mentioned in earlier chapters in connection with the general art program for normal children. Since the gifted can be detected only after a relatively long period of time, they must obviously take part in the art program designed for all until their talent is discovered. When it is clear that an individual possesses gifts above the ordinary, the teacher, using the teaching principles suggested in Chapter 2, will help the

124 *Methods of preparing the silk screen, using wax paper (above) and tusche (below).*

child to progress at his optimum level of accomplishment. This may be done through any art form. In drawing and painting, it means more drawing and painting; in sculpture, more sculpture. Progress in art occurs because the worker keeps producing art. Mere quantity of production, or repetition of forms previously created, of course, is not progress, but production which leads to improved skill, more penetrating insight, greater mastery of media will help to develop his talent.

The principle of teaching in response to the needs of the learner has been emphasized throughout this book. We observed earlier that in order to profit from art at all, some slow learners need to be subjected to a step-by-step method of instruction. With the gifted, just the reverse is necessary. Here the teacher is faced with the necessity for what might be described as "under-teaching." Every attempt must be made to challenge the greater abilities of the gifted child. Whenever he can learn a fact or a technique for himself he should do so. Assistance must in general be withheld until he has explored every possible avenue on his own for a solution to his problems. The gifted pupil who is given this type of educational treatment thrives on it, and so does his art.

Whether in a special classroom or as individuals in a normal classroom, artistically gifted children must be continually challenged with drawing and painting and three-dimensional media of all sorts and with examples of fine production in these media. The artistically gifted child is normally motivated to express himself with the drawing and painting media. The challenge must come from his desire to emulate the achievement of great artists. Thus he should always have access to fine works of art in the media of his choice or, failing the actual works, good reproductions of them. The teacher should urge him to visit art galleries and museums where such are available and suggest certain outstanding works for him to study while visiting these institutions.

Every gifted pupil should be encouraged to see the best art and to read good books on art, and here the teacher will have to make special efforts with gifted pupils from underprivileged homes. The gifted child in a cultured home, as we saw earlier, will probably have many opportunities to add to his knowledge of art. The underprivileged child has probably enjoyed few, if any, such opportunities. Indeed his gift must often be an especially vital one to survive. In his case, the teacher's duty is to supply the inspiration and sources of knowledge which his home environment has denied him.

The teacher of gifted children even as advanced as the sixth grade, like the teacher of normal children, need not necessarily be an expert performer in art. In the case of oil painting or silk-screen printing, for example, he should know a reasonable amount about these techniques, but he need not be a prize-winner in either of them. Knowledge about them may be gained through some practice, some reading, and considerable looking. Then the teacher, who must not be afraid to admit to the pupils that he does not enjoy professional artistic competence, can assist and inspire gifted youngsters. With some insight into the nature of a technique he may suggest which paintings are the best to study and which books are best to read. With sufficient knowledge to give the minimum demonstrations or directions necessary to start a gifted child working, the teacher need only suggest some of the possibilities of the medium under consideration. To do more teaching can often annoy or disrupt the gifted child in his search for a personal idiom of expression.

We noted earlier that gifted pupils, evidently sensing the importance of personal expression in art, tend to prefer individual to group activity. However, when a gifted learner is found in a general classroom, his classmates will often elect him to important positions in the committees established to perform group work. Indeed, he is frequently elected to the head chairmanship of an enterprise. With his special abilities in art, the child is thus placed in a position to do much of the difficult work, thereby depriving his classmates of tasks which they should do themselves. Fortunately, gifted pupils tend to be well adjusted in other ways and a teacher can appeal to their reason and good judgment with better than average results. Hence, when a gifted pupil appears to be assuming more than his share of responsibility in group work, a short, forthright, and friendly discussion about the situation will usually result in his relinquishing some tasks to his fellows.

In cases where a group of gifted pupils shows a disinclination to perform group work in art, it seems reasonable to suggest that the teacher respect their wishes. After all, the pupils are probably well adjusted socially without group work. Whatever further practice they need in working cooperatively can be assigned in other areas of learning, thus leaving them free to exercise their remarkable individual talents in art—the area best suited for a personal contribution.

ACTIVITIES FOR THE READER

1. Study some children considered to be artistically gifted. Make a note of their outstanding personal qualities, work habits, and their attitude toward their fellows.

2. Make a collection of the drawings and paintings of artistically gifted children. Analyze the work for its subject matter, design, and technique. Compare this collection with one composed of the work of normal children having chronological ages comparable to those of the gifted group.

3. Study the home environment of several artistically gifted pupils. How does this environment rate culturally and economically?

4. Buy about six flat hog bristle brushes, reasonably good in quality and ranging in size from about one-eighth to one-half of an inch, and one palette knife. Also buy 6 canvas boards no smaller than 12×18 inches each and at least the following pigments in studio size tubes: Prussian blue, chromium oxide green (transparent), yellow ochre, cadmium yellow medium, cadmium red, burnt umber, and ivory black. Get at least a pound tube of zinc white and a pint of turpentine. Arrange a palette as suggested above in this chapter. Then make a nonobjective painting in oils. Paint a line in thin paint over the surface of the

canvas board so that a number of interesting enclosed areas are formed. Choose any one tube of pigment and black and white. In some areas enclosed by the line, paint grays mixed from black and white. In other areas, paint tints and shades of your color. Somewhere, for a center of interest, use pure black or pure color. Try for different textures by loading your brush with paint, putting paint on with a palette knife, drawing in the wet paint with the palette knife or the wrong end of the brush, or painting thickly in some areas and thinly in others. Experiment, but paint with some thought for unity.

5. Set up a still-life arrangement and sketch it on paper in pencil or ink. Then outline the general composition in thin paint on a canvas and begin to paint. It is wise to keep to a few pigments at first—say, one bright one, like yellow, and then umber, black, and white. Paint with bold strokes with medium thick paint the areas with middle light values. Later add high lights in thicker paint, using a palette knife if desired. Paint the shadow areas in thinner paint.

6. After producing the above two oil paintings, read a book on the subject selected from the list given earlier.

7. Do a landscape or portrait in oils, but continue to keep the number of colors restricted.

8. Do some formal exercises with oil pigments:
(a) In 10 small areas drawn on canvas board, take a hue from its lowest to its highest value by adding black and white.
(b) With one pigment, make a 10-degree texture scale from very rough to very smooth.
(c) Mix about 10 different grays by adding oil-color complementaries from the color chart. Note the differences obtained between a light mixing of pigments and a complete mixing.

9. Repeat some of the drawing and painting activities suggested at the end of Chapter 7.

10. Prepare silk screens according to the directions given earlier. Experiment with all three methods of preparing the screen. Practice printing on paper, using some of the pattern arrangements suggested in activities (6a-f) at the close of Chapter 10. Later, print your favorite pattern on textile.

Relating Art

to the General School Program

Stimulus for artistic expression may arise in any area of a child's life. Providing that a child is genuinely moved by an experience, it makes little difference from an artistic standpoint what the source of stimulation may be. Since children live a large part of their lives in school, one might expect that many situations found in play or study at school promote expression. Such, in fact, is the case. Life at school may be the source of many and varied significant artistic statements.

Correlation and the Unit Curriculum

That other subjects should serve as a basis for children's art work is psychologically sound in principle. It will be remembered from Chapter 1 that whereas the mechanistic psychologists believed that learning can best occur when school subjects are broken down into their smallest parts, the Gestalt psychologists disputed this assertion and proved that just the reverse is true. Wholes, not parts, are primary, asserted the Gestalt psychologists. Learning occurs best, not when subjects are dissected, but rather when they are combined.

These assertions led to a practice known as "correlation" and to an arrangement usually called the "unit curriculum." Through the practice of correlation, school subjects, formerly considered discrete, are closely related. Reading, written English, spelling, grammar, and handwriting, for example, have become one area of study known as the "language arts." History, geography, and civics are called "social studies." Nature study, physics, and chemistry are called "general science." As a result of such groupings of subject matter, the pupils are said to gain greater insight into all the areas of learning involved.

Further grouping occurs in the unit (or "area," or "experience") curriculum. Here, the broad areas of learning which result from correlation are superseded by even broader themes. In the place of "language arts," "social studies," and "general science," one may find in some school curricula such items as "living together in the home," "how people make a living," or "how we are fed, clothed, and sheltered." [1] In working on these themes, children are able to learn many facts related to various subject fields and to develop the necessary skills in spelling, computing, penmanship, and the like. A large part of the day is spent in doing research on the main theme and the problems associated with it, during which time the pupils must draw, write, read, sing, build, measure, and so on. A part of each day is set aside not only for the evaluation of products and procedures, but also for the practice of skills which the learners need to improve. Since this need arises from failure to do well in a planned activity, the pupil is motivated to concentrate upon practice. Hence it is asserted that in a well-conducted unit of work, pupils are able to develop skills in a functional manner which rivals in efficiency the methods of developing skills by drills used when subjects are studied independently.

As well as serving as a means of learning facts and of developing skills, the unit curriculum provides ample opportunities for pupils to participate in democratic procedures. Indeed the unit curriculum is essentially a group endeavor in which children must cooperate for the successful outcome of their efforts. [2] "During the course of a unit of work children . . . have continuous experiences in democratic living whereby they develop . . . characteristics so desired in democratic individuals. The very nature of unit teaching makes it the best method so far devised for children to have these experiences." [3]

---

[1] These units are quoted from Donalda Dickie, *The Enterprise in Theory and Practice* (Toronto: Gage, 1940). See also Lavone A. Hanna, Gladys L. Potter, and Neva Hagaman, *Unit Teaching in the Elementary School* (N.Y.: Rinehart, 1955), and A. Gordon Melvin, *The Activity Program* (N.Y.: Reynal & Hitchcock, 1936).

[2] Review Chapter 2.

[3] Hanna and others, *Unit Teaching in the Elementary School,* p. 72. See also L. Thomas Hopkins, *Interaction: The Democratic Process* (Boston: Heath, 1941), especially Chapters 1 and 2.

125 *"The Queen of Hearts Making Tarts"—a painting in tempera by a first-grade girl.*

Some Effects upon Art
of Correlation
and the Unit Curriculum

The teaching of art has, of course, been affected by both the correlation of subjects and their fusion in the unit curriculum. One may assert that art education has benefited in certain circumstances as a result of the grouping of areas of learning but, in other circumstances, has suffered.

As we have noted on several occasions in earlier chapters, the practice of art is based upon a series of delicate circumstances.[4] Not the least important of these is the need for a person to be moved by an experience prior to expression. Neither child nor adult can produce art unless he is aroused, or, as we have said, motivated, by a situation to the point where he is moved by an inner compulsion towards an expressive act. That is why the teacher must give careful attention to motivation before art production begins.

The production of art, therefore, does not occur automatically as a result of correlation or a general fusion of school subjects. Only the child who is emotionally and intellectually moved by an experience in another area of

---

[4] Review Chapter 2 in particular.

learning is in a position to relate his artistic expression to other school subjects. Then the fusion of art and other subjects may be said to be strong, and learning, both artistic and academic, is gratifying.

It is instructive to study both some of the techniques in developing correlations between art and certain other subjects and some of the results when art is performed as part of a larger unit of study.

Correlations Between Art and Some Other Subjects

THE LANGUAGE ARTS: Experiences in the language arts may lead to strong correlations with art, as shown in Fig. 125. Stories and poems may encourage children in the symbol or later stages of expression to make two- and three-dimensional illustrations. The media associated with picture-making or paper work serve best in this type of work, although modeling materials may also be useful. Either the stories and poems the children read and study in class, or in some cases those they write themselves, may be used as the basis for pictorial or three-dimensional expression. While the child's

126 *"Davy Crockett Making Peace with Red Stick"—a tempera painting by a boy in first grade.*

reactions to the literary output of others may readily be correlated with his art, the same is not as true of the child's own literary expression. Only when the youngster retains a strong interest in the experience suggested in his written work can he be expected to express a similar reaction in art. Should his interest remain high after literary expression, a further expressive act in another medium might lead to further clarification of his reaction. In such a case the teacher may safely encourage a correlated activity.

Even when the child uses stories and poems written by others, however, certain teaching precautions must be observed if the correlation is to be successful. In this instance, the child's experience is vicarious. Only when the literary work has aroused the child to the extent that he strongly wishes to express something about it, is the vicarious experience suitable subject matter for art. If he has failed to respond sufficiently to the work under consideration, he cannot be expected to react artistically to it, and hence no correlative output of this kind should be encouraged.

One of the strongest interrelationships existing between art and another subject may be found in puppetry and other theater arts on the one hand and spoken and written English on the other. The subject matter of a puppet or stage play may be derived, first, from a play already written by someone else; second, from one the children prepare after reading a narrative poem or a story; and finally, from one they write entirely by themselves. All three sources will demand the use of English spoken in a natural, functional setting. The last two require, furthermore, a high degree of ingenuity and creative effort, which is not beyond the capabilities of most groups of children in the elementary school. Drama-making for children is after all a form of make-believe which occurs frequently in their free play.

THE SOCIAL STUDIES: For little children, social studies begin in their immediate environment. Such geography, history, or civics as they first consider is found close to home. Because young children are naturally interested in what goes on around them, few problems arise when they base their art upon this area of learning. Their paintings, murals, and three-dimensional work may depict such themes as "our neighborhood," "the people who call at our house (baker, milkman, or laundryman)," "our waterfront," "families who have lived longest in our district," "what our firemen do (policemen, other civic employees)," "how we travel in our city."

In the lower grades a frequently found topic related to social studies is "our friends and neighbors in other lands" or "boys and girls in faraway places." Here the subject takes the children away from the environment they know and as a result their art work often deteriorates.

The chief reason for this deterioration is that the children frequently do not know enough about the remote region to say much about it, with the

127 *"Paul Bunyan and the Cooks"—a tempera painting by a boy in the fourth grade.*

128 *"A Baby Deer." This painting in tempera by a boy in the second grade is artistically successful but, of course, actually inaccurate scientifically.*

consequence that the teacher may substitute stereotyped adult symbols for true information. How often have we seen in children's work a tulip, a windmill, and a boy in baggy trousers to represent the Netherlands; a man sleeping under a cactus plant for Mexico, or a mounted policeman in a red coat for Canada. These symbols—a species of adult pictogram—give so restricted an idea of a country that they come between the child and the true character of the foreign land. These stereotypes cannot possibly lead to a knowledge and understanding of the country in question, and whatever art forms occur are merely trite and mechanical half-truths. Granted that the Netherlands has tulips, that Mexicans sleep, and that Canada maintains the Royal Canadian Mounted Police, such symbols are not the heart and core of these lands.

Before young children can be expected to give expression in art to a theme based upon remote regions, they must have gained a wide knowledge of them, and they must have been stirred by some aspects of this knowledge. By reading books and looking at moving pictures, by singing songs of the country, by studying the work of its artists, and so forth, in course of time they may gain a body of knowledge and a sense of the true character of distant places which will allow them to express something worthwhile.

The same principle must apply to the output of pupils in the higher grades of the elementary school. Frequently more mature pupils may be inspired by events and conditions remote in time and place. In their national history for example, they may be stirred by events in the American Revolution, the War between the States, the winning of the West, or the exploration of the Antarctic and may be ready to give expression to them. If, for the lack of knowledge, they find it necessary to copy the work of others, say, the well-known picture of "Washington Crossing the Delaware," they are not engaging in art and are probably learning little about history. Hence, their time could be more profitably occupied elsewhere. If, on the contrary, they have equipped themselves with a sufficient background of the period which interests them and are thereby capable of giving a knowledgeable account of it, they are in a position both to gain historical knowledge and to produce art of some consequence.

The drawing of maps is not art but science. It is an extraordinary fact that even today a few teachers seem to consider the making of maps, either drawn and painted or molded in flour and salt or asbestos powder mixtures, to be a form of artistic effort. If a map is to be of any use at all, it must be scientifically accurate and allow no liberties of form for artistic purposes. No personal statement, therefore, can be permitted to influence the outline being produced. The only kind of map-making that even approaches art is the so-called "pictorial map" in which drawings are placed over its areas to indicate industries, products, physical features, and the like.

SCIENCE: Although artists like Audubon have been able to bring art and science into close proximity, it is generally recognized that scientific drawings and artistic expressions do not coincide. Like map drawing, a scientific drawing is an exact statement of fact, allowing no deviation from the natural appearance of an object.

Many years ago, art programs gave considerable importance to the drawing of "natural specimens." The pussywillow was a favorite theme, as were daffodils, tulips, and bunches of grapes. These objects were drawn even by the youngest children with strict respect for photographic accuracy. Since that time we have deepened our insight into the modes of children's thinking and their manner of expression. As was stated in Chapter 6, we now know that children should make use of symbols personal to themselves to represent objects. To a child, a natural object creates feelings and holds meanings which a scientific statement could scarcely express (see Fig. 128). To ask a child in an art session to draw scientifically serves merely to curb his expression.

Most children in elementary school, of course, are incapable of drawing with scientific accuracy. This does not mean, however, that they should be isolated, if this were possible, from natural objects or that they should not use them in their expressive acts. On the contrary, flowers, birds, sea shells, fish, and animals in the zoo, as stated previously, may be used with excellent effect in art. Provided that the child is given freedom to depart from the scientific form he observes, any natural object may be employed as the basis of design.

The fact that this freedom is allowed does not retard his growth in scientific knowledge. In looking at natural objects and experiencing them in other ways, he comes close to nature. Later, should he be of a scientific turn of mind, his art experiences with the natural world will provide him with valuable insights which may lead to scientific inquiry.

The greatest care, of course, must be taken not to supply children with symbols, considered to be artistic, which tend to replace or interfere with a study of natural objects. The cutting of paper "snowflakes," for example, could be approved only if the activity occurred subsequent to a careful study of these lovely forms and then entirely creatively. The drawing of evergreen trees in the well-known bisymmetrical zigzag design which is sometimes seen in children's work occurs more often as a result of a teacher's demonstration than because of the child's observation. A competent teacher realizes that learning in neither art nor science can occur if children copy symbols devised by others. Only when expression happens as a result of direct contact with nature can desirable learning in both these fields take place.

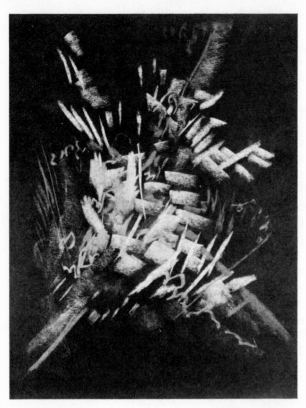

129 *A chalk drawing by a gifted boy in the sixth grade, based upon the "Saber Dance" from Khachaturian's* Gayne Ballet Suite *No. 1.*

MUSIC: Music and art lead themselves to several types of correlation. As an indirect correlation, a background of music is often valuable to children while they are drawing, painting, or working in three dimensions. The music often appears in a subtle fashion to influence the children's visual output.

The teacher may arrange direct correlations between music and art for children at any level in the elementary school. Music having a pronounced rhythmic beat and melodic line may be employed as a basis for nonobjective patterns such as that seen in Fig. 129.[5]

---

[5] "Some Activities for the Reader" at the end of Chapter 3 suggests methods and media suitable both for teachers and pupils.

So-called "classical" selections are usually to be preferred to jazz because the latter is generally too monotonous for painting. The following are well-known and well-loved examples of musical selections suitable for elementary school children:

J. S. Bach—"Brandenburg" Concerto, No. 1
        The Wise Virgins (ballet, arr. Walton)
Beethoven—Overtures: *Leonore*, No. 3
                 Egmont
                 The Consecration of the House
Bizet—*L'Arlésienne*, Suites 1 and 2
Borodin—*Prince Igor*, "Polovtsian Dances"
Khachaturian—*Gayne Ballet Suite* No. 1
Lalo—*Symphonie Espagnole*
Liszt—*Hungarian Rhapsodies*, Nos. 1 to 7
      Mephisto Waltzes
Rossini—Overtures: *The Barber of Seville*
              William Tell
              Semiramide
Von Suppé—Overtures: *Light Cavalry*
                 Poet and Peasant

Music depicting a definite mood may also lead to some interesting pictures, especially in the fifth and sixth grades. The teacher usually discusses the mood of the selection to be heard and then plays the record. After this, a second discussion with the class may occur concerning possible combinations of colors, lines, and other elements of design which might express the mood pictorially. Work, preferably in soft chalk or paint, then begins, with the music playing in the background.

The following are some examples of selections expressing certain moods, suitable for fifth- and sixth-grade pupils.

Bax—*Tintagel*
Borodin—*In the Steppes of Central Asia*
Britten—*Peter Grimes*, "Four Sea Interludes"
Copland—*Appalachian Spring*
        El Salon Mexico
Debussy—*Clair de Lune*
        La Mer
Elgar—*Pomp and Circumstance*, Nos. 1 to 4

Mussorgsky—*Night on Bald Mountain*
Sibelius—*The Swan of Tuonela*
      Finlandia
Wagner—*Die Walküre:* "Ride of the Valkyries"

Music involving a literary theme, or "program music" as it is sometimes called, may also assist in developing noteworthy picture-making by pupils in the symbol or higher stages of expression (see Fig. 130). The teacher gives the outline of the story, plays excerpts from the music, and from time to time draws attention to certain passages obviously depicting specific events in the narrative. Examples of selections suitable mainly for pupils in the fourth or higher grades are as follows:

Beethoven—Symphony No. 6, F Major, Op. 68 ("Pastoral")
Bizet—*Carmen*, excerpts
Grofé—*Grand Canyon Suite*
Humperdinck—*Hänsel und Gretel*, excerpts

130 Danse Macabre *by Saint-Saëns suggested the theme used by a sixth-grade boy in this tempera painting.*

Mussorgsky—*Pictures at an Exhibition*
Prokofiev—*Cinderella,* excerpts
       Peter and the Wolf
Respighi—*The Pines of Rome*
Rimsky-Korsakov—*Scheherazade*
Saint-Saëns—*Danse Macabre*
Tchaikovsky—*Sleeping Beauty*

MATHEMATICS: As soon as a child is capable of using a measured line, mathematics may begin to enter into some of his art work. Activities such as building model houses, making costumes for puppets, or constructing puppet stages lend themselves to this correlation.

Some teachers have attempted to combine the two fields by having the children work during art sessions with mechanical-drawing tools, such as compasses, triangles, and T-squares, to devise geometric designs. While a little of this type of work might be acceptable, any large amount of it is scarcely to be recommended because it tends to be mechanical and hence not particularly expressive.

Unplanned Correlations

The preceding examples constitute correlations of various subject fields with art which the teacher has consciously developed. Many other correlations may occur which are not arranged formally. Should a child develop a harmony of movement in physical education, a sense of balance through number, a concept of unity from some aspect of social studies, or a feeling for rhythm from poetry, there are reasons to believe that these attainments may affect his art output. Many of the general learnings of this nature acquired in art, moreover, are probably incorporated, to some extent, into other areas of his educational program. So subtle are these correlations in learning, however, that the child and indeed the teacher may be unaware of what is taking place. The most we can do for children is to keep all learning upon the highest possible creative and aesthetic levels.

Correlations Through "Workbooks"

Many series of so-called "workbooks" for what is termed "seat-work" in the various academic subjects are on the market. The authors of some of these devices seem unable to resist the temptation of making what they think is a correlation between their subject and what they consider to be art. The reader will no doubt recall many such "exercises." In a series intended to improve reading we may find this printed under a line drawing:

131 *"Lighting the Menorah for Hanukkah"—a tempera painting by a sixth-grade boy.*

"This is a bird; color it red." In number-work: "Here is a top; draw three tops." Most other subjects are given similar treatment.

It is obvious that the authors of these books are either ignorant of the expressive modes in art of young children or determined to ignore them. The symbolic representations normal to little children are never used. Furthermore, the areas in which children are supposed to do their copying of tops, rabbits, balls, and so on are too restricted to suit the child's physiological development. Finally, the drawings found in the books are usually so hackneyed as to do little for the child's taste except degrade it.

If books of this kind are of any value—a debatable point—except for keeping children quiet, it would be a relief were some adventurous authors to attempt to place the activities upon a more creative level. Until this is done, teachers would do a service to art, and probably to education in general, if they would steadfastly refrain from using them. Similar criticism can be made of coloring books in which children learn to scribble colors over line drawings of dubious quality. As one teacher facetiously remarked "Administering chloroform to children would keep them quieter and might do less harm."

Relating Art to Holy Days and Holidays

Important civilizing influences are many of the special days for religious and national observance. In the Christian calendar are Christmas and Easter, for example, and in the Jewish calendar are Hanukkah and Passover. Again, all American children usually observe such national or folk holidays as Independence Day, Memorial Day, Halloween, and Thanksgiving.

Symbols of great antiquity and deep meaning are associated with some of these festivals: the Cross, the Star of David, the Menorah (or sacred candelabrum associated with Hanukkah) seen in Fig. 131. Then there are the "profane" symbols: the Black Cat and Witch, the Christmas Candle, Santa Claus, the Pumpkin, the Horn of Plenty.

Unfortunately, these symbols are often used in a standardized, uncreative way in so-called "art lessons." Year after year the dreary procession of copy work appears—a lily and a Cross for Easter, a witch on a broomstick and a cat with an arched back for Halloween, a horn of plenty bulging with apples and grapes for Thanksgiving.

In being limited to the mere copying of these symbols, the child is prevented from giving his attention to the special significance of these events in his own life. Thanksgiving, for example, is a time in which the community turns to God; it is a day for feasting and for the gathering of family and friends. These are civilizing events, charged with feeling and worthy of thoughtful contemplation. Above all from an art standpoint, they are eminently suitable for expressive purposes. Scarcely a child will be unaffected by them, so that expression may come from deep sources. To suggest to a child, therefore, that he should copy the shopworn horn of plenty instead of offering his own impressions of Thanksgiving seems almost of barbaric. If, of course, a child holds a symbol very dear, he might work with it, not as an isolated object but in close association with the environment in which he found it. As a result he probably will produce an original design in which the symbol is the chief motif. Thus, we can say that pictures, murals, modeling, and other art activities based upon the children's *personal* reactions to holy days and holidays should be encouraged in every grade and can result in output rich in subject matter and artistic quality.

Art in the Unit Curriculum

Excellent art may be produced in school as part of the unit curriculum but continual precautions must be taken to ensure that art does not degenerate into mere handiwork. Perhaps nowhere else in the school program is the danger more apparent for busy work to replace true artistic effort. Some educators seem to believe that as long as children working at the unit curriculum are busy with hammer, nails, orange crates, and paint they are somehow learning about art.[6] Even some books on art education which suggest commendable art activities in most chapters apparently fail to recognize the real nature of art work when activities related to the unit curriculum are discussed.[7]

It is recognized, of course, that the unit curriculum must promote many activities which are not artistic. Such being the case, the teacher would be wise continually to analyze the work being done to see that sufficient time is given to artistic work. If the unit curriculum denies a child a sufficiently broad art education, it may be detrimental to his general education. Vigorous steps must then be taken to see that artistic pursuits are included in the school program, either as part of the work unit of the moment or as a study in itself. If other subjects or groups of subjects suggest artistic expression, so much to the good. But any picture-making, mural-making, puppetry, sculpture, and the like which may arise from other school activities must conform in all respects to the true nature of art.[8]

If such is not obviously the case in the school, then let art itself be the integrating factor in school life; for indeed it is sufficiently all-embracing in its subject matter, its processes, and its educative effects always to serve this purpose.[9]

Some Activities Relating Art to Other School Areas

Former chapters have outlined many activities, media, and techniques which may be used from time to time in connection with artistic themes arising from life at school. Two further types of work might be discussed briefly, however, since they may serve especially useful purposes in both correlative and unit activities. These are poster-making and several three-dimensional picture-making techniques generally known as "dioramas," "panoramas," "movies," and "peep shows."

---

[6] See, for example, A. Gordon Melvin, *The Activity Program*, especially the illustration facing p. 38, in which is shown obvious copywork in the children's drawings of animals.

[7] See, for example, Margaret Hamilton Erdt, *Teaching Art in the Elementary School* (N.Y.: Rinehart, 1954), especially pp. 65–69. While the topic "Shopping in a Market" constitutes in many respects a commendable group endeavor, such suggested activities as making a refrigerator, a freezer, a clock, and scales seem to come perilously close to busy work and to leave little time for expressive work in art.

[8] See Chapter 1.

[9] Such appears to be the theme in Leon L. Winslow, *The Integrated School Art Program*, 2nd Ed. (N.Y.: McGraw-Hill, 1949).

Poster-Making

MEDIA AND TECHNIQUES: From time to time, a classroom project or school activity may require some form of advertising by poster. Then, ways and means must be devised by which the poster may be produced in accordance with sound educational and artistic principles.

An effective poster must fulfill several well-defined basic requirements to be useful. It must be arresting, it must convey its message briefly, it should usually contain only one idea, and it should be easily readable at a distance.

The lettering required in most poster work demands painstaking practice and provides little scope for the imagination. Letter "A" must be letter "A," and very little deviation can be allowed if the letter is to remain readable. Indeed, to produce acceptable letters and layout for a poster requires a technical competence usually beyond the capabilities of an elementary school child.

The solution to this problem is to build upon whatever abilities children possess. Most school systems include a carefully graded program to teach writing. The youngest children frequently begin writing in what is called "print script." This is often subsequently developed into a "joined print script," and after this stage the child begins cursive writing. Competence at each stage is the result of much painstaking teaching. It is wise, therefore, for the child to make use of the abilities he has gained in the writing program in his poster work. Whatever alphabet he has learned and mastered as part of the writing program seems to be the logical one to use in a poster because in both types of work he is employing the hard-earned skill of using words to convey ideas. To teach him "Roman" lettering, or to encourage him to copy or to devise some curious lettering of his own, would be grossly inefficient educational practice.

In poster-making, the beginners in writing should first use the usual large pencils and writing paper to which they are accustomed. Later they can employ wax crayons and drawing paper. By the fifth and sixth grades the pupils are able to use special equipment for poster-making, such as large lettering nibs having round, oval, and square tips and India ink to make the writing bold enough for a poster. Following a little practice in using special pens and inks, the pupils seem to experience no great difficulty in writing in their accustomed style upon the larger scale required for the poster.

What drawings and paintings are used by the children in conjunction with their verbal message should likewise be in keeping with their developmental level and general competence. If a child is in the symbol stage of

132 *A cut-paper poster by a second-grade boy.*

expression, for example, obviously he should use this form in his poster work.

TEACHING: Poster-making can cause problems for an elementary school teacher because of demands made upon the school by officials of local charitable organizations who desire advertising of the worthy causes they sponsor. While in picture-making teachers are contented with work of a technical competence commensurate with the child's developmental level, such is not always the case when posters are being produced for the community. In an attempt to obtain useful posters, the teacher may apply pressure so that the children are forced both to copy the drawings of others and to spend valuable educational time in outlining letters of the alphabet. All this militates against an expressive art program. All overtures from outside sources to have posters made for events remote from the school, therefore, should be resisted. Much as a school wishes to support the community at large, the technical difficulties involved in the making of posters for the community forbid the inclusion of this work in the art program in the elementary grades.

A poster for a school activity is quite a different matter. Then, of course, the teacher should encourage the project and offer assistance as it is required. The size of the poster, its design, the strength of color used, the boldness of the writing, and the like should be discussed. The teacher should also demonstrate the different types of lettering nibs and brushes available, while time for preliminary practice with these tools should be found before an actual poster is made. As pupils become more experienced in the work, the teacher should encourage them to make rough layouts before beginning work in the final project.

Thus the poster, if treated as an extension of writing and picture-making, may be included in the art program of the elementary school to serve a limited but necessary purpose.

"Dioramas," "Panoramas," "Movies," and "Peep Shows"

MEDIA AND TECHNIQUES: These four types of work are especially valuable for correlations between art and literature or history.

A diorama is a display having a backdrop and wings rather like a miniature stage. It may be made simply from a carton or box with the lid and the one side removed. The objects placed in this setting may be made from cardboard, carving materials, or a variety of other substances. The backdrop can be painted or designed in paper.

A panorama is constructed on an open surface and may be seen from any side. The well-known kindergarten "sandtable" is a kind of panorama arrangement. The supporting surface is a tray of convenient size having wooden sides to prevent things from falling off.

All manner of materials and techniques may be used in the making of the panorama. Sand for deserts, glass for rivers, cardboard for houses, papier-mâché for people and animals, paper for trees are among the items one might suggest.

A "movie" is a series of pictures attached to each other to form a ribbon. For displaying the movie, a cardboard carton may be used. An opening for the "screen" should be cut in the bottom of the carton. Two wooden rollers are then thrust vertically through the carton on either side of the screen opening. Old broom handles make good rollers, which must project well beyond the sides of the carton. Pictures are stuck together in a ribbon, the ends of which are tacked to the rollers. By turning either of the rollers the pictures

133 *A diorama produced by pupils in the fifth grade.*

are made to move across the opening. The usual drawing and painting materials are used for the pictures.

The peep show is actually a variation of the diorama. An old shoe box provides a good basic unit for this technique. In a small end of the box a hole about the size of a quarter should be cut. Inside at the other end of the box, and at least half-way up the sides, a background must be painted. Figures and trees coming between the eye and the background are best made from cardboard. Other properties may be constructed of a variety of materials from straw to absorbent cotton.

Interesting effects in lighting can be obtained by covering the top of the box with colored plastics or tissue papers. (When not in use, the peep show should be protected by placing the box lid in position.) Moving a straight beam of light, such as that from a pencil-type flashlight, over the colored material gives the viewer many pleasant and surprising design effects.

TEACHING: These four techniques essentially constitute group work involving from two to, say, a dozen pupils, in any grade and in any stage of pictorial development from the symbol stage up. The teacher's work therefore will be chiefly that of sponsoring group activities according to the principles outlined in an earlier chapter. The techniques of constructing, modeling, drawing, and painting, mentioned in earlier chapters, will also be employed in these activities.

Of greatest concern to the teacher is ensuring that the pupils give maximum attention to developing designs having artistic qualities. Unless the teacher discusses design from time to time, any one of these four types of work could degenerate into busy work. There is no need for this to happen, however, since each type of work can be an art activity in every sense.

ACTIVITIES FOR THE READER

1. Prepare detailed plans for three lessons involving a correlation between art and each of the following: physical education; silent reading; arithmetic.

2. Describe from your observations in classrooms three attempts at correlation between art and other subjects which degenerated into busy work. Explain in each case how you would have altered the lessons to ensure that art was produced.

3. Analyze a unit of work you have seen in a classroom for the art education involved. If you believe that learning about art could have been improved, explain how this could have been done.

4. Study some "workbooks" and list any errors made by the authors when they attempt to correlate what they consider to be art with some other subjects. Suggest art activities to replace those outlined by the authors.

134 *A panorama produced by a group of first-grade pupils.*

Royal Studio

135a *A movie, front view, produced by third-grade children.*

135b *The same movie, rear view.*

136 *A peep show made by two children in the second grade.*

5. List all the symbols related to holy days and holidays which children have been asked to copy in classrooms you have observed. Suggest some art work to replace this copy work.

6. Experiment with a number of lettering nibs. Use your own handwriting but try to eliminate any wiggles and squiggles. Also, in the interest of clarity, reduce the length of ascending and descending letters.[10]

---

[10] For students who wish to become especially proficient in lettering, see Ross F. George, *Speedball Text Book*, 14th Ed. (Camden, N.J.: Hunt Pen Company, 1941). This is a helpful book in spite of some bad designs.

See also Robin Tanner, *Lettering for Children* (Peoria, Ill., Bennett, 1937). This outlines a method of lettering called "Italic." Many educators throughout the world seem to be adopting this type of lettering to replace the current handwriting in schools. So strong has the movement become that some countries, including Canada and England, have formed national societies for the promotion of "Italic handwriting." The script is certainly easily read, is pleasant to see, and is said to be not especially difficult for children to master.

The student who wishes to know more about lettering should see Oscar Ogg, *An Alphabet Source Book*, (N.Y.: Dover, 1947); this is a purely technical work. More historical is Ogg, *The 26 Letters*, (N.Y.: Crowell, 1948).

7.   Make a poster for a school event: (a) select a title for the headline; if a secondary heading is required keep it to three or four words; (b) make a rough layout, including letters and illustration if any; (c) outline the poster on Bristol board; (d) paint the picture if you have included one; (e) do the lettering; (f) analyze your work from a distance of 10 feet, for clarity, brevity, and design quality.

8.   With the help of one or two other interested people experiment with many materials to make a diorama, a panorama, a peep show, and a "movie." In the movie include a title page and captions as well as drawings to tell your story. Relate all four activities to some other classroom work.

Displaying Children's Art

In recent years the display of children's art has become increasingly attractive, and this development is apparently welcomed both by art teachers and by other adults interested in education, from school administrators to parents.

Several obvious educational benefits may occur as a result of effective display techniques. It is the purpose of this chapter, therefore, to discuss some of the most important aspects of children's art displays, including the chief reasons for displaying the work, some methods of selecting pieces for display, some of the techniques and media involved in arranging displays, and the teaching methods appropriate to this aspect of art education.

Why Display Children's Art?

There are many reasons for displaying children's art, most of them psychological and pedagogical. Purely artistic reasons are also important, however, and perhaps the most important reason of all is simply this: the results of children's artistic acts are usually worth observing for their aesthetic qualities. Children's art is often good art, and for this reason alone it should not be hidden in folios but rather brought forth for people to see. The production of any art form is not a casual event but rather an offering of heart and mind from one human being to another. Indeed, the whole character of ex-

137 *Third-grade pupils admire a display of paper fish.*

pression in art has been recognized as *"an overture demanding response from others."* [1] Because the child offers in his work something of his true self, his efforts are worthy of respectful attention.

Displaying children's art constitutes an effective teaching device. One common method is to display work according to topics or themes. When twenty-five or more pupils in a class present their reactions to one theme, it is highly educative for all to observe the reactions of others. If art is suitably taught, no two children make identical statements about an experience. Thus, viewing the various statements, the children may gain a broader insight into the topic as a whole.

In displaying children's art, furthermore, we tend to develop in the pupils certain desirable attitudes towards the school. The young child who sees his artistic efforts on display among those of his fellows tends thereby to sense a oneness with his group. Thus his participation develops a feeling of "belongingness" which often increases the fullness of subsequent participation. Perhaps the child has stated something about his pet at home, his mother, father, brothers or sisters, his toys, or his playmates. It is a comfort-

---

[1] The words are those of I. D. Suttie, in *The Origins of Love and Hate,* quoted by Read, *Education Through Art* (N.Y.: Pantheon, 1945), p. 164.

ing thought to him, not only that all these important aspects of his life have miraculously found their way into his school, but also that the school is interested in them.

The display of children's art also has, of course, its decorative purposes. The classroom is usually a very barren place when first the teacher enters it preparatory to the opening of school. Likewise the halls of many schools are drab caverns until suitable decorations have been arranged. Much of the art work of children has a highly decorative quality which will quickly change the character of a school building. Often bold and colorful, the work adds attractiveness and an intimate feeling to even the most austere surroundings. For some of the older school buildings in particular, the display of children's art may work remarkable improvement upon the architectural horrors in which some classes must still be held. Even the most delightful interior architecture of our splendid modern schools, however, can be improved by a judicious display of children's production.

More and more, schools are serving as institutions of learning by day and as community centers by night. Parent-teacher groups, night-school classes (in which, among other subjects, art may be studied), and other meetings of interest to the members of a community are causing greater numbers of adults to visit the schools than ever before. This is a desirable development, since it provides the school with an opportunity to show the public what is being done with that sacred commodity, the taxpayer's money. Furthermore, it presents the opportunity of arousing or maintaining public interest in education in general and art education in particular.

Arranging Displays in the Classroom

SELECTING WORK: In considering classroom displays, probably the first question in the teacher's mind is how to choose the work for exhibition. The criteria for selection should be both pedagogical and aesthetic. While a child will find interest in the art output of others, he is also interested in his own work and is usually proud of it. This means that every child in a class sooner or later during the school term should find some of his work on display. Since space is limited in a classroom, he cannot expect his work to appear very often, but this fact he will accept if he feels that his chances of showing are equal with those of others. By being aware of this, he tends to become a more active participant in all displays which appear on the classroom walls.

As children mature, they develop an ability to appraise the standards of both their behavior and their artistic output. It is an unintelligent child indeed who is unable to decide whether or not he has exerted himself to a degree approaching capacity. Most children in the upper grades can tell themselves with some accuracy whether they "took it easy" or "worked hard." They are also capable of realizing when their output has not resulted in a success commensurate with their effort. An attempt at expression does not always result in success, as every creating person knows. When a child realizes that his output has not reached an accustomed standard, displaying his work would in all likelihood be an embarrassment to him. Before a particular child's work is displayed, therefore, a teacher would do well to compare it with his previous performances. A deviation from his usual standard may be the result of either a decrease in effort or a "run of bad luck." In either case, the normal pupil would, in all likelihood, not expect to find his output on display.

If work for display is chosen with these ideas in mind, the child of exceptional ability will not create the problems of selection which might otherwise be the case. It would be discouraging for the remaining members of the class to see a more gifted child's work repeatedly occupying a major portion of the displays to the partial exclusion of the work of others. As suggested in an earlier chapter, the gifted child exhibits a range of success in output, just as everyone else does.[2] This being the case, only the most significant items of his expression, as with that of other children, need appear on display.

Sometimes—indeed perhaps frequently—the most finished and apparently competent work of any particular child of no matter what ability may be rejected in the interest of output showing an advance in some specific ability in art, such as an improvement in the handling of a medium or an element of design. On the other hand, sometimes, during what might be described as a burst of growth, a child may pass from one expressive stage or mode to another.[3] On such occasions, his development may adversely affect his technique. Skills then seem to deteriorate, or rather do not keep pace with thought, so that the work appears inadequate in composition or in the handling of media. Nevertheless, because the advance has been made in other directions, the output should be displayed, if the child is willing for this to be done.

In order to summarize the general progress of each child, the teacher will not have to save all the art work of every pupil during the school year. While some of the work may be kept in a portfolio for reference, the teacher will find that he can rely to a great extent upon his memory of each child's earlier performances. This is so because the art output of each child be-

---

[2] See Chapter 13.   [3] See Chapter 6.

comes unique in the eyes of an alert, interested, and sensitive teacher. (More will be said about appraisal in Chapter 17.)

It will be realized that the selection of work for display is a delicate matter. It depends not only upon the outward appearance of each piece, but also upon an intimate knowledge of every child responsible for it. The teacher must be fully aware of each child's potential and judge his work, not from some preconceived standard of attainment, but rather in relation to the pupil's personal abilities.

The question now arises as to the part children should play in the selection of work. This is a difficult question to answer and one which the teacher will probably have to solve for himself. It is obviously desirable that children should have some control of the selection of work. However, the teacher is probably in the best position to recognize both the aesthetic growth in individuals and the true aesthetic quality in a large proportion of the output. Perhaps a satisfactory compromise can be reached if each child is frequently given the opportunity to indicate his preferences for display of his own work, while committees of children are, from time to time, made responsible for selecting displays from the various pieces chosen by individuals. At other times, however, it may be necessary for the teacher to arrange the display on the basis of his own choice. On these occasions, he may still work closely with the children by explaining the reasons for his selection.

With these considerations in mind, we may now turn to the mechanics of display in the classroom.

MEDIA AND TECHNIQUES FOR DISPLAYING TWO-DIMENSIONAL WORK: The display areas on which the work is posted should not be overcrowded. Each piece should be set apart, preferably with a mount or frame. Frames should be chosen so that their color provides a unity to the display but does not conflict with the colors used in the drawings and paintings themselves. Grays, browns, and sometimes black are usually suitable colors for mounts or frames. When the display panels are made of wood, cork, or fiber boards, both mount and picture may most conveniently be fastened to the display area by a gun-type wall-stapler. While pins and thumbtacks may be used here, the staple is the neatest means of fixing the pieces of work to the support.

Mounts or frames may be devised in a number of ways and with several materials. The simplest, cheapest, and, as many think, most attractive method of mounting is to tack a sheet of newsprint, paper, or cardboard to the display board and upon this to tack a drawing or painting having smaller dimensions. A variety of effects may be obtained with this method by altering the proportion of background to picture, by tacking the background

138 *Some methods of mounting pictures.*

diagonally to the picture, by leaving one corner of the background untacked, or by placing the picture over the background so that only two edges of the background paper show.

Another method is to frame a picture by cutting a window in a sheet of paper or cardboard. The simplest method is to cut away an area of paper the size of a picture before tacking the paper in place. For variety, the area cut away might be slightly less than that of the picture and the edges of the cut-out area may be rolled back to form a raised part around the picture.

Mounting and framing may again be varied by using two or more cardboard mounts or frames in different tones of one color. The use of two materials having contrasting textures, such as burlap and plywood, also creates interesting effects.

Sometimes a picture can be supported away from a mount. This may be done by pinning a picture to a cardboard tray which in turn is fastened to the support.

Frames with deep edges are easily made from cardboard, either plain or corrugated, to form still more interesting effects for mounting.

As mentioned earlier, it is often desirable for those arranging a show to exhibit work according to topics or themes. Sometimes a theme depicts a series of events which demand a logical order of display, for example, "Our Trip to the Dairy," which would include leaving the school, the arrival at the plant, the mechanical processes observed, and the return to school. To assist the observer in following the proper sequence of pictures, one can use a series of paper arrows. This display technique may also be used where no particular logical arrangement is required, but where a certain aesthetic order is desired. Those arranging a display will also find string convenient in establishing a sequence. If various colors and types of string, including those with a metallic finish, are strung from one place to another in a panel, some exceptionally interesting rhythms throughout the display can be achieved.

Whenever a display is arranged, a title is usually required. Titles, of course, become part of the general design of a display. A title may be produced in two dimensions with lettering pens and India or colored inks.[4] Three-dimensional titles can be made from cardboard cut-out letters, but this work is usually beyond the ability of most elementary school children. After it is cut out, each letter is stuck on long pins which hold it away from the display board. Attractive background papers of contrasting color or texture help to make this type of title particularly arresting.

---

4 See the section on poster-making in Chapter 14.

The most common and simplest arrangement of pictures on a display panel is one that follows the rectangular shape of the board. The pictures are hung so that their edges are parallel to those of the board. More often than not a formal balance is achieved so that the spectators' attention will be attracted equally around imaginary central axes of the board. The margins established between the picture frames and the outside edges of the horizontal display panel will be such that the bottom margin will be widest, the top narrowest, and the width of the sides in between that of top and bottom. In a vertical panel, the traditional proportions to be observed reverse the sides and top: now the bottom is widest, the top is second in size, and the sides are narrowest. A square panel calls for even margins at top and sides, with a wider margin at the bottom. These classic arrangements are safe, and by using them one may tastefully display any group of pictures (see Fig. 139).

While it is usually desirable that pictures be hung in the traditional manner described above, from time to time some experimental arrangements should be tried. For example, the frames of all pictures might be tilted slightly "off center," but with the pictures themselves remaining in an upright position. Again, all pictures might be placed on the display board to form a full-drop or half-drop repeat pattern. Still again, informally arranged clusters of pictures might be drawn together visually with background papers of contrasting hues. Such experiments, of course, must be used with considerable discretion in order that the display itself does not become so "showy" as to detract from the pictures.

All displays in a classroom must exhibit "order and good government," and should be considered as designs subject to the disciplines of good taste. As each one is added, it must be considered in relation to whatever displays are already on view. In general it is a wise plan to restrict displays to those areas especially designed for exhibits. A classroom can scarcely appear orderly if drawings and paintings are stuck to blackboards, pinned to chalk-rails, or plastered on windows. Blackboards, chalk-rails, and windows are functional parts of the classroom whose efficiency is impaired by displays of art. To interfere with their function through decoration is an act of bad taste.

MEDIA AND TECHNIQUES FOR DISPLAYING THREE-DIMENSIONAL WORK: Many classrooms are not equipped with display cases for three-dimensional output. It is frequently necessary, therefore, for the class to improvise other means of display. If space is available, one may place a table directly in front of a display board. The three-dimensional objects may then be set on the table and descriptions of the work or related two-dimensional work may be pinned to the board. Should it be considered necessary to link a written description to any particular piece on the table, a colored string may be fixed from the description to the piece of work.

The objects should be arranged according to their bulk and height. Obviously the largest and tallest objects will have to be placed well in the background so that smaller objects will not be hidden. Some groups of objects, particularly modeled or carved forms and pottery, will demand the use of pedestals. Made from boxes or blocks of wood, the pedestals may be painted or covered with textiles to provide interesting variety to the display. By placing a sheet of glass over one or more pedestals, one can arrange a convenient series of shelves of varying heights.

Display boards themselves may be used to exhibit three-dimensional work. Metal brackets fixed to the boards with screws to support glass shelves will make attractive display space.

In arranging three-dimensional displays, the exhibitors must give the same attention to design as they would do in displaying flat work. Brilliantly colored pieces, for example, or those having outstanding shapes or textural qualities must be well placed with respect to the centers of interest, the balance, and the rhythm of the design. Having the same background for the objects may be particularly important as a means of bringing unity to the three-dimensional display.[5]

By avoiding straight rows of objects and instead placing them at different heights and various distances from the observer, by grouping objects within a display and yet maintaining a unity throughout all such groups, some striking results may be obtained. Objects, however, do not arrange

---

[5] Review Chapter 3 for a discussion of design.

139 *Standard arrangements for placing pictures on mats.*

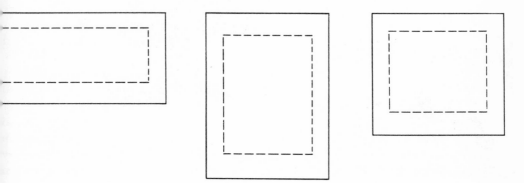

themselves, and to present them with charm and character, one must give considerable attention to the problems peculiar to three-dimensional display.

TEACHING: Because the displaying of art work is an art activity in itself, it is highly desirable for children to take part in it. Moreover display techniques also may lead to excellent group endeavors. The kindergarten is not too soon for children to begin this work. Kindergarten children may participate in quasi-group activities in which individuals bring their work to some central area for display.[6]

As soon as possible, of course, display through the quasi-group activity should lead to group activity proper in which Kilpatrick's stages are in force.

As in all other art activities, the teacher must continually remind the children of the importance of design in display arrangements. Whether the children are drawing up plans in advance for a display or working out a display directly on a display panel or elsewhere, the teacher must encourage the pupils continually to consider the designs being formed.

The teacher should give every encouragement to the pupils to experi-

_____
[6] See Chapter 11.

140 *A display of weaving in which careful attention has been given to the all-over arrangement.*

Royal Studio

ment with new ways of displaying their art. One method is to have members of the class report on any outstanding display techniques observed in store windows or elsewhere. Another of course is for the teacher himself, from time to time, to arrange a display of children's work in which some new ideas for display are demonstrated.[7]

Arranging Displays
Outside of the Classroom

The problems arising from displays arranged in the halls or elsewhere in a school are little different from those related to classroom exhibitions. More people and examples of work are involved, of course, so that organizational problems are intensified.

MEDIA AND TECHNIQUES: Many schools lack facilities for the display of art in the halls. But since the cost of providing suitable panels and even display cases is a relatively minor item in the annual educational budget, school authorities may be expected to provide them. When the panels and cases are being installed, those responsible for the installations must remember to arrange suitable lighting for each one.

On occasion, the school may need additional display facilities. Many extra panels might be required on "Parents' Night" for example, when the school wishes to make an exceptional effort to interest the community. The design of panels for extra display facilities has become almost standard. The panels consist of sheets of building board, usually measuring from four by four feet to four by eight feet, to either end of which legs are bolted. The legs usually take the form of inverted T's, but other ingenious and attractive designs are to be seen. For three-dimensional display, a boxlike construction often having shelves takes the place of the panel.

A second type of portable display board has been designed for space-saving and quick assembly. It consists of panels of building board and sturdy legs with slots cut into two adjacent sides. The panels are fitted into the slots to form a zigzag effect which is pleasing and practical. The panels are made secure by lashing the legs together with cord at the top and bottom of the panels.

The subject matter of art displays for parent and community groups may be different from that in displays for children. Parents and other adults are interested not only in the work as such, but also in the pedagogical rea-

---

[7] Very little worthwhile literature dealing with display techniques for teachers is available. Marjorie East, *Display for Learning* (N.Y.: Dryden, 1952), contains many good ideas, but the design qualities of much of the work shown in the illustrations seem to leave room for improvement.

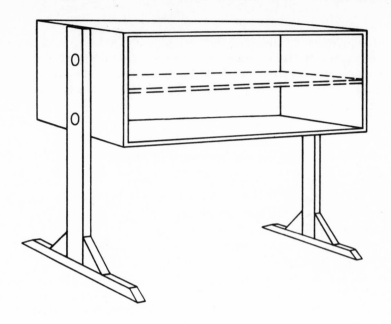

141 *Above, a display case for three-dimensional objects and below, panels for two-dimensional objects.*

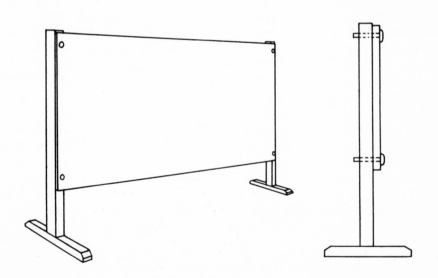

sons supporting the contemporary art program. It must be remembered that for many adults, the present-day program of art in schools is completely different from the so-called art work they were forced to do in their youth. While ignorance of the contemporary program sometimes leads to disapproval, in general parents are quick to react favorably to present-day trends in art, once those trends are understood. For parents, the subjects of the displays of children's art might frequently emphasize some of the pedagogical and psychological implications of the activities. The following are a few sample topics of this nature which have proved satisfactory during Parents' Night:

> Art education—the old and the new
> Personal development through art
> Variety in artistic expression
> Group work in art
> Art and democratic education [8]

For each exhibition, brief but effective signs should be made to emphasize the points demonstrated by the children's work. Each show, moreover, should have a clearly marked beginning, a logical sequence of ideas throughout the body of the exhibition, and a short summary, either written or pictorial or both, at its close.

TEACHING: The display of work outside of the classroom can become a burdensome undertaking if too few people take on the job but can be a real challenge to a large group. In some schools, display committees composed of teachers and pupils are formed. These committees often decide upon the themes and make themselves responsible for hanging the displays. Sometimes arrangements are made in advance so that each class in the school is responsible for a display for a given period of time. At other schools, broad themes of local interest are selected to which each class contributes. Frequently, a combination of both types of display is used.

Actually, the teaching techniques involved in this larger display activity remain the same as those outlined earlier for the classroom display. The teachers must still stimulate the pupils, offer suggestions as they are required, and demonstrate and discuss new techniques.

A few last but highly important words must be said. No matter what type of exhibition is organized, whether in classrooms, in the halls, or else-

---

[8] See Viktor Lowenfeld, *Your Child and His Art* (N.Y.: Macmillan, 1954), which is written to help parents understand their children's art. Many topics which might form the core of a display for parents can be found in this excellent book.

142 *A large zigzag display in a school gymnasium.*

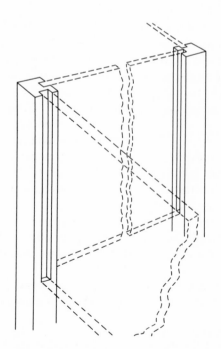

143 *Diagram of posts and panels for a zigzag-type of display.*

where in a school, *an art show must be kept on the move.* To leave it on the walls longer than is necessary is to waste an educational opportunity. Nothing becomes more bedraggled or more quickly out-of-date than an art show left too long on the walls. Perhaps, on the other hand, nothing is more effective as a teaching device than a shiny, new, attractively displayed art show.

ACTIVITIES FOR THE READER

1. Describe the varying criteria by which teachers you have observed have selected children's art work for display. Appraise each criterion according to its educational effects upon the children concerned.

2. Study and compare the display techniques you have observed in various classrooms.

3. Experiment with mounting and framing a picture on a surface such as a drawing board. Try some of the ways suggested in this chapter and then attempt to devise new ways to display the picture.

4. Sketch in pencil or crayon some plans for a display of 5 pictures. Select the plan you like best and use it in actually pinning pictures to a panel.

5. Repeat (4), only this time include at least 12 pictures.

6. Make some plans for the display of 3 pieces of pottery. Carry out the plan you like best.

7. List some subjects for an art display to be used in the main entrance of a school on Parents' Night. The entrance hall is about 25 feet long and 12 feet wide. After selecting the subject which most appeals to you, indicate in detailed sketches (a) the type and position of the display panels; (b) the number and subject matter of the pictures or three-dimensional objects; (c) the captions to be used; and (d) the route which the visitors should follow to view the exhibition and the means by which they are directed along this route.

Developing Children's

Appreciation of Art

Up to this point we have concentrated upon problems in art education arising from the production of art forms. We must now turn to the other side of art education, that of the pupils' appreciation of the work of others. Before we begin our discussion about art appreciation, it might be well to review what we mean by art. What, in other words, is the nature of the phenomenon which the pupil is to appreciate? In the opening chapter, it will be remembered that the nature of art was outlined. We saw that art consists of an artist's statement about his reactions to some moving experience and that this expression is communicated through a design. Such is the quality of a work of art that it holds significance for many who behold it. Reflecting the mind of its creator and the skill he has achieved through a lifelong search for excellence of expression, the work of art is an inspiring record of human achievement.

Because qualities of mind and abilities to develop skill vary from one human being to another, a range of significance exists among art productions. Great artists produce great art in which content and design are fused with incomparable skill and insight, but relatively few people have such greatness. There are many artists of lesser ability, however, who produce significant works which are worthy of attention and respect. Perhaps one artist's skill in designing may be superior to his ability to select significant subject matter, while in the work of another, the profundity of the subject matter suffers through a deficiency of design. In such art there is often much to learn and to appreciate. Only when an artist loses sight of the ideals necessary for the production of art forms is his work unworthy of our attention.

The Nature of Art Appreciation

In considering art appreciation we face intangibles. When the pupil has produced an art form, we have his finished product to study and to compare with the output of others. There can be no such tangible evidence of development in the pupils' ability to appreciate art. However, we have good reason to believe that a pupil's appreciation of art can be heightened and, consequently, his taste developed as a result of certain teaching procedures.

Psychologists who have attempted to probe the mysteries of art appreciation are relatively few and their findings are not conclusive.

> Appreciation can be almost wholly a matter of quiet contemplation, of direct sense perception along with various inward mental and emotional processes aroused by perception. Psychologists now tend to overlook this distinctively aesthetic type of response, at this time when it is fashionable to lay heavy stress upon the active and purposeful aspects of behavior. The aesthetic type is no less real or important though harder . . . to deal with and often ignored in consequence.[1]

Rather than to psychologists, we must refer to certain philosophers for most of our insight into the nature of aesthetic appreciation.[2] It must be noted, however, that much of what has been said in comparatively recent years by philosophers appears to be strongly influenced by the general tenets of Gestalt psychology.

First, as Dewey says, "in the kingdom of art as well as of righteousness it is those who hunger and thirst who enter." This attitude of "hunger and thirst" involves not only the desire but, as we shall see later, apparently the will and ability to transcend personal sentiment which might prevent a full appreciation of the work.

---

[1] Thomas Munro, "Powers of Art Appreciation and Evaluation," in *The Fortieth Yearbook of the National Society for the Study of Education* (Bloomington, Ill.: Public School Publishing Co., 1941), p. 329.

[2] It is interesting to note that typologists exist in this field as well as in that of expression. Edward Bullough is perhaps best known in this connection because of his influence upon Herbert Read. He lists four types of people as follows: objective, physiological, associative, and character. See his " 'Perceptive Problem' in the Aesthetic Appreciation of Single Colours," *British Journal of Psychology,* II: 1906–08, 406–63. See also Read, *Education Through Art* (N.Y.: Pantheon, 1945), pp. 91–92, for a description of these types.

To what do we react in a work of art and how do we react? Fry offers the argument that in all cases our reaction to works of art is a reaction to relationships and not to isolated sensations, objects, persons, or events. He goes on to point out, as an example, that some of the works of the greatest colorists are built up from elements which when taken separately are of no particular significance but which through interrelationships in their composition gain the utmost significance. He carries his observations concerning our reactions to the relationships of elements of composition into the fields of music, poetry, and architecture.[3]

Read, in his *Meaning of Art*, considers that the aesthetic reaction, when it does occur, affects the mind suddenly.[4] The observer (and one should note that Read specifies "of sensibility") does not go through a long process of intellectual analysis before he pronounces himself pleased or otherwise. Ellis supports this viewpoint, at least in part, when he says that throughout his life a revelation of a painter's work has always occurred to him suddenly—"in a flash"—and that henceforth this sudden insight "became the clue to all the painter's work."[5]

The normal condition of our existence is one in which we maintain a necessary state of tension or inhibition. At certain times, however, we cease to maintain this state and instead laugh, cry, and the like. These changes, we say, are a release and among them may be included the aesthetic reaction.

An important distinction has been made between the reaction of "having a good laugh" or "a good cry" at, say, a cinema, and the aesthetic reaction to the screen play. The former reaction, according to Read, is one of sentimentality. ". . . Sentimentality," he states, "is a release, but also a loosening, a relaxing of the emotions; art is a release, but also a bracing."[6]

Thus, in Read's view, to weep over the trials of the heroine of a play as if we were in the place of the sufferer is not to experience the aesthetic quality of the production. A work of art may lead the stream of consciousness away into delightful imaginings, but such a state is beside the point if we strictly agree that the work of art is our single reference for aesthetic appreciation. Dewey sums up the matter thus: ". . . Emotion is esthetic when it adheres to an object formed by an expressive act, in the sense in which the act of expression has been defined."[7] Fry describes the manner in which Dewey's dictum is often violated:

---

[3] Roger Fry, *Transformations* (N.Y.: Doubleday, 1956).
[4] N.Y.: Pitman, 1951, p. 38.
[5] Havelock Ellis, *The Dance of Life* (N.Y.: Modern Library, 1929), p. 314.
[6] Read, *The Meaning of Art*, p. 39.
[7] Dewey, *Art as Experience* (N.Y.: Minton Balch, 1934), p. 76.

144 *Reynolds'* Age of Innocence *is the kind of painting that may, unfortunately, be used for inappropriate lessons in art appreciation.*

> Here we touch the crux of the aesthetic experience for the greater number of people who are accustomed to rely almost exclusively on their interest in, or emotion about, the persons or events called to mind by the imagery of the fine arts. Landscape for such is just reminiscence or revelation of pleasant natural scenes; portraiture interests by the beautiful . . . ladies . . . it represents; figure painting avails by its attractive and provocative nudes. . . .[8]

Art appreciation, as distinguished from sentimentality, seems to involve the total personality, and there is probably much truth in the old saw about "a picture judging a person" rather than the reverse. What a person is—emotionally, intellectually, and socially—will determine his ability to appreciate art. This ability is not innate, but it is built around and upon the innate so that some are able to acquire it more quickly than others. Art appreciation, in fact, appears to be the result of a prolonged education. "As for appreciation, this can undoubtedly be developed by teaching," says Read, although "the faculty is only likely to develop as one aspect of social adaptation. . . ."[9] The problem arises as to what may be done in the elementary school to help children learn to appreciate the art of others. The remainder of this chapter will concentrate upon some practical ways and means of developing appreciation of art.

---

[8] Fry, *Transformations*, p. 3.   [9] Read, *Education Through Art*, p. 206.

Some Teaching Methods
to Develop Appreciation

At least three points of view have been held concerning the teaching of appreciation in the elementary school. The first suggests that there should be no teaching because children are not sufficiently mature to benefit from it. Instead, the teacher should encourage the pupils to express themselves and then "can only stand over them in a kind of protective awe." [10] The second is that formal lessons should be offered from time to time, particularly with regard to "picture study." The third is that appreciation should be taught only when such teaching appears to be expedient; that is to say, when the need is clearly apparent.

The first point of view seems to recommend a position which is practically impossible to maintain. The actions of a teacher during his daily rounds of duty, his appearance, his care of the classroom, and so on must exert some effect, either good or bad, upon the attitudes of children towards art. Furthermore, if expression is to receive any guidance whatsoever, the question of appreciation immediately enters into an art activity. We may assert, therefore, that whether or not a teacher believes in teaching for the development of appreciation, he does so teach.

The second point of view had more advocates twenty-five years ago than it has today. An extraordinary amount of nonsense has been perpetrated in many classrooms through formal lessons in art appreciation, in which questions are asked about certain works of art. Sir Joshua Reynolds' *The Age of Innocence,* for example (Fig. 144), may be the picture chosen for study. Even when the questions pertain reasonably closely to the picture being studied—e.g., "Why is the little girl placed where she is in the picture?" or, "What colors has the artist used to make us look at her?"—there is some doubt as to the value of the teaching procedure. But when, as is not infrequently the case, the questions become artistically remote from the work and include such sentimental or literary ideas as—"Isn't she a pretty little girl? Do you think she is happy? Why isn't she wearing shoes? Will it rain? What will the little girl do then?"—the appreciation of art can never occur. Such questions simply lead the children away from "the sense in which the act of expression has been defined." To offer this type of lesson in picture appreciation, even as a literary exercise, can only intensify an all too prevalent misapprehension as to the nature of art.[11]

---

[10] *Ibid.*

[11] At this time the reader might profitably refer to Margaret H. Bully, *Art and Counterfeit* (London: Methuen, 1925), and, by the same author, the large and less concise but interesting *Art and Every Man: A Basis for Appreciation,* 2 vols. (London: Batsford, 1952).

Indeed, in recent years any formal teaching of "famous masterpieces" to children is held in some suspicion. "Urging people to like things, or preaching about our own likes is not the most effective way to get results." [12] As Dewey says, art can be appreciated only when there is a "hunger and thirst" for it. The formal attempt to motivate children to appreciate famous paintings is rarely as effective as its advocates maintain. But the failure in general of the formal method of teaching appreciation of art in no way obviates the necessity for children to be afforded every possible means of coming into contact with their cultural heritage.

Many teachers devote much of their time, thought, and energy to a program in which an appreciation of art is taught in close relationship to expression. [13] According to this method, a teacher seizes every practical opportunity to introduce the subject of appreciation, not only of drawing and painting but also of three-dimensional work such as sculpture and pottery.

The method is based upon the belief that one cannot logically divorce expression from appreciation. After working with a medium, we know what to look for in similar work of others. We become conscious of the problems, needs, and goals which have influenced our own expressive acts. It does not matter how limited may be our present insight into artistic expression. As long as we have some personal problem which has arisen from our own labors, some goal related to the activity, and some need for enlightenment, we are in a position to increase our insight by intelligently appreciating what another has done. As our insight and appreciation grow, so in turn may our taste and related expressive acts improve.

Learning of the type described above requires that the teacher make extensive use of visual aids and art objects themselves. No matter what field of art may be engaging the child's attention—pottery, textiles, drawing, painting—the teacher will find it necessary to have available suitable works in similar areas for reference, comparison, and study.

Much of this reference material will probably represent the contemporary period. Since this is the era in which the children are living, they are

---

[12] Thomas Munro, "Powers of Art Appreciation and Evaluation," p. 340. The extent to which a child's acquaintance with pictures may be at the mercy of a teacher is well illustrated in many of the books on art appreciation appearing about a quarter of a century ago. A typical example is Agnes Hammell, *Advancing in Picture Study* (Toronto: Gage, 1931). Most of the 110 illustrations chosen by this author are of the "realistic" or story-telling photographic type, by Landseer, Dupré, Breton, Alma-Tadema, Leighton, and others of similar style. El Greco is not represented, nor is Michelangelo, Gauguin, nor Matisse. Rather amazing is the inclusion of some Cézanne apples!

[13] This method is also advocated for adolescents in a report of the Progressive Education Association, *The Visual Arts in General Education* (N.Y.: Appleton-Century, 1940), pp. 72 ff.

probably in a better position to appreciate contemporary than traditional art. Nevertheless, when the children are studying history, they should become reasonably familiar with the production of the artists of the period being considered. Artists convey not only factual statements but also frequently emotional reactions to the epoch during which they live, both of which are important in assisting children to acquire insight into life in the past. The same, of course, may be said of artists from foreign lands. The teacher, therefore, requires a collection of visual aids which illustrate many aspects of art, both contemporary and historical, related to his own and other cultures.

Teaching Aids
for Developing Appreciation

Among the visual aids required in the program for the development of appreciation of art are prints of pictures, pictorial reproductions of other art forms, films, filmstrips, and slides dealing with a variety of art topics, and (if one may call such objects "visual aids") some actual works of art in two and three dimensions.

Pictorial Reproductions

Today any school can possess a good collection of prints of pictures and pictorial reproductions of other art forms. Never before has so large a selection of these been available. With the refinements of printing processes, most prints today are acceptable, accurate, and, no doubt, because of large editions, surprisingly inexpensive. Many stationery stores, book stores, and artists' supply firms act as outlets for both American and imported prints. Books containing excellent reproductions are also available.[14] Finally, popular magazines, such as *Life,* frequently devote pages in both color and halftone to reproduction of art. While the quality of the printing in these periodicals may not equal that in art books, it is usually sufficiently good for the prints to be kept on file for reference in the classroom.

Indeed, the teacher will have to seize every opportunity to add to the classroom collection. In teaching appreciation as the need arises, one never can be quite sure what pictures may be required. If some preadolescents are exploring color, for example, works of such painters as El Greco, Gauguin, Van Gogh, Matisse, and Dufy might be studied. If some are considering social themes, they might look at reproductions of Daumier's or Ben Shahn's drawings and paintings (see Fig. 145). If some are concerned with linear perspective, they might compare some of the output of the Middle Ages with that of the High Renaissance. If a religious topic holds some

[14] For several series especially worthy of note, see Appendix 2.

pupils' interest, they might see reproductions of works as diverse as the twelfth- to fourteenth-century bronzes of South India, the figures on the west portal of Chartres Cathedral, the paintings of Duccio, and those of Rouault and Stanley Spencer.

Not only must the collection of reproductions of works of art be extensive but the teacher must be thoroughly familiar with it, so that the right reproductions may be produced exactly when they are required. He must also be sufficiently familiar with each item in the collection to be able to emphasize any particular aspect of a composition which is related to each pupil's interest.

The reader will observe that little has been said concerning books on art for children. Unfortunately, such books are very rare. Manifestly nothing could be more desirable than to have on hand a well-stocked library of books in which children could read about art and artists. But most writers of childrens' books about art have given too little attention to difficulties of vocabulary so that few publications of any quality exist which can be mastered by children enrolled in the first six grades.[15] A partial solution to this dilemma is for teachers to paraphrase what has been said in some of the standard histories of art, and to tell stories to the children about the lives of famous artists.

Films, Filmstrips, and Slides

If books on art for young children are in short supply, the same cannot be said about films. In recent years several companies have produced some excellent films.[16] This is not to say that the teaching profession is overburdened with art films; quite the reverse. Each year, however, sees worthwhile additions to a growing library of acceptable art films for the young.

---

[15] The following are among the books which might be of use to children in about the fifth and sixth grades:

Alice Elizabeth Chase, *Famous Paintings* (N.Y.: Platt & Munk, 1951). Of the books on art for young children, this is probably one of the most useful in spite of its unfortunate title. Both text and illustrations arranged according to topics of interest to children are to be recommended.

H. W. Janson and Dora Jane Janson, *The Story of Painting for Young People* (N.Y.: Harry N. Abrams, 1952). This is a reasonably well-illustrated history written in fairly simple terms. It gives well-balanced attention to the contemporary period.

V. M. Hillyer and E. G. Huey, *A Child's History of Art* (N.Y.: Appleton-Century, 1938). This is a standard chronological history of art, written in terms which children may understand; the illustrations, however, are noticeably poor in quality.

[16] In the United States there are over eighty commercial sources which release art films, many of which are suitable for young children. For a survey of titles and a list of sources, see William McK. Chapman, Ed., *Films on Art 1952* (N.Y.: American Federation of Arts, 1952). The address of the Federation is 1083 Fifth Ave., New York 28, N.Y.

145 Reconstruction *by Ben Shahn could be among the works studied when pupils are dealing with social themes.*

These art films are designed to fulfill various purposes. Many of them are made both to stimulate children to produce art and to assist them in mastering various techniques. Some are produced largely to develop the children's insight into the art forms of others. Again some films, such as the internationally renowned *Loon's Necklace,*[17] are not produced specifically as art films but prove to be highly effective in the classroom in both the production and appreciation of art. Whatever the main purpose of the producers of a film may be, however, if the art film is a good one, it can scarcely fail to develop a child's insight and taste, provided, of course, that the teacher uses it according to the tenets of a sound pedagogy.

The teacher who uses films in his art program must understand what constitutes a good film. Before using a film with his class, he must obviously preview it, and then decide how effective it may be. What criteria does he use in selecting art films to be shown to young children? First, he expects the film to be technically and artistically competent. Young children see expertly made films in the theaters and on television screens. The day of

---

[17] See listing in Appendix 6.

slovenly work by producers of children's movies has long since passed. Next, of course, the film must be suitable to the children's level of understanding and maturity. To show young children the highly competent but rather intellectual production *An Experience in Cubism* would probably bore them, while *Begone Dull Care*, although based on nonobjective and abstract forms, delights them with its sparkling sound and movement. Next, the film should be chosen because it is closely related to the children's immediate interests. To present the film *Canadian Landscape*—in many respects a fine production—to a class of young children studying Eskimos would not be especially effective. What they should see at this time is perhaps *Eskimo Arts and Crafts* or *How to Build an Igloo*. The landscape film should, of course, be reserved until the pupils are concerned over producing their own landscapes. No matter how excellent a film may be in itself, in other words, when shown out of context, it tends to be a poor educational device. Finally, when a film is of the "how-to-do-it" variety, it must not only stimulate the children but also leave some room for them to use their own initiative. Films in the "Creative Hands Series," for example, are especially designed not "to tell all." They attempt to stimulate production, focus attention upon design, and give a few basic hints about technique. The content of the films stops

The Museum of Modern Art, New York

146 **Christ Mocked by Soldiers** *by Georges Rouault might prove stimulating to pupils who were experimenting with religious themes.*

there, however, and the child is left with many problems he must solve through his own efforts.[18]

Knowing the film intimately, the teacher may then use it at the right moment during the art sessions, either as an introduction to a topic, as an aid in teaching a topic, or as a summary to a series of experiences with a topic. Sometimes the teacher may consider it necessary to comment on the film to the class before it is shown, while on other occasions a discussion might take place after the screening.

To obtain a film for a specific art period is often difficult. A projector and a screen must be scheduled as well as the film, sometimes as much as three or four weeks in advance. Therefore, as much planning in advance as possible must be done so that the film will suit the type of art activity in progress.

The above remarks concerning films also have application to the use of slides and filmstrips.[19] Although these visual aids lack the dynamic qualities of movement and sound, they allow the teacher greater control of presentations. Whereas a film moves at a predetermined speed, the filmstrip frame or slide may be held on the screen for as long as it is required.

Actual Works of Art

Although we may obtain a reasonably accurate idea about many works of art by consulting reproductions of them, nothing can actually replace the work itself. How often one feels he knows a work of art through a study of reproductions, only to be overwhelmed on first seeing the original masterpiece! Colors, brush strokes, textures, and sometimes the scale of the work are never adequately conveyed by a reproduction. It is most desirable, therefore, that children should have the opportunity from time to time of observing original works of art, no matter how familiar they may be with reproductions.

The most obvious sources of originals are art galleries and museums. Schools which are fortunate enough to be situated near such institutions

---

[18] See Appendix 6 for further information on this series and other suitable films and filmstrips.

[19] The main sources of filmstrips in the United States, of which there are about 300, are listed in Frederic A. Krahn, Ed., *Filmstrip Guide* (N.Y.: Wilson, 1954). It also lists and describes over 5,000 filmstrips, many of which deal with art.

Some English outlets are Educational Productions, Ltd., East Ardsley, Wakefield, Yorkshire; Gaumont-British Film Productions, 127 Wardour St., London W.1; Visual Information Service, 168A Battersea Bridge Rd., London S.W.11.

Some Canadian outlets are National Film Board, 3255 Côte de Liesse Road, Ville St. Laurent, P.Q.; United Kingdom Information Office, 1111 Beaver Hall Hill, Montreal 11, P.Q.; J. Arthur Rank-16 mm Division, 277 Victoria St., Toronto.

would be remiss indeed not to make use of them. Even if a relatively long journey is necessary, the time and effort required to make the trip may be considered well spent.

Before a class pays a visit to a museum or gallery, as suggested in Chapter 2, the teacher should take the trip alone. By doing so he will become acquainted not only with the building and the collections, but also with such mundane but important problems as the location of washrooms for the children and the special rules and regulations of the institution concerning the general behavior of young visitors. At the time of his visit he can also make arrangements with museum officials concerning the program for the children's visit and the length of time to be given to it. Then, before the pupils set off, they should have some idea of the reason for their trip. To see an art show may be all very exciting and commendable, but without a focus of interest, the trip could be largely a waste of time. As a general principle, probably subject to many exceptions, it appears wise to organize trips to museums and art galleries only for those pupils who are sufficiently mature to be able to develop a long-range interest in an art problem. In many instances, the little ones may better wait until they can define and retain in their minds a legitimate reason for the visit more closely related to art than to entertainment. However, some museums and art galleries have lecturers who are talented in talking to children and provide exhibits especially designed for the very young. These the children should visit.

Unfortunately it is not always possible for children to handle the three-dimensional objects on display. The teacher might inquire as to the possi-

147 *Pupils studying Henry Moore's* **King** and **Queen** *while visiting the Toronto Art Gallery.*

bilities of allowing certain less delicate objects to be handled. Sometimes a request of this kind brings forth remarkable results, and the children may be allowed to touch many objects and thus learn more about them.

On no account should young children be expected to make long reports or detailed drawings of the objects observed during the visit. If reports or scientific drawings are to be made, they should be mere sketches. To ask young children for detailed reports might rob the whole expedition of its good effects.

Schools which are not located sufficiently close to museums and art galleries for visits by pupils will have to depend upon other means for bringing original works of art before the children. Many museums and art galleries today maintain an extension service by which well-packaged and adequately annotated items are shipped to responsible organizations. The teacher should investigate these opportunities, for by such means, art can be brought not only to the school children, but also to the community at large.

Another possible source of original art forms is the locality in which the school is situated, where very often creditable local painters and craftsmen can be discovered. The teacher should take pains to find these local artists and to help them organize shows of their work for the children and others to see.

Finally, it is not suggesting too much that a school set aside funds for purchasing, not only reproductions but also occasionally original paintings and other works of art. In time a school system of any size can possess a permanent exhibition of good pieces in which it can take both interest and pride.

Practical Objects

The study of "practical" objects—cups and saucers, kettles, knives and forks, telephones, and chairs—can do much to help children to develop an appreciation of art and to elevate their taste.[20]

---

[20] The reader's attention is directed at this time to the *Bauhaus*, a school of design founded in 1919 by Walter Gropius at Weimar and later moved to Dessau in Germany. Although painters of note, including Kandinsky, Klee, and Feininger, gathered there, the *Bauhaus* was primarily an institution dealing with problems related to architecture and industrial design. Here many unique experiments were performed by the students in order to gain experience with materials, tools, and techniques of an industrial nature. Emphasis was placed upon experience with these aspects of industrial production, and as a result, a disciplined and appropriate approach to art forms related to machine production made its appearance. The writings of László Moholy-Nagy and others, describing some of the work at the *Bauhaus*, have been carefully read by art educators, especially those in high schools and art schools, and have influenced their teaching methods. See, for example, László Moholy-Nagy, *The New Vision* (N.Y.: Wittenborn, 1946), and Walter Gropius, Ed., *Bauhaus 1919–1928* (N.Y.: Museum

148 *China by Eva Zeisel—examples of well-designed practical objects.*

Although a functional or practical object may not be as profound an artistic expression as, say, a fine painting or a superb piece of sculpture, it may nevertheless have the attributes of true art.[21] Thus, well-conceived, practical objects, such as those illustrated in Fig. 148, should be brought to the attention of young people as part of the program of art appreciation. Every object shown should be chosen with the highest standards in mind.[22] Usually, these standards are well within the comprehension of most pupils in the higher grades of the elementary school.

A teaching difficulty occurs in developing an appreciation of practical objects because appreciation can only rarely be related to production. While children continually make pictures and produce sculpture which they may compare with professional work, such is not often the case with practical objects. Hence the teacher will sometimes find it necessary to discuss such things as cups and saucers and television cabinets by themselves, rather

of Modern Art, 1938), in which it is stated that among other reasons the *Bauhaus* is important "because it courageously accepted the machine as an instrument worthy of the artist."

[21] See Chapter 3.

[22] *Ibid.*

than in connection with children's work. The children, however, often find a discussion about such articles interesting because these are things with which they come in contact in their daily lives. Thus these objects tend to have real meaning even when not associated with the children's expressive acts. Of course, occasionally in school, especially as part of the unit curriculum, the children may be required to construct models of some practical objects. Then the teacher will strengthen the appreciation lesson by discussing well-designed examples of objects similar to the models under construction.

ACTIVITIES FOR THE READER

1. Select three paintings or reproductions of paintings—the first by a master, the second by a reputable but not renowned artist, and the third by an amateur—and (a) tell what the paintings all have in common; (b) explain the differences in their significance to you.

2. Describe any occasion on which you gained insight into an artist's work which previously had puzzled you. Can you account for the "flash" of insight?

3. Describe any occasion on which you lapsed into "sentimentality" while observing a work of art. How did your reaction affect your appreciation of the work? What did you do to overcome your sentimental lapse?

4. Describe two paintings which you consider to be more sentimental than artistic.

5. Outline some teaching procedures for helping fifth-grade children better to appreciate each of the following: (a) a mural in egg tempera by Thomas Benton or some other well-known painter; (b) the design of a frying pan; (c) the design of living-room curtains; (d) some wood sculpture by Chaim Gross or some other well-known artist.

Appraising Children's

Progress in Art

The basis of appraisal of a pupil's progress in any area of learning can be found only in the objectives of that area. If the objectives of a particular subject field have been accurately stated, however, they will reflect not only the specific contributions which the area has to offer, but also the philosophical purposes and educational practices of the school system. An appraisal of the progress of any pupil enrolled in an educational system involves a judgment, then, of more than the pupil himself. Indeed such an appraisal involves a judgment upon the efficiency of the school system in general and of the teachers' endeavors in particular.

The Process of Appraisal

In general education, a number of necessary steps in the process of evaluation, or appraisal, have been established.[1] First, as has been suggested above, one must define the broad major objectives of teaching a given subject, after which "it is essential to outline more or less specifically the skills and knowledges" required by the subject.[2]

The next step is to select tests from the lists of those available for each

---

[1] See, for example, J. W. Wrightstone, J. Justman, and I. Robbins, *Evaluation in Modern Education* (N.Y.: American Book, 1956), especially Chapter 2; and T. L. Torgerson and G. S. Adams, *Measurement and Evaluation for the Elementary School Teacher* (N.Y.: Dryden, 1954), especially Chapter 1.

[2] Wrightstone and others, *Evaluation in Modern Education,* p. 19.

major objective. If a suitable measuring device cannot be found for any objective, an attempt must be made to devise one.[3] The final step is "to apply the various formal and informal tests and techniques in order to make judgments about individual growth and development in each of the major objectives."[4] In taking this last step, the teacher gathers information which tends to be of use to him in future teaching.

Influences of Objectives of Art Education upon Appraisal

In the opening chapter of this book, a statement was given of the objectives of art education in the schools of a democratic state. These objectives, the reader will doubtless have noted, have colored all subsequent suggestions concerning the selection of art activities, the pupils' approach to these activities, and the role of the teacher as a sponsor of an art program. Now the objectives will once more exert their influence in the matter of the teacher's appraisal of the pupils' progress in art.

The main objective of art education in a democratic school system was said to consist in helping in the emotional, intellectual, and social growth of each child. Through art education we hope in particular that pupils will gain insight into the nature of artistic acts, that they will develop artistic skills, and that they will learn to use wisely the freedom of expression which the contemporary program allows. Through art activities we hope that the pupils will understand their experiences better and will develop their taste. In all their art activities and general relationships with their teacher and classmates, we hope finally that they will gain insight into the democratic ideal.

An analysis of these objectives indicates the points on which the teacher might pass judgment concerning the pupil's progress. First, we have the development of the individual child to consider. This is indicated to a large extent by the work in art he produces and by his reactions to the expressions of others. Next, we have to judge the growth of the child in relation to the group with which he is associated. In sum, we must consider:

1. The quality of each pupil's personal artistic expression.
2. The quality of each pupil's reactions to the work of the others.
3. The quality of each pupil's behavior as exhibited during his participation in all types of art activities.

[3] See Wrightstone and others, Part Two: "Major Evaluation Techniques," for the type of measuring devices which might be used.

[4] *Ibid.*, p. 21.

The above categories of criteria will indicate the close connection which exists between the progress of a pupil and the educational outlook of a school system. If the pupil's work is standardized, probably the teacher and the system engaging him do not believe in personal expression. If the pupil dislikes all "modern art," perhaps his teacher is of like mind. If the pupil cannot get along with his fellows in group work in art, perhaps the school system does not devote sufficient attention to the development of this social skill. How can freedom of expression be judged unless freedom to express exists in the educational environment; how can the development of taste be appraised unless educational conditions encourage such growth; how can growth in democratic living be appraised unless democratic procedures in art prevail in the school?

Categories of Criteria Used in Appraisal of the Art Program

In keeping with the three main categories of criteria to be used in appraising the art program, there follow three lists of questions concerned with each pupil's artistic expression, his appreciation of art, and his behavior during art classes. These lists are not intended to include all questions which might be mentioned, but, rather, are offered as examples of the type of lists which a teacher might devise for himself.

1. *The quality of each pupil's personal artistic expression* [5]

> To what extent has the pupil attempted to express his reactions to his own experiences?
>
> To what extent has he expressed himself emotionally and intellectually in a form commensurate with his apparent stage or phase of aesthetic development? [6]
>
> To what extent has the pupil developed a personal style or technique? [7]
>
> To what extent does the pupil's work show a sensitivity concerning functional design?
>
> Does his work indicate to any extent that he is sensible of the effects of tools and materials upon design?

---

[5] It will be understood that expression, appreciation, and general behavior cannot in practice be isolated from each other, and that the division has been made here only for the sake of convenience to the discussion. A similar situation occurred in Chapter 3 when design was being discussed in terms of its elements.

[6] Review Chapter 6.

[7] Review Chapter 3 for this and the following questions about design.

To what extent does this work show ability to use each element of design: line; mass and space; light and shade; color; texture?

How successful is he in arriving at a unity of design?

How successful is he in arranging a variety in his design?

Does the pupil appear to develop technical skills in art commensurate with his needs of expression?

To what extent is the pupil capable of: (a) relating artistic expression to other school experiences; (b) relating other school experiences to artistic expression?

2. *The quality of each pupil's reactions to the work of others*

To what extent does the pupil look at the work of his classmates and of professionals, and what appears to be his attitude towards this work?

To what extent does he consult books of art?

What is his apparent attitude towards art as shown in his reaction to films, slides, talks, and visits to institutions?

What evidences of a satisfactory development of taste has he shown?

3. *The quality of each pupil's behavior as exhibited during his participation in all types of art activities*

During his art activities, in what respects has the pupil demonstrated a personal initiative?

To what extent does he find a challenge in unfamiliar art materials?

In what respects has he demonstrated through art activities an inner discipline, worthy habits of thinking, commendable attitudes regarding a search for excellence, or other desirable personal qualities?

To what extent does he show good judgment in selecting tools and media for art work?

Once having selected an artistic goal, to what extent does he strive to reach it?

What is his attitude with regard to accepting advice about his artistic production?

To what extent has he demonstrated qualities of leadership in art activities?

To what extent has he shown himself willing to cooperate generally in the worthy art projects of his group?

How willing is he to share in research work in art, in expressive work, and in the less rewarding tasks such as helping to keep equipment, supplies, and the working area used by the group clean and tidy? In general does he seem willing to share ideas about art with others?

Has he shown a reasonable attitude towards the sharing of display space?

Types of Evidence Used in Appraisal of the Art Program

The major evaluation techniques used in general education are employed in art education. Standardized measuring devices for the production and appreciation of art are available. Teachers also devise what are known as objective and essay type examinations to test various aspects of the art program. Anecdotal records and observational techniques are used, as are check lists, interviews, and cumulative records. If experts in the science of testing are available, presumably even the "projective" techniques, or self-descriptive personal reports, and the "sociometric" methods of evaluation, which reveal information about the structure of social groups including the leaders and isolates they contain, might be used in an art program.[8] To discuss in detail all these techniques would go beyond the scope of this book. However, some comment will be made on those devices most convenient for teachers of art and frequently used in the classroom. These include standardized art tests, art tests devised by the teacher, and the less formal methods such as anecdotal techniques and check lists.

Standardized Art Tests

The decade between 1920 and 1930 witnessed extraordinary attempts to develop standardized tests to discover children's ability both to produce art and to appreciate it. High hopes were held for the success of these tests. Thousands of children were involved in the development of the tests, and for each child involved, a scientific indication of his ability to produce or to appreciate art forms was often set down. By the beginning of the 1930's, however, people especially interested in art education began to question the accuracy of the tests. Statements such as the following by Tannahill began to appear:

> Of all the tests in art which have been published, the most successful ones have to do with the testing of art appreciation. It is difficult,

---

Descriptions of all these techniques will be found in Wrightstone and others, *Evaluation in Modern Education.*

however, even in this field to reach an agreement of opinion among art teachers and connoisseurs because personal taste and style are changeable factors, and artists have more or less prided themselves upon their non-adherence to a rigid standard rather than upon their adherence to one. This is true especially of creative expression, where the individuality of the artist, whether child or adult, is so important. It would seem that any attempt to test ability to create is futile. What may be a creation to one is not necessarily a work of art to another.[9]

When one studies some of the tests in question, and at the same time considers the nature of artistic acts, it is not difficult to observe some of their deficiencies. *The Scale for General Merit of Children's Drawings*,[10] for example, may be questioned as an efficient testing device, not only upon the grounds mentioned in Tannahill's statement, but also because its author seems to consider the exact representation of objects observed in the environment to be the chief excellence of artistic expression. Again, *Tests in Fundamental Abilities of Visual Art* [11] appears to overemphasize skills and technical details apart from the total act of expression.

A popular test for the purpose of measuring appreciation is the *Art Judgment Test* by N. C. Meier and C. E. Seashore.[12] Another is the *McAdory Art Test*.[13]

Carroll says of the last two, "Neither of the tests correlates to any extent with the judgment of university art instructors." [14] Actually, both tests are more a guessing game than a serious measuring device of appreciation. Under the title, "A Survey of Recent Research in Art and Art Education," Faulkner lists many of the standardized art tests, but he observes: "The extent to which art abilities may be measured scientifically is still a controversial issue. Viewed objectively, few, if any, art tests have lived up to the expectations and promises of their makers." [15]

In spite of the fact that some writers about educational measurement seem to consider standardized art tests to be valid measuring instruments,

---

[9] S. B. Tannahill, *Fine Arts for Public School Administrators* (N.Y.: Teachers College, 1932), p. 126.

[10] E. L. Thorndike (N.Y.: Teachers College, Columbia University, 1924).

[11] A. F. Laurenz (Los Angeles: Southern California School Book Depository, 1927).

[12] *Meier-Seashore Art Judgment Test* (Iowa City: University of Iowa, 1930).

[13] *McAdory Art Test* (N.Y.: Bureau of Publications, Teachers College, Columbia University, 1929).

[14] H. A. Carroll, "What Do the Meier-Seashore and the McAdory Art Tests Measure?" *Journal of Educational Research*, vol. 26 (May 1933), p. 665.

[15] R. Faulkner, in *The Fortieth Yearbook of the National Society for the Study of Education* (Bloomington, Ill.: Public School Publishing Co., 1941), p. 376.

warnings from art authorities indicate that the teacher of art should not place too much reliance upon tests.[16]

With our present understanding of the human mind and its functioning in relation to aesthetics, we lack the knowledge and ability to measure artistic qualities accurately.[17] Indeed, whether or not we shall ever be able to invent accurate measuring devices for these aspects of human endeavor is a debatable point.

Formal Tests Made by the Teacher

If the standardized art tests devised by experts in measurement apparently fall short of their purpose, what of a test composed by the classroom teacher? Such tests need not be entirely condemned, provided the teacher understands their significance. Sometimes the teacher may wish to use a test to discover whether or not the pupils have grasped some part of the art program. He may, for example, present a few questions based upon the pupils' knowledge of a specific medium, or of facts surrounding an artist's life, or of techniques in using color.

The following completion-type problem could be used to test knowledge of color mixing:

Fill in the blanks—
1. To obtain a *shade* of red tempera paint add _____.
2. To obtain a *tint* of red water color add _____.
3. To turn *blue* into gray add _____.
4. To turn *green* into gray add _____.[18]

An essay-type answer might be obtained from the following question:

Describe two methods of mixing tempera paint to obtain gray.

---

[16] See, for example, Wrightstone and others, *Evaluation in Modern Education,* pp. 276–80, where it is stated during a discussion of art tests: " It is apparent . . . that knowledge about principles and skills as well as some aspects of appreciation [of art] can be measured."

[17] It is interesting to note that art is not the only field of study in which the degree of reliance upon standardized tests is decreasing in some quarters. Saucier says:

"In the past, too often writers on measurement have attempted to judge the worth of an examination apart from objectives of education and teaching procedure. They have written extensively about validity, reliability, objectivity, economy of time, and the like, with little or no regard for what the school has been supposed to be doing for the child. . . . 'The main concept guiding evaluation programs is that *evaluation should be in terms of the extent to which pupils have attained the objectives of elementary education.*' It is encouraging to note that this principle is beginning to be advanced at least in theory."—W. A. Saucier, *Theory and Practice in the Elementary School* (N.Y.: Macmillan, 1941), p. 398.

Perhaps the deficiencies of standardized tests are more apparent in art than elsewhere.

[18] See Chapter 7 for the answers.

One should note that it is possible to devise tests in art which do not require written answers of any kind. For example, one item could be the following:

> With red tempera paint and only one other pigment in each case, mix
> (a) a *shade* of red
> (b) a *tint* of red
> (c) *gray.*

The items tested in these cases are merely facts surrounding art, but are in no way representative of art itself. Therefore, while the teacher may develop a few formal tests related to production and appreciation of art in his classroom, whatever he tests will probably not include the real nature of aesthetic activity. Any test designed to measure art itself or art appreciation will tend to prove invalid. We must conclude, therefore, by asserting that neither the standardized test in art nor the formal test devised by the classroom teacher for specific aspects of the art program can produce a satisfactory indication of a pupil's real ability in this complex field of learning. At best such a test can serve merely as a supplement to less formal methods of appraisal.[19]

Some Less Formal Methods of Appraisal

In the world of art, people are continually making judgments unsupported by scientific measuring devices. They assert, for example, that Seurat's *La Grande Jatte* is a masterpiece in paint; that Da Vinci is not as good an artist as the public believes; that Turner's compositions are flimsy; that Bellows was a master of concise statement with a brush. When the opinions of numbers of well-qualified people coincide upon a work of art, we are inclined to accept their statements as true. If numbers of such people agree for any considerable period of time that a work is excellent, we begin to call it a masterpiece. By this type of informal appraisal, and by this alone, Western man fills his galleries and selects his masterpieces. No great work of art has ever been chosen by any other method.

The method has, of course, demonstrable limitations. The history of art is full of painters, such as Cézanne, now considered significant, who formerly were either unrecognized or disliked by the critics. Then we have

---

[19] "Any evaluation of an individual's future promise in art . . . would have to be based not only on test data, but on a summarization of his experiences in various art activities; and appraisal of his sketches, paintings, or other art products; and observation of his interests and motivation." See Torgerson and Adams, *Measurement and Evaluation,* pp. 370–75. This book contains a good chapter on the construction of tests for classroom use, pp. 220–43.

149 *Appraisal of a pupil's progress in art must be derived largely from the teacher's acquaintance with each child.*

painters like Landseer, who were favored by contemporary critics but who, in the course of time, lost their original high place in the eyes of reputable judges. With full awareness of the limitations of our method of selecting works of art, however, we retain this method because no better practical means of selection has been devised. Likewise, we resort to informal methods in appraising the capabilities of the judges—that is to say, their abilities to appreciate art.

The teacher should recognize that he will be subject to error in his appraisal of the child's patterns of behavior and his ability to produce and to appreciate art. Having accepted this fact, he will probably be cautious in jumping to conclusions, painstaking in his efforts to analyze the pupils' progress, and humble in the weight he attaches to his opinions. Nevertheless, if he familiarizes himself with art, with the children under his care, and with an acceptable pedagogy in relation to art and children, there is nothing to prevent him from accepting with some confidence the task of appraising the progress which the children make in art education.

One of the simplest methods of gathering data about a child's progress in art is to keep a check list. The most difficult part of this method is to devise a practical list. This the teacher must do largely for himself, because check lists made by others rarely are entirely suitable for him.

It is suggested, however, that the list be based upon the three general headings mentioned earlier, namely, expression, appreciation, and behavior. Also, the subheadings might resemble the questions offered under the three general headings. The following is a sample of a short check list for *expression*. It would have to be altered to suit any specific grade or type of art activity.

Artistic Expression: YES | NO [20]

1. Used own experiences
2. Progressed normally through
   manipulative ⎫
   symbol   ⎬ stage
   preadolescent ⎭
3. Produced work showing personal style
4. Produced work which showed
   (a) respect for material
   (b) respect for function of object
5. While using tools showed
   (a) dexterity
   (b) taste
6. Showed ability to use
   (a) line
   (b) mass and space
   (c) light and shade
   (d) color
   (e) texture
7. Work showed unity of design
8. Work showed variety of design
9. Work showed development of skill
10. Successfully related
    (a) art work to school experiences
    (b) other school experiences to artistic expression

A second device, known as the "anecdotal" method, is also valuable. With this method the teacher jots down periodically observations about each

---

[20] An alternate procedure is to use numbers. For example, in a range from 0 to 5 in item 1, 5 in the column would mean "always uses own experience"; 0 in the same column would mean "never uses them."

child, based on the questions in the list. This method is recommended by Saucier, among others, who says of it:

> A cumulative record of such specific reactions may become a rather reliable index of his trend and stage of development in some traits. It at least furnishes the teacher and the child with some concrete evidence of strong and weak points in his character and conduct.[21]

As an example, opposite some of the items of the sample check list previously outlined, the following remarks might be set down for a six-year-old in the first grade:

EXPRESSION	COMMENTS
1. Used own experiences	"in general picture-making, yes, but not in correlation with social studies when he copied a drawing"
2. Progressed normally through symbol stage	"normal until absence from school—then regression to manipulation for two days—after that normal—is putting in sky and ground symbols"
3. Produced work showing personal style	"nothing special yet"
4.	(not applicable)
5. While using tools showed dexterity	"using scissors well"
6. Showed ability to use line	"nervous child—so, nervous line—"

A further use of the anecdotal method is to write from time to time a short paragraph about each child. In this case a check list is necessary but is not completed item by item. The following are examples of notes about children which a teacher might write for his personal file.

John A. [*who is six years old and in first grade*]

John uses a variety of personal experiences in his pictures, and he is certainly getting along well lately in trying to develop symbols of houses. It is strange, however, how his work seemed to deteriorate last week. He works hard, though, and gets along well in a group.

Betty McM. [*who is eleven years old and in sixth grade*]

She has always shown herself to be a sensitive child, and her paintings reflect her feelings. Her work seems overdelicate at times

---

[21] Saucier, *Theory and Practice in the Elementary School,* p. 401.

and to give it more character perhaps she might concentrate a little more on the use of light and shade and bright color areas. She did not seem to care for working on murals with others, but she participated well in the puppet show. She was obviously moved when she listened to music in preparation for a picture. I doubt if she will ever be a vigorous leader, but she is a fine little person who must be treated gently.

Robert L. [who is ten years old and in fifth grade]

What a careless, untidy fellow Robert is; paint in a mess, drawings all thumb marks, brushes unwashed! As stage manager of our play, nevertheless, he worked well. He seems to be more at home with sculpture than he is in the areas of drawing and paintings. Perhaps he needs dirty hands to feel at ease with a task! His last sculpture in clay, if not particularly sensitive, was at least vigorous. He likes to explore new materials and last week brought to school some wood for carving.

While the data derived from check lists and other notations will greatly assist the teacher in arriving at an appraisal of a pupil's progress, he will find it necessary also to keep a file of the child's actual art production. Usually lack of space prevents the teacher from keeping any but the flat work. However, a sampling of each pupil's work should be retained for periodic study and comparison with the written notations.

Having either checked from a list, or noted in some other way, the child's various reactions to the art program, the teacher may then wish to arrive at a concise summary of the apparent progress the pupil has made. It is hoped that the teacher will not attempt to resolve the check list or notations into a scientific measuring instrument. It is possible, for example, to add check marks and to compare the total of one child with that of another. Again, the teacher could give extra mathematical weight to some items before addition took place. With such devices the teacher could arrive at a score for each pupil, but judging from past attempts to measure art education, the results would in all likelihood be entirely invalid.

The check list, the making of notations, or indeed any other method of gathering data about art education is not suggested, therefore, as a means of scientific appraisal, but merely to remind a teacher what a child has done in art over a given period of time. In the end, the teacher can only summarize a child's progress in art in the most general terms. Once made, however, such a summary will prove valuable to the teacher making progress reports to parents and others interested in the child's welfare.

Reporting Progress in Art

From time to time every school system reports to parents concerning their children's progress. This is one of the traditional and necessary functions of a school. Every aspect of the program of studies should be mentioned upon a report form to parents, if only as a notice to parents that their children have been exposed to the subject. The fact that the art program does not lend itself to exact measurement in no way excuses the teacher from making a report on the pupils who participated in it.

In addition to informing parents of the progress of their offspring, some educators feel that reports have other functions. From the teachers' point of view, these are: (1) helping teachers to reach conclusions about their pupils, (2) assisting teachers to make plans for the future, and (3) in general, helping them to appraise the effectiveness of their teaching. From the point of view of the pupils, reports have the purpose of: (1) helping pupils to realize the progress they have made, (2) pointing out to them where they might improve in their work, and (3) indicating to them what they might do in the future to make further progress.[22] From the point of view of some educators, reports provide an incentive for pupils to work harder and more efficiently if the child compares his achievements with those of his fellows.

Whether or not all these functions are legitimate for some subject fields other than art, it is not the purpose of this book to debate. Let it be said emphatically in relation to art, however, that the only legitimate function of a report is to let the parents know how their child is progressing in this field. If a teacher of art has waited until report time to reach conclusions about a child's progress, he can scarcely have acted as an efficient and sympathetic counselor in art. Furthermore, if the pupils must depend upon a report card to help them understand their progress, to improve their work, and to give them clues as to future action, "public relations" in the classroom must have reached an extraordinarily low ebb.

Perhaps the worst use to which a report in art could be put, however, would be as an incentive for the pupil to work harder and more efficiently. The idea of using the report in this fashion is based upon a teacher's threat and upon a child's fear—a threat that the teacher will tell Mother and Father that they have a "bad" child because he fails to perform his art to the teacher's satisfaction. No art was ever produced under these conditions, nor is it ever likely to be. The quicker the teacher who resorts to these methods of reporting retires or seeks other employment, the happier will everyone be.

---

[22] See Torgerson and Adams, *Measurement and Evaluation,* pp. 412–18, for a good discussion about "reporting."

Regarding the mechanics of reporting to the parents, several points must be kept in mind. Perhaps the first of these is that the method of reporting must be easily understood by all parents. Any report which makes use of complicated symbols or what is considered by some to be highly professional language (and by others to be an undesirable "pedagese") will not be appreciated by most parents. The report should reflect objectives and practices of the art program and should attempt to comment upon the child, both as an individual and as a member of a group. A further criterion of any good report is, of course, that it be as accurate and fair as a teacher can make it. In art, while one can be fair, as has been stated earlier, it is probably impossible to be entirely accurate. The teacher can merely try to be as accurate as possible. From the teacher's point of view also, the system of reporting should not demand a disproportionate amount of clerical work.

In general, since reporting in art is characterized by a number of peculiarities arising from the nature of this area of learning, it might be well for the teacher to discuss these peculiarities frankly with the parents and, in fact, with children who are in a position to understand them. Some educators have recommended that a system of reporting by consultation among the teacher, the parents, and some of the older children be devised.

Cooperative reporting, while excellent in theory, may not always work to the advantage of art. Unless parents and others have reached a stage of thinking in which they are willing to forgo a competitive method of reporting, art education may suffer materially. Because art may be likened to a personal gift from a child to his fellows, there is obviously no room for competition in it. To encourage competition between children engaged in art is to be at odds with the whole process of their artistic expression. When they are behaving naturally, children produce art because of an inner compulsion arising from some reaction to experience, not for the sake of a prize or a mark. In the art of children we have, coupled with the compulsion towards self-expression, one of the comparatively rare human manifestations of what appears to be a desire, unmotivated by thoughts of material gain, to be of service to one's fellows. For adults to attempt to interfere with this happy state of aesthetic gift-giving would be a very shortsighted and sad policy.

This attitude of children is closely connected with the artistic tradition in general and is different from that associated with many other areas of human endeavor. In many of his relationships with his fellows, man appears naturally to be a fiercely competitive creature, as his warlike history testifies. While many maintain that competition has its legitimate place in some aspects of our society, obviously man cannot live by competition alone. In his artistic outpourings, he demonstrates another side of his nature, which, in view of our modern engines of destruction, we might do well to foster. In art we find a field of endeavor which depends upon a love of the activity for itself and not upon extraneous rewards. As far as we can tell, no great art has ever been produced whose creator, however much he craved success, was chiefly motivated by a desire for personal gain and dominance over his fellows, rather than by a search for excellence.

The system of reporting a pupil's progress in art, therefore, should avoid any idea of competition between a child and his fellows. Fortunately, the time-honored system of reporting by a mathematical rating, which lends itself directly to competition, has no meaning in art. For reasons outlined earlier, it is virtually impossible for anyone to arrive at a mathematically accurate mark for art either in figures or in letters. The only means of reporting left to teachers of art, therefore, are those generally called "progress reports" and "narrative reports."

The progress report is based upon the use of check marks, symbols, or letters. Often only two marks are used—"S" for satisfactory and "U" for unsatisfactory. Sometimes the letter "O" may be employed to signify outstanding progress. Under the heading "art" on the report form, the subheadings "expression," "appreciation," and "personal and social development" might be listed. The parent would then expect to find either S, U, or O opposite each of these subheadings. This system appears to be theoretically sound for reporting art, in that it is based upon each child's individual progress, rather than upon his progress in comparison with that of his fellows. In practice, however, some children who have formerly been reported in numerical terms quickly begin using it competitively. "Jack's going to 'get it' when he goes home," say these children. "He got four U's and his sister got an O and three S's!" "I beat her," says another. "I got two O's once."

Perhaps a safer device for reporting art lies in the narrative method. Here, in a simple sentence or two, the teacher attempts to tell the parent how well his child has progressed. "Philip produced some good pictures last term," the report might run. "He seems to enjoy films and slides about art and he participated satisfactorily in a puppet show," or "Peter's linoleum printing turned out satisfactorily. If he could try to be a little more tidy with the supplies, we would all appreciate it."

Should the teacher not wish to commit himself, at least until he is thoroughly familiar with every child, he might, with the parents' consent, make his report to them verbally during a short conference. This method tends to be time consuming but because of its flexibility is one which has some obvious advantages over written reports to parents. It demands, of course, that the teacher have some ability to report both good and bad aspects of a child's efforts without arousing the personal wrath of a parent. No teacher, furthermore, can afford to arrange an interview of this type without first being fully prepared. For the school's permanent records, a teacher must keep on file a complete written report of each pupil, even if this report is not presented to the parents.

● ACTIVITIES FOR THE READER

1. Describe some situations in which the art program reflects the educational outlook of (a) a school principal; (b) a school board; (c) a community.

2. Devise some tests in art as follows:
   (a) A "true-false" type to test second-grade pupils' knowledge of handling clay.
   (b) A "recall" or "completion" type to test fourth-grade pupils' knowledge of mural-making.
   (c) A "multiple-choice" type to test sixth-grade pupils' knowledge of linear perspective.
   (d) A "matching items" type to test fifth-grade pupils' ability to use "resist" techniques.
   (e) A "nonlanguage" type to test sixth-grade pupils' knowledge of art terms.[23]

3. From a collection of about ten professional paintings or reproductions of paintings, select the two you like best. Analyze how you arrived at your choice.

4. Make check lists for (a) appreciation of sculpture by sixth-grade pupils; (b) social growth of fourth-grade pupils while doing puppetry.

5. Study over a period of two weeks the art output, indications of art appreciation, and behavior of a group of ten children and write a paragraph of not more than fifty words for each child, summarizing his progress.

6. Describe any results, either good or bad, that you have observed as a result of competitive marking of children's art.

---

[23] See any standard work on measurement, such as Torgerson and Adams, *Measurement and Evaluation,* for a definition of the types of tests.

Growing Professionally

in Teaching Art

Any teacher worthy of the name desires to improve himself professionally. Most of us begin our careers in this important and challenging occupation longing for greater insight into the nature of children and for additional knowledge of subject matter and the skill to use it. We want to know how to get along well with the people with whom we must associate in our new profession—other teachers, the principal, supervisors, superintendents, caretakers, and, above all, the children. Sensing our enormous responsibility in assisting the development of our country's youth, we usually feel humble and inadequate.

In sensing his inadequacies and in desiring to develop professionally, the teacher is adopting an attitude normal in any person who wishes to succeed in his occupation. Any learned profession provides scope for professional growth. In teaching—which involves an acquaintance with much of our cultural heritage, an understanding of many of the skills by which we maintain our culture, and professional knowledge—the scope for growth is unlimited.

When the beginning teacher first assumes his duties, he may feel inadequate in all subjects. It is not long, however, before he recalls much old knowledge and many skills; his background of English, mathematics, and some of the sciences learned in elementary school, high school, and college returns to him. Nearly all teachers possess an academic background upon which they can draw in this way, but relatively few possess a similarly broad background in art. The teacher may have been exposed to a certain amount of art in some of his elementary school grades, but in all likelihood he dropped the study of art around the seventh or eighth grade, never to resume it during his remaining years in a public school. As a graduate of a teachers' college he may again have been exposed to art, but unless he specialized in this field, the time spent learning about it was probably not great. In this and in most other countries, the stress laid upon academic subjects and the time devoted to them all but crowd out a study of fine arts.

These facts are pointed out to emphasize the special scope which exists for professional growth of the teacher of art. Not only must he develop the basic skills of the teacher but also, unless his background is very different from the average, he must develop many new artistic skills and insights. Some of the means available to the teacher who wishes to develop professionally in art will occupy the remainder of this chapter.

Growth Through Teaching Practice

Perhaps the most effective way to develop professionally as a teacher of art is to begin to teach the subject vigorously and thoughtfully. No matter how fearful one may be of launching an art activity, an earnest effort must be made if one is to learn effectively how the activity may best be handled in the classroom. When first teaching art, one must keep firmly in mind two facts of primary importance. First, there are *art* activities and there are other activities which use art tools and materials, but which are not art and are either educationally ineffective or definitely harmful. Second, once a valuable art activity is selected, it must be taught effectively if the pupils are to derive benefit from it. The nature of an art activity and of effective teaching methods was described earlier and need not be outlined again.[1] It is sufficient to say that the knowledge both of what art is and of some efficient means of teaching it are prerequisite to a satisfactory art program.

Having subjected himself to a rigorous mental screening concerning subject matter and teaching techniques, the inexperienced teacher must next acquire an understanding of the tools and materials associated with specific activities. The professionally competent teacher of art has some skill in the type of work he initiates. One may wish to enquire why this should be so, since the good teacher will neither make drawings for children to copy nor touch up a child's work. The primary reason for developing skill in the execution in art is that one learns best by doing. One gains an experience of art

---

[1] Review Chapters 1 and 2.

through a brush or a chisel that no words can describe. By gaining artistic skills, moreover, the teacher tends to develop a fellow feeling between his pupils and himself. Those who can paint or carve often sense an affinity for one another—a strong feeling of kinship. The classroom in which bonds of fellow feeling and mutual respect develop between teacher and pupils during art sessions is evidence of the teacher's professional maturity.

Growth Through
In-Service Reading

In order to grow professionally the teacher of art must do more than develop some technical abilities. He should also do some consistent reading about art, the teaching of art, and education in general. There are some fine histories of art which relate it to mankind's progress towards civilization and others in which a segment of the history of art is highlighted through the progress of one painter. Still other books, often more formidable since they emphasize abstract ideas and employ a special vocabulary, are those that pertain to the philosophy of art, or aesthetics. For the student who perseveres, the philosophy of art reveals a delightful world of the mind. Finally, there is professional reading related either to education in general or to art education in particular. Here the list of books is extensive, and the reader's choice will depend largely upon the grade levels with which he is concerned and the problems arising from his classroom work.

While a program of reading is necessary for professional growth, whatever one reads becomes more meaningful to the reader if the printed statements can be compared with actual happenings. It is important, therefore, for the teacher to test, compare, and revise his ideas gained through reading in the light of his experiences with children working at art in their classrooms. A balance of theory and practice, in other words, is necessary for the most effective professional growth.

Growth Through
Professional Associations

As soon as one becomes a teacher, new and important people such as the school principal and the district superintendent enter one's life. If fortunate, one will be visited by an art official known by a variety of titles including "supervisor," "consultant," and "specialist." In a large school, an internal art specialist may also be appointed. Usually a teacher holds most of these officials in some awe until he, perhaps, in turn, is appointed in one of their places, after which he holds the classroom teacher in awe!

150 *Teachers working in art classes, Ann Arbor, Michigan. Much can be learned during practical in-service sessions.*

The superintendent acts as a general manager of a school system and the principal as a kind of branch head. The principal will probably make calls upon the teacher while he is conducting classes, and the superintendent might do the same, depending upon the supervisory system established locally. Both of these officials usually have much good advice to offer in a general way, but neither makes himself responsible for the details of an art program. These they leave to the visiting art specialist. In matters concerning art education, then, the teacher will deal largely with this supervisor.

Most art specialists hold an advanced degree in art education obtained from a reputable university. As a classroom teacher the specialist probably showed exceptional interest and ability in art education. He was known perhaps for his enthusiasms for displays during Parents' Nights or at local teachers' conventions. More than likely he has always had some talent in one of the major art fields such as painting and sculpture. As well as being artistic, he has also shown that he can be businesslike and can do a good organizational job when the need arises. He is a likeable person and one who uses good judgment whether chairing a meeting or offering advice to a new teacher. Altogether, a competent art specialist may be considered a kind of professional artistic friend—a person of taste, tact, ability, and zeal with whom the teacher feels he can cooperate in improving the art program.

The art specialist has many duties to perform, which vary in detail from one locality to the other but which in broad outline are similar in most school systems. The specialist's primary duty is "to stress the curricular purposes served by art as a school subject or area of experience." [2] Whatever the general educational objectives of a school system may be, in other words, it is the chief duty of the art supervisor to encourage the teaching of art in such a way that the objectives may be realized. Theoretically, this specialist, then, is spokesman for art for the policy makers of a school system whose educational wishes he implements. In practice, of course, the policy makers rely upon the specialist to develop ways and means of conducting the art program according to curricular objectives. In doing so, the wise and efficient supervisor works in a democratic spirit with teachers and others. Of all people, the art supervisor tends to be of greatest assistance in helping the teacher of art to grow professionally.

What can the art supervisor expect of a teacher during one of his visits to the classroom? That he should be received pleasantly and courteously is taken for granted. He can expect the teacher to try faithfully to achieve the objectives of the art program through recommended practices and procedures in the classroom. He should find the teacher cooperative in helping him to assist, demonstrate, observe, or evaluate the art program. He should find the art supplies and equipment in good order, clean, and ready for use. He should see evidence of careful attention to display techniques and should be afforded cooperation in arranging larger exhibits outside of the classroom.

The art supervisor is usually responsible not only for helping to broaden a teacher's knowledge of art, but also for helping him develop his skill in producing art objects. Hence he arranges afternoon or evening workshops at which teachers can work at puppetry, paper sculpture, painting, and the like, and discuss the theory of art education. It is the duty of any teacher who needs to develop skill and increase his knowledge of art to attend these workshops.

The teacher who faithfully and cheerfully supports a competent art supervisor has much to gain. He is likely to broaden his philosophy of education, not only in art, but also in general education. He will be guided away from "tricks" and "fads" and will be helped to recognize only those activities which reside within the great artistic tradition. Thus his taste and artistic insight will develop. He will be inspired and encouraged to do crea-

---

[2] L. L. Winslow, "Current Practices in School Art," *Art in American Life and Education,* p. 480, Fortieth Yearbook of the National Society for the Study of Education, G. M. Whipple, Ed. (Bloomington, Ill.: Public School Publishing Co., 1941).

tive work of his own. He will be kept up to date concerning the rapidly changing ideas of art education and will be made aware of new books about trends in art.

In schools where internal art consultants are employed, the teacher has similar duties and stands to gain many of the benefits mentioned above in connection with an art supervisor. Should the school system have neither supervisor nor consultants, then the teacher must rely to a great extent upon his association with those fellow teachers who show an interest in art and an ability to teach it.[3]

Growth Through Formal Study

Considerable professional growth may occur through attendance at winter or summer courses in art in universities, art schools, and other institutions which offer lectures or workshops in a wide variety of art topics. Much of the work may go far beyond the requirements of the classroom, but this is as it should be. The teacher of art should be more than just one jump ahead of the children. Therefore, as well as studying work having direct application to the classroom, the teacher should welcome the opportunity to go reasonably deeply into such areas as art history or philosophy, oil painting, or ceramics.

The teacher should take some care in selecting the institution in which he proposes to study. Art schools and colleges vary in the quality of teaching and in the type of art, such as commercial art as opposed to fine arts, they teach. If possible, the teacher should visit the studios and classrooms before enrolling. In the best institutions, both the artistic and academic freedoms and disciplines are observed. If the work of the students varies from one individual to another, if design is well related to expression, if a variety of media are put to a disciplined use, if more than one point of view is to be heard in lectures and discussions about the theory and practice of art and of art education, the place of learning shows signs of being a good one in which to study.

In recent years excellent summer tours abroad have been arranged. These tours take students to world-famous galleries and museums and hence are greatly to be recommended as part of a formal program of professional growth. Indeed, anyone's concept of man's artistic achievements can be greatly improved by visits to such institutions as the Prado in Madrid, the Louvre in Paris, and the Uffizi Gallery in Florence.

---

[3] *The 3 R's and Art* (Harrisburg, Pa.: Department of Public Instruction, 1955) gives excellent summaries of the duties of art teachers, supervisors, and consultants. See Chapter 2 for a further discussion about association with other teachers.

Conclusion

Teaching art is an important and a challenging job. So important is art in a program of general education that one may safely assert that no child is truly educated until he has participated in a vigorous program of art education. Although within the grasp of any elementary teacher, the job is a challenging one because it demands of him a number of skills, a fund of knowledge, and a sensitivity and insight requiring considerable effort to achieve. Still a relatively new area of learning, art education is developing rapidly and has a place for every intelligent enthusiast who would like to participate in its growth and to share in the contribution it is unquestionably making to youth, to art, to general education, and to democracy.

A Check List
for Professional Growth

Efficiency of art teaching and the teacher's professional growth go hand in hand. In attempting to outline workable methods of teaching, this book has indicated in each chapter how the teacher may improve his professional background and hence his competence in the classroom. A sample check list follows containing some items to which a teacher might refer from time to time in order to analyze his own professional development.

Check List for Teachers

CHAPTER 1

    YES   NO

(a) Am I aware of the characteristics of the contemporary program of art?

(b) Am I familiar with the traditional nature of art?

(c) Do I understand the influences of the democratic credo upon art education today?

(d) Do I know the relationships which exist between art and general educational thought?

(e) Do I know how and why the art program has changed over the last fifty years?

(f) Do I know and understand the objectives of contemporary art education?

CHAPTER 2

(a) Do I understand the place in art teaching of motivation, isolating and defining a theme for expres-

sion, establishing goals, and selecting the media
and tools of expression?

(b) Can I differentiate between effective and faulty
teaching practices in art?

CHAPTER 3

(a) Do I know the elements of design?

(b) Do I realize the significance of variety, unity, and
function in design?

(c) Am I developing for myself a set of principles of
design?

(d) Can I control the elements of design in drawing,
painting, and other art work?

CHAPTER 4

(a) Do I understand the "choice points" in an art program?

(b) Do I know who should choose an art program?

(c) Am I familiar with the criteria of choice in an art
program?

CHAPTER 5

(a) Have I summarized the general art operations that
occur in my classroom?

(b) Do I know the basic supplies and equipment required to teach art?

(c) Have I analyzed in detail the physical arrangements in the classroom?

CHAPTER 6

(a) Do I know the developmental stages and modes of
expression in children's art?

(b) Do I understand the developments in children's
design?

(c) Do I know the proper sources of subject matter for
children's work?

CHAPTER 7

(a) Do I know the most suitable tools, media, and types
of subject matter, and the assistance children in

various stages of development require while they
are drawing and painting?

(b) Do I know enough about such things as color and linear perspective to help children to use them effectively?

(c) Is my own insight into drawing techniques sufficient for me to help children to develop drawing skills?

(d) Can I help children to improve their pictorial composition?

CHAPTER 8

(a) Do I know enough about picture-making with paper to help children to use this technique?

(b) Can I help children when they are making free-standing forms or mobiles out of paper?

(c) Can I teach the use of paper in plastic forms?

CHAPTER 9

(a) Am I prepared to teach sculpture in wood, either in relief or in the round?

(b) Can I teach the use of other media for sculpture?

(c) Can I teach children how to work with clay?

CHAPTER 10

(a) Do I know enough about various printing processes so that children of all ages under my care could benefit from this work?

(b) Can I teach stenciling effectively?

CHAPTER 11

(a) Do I really understand the nature of a democratic group?

(b) Can I handle group work in art so that pupils may learn about democracy?

(c) Do I know enough about mural-making and puppetry so that I can effectively help the children with these group activities?

(a) Do I know enough about slow learners generally to help them with their art?

(b) Am I familiar with some art techniques suitable for slow learners?

CHAPTER 13

(a) Am I sufficiently familiar with gifted children to help them in their art activities?

(b) Am I clever enough at some art activities to help gifted children to perform them?

CHAPTER 14

(a) Can I distinguish between strong and weak correlations of art and some other school experiences?

(b) Can I analyze the activities arising from the unit curriculum so that sufficient attention is given to art education?

CHAPTER 15

(a) Do I know why we display children's art?

(b) Do I know enough about display techniques to assist children and others to arrange striking shows?

CHAPTER 16

(a) Do I understand something about the nature of art appreciation?

(b) Have I developed some effective teaching methods to promote appreciation of good paintings, films, and other art forms?

CHAPTER 17

(a) Do I know how to appraise the quality of children's art production, art appreciation, and behavior in an art class?

(b) Am I capable of reporting honestly to parents a pupil's progress in art?

CHAPTER 18

(a) Do I read enough about art, art education, and general education to keep up with developments?

(b) Can I get along with my professional associates,   YES | NO
especially my art supervisor?

(c) Have I worked out an effective in-service program of art study?

ACTIVITIES FOR THE READER

1. Plan a professional reading program for the coming year to include books on art, art education, and general education.

2. List all the ways you could be of assistance to (a) a fellow teacher who wants help in art; (b) an art supervisor.

3. Work out a five-year program for yourself for summer art activities.

4. Describe your "dream tour" of art galleries in (a) the United States; (b) Europe.

5. Make a personal check list of items pertaining to your professional growth in art.

Appendices

<table>
<tr><td>

I

</td><td>

*A Recommended Reading List
for the Student of Art Education*

</td></tr>
</table>

Most of these books have been selected from the footnote references in this volume, where they have received comment.

ART APPRECIATION

Bethers, Ray. *Composition in Pictures.* Second edition. New York: Pitman Publishing Corporation, 1956.

Bulley, Margaret H. *Art and Counterfeit.* London: Methuen & Company, 1925.

—— *Art and Every Man: A Basis for Appreciation,* 2 vols. London: B. T. Batsford, Ltd., 1952.

Chase, Edward T. *The Etchings of the French Impressionists and Their Contemporaries.* New York: Crown Publishers, 1946.

Craven, Thomas, editor. *A Treasury of American Prints.* New York: Simon & Shuster, Inc., 1939.

Moholy-Nagy, László. *The New Vision.* Translated by Daphne M. Hoffman. New York: George Wittenborn, Inc., 1946.

Moore, Henry. *Shelter Sketch Book.* New York: George Wittenborn, Inc., 1946.

—— *Sculpture and Drawings.* Introduction by Herbert Read. New York: Curt Valentin, 1949.

Pope-Hennessy, John. *Sienese Quattrocento Painting.* New York: Phaidon Publishers, Inc., 1952.

Rothenstein, John. *Augustus John.* New York: Oxford University Press, 1944.

Schnier, Jacques. *Sculpture in Modern America.* Berkeley and Los Angeles: University of California Press, 1948.

Wilenski, Reginald H. *Modern French Painters.* Revised edition. New York: Harcourt, Brace & Company, 1948.

—— *The Meaning of Modern Sculpture.* London: Faber & Faber, Ltd., 1932.

Zorach, William. *Zorach Explains Sculpture.* New York: American Artists Group, 1947.

ART EDUCATION

Barkan, Manuel. *A Foundation for Art Education.* New York: The Ronald Press, 1955.

Cole, Natalie Robinson. *The Arts in the Classroom.* New York: The John Day Company, 1940.

Eng, Helga. *The Psychology of Children's Drawing.* Translated by Henry Stafford Hatfield. New York: Harcourt, Brace & Company, 1931.

Gaitskell, Charles D., and Margaret R. *Art Education for Slow Learners.* Peoria, Ill.: Charles A. Bennett Company, 1953.

—— *Art Education in the Kindergarten.* Peoria, Ill.: Charles A. Bennett Company, 1952.

—— *Art Education During Adolescence.* New York: Harcourt, Brace & Company, 1954.

Gondor, Emery I. *Art and Play Therapy.* New York: Random House, 1954.

Lowenfeld, Viktor. *Creative and Mental Growth.* New York: The Macmillan Company, 1952.

Munro, Thomas. *Art Education.* New York: The Liberal Arts Press, 1956.

Pearson, Ralph M. *The New Art Education.* Revised edition. New York: Harper & Brothers, 1953.

Progressive Education Association. *The Visual Arts in General Education.* New York: D. Appleton-Century Company, 1940.

Read, Herbert. *Education Through Art.* New York: Pantheon Books, Inc., 1945.

Richardson, Marion. *Art and the Child.* Peoria, Ill.: Charles A. Bennett Company, 1952.

Tannahill, Sallie Belle. *Fine Arts for Public School Administrators.* New York: Bureau of Publications, Teachers College, Columbia University, 1932.

Tomlinson, Reginald R. *Picture Making by Children.* New York: Studio Publications, 1934.

—— *Crafts for Children.* New York: Studio Publications, 1935.

Viola, Wilhelm. *Child Art and Franz Cizek.* New York: Reynal & Hitchcock, Inc., 1936.

Winslow, Leon L. *The Integrated School Art Program.* Second edition. New York: McGraw-Hill Book Company, 1949.

Ziegfeld, Edwin, editor. *Education and Art.* Paris: Unesco, 1953.

ART HISTORY

Blesh, Rudi. *Modern Art U.S.A.* New York: Alfred A. Knopf, Inc., 1956.

Cheney, Sheldon. *The Story of Modern Art.* New York: The Viking Press, 1941.

—— *Expressionism in Art.* New York: Liveright Publishing Corporation, 1948.

—— *A New World History of Art.* New York: The Viking Press, 1956.

Craven, Thomas. *Men of Art.* New York: Simon & Schuster, Inc., 1931.

Faure, Élie. *History of Art,* 5 vols. Translated by Walter Pach. New York: Harper & Brothers, 1921–1930.

Gardner, Helen. *Art Through the Ages.* Third edition. New York: Harcourt, Brace & Company, 1948.

Gropius, Walter, editor. *Bauhaus 1919–1928.* New York: The Museum of Modern Art, 1938.

Hillyer, V. M., and Edward G. Huey. *A Child's History of Art.* New York: D. Appleton-Century Company, 1938.

Janson, Horst W., and Dora Jane. *The Story of Painting for Young People.* New York: Harry N. Abrams, Inc., 1952.

Lehmann-Haupt, Hellmut. *Art Under a Dictatorship.* New York: Oxford University Press, 1954.

Mack, Gerstle. *Paul Cézanne.* New York: Alfred A. Knopf, Inc., 1935.

Myers, Bernard. *Modern Art in the Making.* New York: McGraw-Hill Book Company, 1950.

Ogg, Oscar. *The 26 Letters.* New York: Thomas Y. Crowell Company, 1948.

Orpen, William. *The Outline of Art.* Hollywood-by-the-Sea, Fla.: Transatlantic Arts, Inc., 1955.

Zucker, Paul. *Styles in Painting: A Comparative Study.* New York: The Viking Press, 1950.

ART TECHNIQUES

Baranski, Matthew. *Mask Making.* Worcester, Mass.: The Davis Press, 1954.

Batchelder, Marjorie. *The Puppet Theater Handbook.* New York: Harper & Brothers, 1947.

Betts, Victoria B. *Exploring Papier-Mâché.* Worcester, Mass.: The Davis Press, 1955.

Bradbury, C. Earl. *Anatomy and Construction of the Human Figure.* New York: McGraw-Hill Book Company, 1949.

Brown, Harriette J. *Handweaving: for Pleasure and Profit.* New York: Harper & Brothers, 1952.

Clark, Kenneth. *Landscape Painting.* New York: Charles Scribner's Sons, 1950.

Cockerell, Douglas. *Bookbinding and the Care of Books.* Fifth edition. New York: Pitman Publishing Corporation, 1954.

Constable, W. G. *The Painter's Workshop.* New York: Oxford University Press, 1954.

D'Amico, Victor. *Creative Teaching in Art*. Revised edition. Scranton, Penna.: International Textbook Company, 1953.

Doerner, Max. *The Materials of the Artist*. Revised edition. Translated by Eugen Neuhaus. New York: Harcourt, Brace & Company, 1934.

Duncan, Julia Hamlin, and Victor D'Amico. *How to Make Pottery and Ceramic Sculpture: 20 Graded Projects*. New York: The Museum of Modern Art, 1947.

East, Marjorie. *Display for Learning*. New York: The Dryden Press, 1952.

Gassner, John, and Philip Barber. *Producing the Play,* with *New Scene Technicians Handbook*. Revised edition. New York: The Dryden Press, 1953.

George, Ross F. *Speedball Text Book*. Fourteenth edition. Camden, N.J.: Hunt Pen Company, 1941.

Groneman, Chris Harold. *General Bookbinding*. Bloomington, Ill.: McKnight & McKnight Publishing Co., 1941.

Harris, Ruth Green. *Techniques of Sculpture: A Simple Creative Approach*. New York: Harper & Brothers, 1942.

Hughes, Toni. *How to Make Shapes in Space*. New York: E. P. Dutton & Company, 1955.

Johnston, Mary Grace. *Paper Sculpture*. Worcestor, Mass.: The Davis Press, 1952.

Kennard, Joseph Spencer. *Masks and Marionettes*. New York: The Macmillan Company, 1935.

Kirby, Mary. *Designing on the Loom*. New York: Studio Publications, 1955.

Lanchester, Waldo S. *Hand Puppets and String Puppets*. Sixth edition. Leicester, England: The Dryad Press, 1948.

Langevin, Vige, and Jean Lombard. *Peintures et Dessins Collectifs des Enfants*. Paris: Éditions du Scarabée, 1950.

Leach, Bernard. *A Potter's Portfolio*. New York: Pitman Publishing Corporation, 1951.

Lynch, John. *How to Make Mobiles*. New York: Studio Publications, 1953.

Mayer, Ralph. *The Painter's Craft*. New York: D. Van Nostrand Company, 1948.

McIsaac, F. J. *The Tony Sarg Marionette Book*. New York: The Viking Press, 1930.

McLeish, Minnie. *New Color Cuts*. Peoria, Ill.: Charles A. Bennett Company, 1957.

Merten, George. *The Hand Puppets*. New York: Thomas Nelson & Sons, 1957.

—— *The Marionette*. New York: Thomas Nelson & Sons, 1957.

Norling, Ernest Ralph. *Perspective Made Easy*. New York: The Macmillan Company, 1940.

Ogg, Oscar. *An Alphabet Source Book*. New York: Dover Publications, Inc., 1947.

Randall, Arne W. *Murals for Schools*. Worcester, Mass.: The Davis Press, 1956.

Richmond, Leonard, and John Littlejohns. *The Art of Painting in Pastel*. London: Sir Isaac Pitman & Sons, Ltd., 1918.

—— *The Technique of Water Color Painting*. Second edition. New York: Pitman Publishing Corporation, 1948.

Tanner, Robin. *Children's Work in Block Printing*. Peoria, Ill.: Charles A. Bennett Company, 1936.

—— *Lettering for Children*. Peoria, Ill.: Charles A. Bennett Company, 1937.

Tomlinson, Reginald Robert. *Picture and Pattern Making by Children*. Revised edition. New York: Studio Publications, 1950.

Town, Lawrence. *Bookbinding by Hand*. New York: Pitman Publishing Corporation, 1952.

Woolner, H. *Teaching Fabric Printing in Schools*. London: Evans Brothers, Ltd., [n.d.].

AESTHETICS

Bell, Clive. *Since Cézanne*. New York: Harcourt, Brace & Company, 1922.

—— *Art*. London: Chatto & Windus, 1921.

Croce, Benedetto. *Aesthetic*. Translated from the Italian by Douglas Ainslie. New York: Noonday Press, 1922 [1956 printing].

Dewey, John. *Art as Experience*. New York: Minton Balch & Company, 1934.

Ellis, Havelock. *The Dance of Life*. New York: Modern Library, Inc., 1929.

Faulkner, Ray, Edwin Ziegfeld, and Gerald Hill. *Art Today*. Third edition. New York: Henry Holt & Company, 1956.

Fry, Roger. *Transformations*. New York: Doubleday & Company, 1956.

—— *Vision and Design*. New York: Meridian Books, 1956.

—— *Cézanne*. New York: The Macmillan Company, 1927.

Gill, Eric. *Art and a Changing Civilisation*. London: John Lane The Bodley Head, Ltd., 1934.

Holme, G. *Industrial Design and the Future*. London: The Studio Ltd., 1934.

Moholy-Nagy, László. *Vision in Motion*. Chicago: Paul Theobald, 1947.

Mumford, Lewis. *Technics and Civilization*. New York: Harcourt, Brace & Company, 1934.

Read, Herbert. *The Meaning of Art*. New York: Pitman Publishing Corporation, 1951.

—— *A Philosophy of Modern Art*. New York: Horizon Press, 1953.

—— *Art and Industry*. New York: Horizon Press, 1954.

—— *Art Now*. New York: Pitman Publishing Corporation, 1949.

Reid, Louis A. *A Study in Aesthetics*. New York: The Macmillan Company, 1931.

Shahn, Ben. *The Shape of Content*. Cambridge, Mass.: Harvard University Press, 1957.

Teague, Walter Dorwin. *Design This Day: The Technique of Order in the Machine Age*. New York: Harcourt, Brace & Company, 1940.

GENERAL EDUCATION

Bode, Boyd H. *Democracy as a Way of Life*. New York: The Macmillan Company, 1937.

Burton, William H. *The Guidance of Learning Activities*. Second edition. New York: Appleton-Century-Crofts, Inc., 1952.

Cole, Luella. *Teaching in the Elementary School.* New York: Farrar & Rinehart, Inc., 1939.

Cronbach, Lee J. *Educational Psychology.* New York: Harcourt, Brace & Company, 1954.

Dewey, John. *Democracy and Education.* New York: The Macmillan Company, 1916.

—— *How We Think.* New York: D. C. Heath & Co., 1935.

—— *Experience and Education.* New York: The Macmillan Company, 1938.

Garrison, Karl C. *The Psychology of Exceptional Children.* Revised edition. New York: The Ronald Press, 1950.

Goodenough, Florence L., and L. M. Rynkiewicz. *Exceptional Children.* New York: Appleton-Century-Crofts, Inc., 1956.

Hanna, Lavone A., Gladys L. Potter, and Neva Hagaman. *Unit Teaching in the Elementary School.* New York: Rinehart & Company, 1955.

Hartmann, George W. *Educational Psychology.* New York: The American Book Company, 1941.

Heck, Arch. *The Education of Exceptional Children.* Second edition. New York: McGraw-Hill Book Company, 1953.

Hilliard, Frances Pauline. *Improving Social Learnings in the Elementary School.* New York: Bureau of Publications, Teachers College, Columbia University, 1954.

Hollingshead, Arthur D. *Guidance in Democratic Living.* New York: D. Appleton-Century Company, 1941.

Hopkins, L. Thomas. *Interaction: The Democratic Process.* Boston: D. C. Heath & Company, 1941.

Ingram, Christine P. *Education of the Slow-Learning Child.* Second edition. New York: The Ronald Press, 1953.

Jersild, Arthur T. *Child Psychology.* Fourth edition. Englewood Cliffs, N.J.: Prentice-Hall, Inc., 1954.

Kelley, Earl C., and Marie I. Rasey. *Education and the Nature of Man.* New York: Harper & Brothers, 1952.

Kilpatrick, W. H. *Foundations of Method.* New York: The Macmillan Company, [1925].

—— *A Reconstructed Theory of the Educative Process.* New York: Bureau of Publications, Teachers College, Columbia University, 1935.

—— *Remaking the Curriculum.* New York: Newson & Company, 1936.

Köhler, Wolfgang. *The Mentality of Apes.* New York: Harcourt, Brace & Company, 1927.

Lee, Jonathan Murray, and Dorris May. *The Child and His Curriculum.* Second edition. New York: D. Appleton-Century Company, 1950.

Mort, Paul R., and W. S. Vincent. *Modern Educational Practice: A Handbook for Teachers.* New York: McGraw-Hill Book Company, 1950.

Prescott, Daniel A., chairman. *Emotion and the Educative Process.* Washington, D.C.: American Council on Education, 1938.

Roback, A. A. *History of American Psychology.* New York: Library Publishers, 1952.

Ross, Clay C. *Measurement in Today's Schools.* Third edition, edited by J. C. Stanley. Englewood Cliffs, N.J.: Prentice-Hall, Inc., 1954.

Rugg, Harold O. *Foundations for American Education.* Yonkers, N.Y.: World Book Company, 1947.

Saucier, W. A. *Theory and Practice in the Elementary School.* Revised edition. New York: The Macmillan Company, 1951.

Shane, Harold G., and E. T. McSwain. *Evaluation and the Elementary Curriculum.* New York: Henry Holt & Company, 1951.

Shane, Harold G., and Wilbur A. Yauch. *Creative School Administration in Elementary and Junior High Schools.* New York: Henry Holt & Company, 1954.

Spearman, C. E. *Creative Mind.* New York: D. Appleton-Century Company, 1931.

Torgerson, Theodore I., and Georgia Sachs Adams. *Measurement and Evaluation for the Elementary-School Teacher.* New York: The Dryden Press, 1954.

Ulich, Robert. *Fundamentals of Democratic Education.* New York: American Book Company, 1956.

Witty, Paul, editor. *The Gifted Child.* American Association for Gifted Children. Boston: D. C. Heath & Company, 1953.

Wrightstone, Jacob Wayne, J. Justman, and I. Robbins. *Evaluation in Modern Education.* New York: American Book Company, 1956.

II   *Series of Books for Art Appreciation*

The following titles are selected as being especially helpful for the reader. Catalogues are available giving complete listings.

The Museum of Modern Art, 11 West 53rd Street, New York 19, N.Y.

Abstract Painting and Sculpture in America by Andrew Carnduff Ritchie.
Pierre Bonnard by John Rewald
Georges Braque by Henry R. Hope
Alexander Calder by James Johnson Sweeney
Giorgio De Chirico by James Thrall Soby
Eight Automobiles by Arthur Drexler
Fourteen Americans edited by Dorothy C. Miller
The History of Impressionism by John Rewald
The Prints of Paul Klee by James Thrall Soby
The Sculpture of Jacques Lipchitz by Henry R. Hope
Masters of British Painting—1800-1950 by Andrew Carnduff Ritchie
Masters of Modern Art edited by Alfred H. Barr, Jr.
Matisse: His Art and His Public by Alfred H. Barr, Jr.
Etchings by Matisse by William S. Lieberman

Modern Art in Your Life by Robert Goldwater, in collaboration with René d'Harnoncourt

Modern Drawings by Monroe Wheeler and John Rewald

Modern Painters and Sculptors as Illustrators by Monroe Wheeler

Modigliani: Paintings, Drawings, Sculpture by James Thrall Soby

Henry Moore by James Johnson Sweeney

Picasso: Fifty Years of His Art by Alfred H. Barr, Jr.

The Sculptor's Studio: Etchings by Picasso by William S. Lieberman

Post-Impressionism—from Van Gogh to Gauguin by John Rewald

Georges Rouault: Paintings and Prints by James Thrall Soby

Rouault: Retrospective Exhibition 1953 with an introduction by Jacques Maritain

Henri Rousseau by Daniel Catton Rich

Sculpture of the Twentieth Century by Andrew Carnduff Ritchie

Soutine by Monroe Wheeler

De Stijl with text by Alfred H. Barr, Jr.

Yves Tanguy by James Thrall Soby

Toulouse-Lautrec a catalogue of the exhibition held at the Museum of Modern Art, with an introduction by Andrew Carnduff Ritchie

Twelve Americans edited by Dorothy C. Miller, with statements by the artists

Jacques Villon: His Graphic Art by William S. Lieberman

Edouard Vuillard by Andrew Carnduff Ritchie

Franklin C. Watkins by Andrew Carnduff Ritchie

What Is Modern Painting? by Alfred H. Barr, Jr.

New York Graphic Society, 95 East Putnam Avenue, Greenwich, Connecticut

GREAT MASTERS OF THE PAST

  I *Antonello,* text by Stefano Bottari, English translation by Gustina Scaglia

  II *Italian Painting,* text by Edith Standen

  III *Louvre Masterpieces of Italian Painting,* text by Germain Bazin

  IV *Ravenna Mosaics,* text by Giuseppe Bovini, English translation by Gustina Scaglia

  V *Mosaics of St. Marks,* text by Giovanni Bettini

  VI *Botticelli,* text by Henri Chastel

New Art in America, edited by John I. H. Baur

UNESCO WORLD ART SERIES

  I *India: Paintings from the Ajanta Caves,* text by Mandanjeet Singh, introduction by Jawaharlal Nehru

  II *Egypt: Paintings from Tombs and Temples,* text by Jacques Vandier, introduction by Mohamed Naguib

  III *Australia: Aboriginal Paintings from Arnhem Land,* text by Sir Herbert Read, introduction by Charles Mountford

IV   *Yugoslavia: Medieval Frescoes,* text by Svetozar Radojcic, introduction by Talbot Rice

V   *Norway: Paintings from Stave Churches,* text by Roar Hauglid, introduction by Louis Grodecki

VI   *Iran: Early Persian Miniatures,* text by Basil Gray, introduction by André Godard

VII   *Italy: Frescoes by Masaccio,* text by Sir Philip Hendy

VIII   *Spain: Catalonian Romanesque Painting,* text by Juan Ainaud de La-Sarte

IX   *Ceylon: Shrine and Temple and Rock Painting,* texts by Drs. S. Paranavitana and W. G. Archer

(Other titles in this series are in preparation.)

Penguin Books, Inc., 3300 Clipper Mill Road, Baltimore 11, Maryland

PENGUIN MODERN PAINTERS SERIES
Edward Bawden by J. M. Richards
Duncan Grant by Raymond Mortimer
Ivon Hitchens by Patrick Heron
Frances Hodgkins by Myfanwy Evans
David Jones by Robin Ironside
Ben Nicholson by John Summerson
William Nicholson by Robert Nicholls
Ben Shahn by James Thrall Soby
Stanley Spencer by Eric Newton
Graham Sutherland, 2nd edition, by Edward Sackville-West

PHAIDON PRESS SERIES (distributed by Garden City Books, Garden City, N.Y.)
The Art of India Through the Ages
The Bayeux Tapestry
Bellini and Titian at Ferrara
The Sculpture of Bernini
The Paintings of Bruegel
Paul Cézanne and His Times
Dürer and His Times
El Greco
The Paintings of Fra Angelico
The French Impressionists
Ghiberti
Goya
Hokusai
Holbein: Selected Drawings
Complete Paintings of Hans Holbein
Introduction to Renaissance Painting
The Italian Painters of the Renaissance
Japanese Masters of the Colour Print

Augustus John
Leonardo Da Vinci
Mantegna: Paintings, Drawings, Engravings
Marvels of Ancient Rome
Michelangelo: Paintings, Sculpture, Architecture
Renoir
Sienese Quattrocento Painting
Tiepolo: His Life and Work
Tintoretto
Titian
Towards Modern Art
Paolo Uccello
Vincent Van Gogh

Skira, Publishers, 381 Fourth Avenue, New York 16, N.Y.

For some large contemporary lithographs and reproductions of excellent quality for display in the school, see the catalogue of School Prints, Ltd., 13 Motcomb St., Belgrave Square, London S.W.1, England.

III — *Museum of Modern Art Teaching Portfolios*

These are useful for groups of teachers to study, but are generally too difficult for most elementary school children.

Modern Sculpture: Portfolio No. 1. E. C. Osborn, ed., 1947
Texture and Pattern: Portfolio No. 2. E. C. Osborn, ed., 1949
Modern Art Old and New: Portfolio No. 3. René d'Harnoncourt, ed., 1950
Useful Objects Today: Portfolio No. 4. Greta Daniel, ed., 1955

IV — *Some Art Education Magazines, Journals, and Yearbooks*

UNITED STATES

American Artist. Watson-Guptill Publications Inc., 24 West 40th Street, New York 18, N.Y. Monthly September to June.

Arts and Activities. The Jones Publishing Co., 8150 N. Central Park Ave., Skokie, Ill. Monthly September to June.

Art Education. The official journal of the National Art Education Association, State Teachers College, Kutztown, Pa. Monthly October to June.

Art Education Today. An annual on art education. Bureau of Publications, Teachers College, Columbia University, New York, N.Y.

    1940 Art Appreciation
    1941 Design
    1942 Art and the Community
    1943 Art Education and the War
    1948 (no subtitle)
    1949–50 The Teacher
    1951–52 The Secondary School Program

College Art Journal. The official publication of the College Art Association of America, 432 Fourth Ave., New York 16, N.Y. Quarterly.

Design. Design Publishing Company, 337 S. High St., Columbus, Ohio. Bimonthly September to June.

Eastern Arts Association: Research Bulletin. Kutztown, Pa. Published each April.

    1950 (no subtitle)
    1951 (no subtitle)

1952   Workbooks and Art Education
1953   The Junior High School
1954   The Meaning of Creativity
1955   The Exceptional Child

Eastern Arts Association: Yearbooks. Kutztown, Pennsylvania. Annuals of the Association.

1944   Tomorrow Challenges Art Education
1945   Art Education and This Is Our Town
1946   Art Education for One World
1947   Art Education in a Free Society
1948   Art: The Balance Wheel in Education
1949   Art in General Education
1950   The Integrative Function of Art Education
1952   Art Education in a Scientific Age
1954   Sources and Resources for Art Education

National Art Education Association: Yearbooks. Kutztown, Pennsylvania. Annuals of the Association.

1949   Art Education Organizes
1951   This Is Art Education
1952   This Is Art Education
1953   Art Education and Human Values
1954   Research in Art Education
1955   Art a Frontier for Freedom
1957   Research in Art Education

School Arts Magazine. Davis Press, Inc., Printers Building, Worcester 8, Massachusetts. Monthly September to June.

UNITED KINGDOM

Art and Craft Education. Evans Bros. Ltd. Montague House, Russell Square, London W.C.1. Bi-monthly

Art Education Official organ of the National Society for Art Education. Birmingham, England. Twice yearly.

Athene. The journal of the Society for Education Through Art, Denison House, 296 Vauxhall Bridge Road, London, S.W.1. Semi-annual.

Design. The Council of Industrial Design and the Scottish committee of the council. Tilbury House, Petty France, London S.W.1. Monthly.

The Studio. Studio Ltd., 66 Chandos Place, London W.C.2. (U.S. address: 432 Fourth Ave., New York 16, N.Y.). Monthly.

CANADA

Annual Reports. Canadian Society for Education Through Art, 206 Huron Street, Toronto 5, Ontario, Canada.

Canadian Art. Society for Art Publications, Box 384, Ottawa, Canada. Quarterly.

V   Some Art Programs in the United States

A Guide to Art Activities. Pittsburgh Public Schools, Pittsburgh, Pennsylvania, 1950. 6 Vols.

A Guide for the Teaching of Art. Kindergarten–7th grade. San Francisco Unified School District, San Francisco, California, 1956.

Art and the Child and Texas Education. Pamphlets. Art Curriculum Committee, T.A.E.A., Dallas, Texas, 1950.

Art Education. Art folders. Detroit Public Schools, Detroit, Michigan, 1953.

Art Education for the Elementary Schools of Ohio. Grades 1–6. Ohio State Department of Education, Columbus, Ohio, 1955.

Art: Elementary Schools of Utah. Grades 1–6. State Department of Education, Salt Lake City, Utah, 1951.

Art Experiences. Grades 1–6. Indianapolis Elementary Schools, Indianapolis, Indiana, 1952.

Art (Expression, Enjoyment, Education) in Our Maryland Schools, Baltimore, Maryland, 1954.

Art for Iowa's Children. Department of Public Instruction, Des Moines, Iowa, 1950.

Art for the Elementary Schools of Missouri. State Department of Education, Jefferson City, Missouri, 1952.

Art for the Elementary Schools. Kindergarten–8th grade. St. Louis Public Schools, St. Louis, Missouri, 1955.

Art in Daily Living. Resource materials. Kindergarten–6th grade. Wilmington Public Schools, Wilmington, Delaware, 1954.

Art in the Elementary Schools. Grades 1–6. Board of Education, New York, New York, 1952.

Art in the Lives of Florida Children. Bulletin 37. Kindergarten–12th grade. State Department of Education, Tallahassee, Florida, 1950.

Art in the Madison Public Schools. Grades 1–12. Madison Public Schools, Madison, Wisconsin, 1953.

Art Resource Materials for Elementary Schools. City of Baltimore Department of Education, Baltimore, Maryland, 1956.

Beginning and Elementary Art Program. State Department of Education, Augusta, Maine, 1950.

Creative Art for Use in the Elementary Schools. Grades 1–6. Denver Public Schools, Denver, Colorado, 1949.

Enjoying Art in the Classroom. Curriculum Resource Bulletin. Grades 1–6. Fairfax County Schools, Fairfax, Virginia, 1953.

Ways to Art. Los Angeles Public Schools, Los Angeles, California, 1952.

VI

Films and Filmstrips on Art and Art Education

In the following lists, certain abbreviations should be noted: Prod: producer; dist: distributor; sd: sound; sil: silent; col: color; b & w: black and white; min: minutes; fr: frames; cap: captions; ms: accompanying manuscript.

PRODUCERS AND DISTRIBUTORS OF FILMS

Bailey	Bailey Films, Inc., 6509 De Longpre Ave., Hollywood 28, Cal.
Bouchard	Thomas Bouchard, 80 W. 40th St., New York 18, N.Y.
Brandon	Brandon Films, Inc., 200 W. 57th St., New York 19, N.Y.
ConFlm	Contemporary Films, Inc., 13 E. 37th St., New York 16, N.Y.
Crawley	Crawley Films Ltd., 19 Fairmont Ave., Ottawa; 1467 Mansfield St., Montreal, Canada.
Coronet	Coronet Films, Coronet Building, Chicago 1, Ill.
EBF	Encyclopaedia Britannica Films, Inc., 1150 Wilmette Ave., Wilmette, Ill.
FlmClassic	Film Classic Exchange, 1645 N. LaBrea Ave., Hollywood 28, Cal.
FlmIm	Film Images, 1860 Broadway, New York, N.Y.
French	French American Cultural Services and Educational Aid, 972 Fifth Ave., New York 21, N.Y.
Gotham	Gotham Films, 1947 Broadway, New York 23, N.Y.
Harmon	Harmon Foundation, 140 Nassau St., New York 7, N.Y.
I.F.E.	I.F.E. Releasing Corp., 1501 Broadway, New York 19, N.Y.
IntFlmBur	International Film Bureau, 57 E. Jackson Blvd., Chicago 4, Ill.
MMA	Museum of Modern Art Film Library, 11 W. 53rd St., New York 19, N.Y.
CanNFB	National Film Board of Canada, 630 Fifth Ave., New York 20, N.Y.; 400 W. Madison St., Chicago 6, Ill.; 3255 Côte de Liesse Road, Ville St. Laurent, P.Q., Canada.
Orbit	Orbit Films, 2521 Sixth Ave., Seattle, Wash.
Riethof	Riethof Productions, Inc., 59 E. 79th St., New York 21, N.Y.
Robbins	David Robbins Productions, 200 W. 57th St., New York 19, N.Y.
SVE	Society for Visual Education, 1345 Diversey Parkway, Chicago 14, Ill.
UWF	United World Films, 1445 Park Ave., New York 29, N.Y.
YoungAmerica	Young America Films, 18 E. 41st St., New York 17, NY.

The following is a selected list of films especially suitable for children.

Animules. 1951. Prod IntFlmBur, dist IntFlmBur, sd, col, 11 min.
Art and Motion. 1952. Prod Paul Burnfield, dist EBF, sd, col, 14 min.
Art in Our World (Experiencing Art Series). 1950. Prod Paul Burnfield, dist Bailey, sd, col, 10 min.
Begone Dull Care. 1949. Prod CanNFB, dist IntFlmBur, sd, col, 16 min.
Care of Art Materials. 1948. Prod YoungAmerica, dist YoungAmerica, sd, b & w, 11 min.
Child as a Potter. 1953. Dist Lobett Productions (2002 Taraval St., San Francisco 16, Cal.), sd, col, 17 min.
Children Are Creative. 1952. Prod Central Washington College of Education, dist Bailey, sd, col, 11 min.
Color (Art in Action Series). 1954. Prod Paul Burnfield, dist EBF, sd, col, 6 min.

CREATIVE HANDS SERIES

Art from Scrap. 1955. Prod Crawley, dist IntFlmBur, sd, col, 5 min.
Beginning of Picture Making. 1951. Prod Crawley, dist IntFlmBur, sd, col, 6 min.
Design to Music. 1949. Prod Crawley, dist IntFlmBur, sd, col, 5 min.
Loom Weaving. 1951. Prod Crawley, dist IntFlmBur, sd, col, 6 min.
Making a Mask. 1951. Prod Crawley, dist IntFlmBur, sil, col, 6 min.
Model Houses. 1949. Prod Crawley, dist IntFlmBur, sd, col, 5½ min.
Paper Sculpture. 1949. Prod Crawley, dist IntFlmBur, sd, col, 5 min.
Picture Making at the Gang Age. 1951. Prod Crawley, dist IntFlmBur, sd, col, 6 min.

Family Portrait (Art for the Family Series). 1953. Dist MMA, sd, b & w, 30 min.
Fiddle-de-dee. 1947. Prod CanNFD, dist IntFlmBur, sd, col, 4 min.
Finger Painting. 1949. Prod Crawley, dist IntFlmBur, sd, b & w, 5 min.
How to Make a Puppet. 1953. Prod R. Nisbauer, dist Bailey, sd, b & w, 12 min.
Let's Draw with Crayons. 1952. Prod Coronet, dist Coronet, sd, b & w, 10 min.
Let's Paint with Water Color. 1951. Dist Coronet, sd, col, 10 min.
Let's Play with Clay, Part 1: Animals. 1950. Prod Gene Byrnes, dist YoungAmerica, sd, b & w, 10 min.
Light and Dark. 1954. Dist EBF, sd, col, 6 min.
Loon's Necklace. 1949. Prod Crawley, dist IntFlmBur, sd, col, 10 min.
Make a Mobile. 1948. Prod Dept. of Art, U.C.L.A., dist Bailey, sd, col, 10 min.
Make a Space Design. Dist MMA, sd, b & w, 30 min.
Making a Feeling and Seeing Picture. 1952. Dist MMA, sd, b & w, 30 min.
Paint a Picture of Sounds. Dist MMA, sd, b & w, 30 min.
Romance of Transportation in Canada. 1953. Prod CanNFB, dist IntFlmBur, sd, col, 11 min.
Story of Peter and the Potter. 1953. Prod CanNFB, dist IntFlmBur, sd, b & w, 21 min.
Tell Your Ideas with Clay. 1952. Dist MMA, sd, b & w, 30 min.

Texture. 1954. Prod Paul Burnfield, dist EBF, sd, col, 6 min.
Totems. 1944. Prod CanNFB, dist IntFlmBur, sd, col, 11 min.
West Wind. 1943. Prod CanNFB, dist IntFlmBur, sd, col, 18 min.
Your Child Is a Genius. 1947. Dist Robbins, sd, col, 14 min.

The following is a list of films especially suitable for adults. Some of the films are not recommended for elementary school children.

Art in Our World (Experiencing Art Series). 1950. Prod Paul Burnfield, dist Bailey, sd, col, 10 min.
Braque, Georges. 1950. Directed by André Bureau and F. Duran, dist French, sd (French), b & w, 25 min.
Calder, Works of. 1951. Produced and narrated by Burgess Meredith, dist MMA, sd, col, 20 min.
Canadian Landscape. 1941. Prod CanNFB, dist IntFlmBur, sd, col, 18 min.
Composers in Clay. 1943. Directed by René Lucot; photographed by André Danton; art consultant, Malvina Hoffman, dist UWF, sd, b & w, 25 min.
Creative Art of Japan. 1951. Prod Orbit, dist Brandon, sd, col, 20 min.
Degas, Ballet by. 1951. Produced and directed by Jean H. Lenauer, dist Brandon, sd, col, 10 min.
Fra Angelico at San Marco. 1951. Directed by Giampiero Pucci, dist FlmIm, sd, b & w, 11 min.
Grandma Moses. 1950. Prod Falcon Films, dist FlmIm, col, sd, 21 min.
Dong Kingman Paints a Water Color. 1946. Prod Simon and Herta Moselsio, dist Harmon, sil, col, 30 min.
Fernand Léger in America—His New Realism. 1946. Directed by Thomas Bouchard, dist Bouchard, narration by Léger in French (English translation available), sd, col, 30 min.
The Mystery of Leonardo Da Vinci. 1951. Directed by Pietro Francisci, dist I.F.E. sd, b & w, 10 min.
Looking at Sculpture. 1950. Directed by Alexander Shaw; commentary by Michael Redgrave, dist Brandon, sd, b & w, 11 min.
Maillol. 1944. Directed by Albert Loisel, dist French, sd, b & w, 20 min.
Matisse. 1946. Prod François Campeaux, dist French, sd, b & w, 25 min.
Joan Miró Makes a Colored Print. 1951. Produced and directed by Thomas Bouchard, dist Bouchard, sd, col, 20 min.
Henry Moore. 1947. Prod Falcon Films, dist FlmIm, sd, col, 16 min.
Primitive Painters of Charlevoix. 1947. Directed by Jean Palardy, prod CanNFB, dist IntFlmBur, sd, col, 22 min.
Rembrandt. 1946. Directed by René Hervouin, dist FlmClassic, sd, b & w, 19 min.
The Renaissance. 1950. Made in collaboration with Wendell W. Wright, School of Education, Indiana University, dist Coronet, sd, b & w, 10 min.
Rodin. 1950. Directed by René Lucot, dist UWF, sd, b & w, 23 min.
Rousseau. 1950. Directed by LoDuca, edited by Renée Guerin, dist French, sd, b & w.

Rubens. 1948. Directed by Henri Storck, prod Paul Haesaerts and Henri Storck, dist Brandon, sd, b & w, 45 min.

Sermons in Stone. 1949. Directed by André Bureau, dist French, sd, b & w, 20 min.

The Titan—Story of Michelangelo. 1950. Prod Robert Flaherty, photographed by Curt Oertel, narrated by Fredric March, dist ConFlm, sd, b & w, 1 hr 7 min.

Toulouse-Lautrec: Painter of the Parisian Bohème. 1951. Prod Riethof, dist Riethof, sd, col, 25 min.

West Wind. 1943. Written and produced by Graham McInnis, dist IntFlmBur, sd, col, 20 min.

SOME RECOMMENDED FILMSTRIPS (35 MM)

Art Belongs to All Children. Prod Ohio State University Press, 1950. Accompanied by disc recording, 78 rpm. 25 min, 54 fr, dist Ohio State University, Columbus, Ohio.

ART IN OUR CLASSROOM SERIES

We Make Designs with Needle and Thread. Prod EBF, 1954, 49 fr, dist EBF.
We Make Stick Puppets. Prod EBF, 1954, 49 fr, dist EBF.
We Print Designs and Pictures. Prod EBF, 1954, 49 fr, dist EBF.
We Work with Clay. Prod EBF, 1954, 49 fr, dist EBF.
We Work with Paper and Scissors. Prod EBF, 1954, 49 fr, dist EBF.
We Work with Papier Mâché. Prod EBF, 1954, 49 fr, dist EBF.

ELEMENTS OF ART SERIES

Color. Prod Curriculum Films, 1951, 39 fr, cap, ms.*
More Shapes. Prod Curriculum Films, 1951, 28 fr, cap, ms.
Painting a Picture. Prod Curriculum Films, 1951, 36 fr, cap, ms.
Proportion. Prod Curriculum Films, 1951, 30 fr, cap, ms.
Shapes. Prod Curriculum Films, 1951, 23 fr, cap, ms.

It's Fun to Combine Art Materials. Prod Jessie Todd, 1953, 46 fr, cap, dist SVE.
Let's Look at a Painting. Prod EBF, 1950, cap, dist EBF.
Let's Paint. Prod Jessie Todd, 1953, 47 fr, cap, dist SVE.
Making a Mural. Prod YoungAmerica, 1952, 37 fr, cap, ms, dist YoungAmerica.
Painting with Water Color. Prod YoungAmerica, 1952, 31 fr, cap, ms, dist Young-America.
Potato Printing. Prod YoungAmerica, 1952, 39 fr, cap, ms, dist YoungAmerica.
Pottery Making. Prod YoungAmerica, 1952, 41 fr, cap, ms, dist YoungAmerica.
There Is Art in Cutting Paper. Prod Jessie Todd, 1953, 35 fr, cap, dist SVE.
There Is Magic in a Wax Crayon. Prod Jessie Todd, 1953, 34 fr, cap, dist SVE.
We Like Clay. Prod Jessie Todd, 1953, 35 fr, cap, dist SVE.
You Can Create with Finger Paints. Prod. Jessie Todd, 1953, 37 fr, cap, dist SVE.

---

* Curriculum Films, Inc., is no longer in business, but their filmstrips may be available in library collections.

Index

d

D'Amico, Victor, 234 and *fn.*, 238 *fn.*, 287 *fn.*, 335 *fn.*
Darwin, Charles, 26
Daumier, Honoré, 14, 386
David, Jacques Louis, 173
da Vinci, Leonardo, *see* Vinci
Davis, Stuart, 79
Degas, Edgar, 27, 78, 323
DeHaan, Robert F., 321 *fn.*
Democratic credo, 18–21
Democratic group, 259–60
  activity, 261–63
Derain, André, 16
Design (or form), 11, 56–80
  analysis of, 59 *fn.*
  attitudes and mental processes in production of, 73–75
  balances in, 69–70
  centers of interest in, 68–69
  children's, 142–46
  color in, 64–65
  deterioration of, 143, 145–46
  elements of, 57–65
  as expression of life, 72
  light and shade in, 62–63
  line in, 59–61
  mass and space in, 61–62
  nature as source of, 157–58
  nonobjective, 157
  principles of, 75–76
  related to subject matter, 12
  rhythms in, 67–68
  of slow learners, 294–95
  texture in, 63–64
  unity of, 66–70
  variety of, 70–72
Design Index, Ottawa, 76–77 *fn.*
Design Magazine, 75 *fn.*
Development of children's art, 125–54
Dewey, John, 5 and *fn.*, 6, 8, 11, 12 *fn.*, 23, 39 *fn.*, 43 *fn.*, 44 *fn.*, 72, 75, 381, 382, 385
  philosophy of, 24
  portrait of, *illus.* 25
Dickie, Donalda, 330, 343
Dioramas, 359, *illus.* 360
Displaying art, 365–79
  boards for, 373, 375
  cases and panels for, *illus.* 376
  in the classroom, 367–75
  mounting and framing, 369–72
  outside of the classroom, 375–79
  reasons for, 365–67
  space, 115, 117
  subject matter for, 375–77
  three-dimensional work, 372–75, *illus.* 116
  titles, 371
  two-dimensional work, 369–72, *illus.* 116
  weaving, *illus.* 374
Doerner, Max, 331 *fn.*
Doll, Edgar A., 190 *fn.*

Dow, A. W., 15
Drawing and painting, 160–85
  advances in, 27
  boards, 108
  books, 27–28, *illus.* 28
  development of skills in, 172–78
  figure, 174
  formulas for, 51–52
  for gifted children, 330–35
  landscape, 174–78
  linear, 26–27
  linear perspective, 31, developing facility with, 169–72, *illus.* 172, *illus.* 174
  in manipulative stage, 161–65
  of maps, 348
  from nature, 349
  photographic, 172–74
  portraiture, 174–78, *illus.* 176
  in preadolescent stage, 166–78
  realistic, 173–74
  regressions in, 145–46
  still life, 174–78
  symbol stage, 165–66
Dry-point, 335
Drying shelves, 115
Duccio di Buoninsegna, 70, 139, 387
  Maestà, illus. 139
Duchamp, Marcel, 139
Dufy, Raoul, 386
Duncan, Julia Hamlin, 238 *fn.*
Dunn, Louise M., 279 *fn.*
Dupré, Jules, 385 *fn.*

e

East, Marjorie, 375 *fn.*
Education, general, bibliography, 426–28
El Greco, *see* Greco
Ellis, Havelock, 72, 382
Embroidery, 310–13, *illus.* 311, Plate VIIIa
Emotions, aesthetic, 11, 382
Eng, Helga, 127
England, *see* United Kingdom
Engobe, 232, 234
Epstein, Jacob, 79
Equipment, for art activities, 105–24
Erasers, 108
Erdt, Margaret Hamilton, 126 *fn.*, 356 *fn.*
Essay-type examinations, 401
Etching, 335
Examinations, teachers' college, 29–30
Expression, 125–42
  based on experience, 7, 95
  check list for, 404
  developmental stages of, 126–42
  in later childhood (preadolescence), 140–42
  manipulation as, 127–30
  mode of, 125–26
  of pupils, 397–98
  schemata in, 125 *fn.*
  of slow learners, 290–95
  symbols in, 130–39
Expressionism, 13, 16–17
  as used by Cizek, 31–33

f

Faculty psychology, 23
Faulkner, Ray, 59 *fn.*, 400
Faure, Élie, 11 *fn.*
Feininger, Lionel, 392 *fn.*
Films and filmstrips, 65, 387–90
    Creative Hands Series, 389
    lists, 436–39
    sources, 387 *fn.*, 390 *fn.*, 435
Finger paint, 163–64
Fist puppets, 266–71, *illus.* 267, 268, 269
    costumes for, 269
Form, *see* Design
Formal art tests, 401–02
Formal study, 416
Forms in space, 202–06, *illus.* 203–04
Fra Angelico, 70
Francesco, Italo de, 16 *fn.*
Free-standing forms in paper, 193–99
Freedom of thought, 6, 19
Froebel, Friedrich Wilhelm, 21–23
    basic geometrical shapes, 22, *illus.* 30
    first kindergarten, 22
    portrait of, *illus.* 22
Fry, Roger, 7, 8, 59 *fn.*, 64, 65, 382, 383
Functional psychology, 23
Furniture, 109, *see also* Equipment, Displaying art
    benches, 215
    clock, 123
    cupboards, 122
    desks, 123
    files, 122
    kiln, 123
    kindergarten, 110
    movable, 117
    sinks, 117, 122
Futurists, 139

g

Gaitskell, C. D., and M. R., 34 *fn.*, 134 *fn.*, 142 *fn.*, 144 *fn.*, 290 *fn.*, 299 *fn.*
Gardner, Helen, 62 *fn.*
Garrison, Karl C., 290 *fn.*, 321 *fn.*
Gassner, John, 287 *fn.*
Gauguin, Paul, 179, 385 *fn.*, 386
Gestalt psychology, 5 *fn.*, 25, 57, 58 *fn.*, 73, 381
Gifted children, 320–41
    acceleration of, 328
    art activities for, 330–37
    case histories, 322–25
    drawing and painting for, 335
    enriched programs for, 327
    general activities for, 330–31
    identification of, 321–27
    schools for, 327 *fn.*
    silk-screen printing for, 335–37
    special arrangements for, 327–30
    teaching, 337–40
    tests for, 327 *fn.*
Gill, Eric, 8
Giotto, 169 *fn.*
Glazing, clay, 232–35, *illus.* 227

Glue, 213
Goals, 43
Goddard, H. H., 321 *fn.*
Gogh, Vincent van, 79, 148, 386
    Peasant Woman at Twilight, illus. 149
    The Street Pavers, illus. 149
Goldstein, Harriet, and Vetta, 70 *fn.*
Gondor, Emery I., 34 *fn.*, 289 *fn.*
Goodenough, Florence L., 290 *fn.*, 322 *fn.*
Gorell, Lord, 213 *fn.*
Goya, Francisco de, 12, 14
    Horrors of War, illus. 10
Grandma Moses, 265
Graves, Maitland E., 65 *fn.*
Greco, El, 12, 62 *fn.*, 67, 79, 148, 173, 385 *fn.*, 386
Greece, 13
Groneman, Chris, 315 *fn.*
Gropius, Walter, 392 *fn.*
Gross, Chaim, 394
Group activities, 97, 259–88
    for beginners, 263–65, *illus.* 264
    for older children, 265–87
    role of teacher in, 261–63
    for slow learners, 316–18
Guggenheim Foundation, 17 *fn.*
Guido, Alfredo, 79

h

Hagaman, Neva, 261 *fn.*, 343 *fn.*
Haley, Monica, 33 *fn.*
Hambidge, Jay, 14 *fn.*
Hammell, Agnes, 385 *fn.*
Handicapped children, *see* Slow learners
Hanna, Lavone A., 261 *fn.*, 343 *fn.*
Haptic type of personality, 147–53
Harris, Ruth Green, 238 *fn.*
Hartmann, George W., 5 and *fn.*
Havighurst, Robert J., 321 *fn.*, 327 *fn.*
Haydon, L., 287 *fn.*
Heck, Arch, 290 *fn.*, 327 *fn.*
Helmholtz, Hermann von, 14
Herbart, Johann Friedrich, 21–24
    steps of teaching, 23
    theory of apperception, 23
Hill, Gerald, 59 *fn.*
Hilliard, Frances Pauline, 261 *fn.*
Hillyer, V. M., 387 *fn.*
Hogarth, William, 15
Hokusai, 99
Holidays, correlation with art, 355, *illus.* 354
Hollingshead, Arthur D., 260, 261 *fn.*, 265 *fn.*
Hollingshead, Byron S., 320 *fn.*
Hollingworth, L. S., 321 *fn.*
Holme, G., 8 *fn.*
Hopkins, L. Thomas, 343 *fn.*
Huey, E. G., 387 *fn.*
Hughes, Toni, 202
Hunt, William Holman, 173

i

Iglehart, Robert, 75 *fn.*
Imagination, 95

Museum of Modern Art, New York, 8 *fn.*, 69 *fn.*
Museums, visits to, 390–92, *illus.* 391
Music, correlation with art, 350–53
Musical selections, for correlation, 351–53

n

Neatness, 49–50
Neo-Impressionism, 13–16, 30, 66, 70, 73
Nicolaïdes, Kimon, 77, 183 *fn.*
Norling, Ernest R., 183 *fn.*

o

Oakland Bridge, *illus.* 74
Objective tests, 399–402
Oden, Melita H., 324 *fn.*, 328 *fn.*
Ogg, Oscar, 363 *fn.*
Oil painting, *illus.* 332
  for gifted children, 331–35
O'Keeffe, Georgia, 69, 79
Ontario Department of Education, 52 *fn.*, 87 *fn.*, *illus.* 118, 144 *fn.*, 148 *fn.*, 321 *fn.*, 322 *fn.*, 324 and *fn.*, 326 and *fn.*
Orozco, José, 70, 79
Ostwald, Wilhelm, 14

p

Paint, 108
  aqueous, 335 *fn.*
  for beginners, 161
  on clay subjects, 234
  distribution system of, 115, 168
  finger, 163
  for gifted children, 331–35
  mixing, 168
  for murals, 282
  oil, 331–34
  for preadolescent stage, 167
  for slow learners, 301
  for stenciling, 254
  for symbol stage, 165
  tempera, 161–62, 165, 167–69, 213, 232, 234, 246, 282, 301
  as a texture, 64
  tins, 109
  in vegetable and stick printing, 246
  water color, 165, 168, 234, 246, 335
  on wood sculpture, 213
Painting, 160–85, *see also* Drawing and painting
  alla prima method, 334
  glazing method, 334 *fn.*
  nonobjective, 12, 13
  in oil, 331–35
  Oriental, 139
  religious, 11, 386–87
  Renaissance, 139
Palette, *illus.* 334
  in oil painting, 332–34
Panoramas, 359, *illus.* 361
Paper, working with, 108, 186–211
  box sculpture, 193–95
  free-standing forms, 193–99, *illus.* 194, *illus.* 195, *illus.* 197

  in manipulative stage, 189–93
  picture-making, 187–93, *illus.* 188, *illus.* 189, Plate VIIb
  plastic forms, 199–206
  in symbol stage, 190, *illus.* 189
  techniques, *illus.* 192, *illus.* 203
Papier-mâché, 199–201
Parent-teacher groups, 367
Parents' Night, 375, 377
Paste, 109, 187
Pearson, Ralph M., 38 *fn.*, 75 *fn.*, 77 *fn.*
Peep shows, 360, *illus.* 363
Pencils, 109
Pennsylvania schools, art rooms in, 120 *fn.*, *illus.* 121
  teachers in, 416 *fn.*
Pennsylvania Station, New York, *illus.* 18
Perspective, 31, 169–72, *illus.* 172, *illus.* 174
Pestalozzi, Johann Heinrich, 21–23
  school at Yverdon, 22 and *fn.*
Phearman, Leo T., 320 *fn.*
Picasso, Pablo, 60, 78, 148, 179
Pictorial composition, *see also* Design children's, 178–81
Pictorial reproductions, 386–87
Picture study, 382–86, 390–92
Piper, John, 71 and *fn.*, 79
Pissarro, Camille, 27
Plaster of Paris, 221–23
Plastic forms, 199–201
  dampened paper, 199, *illus.* 200
  papier-mâché, 201
Plasticine, 225, 236
Plato, 21
Play production, 286–87
  correlation with art, 346
Pompeii, 169 *fn.*
Portraits, 174–78, *illus.* 176
Poster-making, 357–59, *illus.* 358
Potter, Gladys L., 261 *fn.*, 343 *fn.*
Pottery, 229–32
  coil method, 230, *illus.* 229
  slab method, 230–32, *illus.* 231
Practical objects, 392–94, *illus.* 393
Primitives, 265
Printing, 240–58
  linoleum, 248–53
  monoprinting, 241–44, *illus.* 241, *illus.* 242
  silk-screen, 335–37
  vegetable and stick, 244–48, *illus.* 245, *illus.* 247, Plate VI
Pritchard, Miriam C., 327 *fn.*
Professional associations, 413–16
Professional growth, in art teaching, 411–21
  check list for, 417–21
  through formal study, 416
  through in-service reading, 413
  through professional associations, 413–16
  through teaching practice, 412–13
Program, general school, relating art to, 342–64
Program of studies in art, 81–104
Progress reports, 407–10